D1030204

PROBABILITY AND OPINION

PROBABILITY AND OPINION

A STUDY IN THE MEDIEVAL PRESUPPOSITIONS
OF POST-MEDIEVAL THEORIES OF PROBABILITY

by

EDMUND F. BYRNE

MARTINUS NIJHOFF / THE HAGUE / 1968

PRINTED IN THE NETHERLANDS

to Edward A. Maziarz
SINE QUO NON

PREFACE

Modern physics has accustomed us to consider events which cannot give rise to certainty in our knowledge. A scientific knowledge of such events is nevertheless possible. The method which has enabled us to obtain a stable and exact knowledge about uncertain events consists in a kind of changing of plane and in the replacing of the study of individual phenomena by the study of statistical aggregates to which those phenomena can give rise. A statistical aggregate is not a collection of real phenomena, among which some would happen more often, others more rarely. It is a set of possibilities relative to a certain object or to a certain type of phenomenon. For example, we could consider the different ways in which a die, thrown in given conditions, can fall: they are the possible results of a certain trial, the casting of the die (in the foreseen conditions). The set of those results constitutes effectively a set of possibilities, relative to a phenomenon of a certain type, the fall of the die in specified circumstances. Similarly, it is possible to consider the different velocities which can affect a molecule in a volume of gas; the set of those velocities constitutes effectively a set of possible values which a physical property, namely the velocity of a molecule, can have.

The properties of a physical aggregate are expressed by means of the concept of probability; more precisely they are expressed under the form of a distribution of probabilities. To each of the possibilities which belong to the aggregate, such a distribution assigns a real number between 0 and 1 to serve in some way as a measure of the corresponding possibility. With those probabilities, as is well known, can be associated an interpretation in terms of frequencies: if a distribution assigns to a possibility P the probability p, this can be interpreted by saying that, if the trial is repeated indefinitely, the relative frequency, in this series of trials, of a result corresponding to the possibility P approaches more and more the value given by the probability p.

A distribution of probabilities is a perfectly determined concept. And the laws which describe how a given distribution changes through time are just as determinate as the laws which describe how an individual entity, such as a particle, behaves in space-time. The difference between a deterministic law and a statistical law does not lie in the nature of the link which the law establishes between the states (of the system under consideration) but in the nature of those states themselves: whereas, in the deterministic law, the states characterize directly an individual entity, in a statistical law they characterize a set of possibilities. Quantum physics has introduced us to a realm of phenomena which can be studied only through a statistical approach. But classical physics did not ignore statistical laws. And several eminent authors have even argued that classical physics is as indeterministic as quantum physics and that the only difference between these two forms of physics concerns the manner in which the probability distributions are superimposed. In quantum physics there is a mutual dependence of the distributions which does not exist in classical physics.

But physics is by no means the only domain of knowledge in which the use of statistical laws has made it possible to give a scientific description of phenomena a direct study of which does not seem feasible. In the biological sciences as well as in the human sciences recourse to statistical methods has shown its great fruitfulness. But these methods, after all, make use of the concept of probability. There exists a mathematical theory of probability which can be axiomatized and which is evidently purely formal. Its aim is to provide methods of calculating, from given probabilities, other probabilities which depend upon the former ones in a more or less complex manner. This theory is of great interest in itself. But from an epistemological point of view, what seems to be of the greatest import is the application of this theory to the analysis of real phenomena. Since it is through the mediation of statistical concepts that the pure theory of probability is applied in the science of the real, it is essentially in the form of a statistical knowledge that a science of the uncertain is constituted. It would not be correct to say that this science replaces the study of certain events by the study of probable events; as has been noted, the method characteristic of this science consists, more exactly, in the replacement of a direct study of events by the study of the configurations of possibilities to which the events of the world can give rise. This reservation being made, we may characterize knowledge which attains to events only indirectly by way of statistical concepts, and thus by way of the concept of probability, as probable knowledge. What the practice of modern science has taught us is that such "probable" knowledge is no less exact than "certain" knowledge.

But the constitution of a science of the probable raises a philosophical problem: what is the foundation, the ground, of such a science? What, after all, is probability? How is it possible to explain that the purely mathematical concept of probability can be applied to the analysis of real phenomena? What is there in reality which corresponds exactly to the aspect of probability through which we attain it? How can statistical aggregates constitute themselves and present configurations which correspond to mathematical laws, obtainable entirely a priori? How does it happen that events which, taken individually, appear to be outside any legality, show themselves nonetheless as submitted to a strict legality from the moment when, instead of considering them in themselves, we look at them through the set of possibilities to which they belong? These different questions must, it seems, be brought back to two fundamental problems which are quite distinct: on the one hand, the problem of the foundation of the theory of probability, on the other hand the problem of the foundation of probable knowledge. The first problem concerns the notion of probability in itself: it consists in the elucidation of the intelligible content of the concept on which the pure theory of probability is based. The second problem concerns the application of the notion of probability to the study of real phenomena. There is of course a link between these two problems: the concept of probability must be such that, according to at least one of its meanings, it lends itself to utilization in the empirical realm. But there is an advantage in treating these two problems separately. And, in particular, if we are interested in knowledge as acquired a posteriori, it is evidently on the second problem that we shall have to focus our attention.

Two types of answers can be given to the problem of the foundation of probable knowledge: in order to give an account of this knowledge, we can invoke either a subjectivist or an objectivist explanation. According to the subjectivist explanation, the introduction of statistical methods is due simply to a limitation of our information. This limitation can be conceived either as a merely de facto limitation, not necessarily insurmountable, or as a limitation in principle. In the two cases, it is admitted that the phenomena which we are studying with the aid of statistical tools could be, in principle and so to say ideally, the object of certain knowledge. For, in themselves, they are entirely determined, in their very individuality: it is only in so far as we have only incomplete information about them that we are obliged to content ourselves with a knowledge of them which is only probable. In the first case it is claimed that this incompleteness of our information is purely contingent, that it is due, for example, to a temporary inadequacy of our measuring instruments or to a lack of time or to a limitation in our systems of calculation. In the second case it is argued rather that the incompleteness of our information is inevitable, by virtue of the fact that our knowledge capacities are inherently limited.

The first point of view, which invokes a contingent limitation, is the one which is found in current justifications of classical statistical mechanics. The second point of view, which invokes a limitation in principle, is the one which is found in the "orthodox" interpretation of quantum mechanics: the probabilistic character of this theory is interpreted as a consequence of the fact that, at the quantum level, it is no longer possible to separate the subject from the object. And this impossibility seems to be a consequence of the difference of scale which separates constitutively our knowledge from the object studied: our knowledge is adapted to macroscopic objects and the separation between subject and object is possible only at this level. Finally, because of this constitution of our knowledge, we are compelled to make use of the classical concepts (built in order to describe macroscopic objects, totally "objectifiable") in order to speak of the objects at the quantum level; and this, according to the "orthodox" interpretation, is at the root of the inseparability between subject and object at the quantum level and, therefore, of the probabilistic character of quantum physics.

According to the objectivist interpretation, the introduction of statistical methods merely reflects, at the level of our knowledge, an indetermination which belongs to the object itself and thus an objective contingency of the reality which is studied. This contingency is interpreted either as a manifestation of a principle of chance in the strict sense, of a non-causality which would affect nature at the level of the elementary events, or as the manifestation of a subjacent or superimposed causality. In the first case we arrive at a realm of non-intelligibility. In the second case contingency is considered as a consequence of the distribution of the natural phenomena in a hierarchy of levels: a phenomenon of a given level, which appears as non-determined at the level to which it belongs, must be considered as resulting in a determined manner from processes which belong to an inferior or to a superior level. (The interpretation of contingency as resulting from universal interaction could be reduced to this type of explanation: the universal system, as an all-embracing system, defines a level which is superior to that of the contingent phenomena.) This interpretation of contingency, of course, is very close to the interpretation of the subjectivist type: a phenomenon appears to us as contingent because we do not have access to the level of phenomena which determines it. But since on this view the insufficiency of our information is said to correspond to a plurality of levels in physical reality, it has an objective foundation, in such a way that the explanation is in effect based on an objective character of reality.

Either explanation requires, in turn, a justification. If the subjectivist explanation is adopted, a justification must be given telling why and how we have the right to suppose that the natural phenomena are entirely determined in themselves, and also why and how our knowledge, supposedly inadequate (be it in principle or merely in fact), turns out nevertheless to be quite adequate at the level of the statistical aggregates. If the objectivist interpretation is adopted, a justification must be given telling why and how contingency appears in the natural phenomena, and why and how phenomena which are supposedly undetermined in themselves can give rise to statistical aggregates which are, for their part, entirely determined.

With regard to the notion of probability, taken in itself, we find again the same division between subjectivist and objectivist interpretations. According to interpretations of the subjectivist type, probability is a measure attached to a certain disposition of the subject, in general to a certain state of his knowledge. It corresponds, for example, to a degree of certitude or to a degree of belief; according to a more subtle interpretation, it corresponds to the attitude with which a rational agent will approach a given situation that is open to chance, for example the attitude with which he will be willing to place a bet on an event whose outcome is not definitively known in advance. According to interpretations of the objectivist type, probability is a measure attached to certain objective aspects of reality. For example, it is understood as the ratio of the number of possible outcomes of a specified type, in a given type of trial, to the total number of possible outcomes of this type of trial. Or it is understood as the limit towards which tends the relative frequency of a certain event (with respect to a well-defined class of possible events) in a series of repeated trials, supposed to be indefinitely long. Or again it is understood as the mea-

sure of the confirmation given to a particular hypothesis by some
particular datum, and this measure itself is understood as a numerical
evaluation of the relative extension, with respect to all the possible
universes in which the hypothesis in question might be verified, of those
possible universes where this hypothesis is verified together with the
datum in question. Or again it is understood as a measure of a physical
property of a certain experimental set-up, namely the "propensity" of
this set-up to produce such and such relative frequencies.

Although there is an evident parallelism between the two sets of
problems which have just been evoked, they must be distinguished one
from the other. Nevertheless, they are not without any mutual
relationship. The subjectivist interpretation of probability is evidently
quite compatible with the subjectivist interpretation of the foundation
of probable knowledge, and in the same way the objectivist interpretation of probability is quite compatible with the objectivist explanation of the foundation of probable knowledge. But these parallels
are by no means obligatory. A subjectivist concept of probability can
well be used as a tool for the knowledge of an objective contingency,
and in the same way an objectivist concept of probability can well be
used as a tool for the knowledge of a reality which is strictly determined
but inaccessible in its details.

It appears, in any case, that the elucidation of these two categories
of problems, which belong to the field of epistemology, demands
recourse to special considerations of the world on one hand and of
man on the other. Be the objective reality conceived as entirely
determined or as marked by contingency, this implies finally a certain
understanding of the nature of the world. And on the other hand, be
the concept of probability conceived as a subjective or as an objective
property, this implies finally a certain understanding of the nature of
knowledge. Thus the relationship which is established between the
notion of probability and knowledge of the real world depends upon
the manner in which the interactions between man and nature are
understood. It would seem, then, that the explicitation of all that is
implied in the problematics of probable knowledge can be achieved
only in the context of a multi-dimensional philosophical interpretation.

It is not at all evident, however, that we have at our disposal already
today philosophical instruments which would be adequate for thinking
correctly the foundational problems raised by the notion of probability
and its applications. We can even wonder if the philosophical traditions
in which we continue to find our inspiration, whether rationalism or

empiricism, are not of a nature such as to prevent a true understanding of probability. Both traditions are inherited from a certain conception of knowledge and, correlatively, of truth, which has been forged in antiquity, from knowledge experiences which were relatively simple. According to this conception, knowledge is a sort of image of reality and is perfect to the extent that the image faithfully reproduces the reality. For rationalism, the image is conceptual in nature, for empiricism it is perceptual in nature; but on both sides there is a kind of immediacy of knowledge with respect to its object.

The language of probability, however, is not at all constituted from some given epistemology, but from certain concrete problems which the traditional methods were not able to solve. The development of the theory of probability represents an intellectual experience which cannot be considered simply as a prolongation of well established procedures, but it is a procedure in which gradually a new type of knowing has emerged. In the history of thought, actual experience always precedes man's understanding of it. And this understanding emerges only very slowly. In general, a new experience is first interpreted in the framework of preexisting theories and it is only step by step that its true nature appears and that there is discovered the true novelty which it involves. And so it is for the theory of probability. We suspect that there is, in the probabilistic procedures, the emergence of a type of knowledge profoundly different from the ones which are described by the traditional epistemologies; and we begin to realize that full consciousness of what is involved in knowledge of this sort is going to oblige us to modify considerably our concept of truth.

The very terms in which the problematics of probability has been presented above are still marked by the classical epistemologies and are without doubt inadequate. But, as always, we are obliged to formulate our questions in a language which is familiar to us, to use such instruments as are available to us, even when we begin to suspect that they are inadequate. We realize full well that probable knowledge cannot be considered as an image of reality; through it, to be sure, we aim at reality and we learn something about it, but the relationship between our knowledge and its object becomes indirect and remote. We approach the real, using probable knowledge, only through an abstract construction which involves the possible, that is to say a sort of systematic and a priori variation, which certainly does not reflect the real but which is rather like a detecting device through which we grasp some aspects of reality. This should be understood not in the sense that there would be a correspondence between the structure of our detecting device and that of reality, but in the sense that, thanks to our detecting device, we can register certain reactions of reality and thus know it, not through an image of it, but through the answers which it gives to our questions.

In the works of the contemporary authors who have studied the foundations of the notion of probability, there is announced a new epistemology the ultimate philosophical implications of which are still very far from being apparent. We already realize, however, that the concept of truth has begun to undergo a radical mutation. This does not gainsay that, until quite recently, probable knowledge has been interpreted in the framework of the old epistemologies, inspired, in one way or another, by the traditional idea of truth as a correspondence between knowledge and the thing known. According to this concept, the ideal of knowledge is that of a knowledge fully conformed to its object and fully conscious of this conformity. From this point of view, probable knowledge can appear only as an imperfect, inadequate knowledge: in this perspective, the probability attached to knowledge is interpreted as the measure of the distance which separates actual knowledge from the ideal, that is to say from a fully adequate re-presentation.

If we want to arrive at a clarification of the philosophical problems implied in the theory of probability, we must begin by becoming as conscious as possible of the epistemological and even ontological presuppositions which are at the root of the traditional interpretation. If today we have reason to think that this interpretation is inappropriate and makes it difficult for us, by its historical weight, to have access to a true understanding of probable knowledge, our first task must be to situate it exactly, because it is only on that condition that we shall be able to overcome it. Now, as it is known, the epistemological principles which are at stake here are rooted in large measure in the philosophical tradition derived from Aristotelianism. Mr. Byrne has precisely set himself the task of contributing to an elucidation of the problematics of the philosophical foundations of probable knowledge by studying the interpretation given to probable knowledge by one of the most eminent historical representatives of the Aristotelian episte-mological tradition, Thomas Aquinas.

As a matter of fact, Thomas Aquinas, following Aristotle, has made a place in his theory of knowledge, both on the theoretical and on the practical level, for probable knowledge. If, then, one should wish to elucidate clearly the epistemological foundations of the traditional interpretation, he might well examine how the proponents of the epistemology on which, historically, this traditional interpretation is based, understood probable knowledge before the appearance of the calculus of probability and of the modern notion of probability. It is most commendable of Mr. Byrne to have undertaken and achieved in the most illuminating manner this study of the Thomist theory of probable knowledge. Of course, we cannot expect to find in the works of Thomas Aquinas a problematics which it became possible to formulate only in recent times, after the mathematical theory of probability and knowledge of a statistical type were developed. The Thomist theory of probability cannot, therefore, be considered as furnishing a kind of anticipation of the classical interpretation of probability. But we can find in the Thomist theory of probable knowledge the presence of epistemological presuppositions which have played a decisive role in this interpretation.

In conformity with his general purpose, Mr. Byrne has sought to make manifest those presuppositions and this has led him, by degrees, to evoke the whole philosophical framework in which those presuppositions are located and from which they take their meaning. Indeed, when a careful study is made of the significance and role of the notion of probable knowledge in the works of Thomas Aquinas, it is found that it is involved in all aspects of his thought. It is present, of course, in his theory of knowledge; but, inasmuch as it plays a role both on the level of theoretical knowledge and on the level of practical knowledge, it intervenes not only in epistemology but also in morals. On the other hand, inasmuch as it concerns the knowledge of nature, it is founded proximally in a cosmological theory which gives physical contingency its place in nature. And inasmuch as it concerns the realm of human decision, it is founded proximally in a theory of man which locates historical contingency in the concrete situations which man has to face. On a higher level, this twofold contingency is founded on the one hand in a metaphysics of creation and on the other hand in a metaphysics of liberty. Ultimately, however, probable knowledge as such is interpreted within the global context of a philosophy which tries to understand all observable reality in the light of the supereminent reality of the being of God and to found all the levels of perfection, both in the realm of being and in the realm of knowledge, upon the absolute perfection of God. Human knowledge is here seen as a kind of analogical approximation of perfect knowledge, which is the knowledge of God, and even such an apparently deficient mode of knowing as probable knowledge must be viewed in that perspective. Probable knowledge is the most satisfactory form which rationality can take at the level of contingency; for, a being with the status of a mere creature cannot know contingent realities in their origin but only in their manifestation. On the basis of an admirable knowledge of the texts, Mr. Byrne shows in considerable detail the various interconnections which are to be found, in the work of Aquinas, among the themes which are in any way implied in the concept of probable knowledge. He argues in effect that it is only by replacing this concept in the totality of Thomas's thought and by following rigorously the threads which connect it with all aspects of this thought that we become able to grasp its full meaning.

But Mr. Byrne, again in conformity with his general intention, has not limited himself to this exhaustive study of the concept of probable knowledge in Thomas Aquinas. In order to prepare the way for a precise understanding of the true epistemological scope of the concept of probability, Mr. Byrne wanted to separate as far as possible the modern forms of probable knowledge, which are founded upon the mathematical theory of probability and its applications, from the epistemological interpretations which have been associated with them, on diverse grounds, precisely along the lines of the traditional episte-mology of Aristotelian inspiration. This has led him to examine some of the modern theories of probability and to establish a systematic comparison between the Aristotelian-Thomist notion and the modern notion of probable knowledge. As Mr. Byrne notes, Thomas Aquinas, obviously, had no idea of what the notion of probability was to become in modern times and it cannot be claimed that there existed already in the Middle Ages any genuinely mathematical theory of probability. Modern use of the formal tools of analysis has made possible a treat-ment of probabilities by means of a calculus and has thus opened the way to a precise application of the notion of probability in the study of empirical phenomena; it has also shown that the notion of probability is not univocal and has thus obliged us to distinguish several concepts of probability. The modern notion of probability is thus considerably richer and more diversified than the medieval notion. This being the case, a comparison between the Thomist notion and the modern notion of probability is, of course, of a very limited scope, at least if we view it in its positive aspects. But it has a considerable scope if we consider it in its negative aspects. It enables us, indeed, to discover better, by contrast, what differentiates the modern notion, or rather the modern notions, from this medieval notion, and, thereby, to see better the error of interpretation which is committed when one tries to understand the modern notions in the framework of an epistemology which remains marked by the tradition of which Thomas Aquinas is one of the most eminent representatives.

By stressing, then, what is original and new in the modern forms of probable knowledge, Mr. Byrne has helped prepare the way for a true philosophical reflection on their meaning. Not only has he attempted to show what is original in them, but he has also indicated to us with much precision the context in which the foundational problems relative to probable knowledge can and must be posed. From this point of view, the present study of Thomas Aquinas makes his philosophy appear as having an exemplatory character: it shows us indeed that it is only in the context of his whole philosophical outlook that Thomas's notion of probable knowledge has its full meaning. It shows us also how a preconstituted philosophical framework can become an obstacle to the full understanding of a notion. On the one hand, then, it helps us understand, by virtue of an historical analogy, that the foundational problems, such as we can pose them today, have a significance which extends very far, that, by degrees, they touch upon numerous problems, not only with regard to the theory of knowledge but also with regard to the philosophy of nature, the philosophy of action, and perhaps even metaphysics, and that their complete elucidation necessarily involves philosophical implications of great depth and magnitude. It shows us on the other hand that the very complexity of the intellectual experience which probable knowledge represents for us today, the plurification of the notion of probability, the flexibility of the interpretations which make it possible to connect the pure theory to the different empirical domains to which it can be applied, prevent us from thinking that we shall be able to elucidate the foundations of probable knowledge in the framework of an absolutist epistemology.

What Mr. Byrne suggests to us, finally, is that not only does the modern theory of probable knowledge oblige philosophy to transform the traditional conception relative to knowledge and to truth but it also calls for a kind of multi-dimensional reflection. There is, in the modern developments of probable knowledge, a proliferation of the modes of truth which renders less and less likely the possibility of fully expressing our intellectual experiences in any one single system. What is called for is an "open philosophy" rather than the substitution of one philosophical system for another. By allowing us to discern those perspectives, Mr. Byrne opens a path, as it were, to a constructive reflection upon the foundations of probable knowledge. And thus his work has value not only as an historical study but also and more deeply as a work of reflection. If he has devoted his attention to a philosophy of the past, it is in order to interrogate it in light of a present problematic. Thereby he has, as it were, brought it forth into the present; he has taken from the thinking of the past what makes it ever living and has restored this thinking to the active thought of today. The historical aspect of the work of Mr. Byrne is only the accompaniment of its reflective aspect and it is from the latter that it must be understood. By helping us to understand the meaning of the considerations of Thomas Aquinas about probable knowledge, Mr. Byrne has, in a way, suggested a context in which the foundational problems relative to a knowledge by probabilities can be adequately posed. As such his work constitutes a precious contribution to the yet unfinished task of reflecting philosophically upon those foundational problems.

We therefore owe a debt of gratitude to Mr. Byrne for having undertaken this meditation and for having conducted it in the double perspective of precise and complete reactualization of Thomas's thoughts on probable knowledge and of an attentive openness to the contemporary problematics of probability. His work represents an exemplary essay in interpretative interrogation and in prospective understanding.

JEAN LADRIÈRE
Louvain
Belgium

AUTHOR'S PREFACE

For many years, man has been seeking after truth. He seeks it in many different ways, from many different sources, and he has by this time found a considerable variety of ways in which to describe it. He is not even sure, at times, that there is such a thing as truth or, if truth does exist, that it is attainable. Still, man seeks truth. And, being the orderly creature that he is, he wants truth to be orderly as well. Thus he has always shown a marked tendency to make truth after his own image, so that he might present it in a neat and, if possible, little package. This, of course, has not infrequently required considerable ingenuity. For, whatever truth may be in the final analysis, it seldom appears to us to be neat and orderly. Man realizes this, at least in those moments when he is honest with himself, but the realization disturbs rather than pleases him. He simply does not like an untidy world. Thus, the more he learns about the complexity and intricacy of the world in which he lives, the more he seeks to express what he has learned by means of pregnant words, symbols, and formulas. These are, to be sure, often no more than time- and labor-saving devices by means of which he avoids the unpleasant task of pointing out (at some length, it must be added) that the world really is not as simple as all that.

Take, for example, that hoary crisis which arose in the intellectual circles of ancient Greece when it was discovered that the diagonal of a square is incommensurate with its side. Try though one might, the poor Greeks found to their dismay, there just is no way to compare the diagonal to the side without involving oneself in a messy sort of number that has ever after been known as an "irrational." So alarming, in fact, was this discovery, that members of the mathematical society of Pythagoreans are said to have sworn an oath never to reveal the secret to the impressionable masses.

The attitude of the Pythagoreans, no doubt, strikes us as having been somewhat bizarre. But it is not hard for us, for all that, to understand how they must have felt. No one, after all, likes to admit that there is disorder in the universe! As has been shown by modern psychology, not even the hallowed "evidence of one's senses" can keep the average adult from seeing order and perfection even when it is not there to be seen. Similarly, anyone living in the temperate zones of our planet is so accustomed to the simple fact of four seasons in the year, each with its appropriate characteristics, that he will find it hard to accept either a warm day in winter or a cold day in the summer. On many different levels of human life, the "conservative" tendency resists any change in that to which one is accustomed, just as the "progressive" seeks to introduce changes intended to rectify irregularities in the *status quo*. We are, in short, irremediably committed to the quest for order and as often as not we are willing to achieve that order at almost any price – even, paradoxically enough, at the price of insufferable turmoil.

One of the early victims of this decidedly human quest for order was the Greek philosopher Parmenides, who divided the universe into two neat categories: being and non-being. Being, for this ancient sage, is forever stable and constant; whatever is not so endowed is non-being, that is, simply speaking, is not. Anyone who recognizes the difference (or, as we might say, "knows the score") has truth; anyone who does not has only opinion – which therefore, for Parmenides, is not very different from error. Plato and Aristotle modified this oversimplified world-view, but each of them remained a confirmed proponent of the Greek ideal of order and regularity. In their writings as in the writings of their forebears, the complexity of things tends to be viewed, in one way or another, in the light of simple principles to which all change and irregularity is subject and in terms of which all is explained.

Medieval thinkers, taking their cue from their Hellenic ancestors, were no less imbued with a love for order. Just as Roman law smoothed out the unpleasant complexities of political life for the sake of what is still known as "the common good," so too did the Scholastics maintain order and discipline in matters intellectual. Greek cosmology remained important as a foundation for the medieval world-order, but became in fact but a visible sign of a higher, spiritual order: the order of faith. Thus the guardian of order and regularity was no longer merely the political ruler nor even the religious leader, but the leader of the new intellectualism, the theologian, to whom fell the awesome task of describing and at times even creating order in a universe permeated with the divine.

Since that time, of course, a few changes have been made. The science of order *par excellence*, mathematics, has blossomed forth in marvelous profusion; and with the aid of the new mathematics undreamed of patterns of regularity have been partly found, partly introduced into the physical universe. The mathematician – or, in the eyes of the masses, the physicist – has become the new guardian of order in the universe. So powerful, indeed, has become the new mathematics, both in its pure and in its applied aspects, that one can no longer say readily where "science" leaves off and its object begins. The "universe," once somewhat naively looked upon as something to be discovered and explained, tends to be more and more the product of man's cogitation and creation. Thus, at least, did the great German philosopher Immanuel Kant envision the relationship between scientific thought and its object. It is no longer *au courant* to refer to oneself as being Kantian; but few philosophers of science have been able to escape Kant's radical dichotomy between subject and object. The denouement of post-Newtonian absolutism, which was in fact a kind of naive mathematical realism, has led to what might be called, by comparison, mathematical idealism. The search for order is by no means less intense than in former days; quite the contrary. It is just that man is now much more conscious of the fact that the order of which he speaks is perhaps due as much to thought as to things; and the thought from whence that order arises is, as often as not, the thought of the mathematician.

This new epistemology, which might be described as critical rather than sceptical, is perhaps not essentially different from the epistemology of the medievals or even of the ancients. The problem of Parmenides is still, at least fundamentally, the problem of today, in spite of countless nuances that have come to be recognized as relevant down through the centuries. That problem, simply stated, is this: how correlate the fixity of thought with the flux of things? For the ancient Greeks, this problem was formulated primarily as the problem of change; for the medievals, the focus of attention became the problem of universals; for philosophers of the Enlightenment, it was the problem of certitude; now, in an age marked by the maturity of science, it is seen primarily as the problem of induction. In short, the epistemological problem at least in its essentials has not changed from antiquity to our own days.

To say, however, that the problem has not changed does not imply that the emphasis has not changed. The epistemological emphasis, if one may so speak, is in fact now exactly the opposite of what it was for the Greeks. The difference, to state it in brazen generalities, is the difference between naive realism and critical idealism, between order in things and order in thought. To show what we mean, let us take for consideration the simple proposition: *There is order in the universe.* Allowing for pedantic qualifications, both Greek and modern would accept this proposition as fundamentally accurate; but each, in accepting it, would mean something quite different from what is meant by the other. For Greek as well as for modern, the idea of a "universe" implies order, namely, the order of parts in a whole. But for the Greek that order is above all qualitative or, if you will, ontological; for the modern, it is quantitative, or mathematical. For the Greek, "the universe" is something objective, real, existential – in short, a *Ding-an-sich*. For the modern, it is considerably more subjective, ideal, essential – in short, a *Wesen*, a *Ding-vor-mir*. Thus, for the Greek the crucial problem was: how can there be *disorder in* the universe (of things)? The modern asks rather: how can there be *order outside* the universe (of thought)? The difference, to say the least, is remarkable; and it is due in no small measure to a gradual liberation of mathematics from the flux and instability of matter, which in turn has made possible a mathematical domination over that very flux and instability.

A complete history of this ideological transformation, assuming that it is even possible, has yet to be written. It seems clear, however, that a most important ingredient, perhaps even the leitmotiv, of such a history would have to be that of the role of mathematics in human thought and human endeavor. And of all the branches of mathematics which man has developed in the course of his long history perhaps none has had a more profound influence upon human thought patterns than that comparatively recent arrival, the calculus of probability.

It is a basic contention of this book that the notion of probability as such has had a much longer history than the mathematical expression thereof. But, as we shall see, the notion of probability assumed a primordial role in human thought only after it was given a mathematical expression and that mathematical expression in turn found its way into the very heart of the empirical sciences. It is not our purpose to evaluate this mathematization of the contemporary notion of probability. But, we shall maintain, mathematization of the probable has resulted in a somewhat top-heavy restriction of "probability" to a meaning which is a function of the mathematical theory. This restriction of meaning, we intend to show, is somewhat arbitrary, involving as it does a widespread disregard for pre-mathematical nuances of the term. Current usage notwithstanding, these nuances are still alive. But they live, like spirits from the past, under assumed names.

Be that as it may, an effect of the modern mathematization of the probable is that this notion has been caught up in the exaggerated ideal of "objectivity," the usual meaning of which is roughly equivalent to "mathematicized." As a result, many authors tend to speak of any non-mathematicized (and hence "non-objective") aspect of probability as being "subjective" or "psychological" and, by implication, "non-scientific." For a host of reasons as diverse as the discovery of non-Euclidean geometries and the "scientifically objective" annihilation of six million Jews, many more recent authors are seeking to explode this myth of objectivity and the Cartesian-Kantian dichotomy upon which it depends by showing that so-called subjective, or, better, personal and social factors play an important role in all human endeavors including that of science. In a few instances, this has led to a broadening of the notion of probability; but most of the authors involved seem content to leave probability to the mathematicians and to make their point in other terms.

In the Middle Ages, by contrast, the notion of probability was relatively innocent of mathematical connotations and yet had a rather wide gamut of nuances which express at least germinally what modern authors are seeking to say in other terms about the non-mathematical aspects of probability. Of particular importance in the medieval view of probability is the fact that this notion is intimately associated with that of opinion. For the medieval, it is an opinion which is or is not probable, or is more or less probable; and the notion of opinion refers not only to an "objective" proposition but to a "subjective" com-mitment to that proposition. Hence for the medieval there is no opinion, and hence no probability, apart from a subject or subjects who assent to that proposition as being true.

To illustrate the medieval usage and theory of probability we have chosen for consideration the best known and in some ways the most important of all medieval masters, Thomas Aquinas. For, in the writings of this thirteenth century scholastic we find an expression of medieval thought-patterns unsurpassed in breadth and depth by any of his contemporaries or predecessors. *We shall not find his thoughts on and in terms of probability of any significant help in connection with the modern problem of the foundations of mathematical probability. But we shall be able to add historical perspective to current discussions of both mathematical and extra-mathematical probability.*

To be sure, we shall have ample occasion to point out weaknesses and inadequacies in Thomas's approach to and use of probability. But of far greater importance to us than the defects in his theory are the ideological roots of these defects. For, by uncovering these ideological roots we shall come to a clearer understanding as to how a given intellectual milieu can retard as well as advance the quest for knowledge. What we shall have to say in this regard, however, will be misunderstood if it is taken as another knowing leer at the darkness which preceded the light. For, in the end, we shall have learned something not only about medieval ideology but about any ideology, including our own.

In the light of these considerations, the work before us can be seen to fall into three distinct parts. In the first part we shall draw out of a survey of contemporary thought about probability the assertion that the notion of probability refers not only to a formal system but to all non-demonstrative reasoning. In the second and principal part of our study we shall show from various points of view that this reference to non-demonstrative reasoning is the central feature of a medieval theory of probability, namely that of Thomas Aquinas. In the third and concluding part we shall indicate briefly the manner in which this medieval usage influenced the classical theory of probability and thus indirectly set the stage for contemporary discussions.

Part One, then, will consist of a survey of representative modern views of probability and non-demonstrative reasoning. The chief purpose of this survey will be to show that, contrary to a rather widespread assumption, the notion of probability transcends the bounds of the mathematical theory of probability. (Ch. 1)

Part Two will consist of five chapters. First we will concentrate upon the notion of opinion within the broad context of Thomas's views on the limitations of human knowledge as seen against a background of ideal types of knowledge. This will enable us to characterize an opinion as imperfect but properly intellectual knowledge. (Ch. 2.) Having thus localized opinion statically within the perspective of merely human knowledge, we will then consider the opinion dynamically, insofar as it has a history as a proposition assented to or rejected by men in the course of time. This will introduce us to a consideration of how Thomas weights opinions, thereby allowing us to associate his usage of probability with what we could call the probity (that is, the authority) of those who accept or reject the opinion in question. (Ch. 3.) If the aforementioned analysis can be characterized as dealing with the passive dynamism of opinion, what ensues has to do rather with the active dynamism of opinion, that is, the role which men themselves play in the formulation, development, and defense of opinions. What is in question here is dialectical argumentation or disputation, the ordinary human means of analyzing and evaluating opinions. In this context probability assumes its basic meaning as indicative of the relationship between an opinion and an argument (*probatio*) or arguments brought forth in its favor (hence, "provable" or perhaps "approvable"). But the ultimate goal of argumentation is to establish a given opinion (or its opposite) demonstratively. Thus the fact that an opinion is said to be probable, though positive on the level of opinion as such, takes on a negative or pejorative signification ("probationary" in the sense of tentative) when seen in the light of the desired culmination, demonstrative or "scientific" knowledge. (Ch. 4.) Everything to be said up to this point will have suggested that for Thomas probability is a logical relationship. In the next chapter, however, we shall point out certain aspects of his thought which suggest an empirical or perhaps even a "relative frequency" theory, expressed discontinuously. (Ch. 5.) Finally, we shall return to the notion of ideal knowledge to show that Thomas ultimately founds certitude not upon the created universe, which he considers to be of finite duration, but upon God, intellectual union with whom is the sole means of transcending the fallibility of opinion and satisfying the quest for comprehensive knowledge of all things. (Ch. 6.)

Part Three, our concluding section, will discuss the historical meaning of probability both in general and with respect to the calculus of probability as such.

As is true of any work of this kind, the pages which are to follow have been written in such a way as to suggest a kind of autonomous omnicompetence on the part of the author. This amounts to what the scholastics might have called a total abstraction from the complex details of real life. It allows a certain simplicity of presentation which would otherwise be stifled by the constant need to indicate, if even possible, the sources of and the influences upon what the author has to say. This procedure has the excellent advantage of confining to the author alone responsibility for the many defects in the work. But it suffers the disadvantage of leaving in obscurity the fact that the work as a whole is at best a reflection of the author's dependence upon others. This dependence is both ideological and personal, although the author himself would be the last one to try to determine in a number of cases the relative importance of one or the other. For the most part, however, the ideological dependence is rather clearly indicated in the form of footnotes and a bibliography. But one's personal dependence upon others is of its very nature more difficult to delineate. Be that as it may, the author's awareness of his decidedly human condition compels him to descend momentarily from his ivory tower in order to acknowledge that even he is but a man. This acknowledgement takes the form of a series of names which, though inconsequential to the casual reader, are to the author but inadequate symbols of his profound gratitude to many. Since the list must of necessity be finite it is restricted to those whose assistance has been more direct and immediate. Without further ado, then, I wish to thank: Professor Jean Ladrière, for his patient guidance and unforgettable example of dedication to truth; Professors A. Dondeyne, Fernand Van Steenberghen, Joseph Dopp, A. Wylleman, and, in general, the faculty of the Institut Supérieur de Philosophie of the University of Louvain; Rev. Edward A. Maziarz, C.PP.S., for reading the manuscript and for other reasons more than sufficient to justify dedicating this work to him; the Fulbright Commission and the United States Educational Foundation in Belgium, which made financially possible the two-year sojourn in Belgium during which this work was written; and Madame Jos. Raemaekers, for her excellent job of typing the manuscript. Finally, a word of thanks to Mrs. Cecilia M. Byrne, my mother, whose presence with me in Belgium was above all a personal consolation but also a frankly practical advantage.

Louvain, Belgium

TABLE OF CONTENTS

PART ONE

MODERN NOTIONS OF PROBABILITY

CHAPTER I

SOME MODERN VIEWS ON PROBABILITY

In approaching our study of the theory of probability in Thomas Aquinas, we are compelled to specify as carefully as possible what it is we hope to learn from such a study. For, it is anything but self-evident that one would wish to look to the Middle Ages, still less to a medieval theologian, for insights about a branch of knowledge which was formulated only subsequently and which has not really become important in the history of thought until the twentieth century. What, one could quite legitimately ask, could we possibly gain from a clearer knowledge of a medieval notion of probability? The answer to this question is nothing less than the purpose of the study before us.

HISTORICAL ORIGIN OF PROBABILITY

On the surface, at least, the study which we propose to make might be considered an inquiry into the non-existent. For, as anyone familiar with the history of the subject would know, the theory of probability was not discovered during the Middle Ages but considerably later – by Cardano, according to some; by Pascal and Fermat, according to others. If, then, the theory of probability was discovered at the time of either of those mentioned, it obviously was not discovered sooner. Moreover, there is some reason for saying that a theory of probability was not developed during the Middle Ages precisely because such a development was impossible at that time. After all, the mathematical equipment of those days was primitive by comparison to that of our own day. What did the medieval know about the complex structures which go to make up the modern theory of probability: highly refined statistical procedures, set theory, stochastic processes, infinitesimal calculus, and so forth?

On the other hand, it is misleading to identify the theory of probability with its current state of development. It is equally misleading to assume that currently available mathematical tools would have been prerequisite to any medieval endeavor in this direction. For, little mathematical acumen is needed to count the number of times a coin turns up heads, or that a die turns up "six"; and for such elementary, but important, calculations both mathematics and material were available already to the ancient Greeks, to say nothing of the medieval Europeans. Thus, it would seem that the beginnings of a theory of probability were not, if we may so speak, medievally impossible.

In the second place, as has been shown in a wide variety of more or less recent studies, a number of scientific developments whose formal "discovery" is usually dated some time after the close of the Middle Ages were nonetheless given a thorough prescientific inauguration in medieval speculations. To mention just a few examples, we are at once reminded of Boyer's findings with regard to medieval foreshadowings of both infinitesimal calculus and analytic geometry.[1] The somewhat bizarre ideas of Ramon Lull, a thirteenth century writer, are also thought to have had some bearing upon Leibniz's dream of a universal language, a dream which has since burst forth into life as symbolic logic.[2] Nor would any serious historian of science wish to deny at least the title of precursors to the thirteenth century experimentalists, Robert Grosseteste and his weighty protégé, Roger Bacon.[3] Another recent study further shows that experimental studies of light owe not a little to the work of yet another medieval, Theodoric of Freiberg.[4] Lest our point here become unduly belabored, let us simply allude to the numerous indications of medieval scientific accomplishments to be found in such works as those of Thorndike, Sarton, Randall, and Clagett.[5] In short, many if not most of the currently pursued mathe-

[1] Carl B. Boyer, *The History of the Calculus and its Conceptual Development* (New York, 1959); *History of Analytic Geometry* (New York, 1956).

[2] The relationship between Lull's *Ars Magna* and Leibniz's ideas about a universal calculus is brought out by I. M. Bochenski, *A History of Formal Logic* (Notre Dame, Ind. 1961), pp. 272–273, 274–276. For some details of the *Ars Magna* see Martin Gardner, *Logic Machines and Diagrams* (New York, 1958).

[3] See A. C. Crombie, *Robert Grosseteste and the Origins of Experimental Science*, 1100–1700 (Oxford, 1953). For an account of Roger Bacon's science see this work, pp. 139–163 as well as other works cited in a bibliographical footnote, p. 139. Crombie has also contributed greatly to our knowledge of medieval science with his *Medieval and Early Modern Science*, of which a revised second edition appeared (Garden City, New York, 1959).

[4] William A. Wallace, *The Scientific Methodology of Theodoric of Freiberg* (Friburg, Switzerland, 1959).

[5] The authors mentioned here are responsible for a large number of works; but we are thinking in particular of the following: George P. Sarton, *The Appreciation of Ancient and Medieval Science during the Renaissance* (Philadelphia, 1953); John Herman Randall, Jr., *The Career of Philosophy from the Middle Ages to the Enlightenment* (New York and London,

matical and physical sciences have some sort of roots in medieval investigations. Thus, again, it would seem that the beginnings of a theory of probability were not medievally impossible.

In the third place, as certain tendencies in modern thought would point out, it is the problem which demands a solution; and thus, if a problem is recognized as such, someone will at least try, with or without success, to resolve it. It might accordingly be postulated that if problems requiring probabilistic solutions were recognized as problems during the Middle Ages, then there might have been at that time some attempt at solutions which we, at least, could recognize as probabilistic. One would, of course, be expecting too much if he were to look to the Middle Ages for problems even germinally related to a Brownian movement or, *a fortiori*, a dispersion pattern of electrons, problems which have been so forcefully dealt with by means of probability equations. But it is by no means so unreasonable to suppose, even *a priori*, that people in the Middle Ages played games and even upon occasion gave themselves to gambling; that they were born, contracted diseases (which even then were classified), and eventually, each after a determinate number of years, died; that they, like us, were faced with many decisions, personal and professional, which could only be made on the basis of some more or less rudimentary calculation of "the odds"; that, in short, they like us were in daily contact with the puzzling uncertainties of the contingent, the accidental, the chance event. If this was in fact the case, then it would again seem that the beginnings of a theory of probability were not medievally impossible.

In the fourth place, a not insignificant ingredient of traditional Roman Catholic moral theology, that of the various problem-solving "systems," does in fact originate in a medieval notion of probability. These systems were developed down through post-medieval times in order to provide practical rules of thumb on the basis of which a person, doubtful as to what course of action to pursue, might resolve his doubt in order to act. It is important to note in this regard that the problems envisioned are such that under the circumstances one cannot know with certitude what is right, and hence must fall back upon

---

1962); L. Thorndike, *A History of Magic and Experimental Science* (New York, 1923–1943), 6 vols.; M. Clagett, *The Science of Mechanics in the Middle Ages* (Madison, Wis., 1960). The forefather of these reevaluations of medieval science was and still is Pierre Duhem, among whose many works the most important and most influential was his *Le Système du Monde; Histoire des doctrines cosmologiques de Platon à Copernic* (Paris, 1913–1917), 5 vols. For an appreciation of Duhem, see A. C. Crombie (ed.), *Scientific Change* (London, 1943), p. 809. For a more comprehensive bibliography of works dealing with science in the Middle Ages, see Crombie's *Robert Grosseteste and the Origins of Experimental Science*.

extrinsic criteria of judgment in order to reach a decision. The typical problem, and an important one at that, is that of an individual who cannot decide simply on the basis of the facts at hand whether he is free of or bound by a given law. To help such an individual the moral theologians gradually devised various systems which were called, in ascending order according to the amount of emphasis given to liberty over law: tutiorism, probabiliorism, equiprobabilism, probabilism, and laxism. In view of the rather legalistic approach which characterized post-Tridentine moral theology, it should not be surprising that the differences between these various systems were, until very recently, the subject of much internal debate and disagreement, so heated at times as to necessitate papal intervention.[1] If, therefore, it is correct to assume from subsequent theological developments that there were in fact medieval discussions about probability, one might also suspect that during the Middle Ages some attempt was made (rudimentary, no doubt, but real) to calculate probabilities. Thus we are once again led to the idea that the beginnings of a theory of probability were not medievally impossible.

Whatever the value of the foregoing dialectic, it cannot, of course, be said to indicate any more than what it claims to indicate, namely that there might have been a theory of probability, however rudimentary, during the Middle Ages. If, however, there is any basis for this conjecture, it is hardly acknowledged by the standard histories of the subject. I. Todhunter, in his venerable *History of the Mathematical Theory of Probability* (1865), notes a reference to the probabilities associated with three dice in a late medieval commentary on Dante's *Purgatorio*, then skims over other more or less relevant observations in the writings of Cardano, Kepler, and Galileo; but he traces the true origin of the science to a famous correspondence between Pascal and Fermat with regard to questions proposed by the Chevalier de Mere,

---

[1] As a matter of fact, the literature which has resulted from discussions of these moral systems is far more extensive than the uninitiated could ever imagine. But, unfortunately, the vast majority of the works in question were written and have remained in Latin. Most readily accessible as an introduction to the moral systems are any of a number of scholastic manuals of moral theology, a recent example of which is that of E. F. Regatillo and M. Zalba: *Theologiae Moralis Summa* (Madrid, 1952), Vol. I, pp. 270–311. A not altogether successful attempt to integrate probabilism in particular into a more love-orientated morality will be found in Gérard Gilleman, *The Primacy of Charity in Moral Theology* (Westminster, Md., 1961), pp. 262–279. A good summary of the historical development of and controversies over the various systems is given by Ulpanius Lopez, *Thesis Probabilismi ex Sancto Thoma Demonstrata* (excerpta ex *Periodicis de Re Morali Canonica Liturgica*, Tom. 25 et 27) (Rome, 1937). A far more extensive treatment, and perhaps the best available in a modern language, is that of Th. Deman, "Probabilisme," *Dictionnaire de Théologie Catholique*, Tome 13, première partie, cols. 417–619. Abundant bibliographical material will be found in Regatillo-Zalba, Lopez, and especially Deman.

whom Boole calls, in his *Laws of Thought*, "a reputed gamester." [1] This view of historical origins went unchallenged for a century and is still found, for example, in an historical summary undertaken by Pius Servien in a work dated 1949.[2] In the past few years, however, renewed interest in the history of the theory of probability has helped somewhat to fill in the gaps left by Todhunter's vague references to Dante and Cardano. Cioffari had already studied the concept of fortune in Dante, in Dante's fourteenth century commentators, and even before.[3] But far more influential was the recent appearance in English (1961) of Cardano's *Liber de Ludo Aleae*, which has convinced many that he rather than Pascal and Fermat deserves the title of founder of the theory of probability.[4] Thus, for example, King and Read, in their popular history of the subject, entitled *Pathways to Probability* (1963), begin with Cardano.[5] In his *Games, Gods and Gambling* (1962), F. N. David spends considerable time on Cardano, but in four preceding chapters traces the origins of probability and statistical ideas all the way back to ancient times. However, the Middle Ages come out badly in David's presentation. As he sees it, these are the Dark Ages, at least as far as the theory of probability is concerned. Christian theology, he says, replaced the pagan notion of a random event with that of divine providence and considered both secular learning and *a fortiori* gambling to be sinful.[6] Thus, if we are to believe the historians, however possible it might have been for someone to develop a theory of probability during the Middle Ages, to all appearances this simply did not happen.

---

[1] I. Todhunter, *A History of the Mathematical Theory of Probability from the Time of Pascal to that of Laplace* (reprinted: New York, 1949), pp. 1–21. For Boole's observation, see *An Investigation of the Laws of Thought* (New York, 1962), p. 243.

[2] Pius Servien, *Hasard et Probabilités* (Paris, 1949), p. 31. See also the same author's study, *Probabilités et Physique* (Paris, 1945), p. 9, and especially his *Science et Hasard* (Paris, 1952), pp. 65–71 and following, where he raises the question as to how one should determine the historical origins of the calculus of probability.

[3] V. Cioffari, *Fortune and Fate from Democritus to St. Thomas Aquinas* (New York, 1935); *The Conception of Fortune and Fate in the Works of Dante* (London, 1941); *Fortune in Dante's 14th Century Commentators* (Cambridge, Mass., 1944).

[4] Gerolamo Cardano, *The Book on Games of Chance: "Liber de Ludo Aleae"*, translated by S. H. Gould and others (New York, 1961).

[5] King, Amy C., and Cecil B. Read, *Pathways to Probability; History of the Mathematics of Certainty and Chance* (New York, 1963).

[6] F. N. David, *Games, Gods and Gambling: the Origins and History of Probability and Statistical Ideas from the Earliest Times to the Newtonian Era* (London, 1962), pp. 24 and 30. It is fascinating to note in connection with David's dislike for the notion of providence that at least one scientist sees a reconciliation between science and religion precisely in terms of the scientific notion of chance and the theological notion of providence. See William G. Pollard, *Chance and Providence: God's Action in a World Governed by Scientific Law* (London, 1958).

THE FOUNDATIONS OF PROBABILITY

In spite of all indications to the negative, we are still not sure whether a theory of probability did or did not exist during the Middle Ages. But, unlike previous historians of the subject, our lack of sureness is due not in the least to any lack of relevant data, but rather to the fact that the very notion of a "theory of probability" is fraught with ambiguity. What, after all, do we mean by a theory of probability? To what extent, if any, must a theory of probability be mathematically formalized? Under what conditions does a theory *about* probability deserve to be entitled a theory *of* probability?

Up to this point, it will have been noticed, in speaking of "the theory of probability" we have tacitly assumed that the theory of probability is essentially mathematical, pure and/or applied. Having thus restricted ourselves to the confines of a current and widespread presupposition, we conceded that to all appearances there was no serious attempt to develop a theory of probability before the time of Cardano. We should now like to modify that conclusion by asserting instead that as far as we know, no one before the time of Cardano seriously attempted to develop a professedly *mathematical* theory of probability – and thus that no one calculated probabilities in the way in which probabilities are calculated today. But we by no means concede that no one attempted to calculate probabilities; for, in fact, we are prepared to show abundant evidence to the contrary.

To clarify the meaning of the distinction just suggested, then, permit us to resort to the French, in which language what we call the (mathematical) theory of probability is called the *calcul des probabilités*. Transliterating this expression, we shall henceforth follow the custom of Bertrand Russell and speak of a *calculus of probability* when referring to the formal (mathematical) system as such. When we speak of *calculating* probabilities, we may mean calculating with the aid of the calculus or without such aid. Whether the latter is mathematical or not will be left up to the reader to decide.

This being said, we must next go on to an even more important clarification. For, just as we began by tacitly assuming that a theory of probability is mathematical, so too we assumed that whatever the theory, the notion of probability as such is clear. But, as even a casual perusal of the literature would show, there is by no means any general agreement as to the meaning of probability. That the term has mathematical implications is more or less taken for granted. After all, it has come to play such an important role in scientific theory precisely on account of what we have chosen to call the calculus of probability. Thus it is only to be expected that, as has been the case for many years now, discussions about probability are conducted along more or less formal lines, and with a view to greater accuracy in the mathematical representation of "probabilities." The value and the effectiveness of these mathematical analyses of probabilities are, of course, nothing less than astounding; nor can anyone foresee a limit to the number and kinds of uses to which this powerful instrument of calculation may sooner or later be put. But it would be a mistake to suppose that because the calculus of probability is so highly developed the notion of probability as such has thus been made that much clearer.[1]

On the other hand, important developments within mathematics do stimulate metamathematical inquiries into the underlying significance of what the mathematician has been doing; and these inquiries, in turn, tend to engender so-called philosophical speculations. The end result of such multi-faceted cooperative reflection upon what one has been and is doing within and with a given mathematical discipline is, at the very least, a deeper understanding of the human cognitive process and its possibilities.[2]

[1] For a thorough treatment of this whole question, see Lancelot T. Hogben, *Statistical Theory: The Relationship of Probability, Credibility and Error; An Examination of the Contemporary Crisis in Statistical Theory from a Behaviorial Viewpoint* (London, 1957).

[2] These remarks have to do, of course, with what has come to be known, expressively enough, as studies in "Foundations." What started as an investigation into the foundations of arithmetic in time grew to encompass all of mathematics. In the process, the very instrument of investigation has itself become the object investigated, so that the whole development might simply be referred to as studies in the foundations of logic. For a time, these studies were vigorously pursued with the expectation that one would ultimately arrive at what might here be called the "rock-bottom" foundations, that is to say, the ultimate formalization of any axiom-system. These premature expectations were, however, put to rest once and for all once logicians began to study the very study of foundations. Especially damaging to the formalist's dream was the long-ignored but telling demonstration by Kurt Gödel (1931) that a formal axiomatic system must necessarily contain internal limitations which make impossible perfect axiomatization. Some interpretations of Gödel's "incompleteness theorem" have appeared suggesting everything from scientific agnosticism to the need for a special type of intuition. Whatever the relevance of these views to Gödel's work, we prefer the more modest conclusion of Nagel and Newman that "the resources of the human intellect have not been, and cannot be, fully formalized." As these same authors go on to observe, in the case of formally indemonstrable truths one must simply resort to "informal" meta-mathematical arguments which, they suggest, are not merely based upon "bare appeals to intuition." See Ernest Nagel and James R. Newman, *Gödel's Proof* (New York, 1958), esp. p. 101. See also Jean Ladrière, *Les Limitations internes des formalismes* (Louvain-Paris, 1957); Bernard J. F. Lonergan, *Insight: A Study of Human Understanding*, revised student edition (New York, 1958), pp. XXIV–XXV and 574. Ladrière provides what is considered by many the best analysis of Gödel's work on a technical basis. Lonergan, on the other hand, is interesting as a masterfully developed philosophical treatise not a little influenced by the incompleteness theorem. A brief but excellent technical summary of the theorem will be found in William and Martha Kneale, *The Development of Logic* (Oxford, 1962), pp. 712–724.

To come right to the point, the development of the calculus of probability has, as is true of other branches of mathematics, led to a deep interest in the question of its foundations. The chief reason for this metamathematical interest has been, of course, a desire to establish the axiomatic basis of the science with formal rigor. At first conducted as it were within the confines of the calculus of probability itself, investigations into the formal foundations have in time become a distinct branch of mathematics in its own right; and, more recently, the technical problems uncovered by such investigations have been taken under the wings of formal logic as such.[1] In short, the development of what Rudolf Carnap calls the logical foundations of probability bears certain close analogies to the development of foundational studies in general.

But the development of probability studies also involves problems which are associated specifically with the notion of probability itself, and it is about these problems that we are most directly concerned. For, on the one hand, in order to formalize the calculus of probability it has been customary to build into the formal system an abstract definition of probability. Once this has been done, of course, the formal system as such stands or falls on the merits of its logical consistency; but the question still remains as to whether in fact it is "probability" that has been formalized. And thus, on the other hand, the *meaning* of probability is not in fact determined by formalization but remains dependent in part upon the history and in part upon the application of the calculus of probability.

Historically, we recall, the calculus of probability grew out of an at first casual and ultimately very serious study of games of chance. Whatever the merits of Cardano's work, the real impetus to such studies was given by the investigations of Pascal and Fermat. Their point of departure, games of chance, remained the focal point and in a sense the model for the research of later mathematicians such as the Bernoullis, De Moivre, Bayes, Lagrange, Condorcet and Laplace. As a result of these ever more extensive analyses, the calculus of probability gradually came to be concerned not merely with games of chance but with all kinds of complex events the outcome of which, as in games of chance, cannot be precisely determined on the basis of initial conditions alone. The fundamental problem, regardless of the particular form which it took, was simply this, if we may so express it: how calculate

---

[1] For a good over-all view of the scope and the various aspects of contemporary studies in the calculus of probability, see the excellent bibliographical survey in Emanuel Parzen, *Modern Probability Theory and its Applications* (New York-London, 1960), pp. 28–31.

indirectly what of its very nature cannot be calculated directly? To put it somewhat differently, these early students of the calculus of probability were seeking to discover and to express mathematically the aspects of order and regularity contained even in events which occur without any obvious order and regularity. What they were seeking, in other words, was a mathematics of the contingent, a means of predicting rigorously in general what in the particular cannot be rigorously predicted.

Now, whatever interest was shown during this early period in the notion of probability as such, the notion itself was not really considered to be problematic. Definitions of probability, though not merely makeshift, *were based on commonly accepted usage,* and usually involved some assertion to the effect that all events under consideration must be equally possible. In time, however, mathematicians such as Poincaré came to see that such a definition of probability is circular, since, at least from a mathematical point of view, there is hardly any difference between possibility and probability.[1] More recently, new formulations, notably that of Keynes and Jeffreys and that of Von Mises and Reichenbach, have sought to surmount the difficulties inherent in what has come to be known as the classical definition.[2] The efforts of these men, representing respectively what are known as the logical and the frequency theory of probability, have been of great practical value; but, as can be seen from the many subsequent attempts to improve their theoretical formulations, they have by no means succeeded in giving an ultimate mathematical expression to the notion of probability.[3]

It is important to note that the difficulties to which we here refer are only indirectly of importance to the formalization of the calculus itself. The introduction of set theory and the axiomatization carried out by

---

[1] Poincaré will be considered briefly when we take up the views of J.-L. Gendre and of Pius Servien, the latter of whom maintains that it is basically impossible to escape the problem uncovered by Poincaré so long as it continues to be posed in the same way.

[2] The chief works of these authors, which must be considered contemporary classics in the field, are the following. John Maynard Keynes, *A Treatise on Probability* (Oxford, 1921; New York, 1942). Harold Jeffreys, *Theory of Probability* (Oxford, 1939); 3rd ed., 1961). Richard von Mises, *Probability, Statistics and Truth,* 1st German ed. Vienna, 1928; 1st English ed., New York, 1939; 2nd revised English ed., New York and London, 1957. Hans Reichenbach, *The Theory of Probability,* 1st German ed., Leiden, 1935; English transl., with new additions, Berkeley, 1949.

[3] The historical development here in question is given thorough treatment by Rudolf Carnap, *Logical Foundations of Probability* (Chicago, 1950), pp. 23–36, 182–192. See also the critical analysis of both the logical and the frequency theory of probability in Bertrand Russell, *Human Knowledge: Its Scope and Limits* (paper ed., New York, 1962), pp. 333–418, as well as the excellent survey by Ernest Nagel, *Principles of the Theory of Probability* (International Encyclopedia of Unified Science, Vol. I, no. 6; Chicago, 1939).

Borel, Lévy, Kolmogorov and others have put the mathematics as such on a firm footing.[1] The difficulties and disagreements, and they are many, have to do rather with the interpretation of the formal system.[2] It is on this level that more or less philosophical commitments come to play a role, at least implicitly, in the discussion; and these, in turn, are brought into the open because of the fact that the calculus of probability has in this century become a key instrument in the formulation of physical theory.

The effective use of a probabilistic approach to describe certain problems in genetics and in physics in the last century paled into insignificance in the early part of the twentieth century when Bohr, Heisenberg, and Schrödinger recast the whole structure of nuclear mechanics along "probabilistic" lines. And thus with the rise of quantum physics the calculus of probability lost the innocence and naiveté of its childhood. No longer was it dealing merely with games of chance or with carefully delimited chance events, but with the very structure of the universe and, in the opinion of some, of our knowledge thereof. No longer did the calculus of probability suggest merely that certain aspects of our experience are "probabilistic," but rather that experience as such and/or that which is experienced is essentially probabilistic. What it means to say that *the world* is probabilistic in structure is by no means clear; but this has not prevented a host of scholars, physicists and otherwise, to philosophize on the implications.[3] In short, the notion of probability has in our times become significantly problematic, and thus there have been reintroduced to the community of scholars those aspects of probability which can well be described as *epistemic*.[4]

[1] Emile Borel's contribution will be found chiefly in the work of which he is editor, *Traité du calcul des probabilités et de ses applications*, 4 vols. (Paris, 1925 ff). For Paul Lévy, see his *Calcul des probabilités* (Paris, 1925). The first systematic presentation of probability theory on an axiomatic basis was made in 1933 by A. Kolmogorov in a monograph available in English translation as *Foundations of the Theory of Probability* (New York, 1950). For subsequent developments in the field, see references given by Parzen, *Modern Probability Theory and its Applications*, p. 30.

[2] See Bertrand Russell, *Human Knowledge: Its Scope and Limits* pp. 339, 344–345; Pius Servien, *Hasard et Probabilités* (Paris, 1949), pp. 2–3 and *passim*; Ronald A. Fisher, *Statistical Methods and Scientific Inference*, 2nd ed. (London-Edinburgh, 1959), pp. 31–32. The foregoing express the common view that the mathematics of probability is well established and only the interpretation is open to question. Karl Popper, however, goes even farther. Noting that "we still lack a satisfactory, consistent definition of probability," he goes on to make this roughly equivalent to saying that "we still lack a satisfactory axiomatic system for the calculus of probability." *Logic of Scientific Discovery* (New York, 1959), p. 146.

[3] Though this tendency to base all kinds of speculations upon the calculus of probability has by no means disappeared from contemporary thought, it was especially *au courant* in the 1930's, that is to say, in the wake of the new quantum physics.

[4] The most important thought along these lines centers around the problem of induction.

In speaking of the epistemic aspects of the theory of probability, it is well to point out at once, however, that not everyone who has devoted himself to the newly posed problem of defining probability would think of himself as being involved in epistemology. Quite to the contrary, most of the important work along these lines has been done by logicians, mathematical theorists of probability, and statisticians interested in the foundations of their particular field of specialization. Accordingly, it is perhaps more accurate to say that the contemporary discussion of the problem, if not overtly epistemic, at least has important epistemic implications.

Now, it is precisely these epistemic aspects of contemporary discussions about probability which we wish to bring into the open. The literature, as just suggested, is such that to do so we must place ourselves more or less within the context of logic and mathematics or, more generally, of what one likes to call the philosophy of science. But in so doing we adopt the point of view neither of the logician nor of the mathematician. For, what we wish to show is that probability, or probable knowledge, transcends the bounds of these disciplines and cannot therefore be adequately analyzed by either.[1] Accordingly, we must as it were stand on the outside and look in at what the mathematician and the logician are doing with probability.

Before we can effectively undertake this observation from the outside, however, we must make sure that we are in fact on the outside looking in and not merely on the inside looking around. At the very least, this requires that we free ourselves of linguistic restrictions, that we escape from unnecessary terminological imprisonment. Very simply, this means allowing, at least as a working hypothesis, that an idea cannot be arbitrarily restricted to one specific domain if in fact it transcends the bounds of that domain. More specifically, if in fact *probability* has meanings which transcend the modern scientific usage, then it would

---

Of particular value as a general survey is the work of Milic Capek, *The Philosophical Impact of Contemporary Physics* (New York-London-Toronto, 1961). With regard to induction as such, a good general survey of the state of the question is that of John P. Day, *Inductive Probability* (New York, 1961).

[1] To avoid any possible misunderstanding, we are in no way suggesting here that either logical or mathematical research is somehow unnecessary or, to be even more ridiculous, irrelevant to the notion of probability. Quite to the contrary, we readily admit that to disregard the logical and mathematical study of probability is simply unthinkable. The point is, as should become clearer in the pages to follow, that we do not think the study of probability need be or should be restricted to formal treatment. For, by so doing one unnecessarily confines himself to a truncated and unrealistic view of what the science is all about. An excellent illustration of what is here involved will be found in C. C. Gillispie, "Intellectual Factors in the Background of Analysis by Probabilities," *in Scientific Change* (ed. A. C. Crombie: London, 1963), pp. 431–453.

seem to be somewhat gratuitous to insist that the term be restricted to a "scientific" meaning. This, in turn, suggests the possibility of two alternative views of the question. On the one hand, it might be asserted that a term, namely, *probability*, cannot be arbitrarily restricted to one definition or meaning if in fact its usage is more extensive. On the other hand, it might be asserted that, if one insists upon such a terminological confinement, thereby allowing only a predetermined meaning for *probability*, he must find another term or terms to express what could otherwise be expressed by that same term.

We shall not here opt for either alternative, for the simple reason that we consider the idea in all its richness of meaning to be of far greater importance than the term or terms used to express it. We cannot, after all, legislate usage. But we can, and shall, point out what happens when an attempt is made to do so, when the desire for "scientific precision" does violence to accepted usage.[1] In the light of these observations, we shall conclude to the desirability of recognizing a broader notion of probability.

This being said, we are now in a position to watch "from the outside." First we shall consider a few mathematicians who assume that the notion of probability is known *par excellence* if not exclusively through mathematics. Then we shall look at two widely differing logical empiricists who assume that the only important meaning of probability is "objective" and that objectivity is roughly equivalent to formalization. Thirdly, we shall see a few people from various disciplines who are struck by the thought that "probability" might be or in fact is read into the calculus of probability. Finally, we shall turn to the founders of two movements of thought which grant the restriction of "probability" to a mathematical meaning but deal in other terms with what was once in all security considered the realm of the probable.

MATHEMATICIANS AND PROBABILITY

Turning first to what mathematicians have to say about the notion of probability, we need not be surprised that their views on this

---

[1] As a matter of fact, there is a great deal of discussion as to whether or not the scientific usage is related to common usage. Richard von Mises, for example, feels compelled to establish a scientific definition more or less independently of common usage: *Probability, Statistics and Truth* (London-New York, 1957), pp. 1–29. Rudolf Carnap, however, led by his desire to establish an inductive logic, feels that a direct relationship can be shown. See his *Logical Foundations of Probability* (Chicago, 1950), pp. 233–252, 279, 511–520. See also the research, inspired by Carnap, which Arne Naess reports as *An Empirical Study of the Expressions "True," "Perfectly Certain," and "Extremely Probable"* (Oslo, 1953).

subject have a decidedly mathematical slant. Probability is at heart a mathematical notion and is subject to scientific analysis only to the extent that it is mathematical. To illustrate this point of view, we shall consider in order Marcel Boll, Emile Borel, and G. Polya.

As Boll sees it, the calculus of probability defies common sense in that it is "the exact determination of the uncertain." Following the lead of Guido Castelnuovo, he describes the calculus of probability as "a science of the unknown," a substitute for certitude; it is, in other words, "an *engin d'avant-garde,* which allows one to go where other means of research cannot for the moment reach." [1] The assertion that the founding definition of probability involves a vicious circle does not trouble him because, as he learns from Gonseth, the problem is really no more than a paradox of language.[2] He does admit in this vein, however, that there are certain language difficulties with regard to the respective meanings of "possible" and "probable." These difficulties he overcomes quite facilely by making the "impossible" and the "certain" nothing but "limit-cases" of the generic term "probable," which, in turn, is subject to a gradation of degrees of confirmation.[3] Anything beyond this mathematical representation of human knowledge is, he concludes, nothing more than "insignificant nuances of style." [4] Thus does he reduce all of epistemology to the arithmetic of proper fractions and at the same time resolve a host of problems which have taxed men's minds for centuries.[5]

Although Boll puts the calculus of probability out in front of science, he is still able to assert that science and the laws which it formulates about the universe are permeated with probability.

[1] Marcel Boll, *Les Certitudes du Hasard* (Paris, 1941), p. 17.

[2] Boll, *Les Certitudes du Hasard,* p. 15.

[3] Boll, *Les Certitudes du Hasard,* pp. 10–11, 17, 19, 59.

[4] Boll, *Les Certitudes du Hasard,* p. 19: "Scientifiquement parlant, il n'y a pas de distinction à faire entre les deux notions de certitude et d'impossibilité: nous savons, en effet . . ., que ce sont deux probabilités complémentaires. Affirmer qu'un événement futur est certain revient à affirmer que l'événement contraire est impossible; une double négation équivaut à une affirmation. Le reste n'est que nuances insignifiantes de style."

[5] It would be grossly unfair to the thought of Bernard I. F. Lonergan to place his analysis of probability on a level with that of Boll. Yet it must be said that the weakness of Lonergan's position consists precisely in a tendency to be overly influenced by a mathematicized concept of probability. He himself is aware of the danger, and thus goes to great pains to distinguish between what amounts to a frequency and a logical interpretation of probability. But when dealing with what he calls "probable judgments" he describes these as "probably true in the non-statistical sense of converging upon true judgments, of approaching them as a limit": *Insight,* rev. student ed. (New York, 1958), p. 300. See also pp. 53–68, 299–304, and especially p. 48, where he notes that failure to distinguish these two kinds of probability (both of which, in our opinion, remain essentially mathematical as he describes them) "would wreck our analysis." The fundamental importance of Lonergan's observation at this point deserves detailed investigation at some future date.

"Chance," he says, "intervenes certainly (sic) in *all* the laws of the universe, without exception." [1] This does not mean, as Kant supposed, that our instruments (mathematical or physical) are imperfect, but that the universe itself is essentially in the hands of chance. Somehow (he does not explain precisely how) the Gauss curve rules over chance.

Dedicated to the great ideal of "objectivity," Boll insists in effect that we must know all things in general before we can begin to know anything about man in particular; for, as he says, "man is not the measure of *anything*." [2] Thus, not surprisingly, he considers Laplace the greatest of all scientists and, perhaps not irrelevantly, opts for the statistical interpretation of the calculus of probability. In line with this interpretation, he vituperates the philosopher Joseph Segond for having suggested that one can at times guess the outcome of a single event.[3] Yet in spite of himself he has to assert that the calculus of probability "naturally applies, at the limit, to isolated cases." Even more, he maintains that there simply is no problem about the relationship between the mathematical generalization and the individual event, and that even to raise a question about it involves a contradiction in terms.[4]

If we must comment upon Boll's rather confused mathematicism, let our comment be, in all simplicity, that we do not agree with his observation that there is nothing to be learned on the subject of probability from the ancients.[5]

Consider now the extra-mathematical musings of the great mathematical probabilist Emile Borel. Here again we are faced with a kind of mathematicism of the probable, but one which is more carefully nuanced than that of Boll. For, in particular, Borel is struck by the fact that *the notion of probability, which was once opposed to that of certitude, is now considered to be the equivalent of both practical and physical certitude.* Borel is convinced that one can have absolute certitude not only about mathematical truths but also about physical laws and even matters of everyday life; and thus his problem is how to justify speaking of certitude in such cases. The solution to the problem,

---

[1] Boll, *Les Certitudes du Hasard*, p. 114: "Le hasard intervient certainement dans *toutes* les lois de l'Univers, sans exception." See also p. 18.

[2] Boll, *Les Certitudes du Hasard*, p. 118: "l'homme n'est la mesure *de rien*."

[3] Boll, *Les Certitudes du Hasard*, p. 117.

[4] Boll, *Les Certitudes du Hasard*, pp. 106–108.

[5] Boll, *Les Certitudes du Hasard*, p. 7. For an even more bizarre mathematicism of probability, see Albert Verley, *Nouvel Aspect de la Théorie des Probabilités* (Ile-Saint-Denis, Seine, 1958), in which the author hopes to show on the basis of the law of large numbers that "les événements futurs préexistent au même titre que les événements antérieurs" (p. 3).

as he sees it, is in effect to show that the calculus of probability itself justifies certitude of this kind. For, as he puts it, "human knowledge merits the name of Science to the extent that measure or number plays a role." [1] For Borel, of course, measure and number are provided by the calculus of probability, whereby one determines the probability of complex phenomena on the basis of the probability (presumed known) of simpler phenomena.[2] In this way, one is able to study "the laws of chance" and in particular what he calls "the unique law of chance." As Borel sees it, what is in question here is "a probability which differs from unity by a quantity sufficiently small." Where one finds such a probability he may, according to Borel's unique law of chance, assert that "an event the probability of which is sufficiently weak never happens" and in practice can be considered "impossible." [3] Thus, the study of such probabilities not only justifies practical certitude but affords a better understanding of "the universal role of probability in scientific knowledge." [4]

Thanks to his unique law of chance, Borel is able to take what he considers "an important step in the evolution of my thought." [5] This important step has to do with the way in which one should speak of Jeans' famous "miracle" of the temperature of water rising instead of falling as it turns to ice. Early in his career, Borel had agreed with Jeans that such a divergence from physical regularity should be considered only "highly improbable." Now, says Borel, the unique law of chance allows him to say that the miracle is not merely highly improbable but is in effect "impossible" [6] Similarly, the chance production of the works of Shakespeare is so improbable that it may be considered absolutely impossible.[7] But in some cases, he admits, the law is less strictly applicable, if applicable at all.[8]

Be that as it may, Borel considers the law as such to be intuitively evident and, though not demonstrable, solidly supported by its many

---

[1] Borel, *Probabilité et Certitude* (Paris, 1950), p. 10: "On sait que c'est dans la mesure où le nombre y joue un rôle qu'une connaissance humaine mérite le nom de Science." See pp. 8–10. See also Borel, *Le Jeu, La Chance et les théories Scientifiques Modernes* (Paris, 1941), Preface.

[2] Borel, *Les Probabilités et la Vie* ((Paris, 1943), p. 5.

[3] Borel, *Probabilités et Vie*, p. 8: "*Les événements dont la probabilité est suffisamment faible ne se produisent jamais;* ou du moins, l'homme doit agir, en toutes circonstances, comme s'ils étaient *impossibles.*" See also the slightly stronger interpretation of this formulation in *Le Jeu, la Chance*, p. 98.

[4] Borel, *Probabilité et Certitude*, p. 6.

[5] Borel, *Probabilité et Certitude*, p. 5.

[6] Borel, *Probabilité et Certitude*, pp. 60–61, 119.

[7] Borel, *Probabilités et Vie*, pp. 11–12. See also *Le jeu, la Chance*, pp. 98–103 and pp. 125–127, where Borel states his earlier view.

[8] Borel, *Probabilités et Vie*, p. 75.

successful applications in the physical sciences.[1] We have certitude about this law, he says; the certitude in question, however, is not mathematical but of a sort not unlike our certitude about the existence of historical personages or of the external world.[2] Accordingly, the law cannot be taken as strictly, he says, in matters of daily life as it is in the sciences. In general, the extent to which the law applies depends upon what he calls the "level (echelle) of probability" appropriate to the problem under consideration. On the "human" level, the criterion of risk is the prudent man; on higher levels (terrestrial, cosmic, and super-cosmic) the demands of evaluation are, in ascending order, much stricter.[3] Since, however, one does "calculate" probabilities in his daily life, it is more advantageous to do so with the kind of precision attainable through the calculus of probability than without it. But the calculus as such, like the price of an object for sale, will always remain subordinate to the individual's free decision: knowledge does not determine choice.[4]

There is in all of this, it will be noted, a hint that probability and certitude transcend the bounds of mathematics; but in Borel this never becomes more than a hint. For him, the key to certitude is number and its correlative, "objectivity." Practical certitude, he says, is "in a way subjective" so long as it is restricted to a single individual; objective certitude depends upon the common agreement of many. This numerical criterion of certitude, which is itself founded upon "high probability," applies to Jeans' miracle as well as to mathematical demonstrations as such. "The only reason," he says, "why we regard as certain some well demonstrated mathematical facts . . . is that the demonstrations have been reconsidered and verified by a large number of persons." [5] Thus, in the final analysis, Borel's critique of science rests upon a law of large numbers.

A somewhat similar view as to the grounds for scientific certitude is expressed by G. Polya in his two-volume study of *Patterns of Plausible Inference*. Concluding this interesting analysis of non-

[1] Borel, *Probabilités et Vie*, pp. 8 and 10; *Le Jeu, la Chance*, pp. 7–8, 149–189.
[2] Borel, *Probabilités et Vie*, p. 12.
[3] Borel, *Probabilités et Vie*, pp. 38–39; *Le Jeu, la Chance*, pp. 103–110.
[4] Borel, *Probabilités et Vie*, pp. 40–50.
[5] Borel, *Probabilité et Certitude*, p. 114: "La seule raison pour laquelle nous regardons comme certains des faits mathématiques bien démontrés . . . c'est que les démonstrations ont été reprises et vérifiées par un grand nombre de personnes, parfois des milliers, parfois même des millions pour les démonstrations qui remontent à Euclide. La probabilité pour que toutes ces personnes aient commis la même erreur est évidemment tellement faible que notre certitude absolue est justifiée." See also pp. 116, 119–121.

demonstrative reasoning, especially as relevant to mathematics, Polya notes:

Analogy and particular cases are the most abundant sources of plausible argument; perhaps, they not only help to shape the demonstrative argument and to render it more understandable, but also add to our *confidence* in it. And so we are led to suspect that a good part of *our reliance on demonstrative reasoning may come from plausible reasoning*.[1]

Be that as it may, Polya tells us more by what he does not say than by what he does. For, as the very title of his work indicates, he tacitly assumes that the notion of probability must be restricted to a mathematical meaning, and that therefore to speak of non-demonstrative reasoning he must utilize another term. We suspect, however, that few would find in the term "plausible" all the nuances of meaning which the scope of Polya's investigation demands. After all, he does not mean what is ordinarily meant by "plausible"; he means what is ordinarily meant by "probable." He cannot say this, however, because his mathematics is in the way.

"OBJECTIVE" THEORIES OF PROBABILITY

We have already noted a concern for "objectivity" in the mathematicism of both Boll and Borel. Now, however, we wish to consider two views of probability which, for all their differences, make "objectivity" a fundamental prerequisite for any scientific theory of probability. For, both writers think within the framework of logical empiricism – one as the living embodiment of the Vienna Circle, the other as its "loyal opposition." Here, then, is the notion of probability according to Rudolf Carnap and Karl Popper.

Carnap, first of all, sees the notion of probability as one important aspect of the problem of "confirmation," which is central to his heroic efforts to formalize inductive (i.e. non-demonstrative) logic. With this goal in mind, he undertakes a rather detailed analysis of past and present attempts to give a scientific definition of probability. For, as he sees it, the historical development of the calculus of probability is in effect "the history of attempts to find an explication for the prescientific concept of probability." [2] But, he insists, there is no one single "common sense" concept of probability, and conse-

---

[1] G. Polya, *Mathematics and Plausible Reasoning*, Vol. II: *Patterns of Plausible Inference* (Princeton, 1954), p. 168.
[2] Carnap, *Logical Foundations of Probability* (Chicago, 1950), p. 23. For the following see pp. 24–29.

quently the explicandum (that which one wishes to define) has not always been the same. As a matter of fact, quite a variety of distinctions have been and still are proposed in an effort to indicate the different meanings of probability. Thus, there are distinctions of more or less historical importance between objective and subjective, logical and statistical (the frequency theory), *a priori* and *a posteriori*, classical and modern. Carnap takes all these various notions (explicanda) into consideration, but maintains that "in all essential respects, leaving aside slight variations," they boil down to "very few and chiefly two."

The two common-sense concepts of probability which, according to Carnap, scientists have sought to explicate are: (i) degree of confirmation; (ii) relative frequency in the long run. The first concept, which Carnap chooses to designate as probability$_1$, is, he says, the concern of inductive (non-demonstrative) logic. The second concept, which he designates as probability$_2$, is that commonly explicated by mathematical statisticians. As Carnap sees it, the explicandum has in the course of time gradually shifted from probability$_1$ to probability$_2$, with the latter first making its appearance about a century ago. The early theorists, notably Bernoulli and Laplace, are often accused of having formulated a "subjective" definition. But this so-called classical definition (the ratio of "favorable" cases to all "possible" cases) is, in the opinion of Carnap, subjective not in intent but only to some extent in the manner of expression. In any event, he maintains, the explicandum of such definitions was always in one way or another a degree of confirmation (probability$_1$).[1] The frequency concept, he says, was first suggested by Leslie Ellis (1842) and A. Cournot (1843).[2] In 1866 John Venn became "the first to advocate the frequency concept of probability$_2$ unambiguously and systematically as explicandum and also the first to propose as explicatum for it the concept of the limit of relative frequency of an infinite series."[3] As in so many other matters, C. S. Peirce was here also something of a prophet (1878). This development towards taking probability$_2$ as the explicandum at length culminated in the elaborate systems of Richard von Mises and Hans

[1] Carnap, *Logical Foundations*, pp. 47–50.

[2] Ellis's views were stated in a paper entitled "On the foundations of the theory of probabilities" which was subsequently printed and then reprinted in *The Mathematical and other Writings of Leslie Ellis* (Cambridge, England, 1863). Cournot is singularly famous for having developed a philosophical system around the notion of probability. See *his Exposition de la théorie des chances et des probabilités* (Paris, 1843). For the more philosophical aspects of Cournot's thought, see his *Considérations sur la marche des idées et des événements dans les temps modernes*, 2 vols. (reprinted Paris, 1934), and also his basic philosophical work available in English as *An Essay on the Foundations of our Knowledge* (New York, 1956).

[3] Carnap, *Logical Foundations*, pp. 182–187.

Reichenbach, and, as suggested above, is prevalent among mathematical statisticians, in particular, Fisher, Neyman, and Pearson.[1] Our own day is marked by heated controversy between proponents of the relative frequency view and proponents of the degree of confirmation view, the latter having been most articulately expounded by Keynes and Jeffreys. This controversy Carnap considers unnecessary and futile, inasmuch as, in his opinion, each side is in fact defining a different explicandum.

For Carnap both the explicandum of probability$_1$ and that of probability$_2$ are "objective" concepts. As far as he is concerned, "psychologism" has been fairly well eliminated from logic both deductive and inductive. This, he insists, is all to the good, since he wants to maintain the "boundary line between logical and psychological concepts."[2] Speaking therefore from the viewpoint of the logician, he insists: "A definition of an explicatum for probability$_1$ must not refer to any person and his beliefs but only to the two sentences and their logical properties within a given language system."[3] He does recognize, however, what he considers a *subjective, psychological concept of probability*, which he admits is of importance in psychological and social sciences. "But," he says, "it cannot serve as a basis for inductive logic or a calculus of probability applicable as a general tool of science."[4]

It is important to remember that the whole purpose of Carnap's analysis of probability is to prepare the way for his great dream of formalizing, i.e. mathematicizing, nondemonstrative logic, a task which not everyone would consider possible. The problem, of course, iswhether or not there is any consistent way of assigning a numerical value to the "degree of confirmation" of ordinary opinionative judgments. As far as Carnap is concerned, the question, though controversial, is still open, and no one has demonstrated impossibility.[5] Thus encouraged in his efforts, he proposes a tripartite division of the kinds of definitions that might be given as explicatum for probability$_1$. Such a definition, he says, may be either classificatory, comparative, or quantitative. There

---

[1] We have already had occasion to list the basic works of von Mises and Reichenbach as well as those of Keynes and Jeffreys, who are mentioned immediately below. For the viewpoint of the mathematical statisticians, see Ronald A. Fisher, *Statistical Methods and Scientific Inference*, 2nd ed. (London-Edinburgh, 1959). Fisher's work is especially valuable from our point of view for his introductory chapter on the historical development of the statistical concept of probability.

[2] Carnap, *Logical Foundations*, p. 44.

[3] Carnap, *Logical Foundations*, p. 43.

[4] Carnap, *Logical Foundations*, p. 51.

[5] Carnap, *Logical Foundations*, p. 231.

is only technical discussion about the first two types of definition; the controversy which is of concern to Carnap centers around the third, which some insist cannot be made meaningful in inductive logic.[1]

Of course, the mere construction of a system of logic, even a"quantified inductive logic," would not be beyond the realm of human ingenuity. The real problem is not of constructibility but that of effectiveness. Accordingly, Carnap devotes considerable space to the basic problem created by the complexity of the singular event.[2] But everything he says suggests a tacit identification between mathematico-logical construction and effectiveness; if it can be constructed, it will work.[3]

That formal logic is incapable of the task which Carnap has set for it is strongly suggested by two important theorems demonstrated within logic itself: Craig's theorem and Gödel's theorem, the first of which suggests the empirical difficulties of such an enterprise, and the second of which manifests the limitations of formalization.[4] The theorem developed by William Craig has to do with the problem of replacing a formal linguistic system, L, containing theoretical expressions by another formal system, L*, having no theoretical terms and yet having the same empirical content as the initial system. Craig's method of replacement, beautiful and impressive though it is in a formal presentation, becomes impossibly cumbersome if the axioms of the subject in question are very numerous.[5] But that the axioms of opinionative reasoning, formerly called "commonplaces," are numerous and, in principle at least, unlimited was clearly recognized as long ago as Aristotle.[6] Moreover, it does not seem likely that the number or even

[1] Carnap, *Logical Foundations*, pp. 220–226. See also pp. 21–23, 233–241.

[2] Carnap, *Logical Foundations*, pp. 241–345.

[3] See, for example, *Logical Foundations*, p. 242, where Carnap assumes for the sake of argument that an inductive logic in his sense is constructible and then sets himself the task of showing (on the basis of a variety of quantitative maxims) how useful it would be both for theoretical and for practical problems. It is already here, we think, that Carnap misses the point and clouds the issue. For, the real issue is not whether a logical system can be constructed but whether ordinary opinionative judgments about contingent events are in fact primarily or even incidentally quantitative and hence susceptible to mathematical formalization. It is at least open to question whether an issue of this kind can be appropriately resolved within the confines of formal logic as such.

[4] For Gödel's theorem, see above, p. 9 fn. 2.

[5] "Moreover," says Ernest Nagel, "in order to specify the axioms for L* we would have to know, *in advance* of any deductions made from them, *all* the true statements of L* – in other words, Craig's method shows us how to construct the language L* only *after* every possible inquiry into the subject matter of L* has been completed." – Ernest Nagel, *The Structure of Science: Problems in the Logic of Scientific Explanation* (New York-Burlingame, 1961), p. 137. Our discussion of Craig's theorem is based upon Nagel's analysis in the work here indicated, pp. 134–137. But it is we and not Nagel who relate the theorem to the problem of probability.

[6] See William and Martha Kneale, *The Development of Logic* (Oxford, 1962), pp. 34, 178–

the kinds of "probable" judgments that can be made will be successfully catalogued in the near future. If, then, we add to these considerations the factor of formal incompleteness demonstrated by Gödel, it would seem that both materially and formally the task of constructing an all-inclusive inductive logic is a formidable one indeed.

This is in fact borne out by a careful perusal of the writings of Carnap himself. For, in spite of his effort to delimit the explicanda of probability for purposes of formalization, he is himself compelled, wittingly or unwittingly, to go beyond the linguisitc limitations which he has imposed upon himself. After telling us that all the meanings of "probable" can be reduced to essentially two, one of which (degree of confirmation) covers the realm of opinionative reasoning, he himself utilizes Polya's term, "plausible," for what he would no doubt consider "informal" if not "psychological" observations *about* probability[1].[1] If, then, we may take Carnap at his word that "the psychological" has been eliminated from the consideration of logic and that nevertheless studies of "the psychological" are legitimate human enterprises, it would seem to follow that there is more to say about "probable" reasoning than can be said by the logician.

Karl Popper, whom we have described as the loyal opposition of logical empiricism, does in fact have quite a bit to say about non-formalized probability. It is just that in saying it he does not use the term "probability." For, Popper, like Carnap, takes the notion of probability to be essentially mathematical. As he says, considering himself on this point in complete agreement with Carnap, probability is, in general, "*something that satisfies the laws of the calculus of probability.*" [2] He admits that there is such a thing as a non-numerical probability statement, but such a statement assumes importance in his eyes only insofar as it is or can be numerically, that is, mathe-

181, 193, 216; Neal Ward Gilbert, *Renaissance Concepts of Method* (New York, 1960), pp. 95, 108–110; Chaim Perelman, *La Nouvelle Rhétorique; Traité de l'Argumentation* (Paris, 1958), Vol. I, pp. 112–132.

[1] For example, in speaking of the opposition to his hope of constructing an inductive logic Carnap says: "It seems to me that the arguments of those who assert the impossibility are very far from proving this point or even making it plausible." *Logical Foundations*, p. 231. See also p. 237. "Plausible," as here used, is roughly equivalent to the medieval *probabilis*. The latter, as we shall see at length, took meaning A of "probable" in Lalande's *Vocabulaire de la Philosophie:* "Qui peut être *approuvé* – et non *prouvé*), qui n'a rien d'absurde ou de contraire à l'autorité." Thus J. Lachelier is led to remark in a note on the entry (specifically, with regard to meaning B. "vraisemblable.") that in saying *probabilia* Cicero means "des opinions plausibles." Not surprisingly, then, it is said under meaning A: "Ce sens est tombé en désuétude." The whole purpose of this chapter is, in effect, to investigate the reasons for this interesting historical phenomenon.

[2] Karl Popper, *Conjectures and Refutations* (London, 1963), p. 286. This work will hereafter be identified as *Conjectures*.

matically, formulated. Thus the question for Popper is this: given a numerical probability statement, how shall it be interpreted? His answer: when it comes to interpreting a probability statement, one is involved in the probability of "events." [1]

This emphasis on "events" is, in turn, just another way of stating the logical empiricist's insistence upon "objectivity." In various places, accordingly, Popper sorts out interpretations of probability statements according as they are "subjective" or "objective." He would consider as subjective either what he calls the psychologistic or the logical interpretation. The relative frequency theory he recognizes as objective, and further insists that his modification of this interpretation, which he calls a propensity theory, is at least "formally" objective. In a subjectivist interpretation, on the other hand, the degree of probability is taken to express a degree of rational belief. [2] Thus, the "psychologistic" (that is, the classical) interpretation sought to justify mathematical *expectation* or to provide a normal law of *error*. This, says Popper, was an effort to provide a basis for "subjective adherences," which, he adds, is appropriate to non-numerical but not to numerical probability statements. The logical interpretation of probability (of Keynes and others) is an improvement, but does not escape subjectivism. Based on a proximity criterion of the degree of probability, this theory defines probability as a "degree of rational belief" determined by a logical relationship between two statements.

Also subjectivist is the notion of chance, which implies that we are still unable to predict, say, the throw of a die. [3] For, as we shall see, Popper dislikes what he calls a "conspiracy theory" of error and accordingly will not admit that probability is used to fill in incomplete knowledge. The problem which any theory of chance must answer, he insists, is how a statement of ignorance, interpreted as a frequency statement, can be empirically tested and "corroborated."

Herein, in fact, lies the weakness of any subjectivist interpretation: there is no reason why an empirical frequency should equal a degree of rational belief, nor can any such relationship be proven. Granted, there

---

[1] See Popper, *Conjectures*, p. 58; *The Logic of Scientific Discovery*, (New York, 1959), pp. 118–119, 147, 173, 234–276, 309, 316. It is important to note here that Popper's insistence that probability statements have to do with events in no way implies his acceptance of the view (held by von Mises and especially Reichenbach) that science is "probable." As we shall see, Popper insists that scientific hypotheses are of necessity "improbable." This unorthodox position he defends by insisting that a scientific hypothesis cannot be considered a type of probability statement. See *Logic*, p. 256, fn. *2.

[2] Popper, *Conjectures*, p. 227.

[3] Popper, *Logic*, p. 206.

are few problems for a subjectivist theory, but the point is that such an interpretation makes probability statements non-empirical tautologies. It might be acceptable, Popper admits, provided we allow our "rational beliefs" to be guided by an objective frequency statement, that is, by the information on which belief depends.[1] But, in short, "only an objective theory can explain the application of the probability calculus within empirical science."[2]

Indeed, this concern to understand the significance of the calculus of probability as applied in the sciences is the motive force behind Popper's internecine criticisms of logical empiricism. Primarily interested in what he calls the problem of demarcation, that is, the distinguishing characteristic of physical science, he argues that, contrary to common opinion, the distinguishing characteristic is not that science is inductive, for induction is a myth. Nor, he adds, does the problem become more manageable by admitting in all humility that induction gives only probability, thereby making some degree of probability the criterion. Those who believe in the constructibility of a system of inductive logic (and Popper is not one of them) argue on the basis of "inductivist decisions" that it is possible to ascribe degrees of probability to the hypotheses themselves and to reduce this concept to that of the probability of events.[3] However this view is developed, truth (equal to 1) and falsity (equal to 0) are considered as limiting cases of probability, the intermediate degrees of which must accordingly be determined in some methodical way. Such, in short, is the rationale behind Carnap's search for degrees of "confirmation." Popper, however, feels that the use of the term "confirmation" prejudges a problem that is by no means solved; for, in his view, it is at least problematical whether the calculus of probability can be applied meaningfully to empirical evidence or to scientific hypotheses as such. Thus he prefers to use the term "corroboration," which he considers to be neutral. [4] But, he insists, the "degree of corroboration" cannot be made equivalent to a mathematical probability.[5] For, it can be shown that every theory has the same probability, namely O. For, the more a statement asserts, the less probable it is; and the scientist aims not at high probability but at a high content – he does not seek a highly probable theory

[1] Popper, *Logic*, p. 211.
[2] Popper, *Logic*, p. 150.
[3] Popper, *Logic*, p. 255.
[4] Popper, *Logic*, p. 251.
[5] Popper, *Conjectures*, p. 192.

but explanation, that is, powerful and *improbable* theories.[1] Probability, in short, is simply "ersatz" for certainty.

Be that as it may, the basic reason why inductive argument cannot be explained by probability theory is that such an explanation still leaves unexplained, as noted already by Hume and more recently by Heymans, the arch-difficulty of induction as such: there is more in the conclusion than in the premisses.[2] Nor is the difficulty evaded by attempting to relate the probability of a statement to the probability of events. If you say a hypothesis is "probable" you cannot translate this into a statement about the probability of events – and if you knew the hypothesis to be true, you would not need to speak of its probability. A probability statement as such, then, is completely undecidable ("metaphysical") unless, in Popper's terminology, made falsifiable by some methodological rule.[3]

Thus, in spite of Popper's strong and constant wish to establish a rapport between the theory of probability and its physical applications, he insists that the physical and the mathematical concepts of probability are distinct.[4] Taken as it stands, a probability statement is "metaphysical," non-falsifiable, without empirical significance. It is only when used to describe a state of events that it can be falsifiable and thus empirical. The question, then, is to determine the relationship between probability statements as such and properly formulated empirical statements, what Popper calls "basic statements." It is in dealing with this problem that one encounters a closeness of approximation and thus "degrees." The determination of this degree of approximation, says Popper, is one of the main problems of mathematical statistics and of the theory of corroboration, namely, the problem of *decidability*.[5]

Decidability, as Popper explains it, is in effect the problem of how to apply a theory of errors. One establishes in principle a norm of allowable error, which Popper calls the "interval of imprecision." The problem of decidability is then to determine how much of a deviation beyond that norm may be disregarded as "negligibly small." Needless to say, this is not a purely mathematical question but involves the physicist, who must decide how much imprecision he can allow in the light of the experimental situation.

[1] Popper, *Logic*, p. 58.
[2] Popper, *Logic*, pp. 202, 264–265.
[3] Popper, *Logic*, pp. 257, 259, 262.
[4] Popper, *Logic*, p. 200.
[5] Popper, *Logic*, p. 191 fn.

These somewhat unorthodox views on the nature and role of mathematical probability are best understood in the light of Popper's
conviction that science seeks truth. For, whatever his doubts about
our attainment of truth, Popper in convinced that the scientific
enterprise is inexplicable except as a search for truth, that is, as an
effort to know the world as it is.[1] Speaking in somewhat ambivalent
terms, he insists that science has nothing to do with a quest for
certainty or probability or reliability but very simply seeks truth.
How else, he points out, can error have meaning? Truth, then, is a
regulative idea, the goal of science: the scientist seeks unceasingly to
bring his theories into conformity or correspondence with reality.
This, according to Popper, is an *objective* theory of truth, a "metalogical" theory. *Subjective* (or, interestingly enough, "epistemic") theories
of truth *"all stem from the fundamental subjectivist position which can
conceive of knowledge only as a special kind of mental state, or as a
disposition, or as a special kind of belief..."* [2] Thus, among what he
considers subjective theories he includes the views that truth is co-
herence (mistakes consistency for truth) or evidence (mistakes "known
to be true" for "true"), or that truth is pragmatic or instrumentalist
(mistakes usefulness for truth).

If, then, truth is an absolute (Popper's own word), how are we to
describe our present state of knowledge? To handle this problem,
Popper imitates the terminology of the Presocratics and distinguishes
between truth without content (*probability*) and truth with content
(*verisimilitude*). Probability, that is, logical probability, suggests an
approach to logical certainty, or tautological truth, by diminution of
informative content. Verisimilitude ("like the truth") suggests an
approach to comprehensive truth. Thus the latter is not a probability,
at least not in the sense of the calculus of probability.[3] Popper also goes
back to Greek terminology to describe modern science as *doxa*, i.e.
opinion. According to Popper, the correlative of *doxa*, *episteme* (certitude), is a fallen idol. Thus, with *episteme* no longer considered
attainable (any more than Bacon's *interpretatio naturae*: "the spelling
out of the open book of Nature"), man is left with *doxa* (Bacon's

---

[1] Popper, *Logic*, p. 15. Popper's position in this regard, it should be noted, is heavily
dependent upon Tarski. Since the latter first introduced the correspondence theory of truth
into semantics and provided a method of utilizing the Aristotelian definition in formal languages, Popper has been a staunch supporter of the view that truth is correspondence with
"the facts" or with "reality." See *Logic*, pp. 223 and 274 fn.

[2] Popper, *Conjectures*, p. 225.

[3] Popper, *Conjectures*, pp. 219, 237.

anticipatio mentis).[1] As for this state of affairs, Popper could not be happier. *Anticipatio mentis*, according to Bacon, is the prejudice of the mind that wrongly prejudges, and perhaps misjudges, Nature, thus leading to *doxa*, or mere guesswork. "This latter method," says Popper, "rejected by Bacon, is in fact a method of interpretation, in the modern sense of the word. It is the *method of conjecture or hypothesis* (a method of which, incidentally, I happen to be a convinced advocate)." [2]

This epistemological stance Popper refers to as critical rationalism. Viewing "essentialism" as the assertion that a theory can ultimately be established, he rejects it on the grounds that theories are never conclusive and that outside of mathematics and logic, problems of definability are mostly gratuitous.[3] Opposed to any "authoritative" theory of truth, he admits that truth is above human authority (not established by decree); but he denies that we must *justify* our knowledge by *positive* reasons which either establish it or make it "highly probable." As he sees it, an authoritative theory of truth presupposes that truth is manifest and that, therefore, if it is not attained it is the potential knower who is at fault – a corollary which Popper identifies as "the conspiracy theory of ignorance." He finds this authority-conspiracy attitude in the Greeks, in Bacon, in Descartes, and, generally, in anyone who supposes on the one hand an ultimate source of knowledge, and on the other the precognitional need for some sort of self-purification. According to Popper, one should not ask, What is the ultimate source of our knowledge? but rather, How can we hope to detect and eliminate error? The answer of his critical rationalism: by guessing at theories and criticizing them, i.e. by "conjectures and refutations."

Thus, in short, does Karl Popper attempt to place the calculus of probability within the wider scope of human knowledge as such.

---

[1] Popper, *Logic*, pp. 279 fn *1, 280.

[2] Popper, *Conjectures*, p. 14. Because of this view of science as a matter of conjectures and refutations, Popper can say that Bellarmine had better insight into the nature of physical science than did Galileo. For while Galileo considered his theory certain (*episteme*), Bellarmine insisted that it had only verisimilitude (*doxa*). The latter view, says Popper, is today the accepted view. For much the same reason, Popper continues, we are no longer concerned with Kant's problem or with his theories because we realize, as Kant did not, that Newton did not achieve *episteme* but only *doxa*. There is, of course, much to be said for Popper's theory of science, providing that one consider science only in the abstract as a set of hypotheses. It is somewhat difficult, however, to accept Popper's dislike for anyone, such as Bacon, who has proposed a subjective source of human fallibility, since Popper himself makes quite a virtue out of the recognition of that very fallibility and accordingly considers himself a descendant of Erasmus, Nicholas of Cusa, Montaigne, Locke, Voltaire, Mill, and most recently, Russell. See *Conjectures*, pp. 16, 27, 48.

[3] Popper, *Logic*, p. 279.

Caught up in the milieu of logical empiricism, he does not, for all his criticisms, escape that which he so strenuously criticizes. Sharing his confreres' fear of the merely "subjective," he opts for an "objective" interpretation of the calculus of probability which would be acceptable to the most meticulous of Pythagoreans. The world, in short, is mathematical – at least insofar as it is scientifically intelligible – and what there is to say about it can best be said on the basis of mathematical structures. A view difficult enough to live with, surely, and Popper himself proves no more successful at living with it than would a committed "subjectivist." For, however guarded his passing references to non-mathematical statements, he implicitly says a great deal about just such statements. That his restriction of the term "probability" to mathematics forces him to resort to the Greek *doxa* and the Latinism *verisimilitude* in such non-mathematical contexts in no way alters the truth of the matter. What men understand by probability is broader than a mathematical formulation; and if they are not to call it "probability," they will simply call it something else.

PROBABILITY AS AN EXTRA-MATHEMATICAL INTERPRETATION

Dismayed by what he considers a dearth of clear thinking about the calculus of probability, a French mining engineer, J.-L. Gendre, came forth in 1947 with an *Introduction à l'étude du jugement probable*.[1] This brief work resolves none of the problems, yet in a few scant pages manages to spell out just how serious they really are. Gendre begins his study by noting that the very notion of probability, which is supposedly the basis of the calculus of probability, has escaped definition. Suspecting therefore that what has come to be known as "the crisis of determinism" is rather more likely "an indetermination of thought," he sets himself the task of providing, without recourse to metaphysics, a workable definition.[2] What he comes up with in the end is nothing more than the frequency interpretation of probability. But he is nonetheless remarkable for having put his finger on the very heart of the problem from the viewpoint of the working scientist.

Gendre grants mathematicians the right to restrict the meaning of "probability" to cases susceptible of algebraic treatment; but he notes that so long as they use this term to identify the object of their

---

[1] Published Paris, 1947, with an introduction by André Lalande. Gendre's work will be referred to here as *Jugement probable*.

[2] Gendre, *Jugement probable*, pp. 9–12.

analysis they invite philosophical criticism.[1] Not adverse to introducing such criticisms himself, he concentrates upon the so-called "law
of large numbers." This, he says, is at best contingent and by no means
deserving the title of a "law." Bernoulli's theorem, he points out,
cannot be proposed as a demonstration of the law of large numbers,
since it is only after verifying this theorem empirically that one finds
he was justified in using it in the first place. Furthermore, in order to
utilize Bernoulli's theorem for empirical work, it is necessary to
replace the factorial in the exact formula with an approximative
value thereof given by Stirling's formula.[2] Overlooking this artifice,
Gendre observes, some authors imply both that the law of large
numbers is demonstrated by Bernolli's theorem and that, at the same
time, it is an "approximative law."[3] But, he notes, one cannot infer
from approximation of results to approximation of a law; for, the very
idea of "approximation" implies the possibility of an exact result
postulated *a priori*. Similarly, the Gauss curve, non-verification of
which is usually attributed to some "perturbation," cannot be taken
uncritically as a law of nature.[4]

In spite of these and similar reservations, Gendre feels that even if
there is no law of large numbers as such, one can no longer doubt a
certain average regularity of physical events which are more or less
accurately represented in terms of statistical frequencies. Because of
this experimentally verifiable regularity, which has been recognized
at least since Aristotle, Gendre refuses to dissociate the calculus of
probability from physical science.[5] To do that would be equivalent to
falling into the "conventionalism" of Henri Poincaré. Wanting no part
of this, Gendre opts instead for what he considers the "realism" of
John Venn.

The issue at stake here is so important that we must spell it out in
detail. For, in spite of Gendre's felt need to choose between what he
takes as two opposing views, Poincaré and Venn, for all their differences,
are speaking of the same thing; and in their words we find expressed
the very essence of the contemporary problem of probability.

John Venn, first of all, writing in his *Logic of Chance* (1886), notes

---

[1] Gendre, *Jugement probable*, p. 17.
[2] For a brief treatment of Stirling's Formula, see William Feller, *An Introduction to Probability Theory and its Applications*, 2nd ed. (New York-London, 1957), Vol. I, pp. 50–53, 169.
[3] Gendre, *Jugement probable*, p. 31. See Ch. II.
[4] Gendre, *Jugement probable*, pp. 12–15, 38, 51.
[5] Gendre, *Jugement probable*, p. 39. With regard to the reference to Aristotle, about whose views we shall have much to say in Chapter 5, see p. 90.

the following: "When Probability is... divorced from direct reference to objects, as it substantially is by not being founded upon experience, it simply resolves itself into the common algebraical or arithmetical doctrine of Permutations and Combinations." [1]

Henri Poincaré, in turn, in spite of his mathematical prowess, simply admits in his *Calcul des Probabilités* that he is unable to provide a satisfactory definition of probability. Reflecting upon this unusual difficulty, he says:

In each application (of the calculus of probability) we must make some conventions and say that we consider some particular cases equally probable. These conventions are not altogether arbitrary, but they are outside the competence (*échappent à l'esprit*) of the mathematician, who will not have to examine them once they are admitted. Thus every probability problem involves two levels (*périodes*) of study: the first – metaphysical, so to speak – justifies this or that convention; the second applies to these conventions the rule of the calculus.[2]

Unduly frightened by Poincaré's reference to the first part of the study as "metaphysical," Gendre suspects the great mathematician of a "syncretism" that would allow the metaphysician to do the job of the mathematician, and, even worse, of a conventionalism that would reduce the calculus of probability to "pure algebraic symbolism." In actual fact, however, it seems clear that what Poincaré is here describing is basically Popper's problem of decidability: the practical problem of physical approximation to mathematical norms, the very same problem, in short, to which Gendre's own study is directed. It is, then, without cause that Gendre seeks refuge in Venn. For, the latter

[1] John Venn, *The Logic of Chance*, 4th ed. (unaltered reprint of 3rd ed. of 1888: New York, 1962), p. 87. It is also interesting to note that when Venn first wrote this work (1866) he was still able to argue that the study of probability is not necessarily and not even primarily mathematical in character. See his observations in this regard in the Preface to the first edition, especially pp. vi, vii, viii, and xi of the 1962 edition.

[1] Henri Poincaré, *Calcul des Probabilités*, 2me éd. (Paris, 1912), ch. I, n. 5: "La définition complète de la probabilité est donc une sorte de pétition de principe: comment reconnaître que tous les cas sont également probables? Une définition mathématique ici n'est pas possible; nous devrons, dans chaque application, faire des *conventions*, dire que nous considérerons tel et tel cas comme également probables. Ces conventions ne sont pas tout à fait arbitraires, mais échappent à l'esprit du mathématicien qui n'aura pas à les examiner, une fois qu'elles seront admises. Ainsi tout problème de probabilité offre deux périodes d'étude: la première, métaphysique pour ainsi dire, qui légitime telle ou telle convention; la seconde, mathématique, qui applique à ces conventions les règles du calcul." Poincaré takes up this problem again, still without resolving it, in *La Science et l'Hypothèse* (Paris, 1929), Ch. XI, esp. pp. 213–219, 243–244. At the latter place he somewhat clarifies what he has said in his *Calcul des Probabilités*: "Pour entreprendre un calcul quelconque de probabilité, et même pour que ce calcul ait un sens, il faut admettre, comme point de départ, une hypothèse ou une convention qui comporte toujours un certain degré d'arbitraire ... Enfin, les problèmes où le calcul des probabilités peut être appliqué avec profit sont ceux où le résultat est indépendant de l'hypothèse faite au début, pourvu seulement que cette hypothèse satisfasse à la condition de continuité."

as well as Poincaré is but calling attention to the fact that the use or interpretation of the calculus of probability cannot be simply identified with the formal system as such. To bring out the significance of this distinction between formal system and interpretation, we turn to the thoughts of Pius Servien [1] and Bertrand Russell.

For Pius Servien, first of all, the so-called calculus of probability has nothing to do with probability and still less with chance. In fact, he maintains, the referenda of these terms are such that they are opposed to science. This rather exceptional position he bases upon a fundamental distinction between the language of science and the language of literature (la langue lyrique).[2] The former is characterized by the fact that a statement within it admits of an infinite number of equivalent statements none of which falsifies the original statement. The language of literature, on the contrary, is such that no statement can be replaced without its being falsified. Applying this distinction to the calculus of probability, Servien finds that the latter is essentially indistinguishable from the arithmetic of proper fractions and that any reference to "probability" or to "chance" is nothing more than an etiquette. The true basis of the calculus of probability (that is, of proper fractions) is, in the final analysis, the relationship of equality. Accordingly, the term "probability," or chance," can be replaced by any other term one might choose without in any way affecting the structure of the formal system. That these notions are thought to be associated with that structure is nothing more than an historical accident, of scientific importance only negatively insofar as the resulting confusion of languages has made intelligent analysis of foundations practically impossible.[3]

For Servien, then, the present confusion over probability requires not just further clarification but a completely new approach – not unlike that which brought forth non-Euclidean geometries out of the impasse over Euclid's axioms.[4] Theorists concerned with the problem

---

[1] The full name is Pius Servien Coculesco. However, perhaps in deference to his father, who also wrote along the same lines, he never uses the last name. Thus we too speak of "Servien" rather than of "Coculesco."

[2] For a brief explanation of this distinction, see Hasard et Probabilités (Paris, 1949), pp. 52–59. The full implications of the distinction are brought out in a number of treatises which form part of the series, published by Hermann, Paris, entitled Actualités Scientifiques et Industrielles. Servien himself is responsible for studies dealing with "Esthétique" and with "Langage Scientifique." Those of which he himself is the author, and to which we shall have occasion to refer, are concerned precisely with the calculus of probability. His most extensive study is a later work entitled Science et Hasard (Paris, 1952); but the essence of his thought will be found in Hasard et Probabilités (Paris, 1949).

[3] Servien, Hasard et Probabilités, pp. 40–43; Science et Hasard, pp. 63–96.

[4] Servien, Hasard et Probabilités, p. 15.

of "equally probable" have not gone beyond Poincaré, and they have not because they have been in a Platonic cave looking at "probability," which is but a shadow cast by "chance." [1] As a result, when they do speak about "chance" they are not infrequently off in realms metaphysical or even theological.[2] This muddled state of affairs suggests clearly enough that the problem has not been well posed. But this one might have known had he but taken seriously the admission of Poincaré, elsewhere always so precise, that his definition of "probability" is circular.[3]

Nor, says Servien, can one escape the difficulty by saying that this mathematical science deals not with probability as such but with chance. For, there is no such idea as chance as far as science is concerned. To the extent that science is mathematical, it achieves scientific status by reducing problems involving "chance" to problems in which there is no chance. In other words, it is only by reducing the disorderly, the "random," to some determinate order that mathematics (and hence physics) can deal with it. This having been done, one is from that point on involved in pure arithmetic, which deals not with chance but only with certitudes.[4] To say, then, that this arithmetical study is concerned with "chance" or "probability" is no more and no less indicative of its mathematical structure than to say that it is a Calculus of Sensations.[5]

Why, then, did the early theorists take as their model the so-called games of chance? Precisely because they were interested in what these games involve: a choice. But as formulated mathematically this choice is by no means "random"; for, the very formulation has as its task to remove the "guesswork" by enumerating and relating all possible permutations and combinations. To say, therefore, that there is no more reason to choose one alternative than another is simply to say in different words that all possible outcomes are "equally possible" –

[1] Servien, *Hasard et Probabilités*, pp. 16–23.

[2] To manifest what he considers to have been a confusion between two different languages (the scientific" and the "literary"), Servien satisfies Gendre's desire for an historical review of the "philosophical" background. Here we see Pascal proclaiming that his new "geometry of dice" encourages belief in God, Bernoulli finding divine providence in the regular frequency of births, and so on through Condorcet, Laplace, Poisson, and Voltaire. Thus, suggests Servien, did the earlier probabilists move easily from playing dice to playing God, and in the process they failed to establish any more than a kind of historical unity to their investigations. See *Hasard et Probabilités*, pp. 30–36; *Science et Hasard*, pp. 13–17, 60–63.

[3] Servien, *Hasard et Probabilités*, pp. 26–28, 91. For a detailed consideration of Poincaré's impasse, see *Probabilités et Physique* (Paris, 1945), pp. 12–20; *Base Physique et Base Mathématique de la Théorie des Probabilités* (Paris, 1942), pp. 16–17.

[4] Servien, *Hasard et Probabilités*, pp. 99–100.

[5] Servien, *Hasard et Probabilités*, p. 93.

which is nothing else than the classical *petitio principii*. Thus, the much-discussed "axiom of choice," so important to Von Mises's interpretation, is "utterly illusory"; a choice of this kind is no more possible to a mathematician than it was to Buridan's ass.[1]

If, however, we turn from pure mathematics to its practical applications, we do find ourselves in a situation demanding choice – not a choice between things "equally possible" but a choice as to what physical phenomena to consider "equal." This, however, is not a question of "probability" but of rules of correspondence and a theory of errors.[2]

What, then, in view of all this, is the calculus of probability? Quite simply, according to Servien, it is a mathematical structure all of which can be built up on the basis of elementary set theory. It is, basically, an arithmetical study of "equal things," more specifically, of the set of proper fractions (fractions less than or equal to 1). Such a study has no need of special axioms relating to "probability" or to "randomness." To use Servien's expression, then, the calculus of probability as such does not deal with the fall of a die but only with "dice in the air."[3]

There is, we think, much to be said for Servien's insistence upon the integrity and independence of mathematics as well as upon the need for a clear distinction between a formal system as such and an interpretation thereof. One feels, however, a certain narrowness or one-sidedness in his position. For, in stressing the abstractness of the formal system and in particular of the calculus of probability, he tends to minimize the relationship of the formal system both to its historical origins and to its use. To put it another way, there is in Servien a tacit assumption that mathematics is a kind of Platonic world of ideas, coming from no one knows where, whose successful application to the things of experience is, however beneficial, nonetheless somewhat fortuitous. In view of the opposite extreme of panmathematicism against which Servien is reacting, however, it must be admitted that what he says needs to be said. It goes without saying, at any rate, that

---

[1] Servien, *Hasard et Probabilités*, Ch. VIII and especially pp. 94–97, where the author attacks the frequency interpretation of the calculus of probability. See also *Science et Hasard*, pp. 140–173, and, for the reference to Buridan's ass, *Hasard et Probabilités*, pp. 106–107.

[2] Servien, *Hasard et Probabilités*. Chs. X and XI, pp. 100–117; *Science et Hasard*, pp. 202–229. This whole question of the relevance of "choice" to physical theory is treated in detail in *Le Choix au Hasard: Mesure d'Egalités physiques et Calcul des Probabilités* (Paris, 1941).

[3] Servien, *Hasard et Probabilités*, pp. 118–128 and especially pp. 122–123; *Science et Hasard*, pp. 185–198. This somewhat figurative distinction between a die in the air and a fallen die is meant to express Servien's key concern to keep separate the "*Base physique et base mathématique de la théorie des probabilités.*" See the work of the same title, Paris, 1942.

he adds considerable support to our contention that the notion of probability has meanings which are independent of mathematical formulations. To solidify this contention, then, we need only show, as Servien does not, that independence need not imply irrelevance. This task, we think, Bertrand Russell carries out very well by means of his theory of "interpretation."

"The pure mathematical theory," says Russell, "which merely enumerates possible cases, is devoid of practical interest unless we know that each possible case occurs approximately with equal frequency, or with some known frequency." [1] In tacit agreement with Servien, he allows that "ignorance is not involved in the (mathematical) concept of probability, which would still have the same meaning for omniscience as for us." But it is precisely our limited knowledge about the processes of nature "that makes it *useful* to apply probability to definite objects, and not only to wholly undefined members of classes."[2] With these points in mind, Russell provides us with an analysis of probability the order, clarity, and scope of which can here be only feebly suggested.

For Russell, the controversy over probability has to do not with the calculus of probability as such but with its interpretation. To resolve this controversy he adopts a position analogous both to that of Servien and to that of Carnap and in some ways a synthesis of the two. Briefly, this position involves a division between two concepts of probability each of which is in turn subdivided. First of all, he makes a sharp distinction between mathematical probability and "degree of credibility." With regard to mathematical probability he makes an equally sharp distinction between the formal axiomatic system as such and an interpretation which satisfies the axioms of that system.[3] With regard

[1] Bertrand Russell, *Human Knowledge: Its Scope and Limit,* paperback edition (New York, 1962), p. 366. This work will be referred to hereafter as *Human Knowledge.*

[2] Russell, *Human Knowledge,* pp. 353, 354.

[3] As we shall have occasion to point out in our conclusion, this distinction between the calculus of probability and what Russell contents himself to call its "interpretation" does not of itself resolve the question of the "meaning" of the calculus of probability. This is not the place to enter into a precise consideration of the logical relationship between a given formal statement and another statement which "interprets" it. However, it is perhaps not out of place to indicate the gravity of the problem that is at issue. From a strictly logical point of view a statement which "interprets" a formal statement and is, accordingly, what is sometimes called an *interpretant* of that formal statement, is as such no more "meaningful" or "meaningless' than the statement which it interprets. An interpretation of a formal statement does not determine a "meaning" for the statement interpreted; it merely establishes a correspondence between the statement interpreted and the interpretant. If in fact the interpretant has "meaning" this is due to factors which transcend the logical relationship of interpretation. What these factors might be with regard to the calculus of probability we shall discuss in terms of the "historical meaning" of the calculus of probability.

to probability understood as a degree of credibility, which he takes to be much broader in scope than the mathematical concept, he distinguishes clearly though less sharply between rational belief the evidence for which includes applications of the calculus of probability and that (much more extensive) the evidence for which cannot be of a mathematical nature.

Setting forth six axioms for the calculus of probability according to the formulation of C. D. Broad, Russell notes that three of the six (those which associate the calculus with numbers between 0 and 1 inclusive) are conventional. Thus, though not all the axioms may be necessary, they are at least sufficient for developing the system as a whole. But the formal system as such is one thing and the interpretation thereof is quite another. From a mathematical point of view, says Russell, any interpretation which satisfies the axioms can be called "probability"; any concept which satisfies the axioms may be taken to *be* mathematical probability. Which interpretation one will in fact adopt is a matter of choice, and the motives of choice are extrinsic to mathematics. The choice, however, may well depend upon the context, and thus some interpretations prove to be more important than others.[1]

This important clarification made, Russell then presents three interpretations of the calculus of probability. Taking up first what he calls a finite-frequency interpretation, then the infinite-frequency interpretation of Von Mises as formulated by Reichenbach, and finally the logical-relationship interpretation of Keynes, Russell maintains that the first satisfies the axioms but is limited in scope, and that the others, though basically sound, require certain modifications.

The difficulty of the finite-frequency interpretation, which involves restricting the values of the probability ratio to rational numbers, is that this interpretation can be extended to infinite collections only if it is possible to establish a series and proceed to a limit. Even if this were possible, one would in order to apply it have to assume some kind of inductive axiom about the course of nature.[2]

However, there are even greater difficulties arising out of the theory which assumes infinite series; and these difficulties, in Russell's opinion, are unnecessary. For, if Reichenbach's interpretation be taken strictly, the notion of probability applies not to classes but to series, and is, in effect, the limit of a series. "But outside pure mathematics," says

---

[1] Russell, *Human Knowledge*, pp. 339–340, 345.
[2] Russell, *Human Knowledge*, pp. 357–358.

Russell, "no series are known to be infinite, and most are, as far as we can judge, finite." [1] For this and other reasons Russell prefers to view Reichenbach's formulation as a kind of mathematical shorthand in which infinity simply means "a good deal more of the series than we have investigated hitherto." [2] (To say otherwise one must, contrary to Reichenbach's own intentions, introduce into abstract theory features of the world, e.g. time.) But even with this restriction, as soon as one goes beyond actually observed instances in order to predict the future course of similar events he is extrapolating from his empirical findings on the basis of some assumption about the efficacy of induction. That this is done, and successfully, is obvious enough; but its justification must be based on an "intentional treatment," whereas mathematical logic has been predominantly extensional. In particular, Reichenbach complicates the issue by tying probability so intimately to induction as to identify it as essentially statistical and yet maintaining at the same time that all propositions are only probable. For Russell, for whom even data may be more or less uncertain, there is no escape on this theory from an infinite regress unless one grant that the empirical estimate of probability (what Russell calls "probable probability") is based on either actual or postulated certainty.[3] For this and similar reasons, Russell qualifies Reichenbach's theory of different levels of frequency ("more or less probable") by insisting that so-called probability judgments, like any others, fall within the absolute true-false dichotomy.[4] In short, Reichenbach's interpretation, though valuable in many ways, presents a definition of probability unacceptable to Russell for the reason that "the frequency on which it depends is hypothetical and forever unascertainable." [5]

Keynes's theory also has much to offer, according to Russell, especially in that it identifies probability as a logical relationship. This relationship, however, is not between propositions, as Keynes would have it, but between propositional functions. "The application to propositions," says Russell, "belongs to the *uses* of the theory, not to the theory itself." [6] Failure to take into account this important distinction is, as Russell sees it, the chief *formal* defect in Keynes's theory,

---

[1] Russell, *Human Knowledge*, p. 367.
[2] Russell, *Human Knowledge*, pp. 365–366.
[3] Russell, *Human Knowledge*, pp. 368–369, 414–416.
[4] Russell, *Human Knowledge*, p. 417. As will be seen below, however, even granting a dichotomy between the true and the false, Russell still allows that a given proposition – a probability judgment – may ultimately be justifiable only in terms of degrees of credibility.
[5] Russell, *Human Knowledge*, p. 372.
[6] Russell, *Human Knowledge*, pp. 379–380.

leading as it does to the following dilemma. If probability cannot be defined, then probability propositions must be premises of knowledge; if it can be defined, then perhaps all propositions in which it occurs can be inferred (i.e. logically deduced within the formal system). Be that as it may, Keynes's work was important in that, by means of what he called the principle of indifference (otherwise known as the principle of non-sufficient reason), he sought to escape the contradictions implied by the reference to "equally possible" in the classical definition.[1] Understanding this principle in terms of propositional functions rather than (as did Keynes) of propositions, Russell considers it extremely valuable, not for the mathematical system as such but for its empirical applications. For, he points out, in the mathematical theory as such there is no assumption of "equally possible"; there, one need only know the numbers of various classes, that is, that each member of the class is to count as one. But in the application of the mathematical theory, which involves degrees of credibility, one must further assume that each case is equally credible – what Keynes meant by "indivisibility" and what Russell calls "relative simplicity." In other words, one must suppose that no structure is definable in terms of the relevant data: "All *calculations* of probability have to do with classes which can be defined in terms of the fundamental class. But the fundamental class itself must consist of members which cannot be logically defined in terms of the data." Being thus in agreement with Keynes, Russell restates the principle of indifference as follows: "Given two propositional functions ϕx, ψx, neither of which mentions a or b, or, if it does, mentions them symmetrically, then given ψa and ψb, the two propositions ϕa, ϕb have equal credibility." [2]

This translation of mathematical probability into a degree of credibility is possible, according to Russell, only in certain particular circumstances. When applicable, it measures the degree of credibility. But in general, the degree of credibility is increased or decreased rather by argument, the change effected by which cannot be estimated simply. For example, as Hume has already observed (and, as we shall see, Thomas Aquinas before him), a long argument is less reliable than a

---

[1] As described by Russell, Keynes, on the basis of the notion óf "irrelevance" (an added proposition is irrelevant if it does not change the probability), asserts: the probabilities of a and b relative to a given evidence are equal if (1) there is no relevant evidence relating to a without corresponding evidence relating to b (that is, if the evidence is "symmetric") and if (2) a and b are "indivisible" relative to the evidence. Russell, *Human Knowledge*, pp. 374–375.

[2] Russell, *Human Knowledge*, p. 387.

short one, because of the greater number of steps to which credence must be given. The number of steps involved can, of course, be incorporated into a mathematical theory, but the latter cannot encompass the private conviction of the individual mathematician as he takes each step. The same is true of non-demonstrative reasoning, of data in general, and of problems of human conduct.[1] Stated generally, "In some cases the degree of credibility can be inferred from mathematical probability, in others it cannot; but even when it can it is important to remember that it is a different concept. It is this sort, and not mathematical probability, that is relevant when it is said that all our knowledge is only probable, and that probability is the guide of life." [2]

Having thus covered the spectrum of probability in its scientific usage, Russell makes various other distinctions which indicate the depth and breadth of the question as he sees it. He distinguishes between "scientific" (mathematical) and "philosophical" doubt, and speaks of a "hierarchy of probability" involving the three levels of philosophy, science, and common sense. He notes that error may be not only absolute (taking the false for true, or vice versa) but also "quantitative," that is, giving more credibility to a proposition than is warranted by the evidence – a tendency, he says, which it is the purpose of scientific method to regulate. Finally, in speaking of "subjective certainty," he distinguishes three kinds; (1) *logical* (appropriate to mathematical probability); (2) *epistemological*, or "highest degree of credibility," which, whether intrinsic or due to argument, is a function of knowledge; and (3) *psychological*, which is simply the absence of doubt as to the truth of a proposition.[3]

To this wide-ranging analysis of the contemporary meaning of probability we have at this point nothing to add. Let it be said only that with the notion of interpretation as suggested by Servien and developed by Russell, we have come a long way from the mathematicism of a Boll or even of a Popper. But, as will now be seen, there is still further to go.

---

[1] Russell, *Human Knowledge*, pp. 383, 395, 398–399.

[2] Russell, *Human Knowledge*, p. 344. The assertion that all our knowledge is only probable Russell attributes to Reichenbach; the assertion that probability is the guide of life he attributes to Bishop Butler.

[3] Russell, *Human Knowledge*, pp. 359, 396–398.

"NON-OBJECTIVE" ASPECTS OF PROBABILITY

To complete our survey of modern views on the notion of probability, we turn now to two independent thinkers who, as a matter of fact, say little about probability as such. One, Michael Polanyi, is interested in what he calls "personal knowledge." The other, Chaim Perelman, devotes his attention to non-demonstrative reasoning in the hope of developing a "theory of argumentation." Each in his own way is reacting against the tendency to consider only "objective" or scientific thought as reasoning. Each also takes it for granted that the notion of probability has been more or less expropriated by the mathematicians. We shall not quibble over words. What is important is the fact that each is restoring to a position of dignity yet another aspect of what was once called probable reasoning.

Arguing forcefully for what he calls "a post-critical philosophy," Michael Polanyi presents a strong case for his contention that the exaggerated ideal of "objectivity" in science involves a disregard of a whole dimension of the scientific enterprise, a dimension which he chooses to describe as "personal knowledge." [1] Eliciting innumerable cases from the history of science recent and remote, Polanyi shows that personal opinions and beliefs (prejudice, in the etymological sense of pre-judgment) are a major factor in every phase of scientific activity, including research, evaluation of evidence, and position taken in controversies.[2] Writing therefore from a viewpoint which might be described as the social psychology of science, he insists that a complete view of science must take into consideration the human, that is, the personal, factors which transcend any formulation, however precise, of the supposed content of scientific knowledge.[3] These personal factors which enter into and influence judgments passed on otherwise "objective" matters of science can be considered in terms of a particular individual, as he does with Kepler; but, because of the very nature of science as a cooperative and traditional endeavor, the factors in question are more meaningful on a social level.[4] The social influences upon the judgment of a scientist might be specifically tied up with a

---

[1] Michael Polanyi, *Personal Knowledge: Towards a Post-Critical Philosophy* (Chicago, 1958). This work will be referred to as *Personal Knowledge*.
[2] All of this could well be summarized by what T. S. Kuhn refers to as "dogma." See his excellent article, "The Function of Dogma in Scientific Research," in *Scientific Change* (ed. A. C. Crombie; London, 1963), pp. 347–369.
[3] See especially Polanyi, *Personal Knowledge*, p. 164.
[4] For Kepler, see Polanyi, *Personal Knowledge*, p. 161.

particular school of thought, as in the case of Marxist and non-Marxist approaches to genetics.[1] But it is more likely that the influences derive from the cultural heritage of a civilization as a whole. The latter type of influence Polanyi calls "superior knowledge," that is to say, "all that is coherently believed to be right and excellent by men within their culture." [2]

Having thus familiarized ourselves with Polanyi's general outlook on science, we are now in a position to summarize his particular views on the theory of probability. As might be expected, he places great weight on the logical demonstrations of Tarski and Gödel to the effect that a given language system, such as the formalization of a science, is so restricted as a result of axiomatization that a statement within that language can only be judged on the basis of a richer language.[3] This need for richer languages results in what Polanyi calls "logical levels"; that is to say, any given science can be judged only by an appropriate meta-science.[4] In the light of these considerations, Polanyi rejects as unattainable Carnap's dream of a formalized logic of probable reasoning. He explicitly adopts Carnap's distinction between probability as relative frequency and probability as degree of confirmation, referring to the first as a statement about probable events and to the latter as a probable statement about events.[5] But in either case, he notes, probability statements are "impersonal" and as such are all "incomplete symbols, requiring to be accompanied by the utterance of a personal commitment in order that they may become the content of an assertion." Thus, in Polanyi's opinion, though "partial" formalization of probability statements may be possible, such formalization "must remain within a framework of personal judgment." [6] Thus for practical purposes he would consider the calculus of probability, however handsomely developed, to be no more than "a maxim like other maxims." As corollaries to this view of the calculus of probability, Polanyi defends the priority of acts of "personal knowledge" with regard to scientific discovery, with regard to appraisals of order and/or randomness in the universe.[7]

[1] Polanyi, *Personal Knowledge*, pp. 158, 159.

[2] Polanyi, *Personal Knowledge*, pp. 374–375.

[3] Polanyi, *Personal Knowledge*, pp. 259–261.

[4] Polanyi, *Personal Knowledge*, pp. 343–344. It is interesting to note in this regard a close similarity between the thought of Polanyi and that of Bernard J. F. Lonergan. See the latter's *Insight* (rev. student ed., London, 1958), which is in many ways an elaborate metaphysical development of the theme provided by Gödel's incompleteness theorem.

[5] Polanyi, *Personal Knowledge*, pp. 24–25, 32.

[6] Polanyi, *Personal Knowledge*, p. 29.

[7] Polanyi, *Personal Knowledge*, pp. 30, 36, 40.

Thus does Polanyi make explicit and extremely important what other analysts of science, especially Russell and in a way Popper, perhaps admit but do not attempt to incorporate into a total view of the scientific enterprise. For, in spite of fundamental differences of outlook and interest, almost all the writers we have considered recognize in one way or another that logical and/or mathematical formulations cannot or at least have not been able to encompass the full scope of human processes of reasoning. But few of these writers consider the non-demonstrative or the fact of non-demonstrability to be in itself worthy of consideration. Carnap, be it noted, is no exception, for his only interest is to reduce the non-demonstrative to a formal system. What Polanyi adds to the observations of others, then, is the contention that factors both personal and social play a role which is not extrinsic but intrinsic to the structure of science itself, and that, therefore, a full view of science must take such factors into consideration.[1]

But even Polanyi himself, it must be noted, considers the non-demonstrative only with regard to "science." For an extension of Polanyi's ideas to the whole range of non-demonstrative reasoning as such we must turn to Chaim Perelman.

Unlike Carnap, Perelman has no ambitions of reducing the informal to the formal; quite the contrary, he seeks to understand the informal as it were on its own terms, precisely insofar as it is not formalizable. What Polanyi says about personal and social factors in science, Perelman says all the more strongly with regard to every attempt of man to persuade his fellow man. For he, not unlike Emmanuel Levinas, is concerned about the dangers of obliterating personal responsibility in a formal maze of "objectivity." [2] Directly influenced by Bachelard, Bernays, Dupreel, and especially by Fernand Gonseth, Perelman has moved from studies of ethical reasoning to a general study of all forms of nondemonstrative reasoning. This refreshing and timely development he refers to as the New Rhetoric. As we shall see, however, the object of his investigations is so broad that his referring to this study as "rhetoric" is perhaps as misleading as it is enlightening. Much more

1 For an idea of the scope and influence of Polanyi's thought, see the volume dedicated to him under the title, *Personal Knowledge* (New York, 1961).

2 Though as yet little known in the English-speaking world, Emmanuel Levinas has come to enjoy a considerable renown for his criticism of overly systematic thinking, especially as a result of his major work, *Totalité et Infini* (The Hague, 1961).

indicative of what he is doing is the alternate title, a theory of argumentation.[1]

Following the general lines of Aristotle's study of nondemonstrative reasoning, Perelman carefully distinguishes his field of interest from that of formal logic by pointing out, among other things, that whereas the aim of the latter is to *convince*, the aim of rhetoric is to *persuade*. Persuasion, in turn, is a responsible act of a person in relationship to others. The others, that is, those whom one seeks to persuade, constitute what Perelman idealizes as "the universal audience" (*l'auditoire universel*). This universal audience may consist of listeners or readers, since the means of persuasion may be spoken ("rhetoric" in the narrower sense of the word) or written. But in either case the kinds and the number of arguments that one would use must be relative to, and hence are a reflection of, the understanding and attitudes of the audience. For, as Perelman puts it, the aim of logic may be validity, and the aim of grammar may be correctness, but the aim of rhetoric is effectiveness.[2] This implies that the "orator" must be guided not by what is most persuasive to him personally but by what will persuade the others. Hence the need, traditionally recognized by rhetoricians, to know the maxims, the "commonplaces," accepted by the audience.[3] In short, as Perelman sees it, the rhetorical situation is an intersubjective situation, involving action and reaction on the part of both rhetorician and audience. Accordingly, the study of means of persuasion must encompass the social factors which have a bearing upon success or failure of an attempt to persuade. Thus, with conscious affinity to the sociologists of knowledge, such as Karl Mannheim and Pitirim A. Sorokin, Perelman develops what might well be called a social psychology of nondemonstrative reasoning.[4] The title is ours, not his. For him, his "new rhetoric" is simply a "theory of argumentation," the

---

[1] Perelman's major work in this field, written in collaboration with L. Olbrechts-Tyteca, is *La Nouvelle Rhétorique: Traité de l'Argumentation*, 2 vols., Paris, 1958. As the subtitle suggests, this work develops in almost text-book order, the various aspects of nondemonstrative reasoning to which we can here refer only in the most general terms. An earlier work by the same two authors is by its very nature more susceptible to summarization: *Rhétorique et Philosophie; Pour une théorie de l'argumentation en Philosophie*, Paris, 1952. Also useful for an understanding of the purposes of the New Rhetoric is a special combined edition of the quarterly *Logique et Analyse* (Nouvelle Série, 6e année, 21 à 24: December, 1963) entitled *La théorie de l'Argumentation*. From the latter we draw rather heavily upon Olbrechts-Tyteca's introductory article, "Rencontre avec la Rhétorique," pp. 3–18. For the sake of simplicity, we refer to Perelman alone the aforementioned works as well as the ideas contained therein.

[2] Perelman, *Rhétorique et Philosophie*, p. 38: "Nous dirons que ce que la correction est pour la grammaire, la validité pour la logique, l'efficacité l'est pour la rhétorique."

[3] Perelman, *Traité de l'Argumentation*, Vol. I, pp. 112–132.

[4] Perelman, *Rhétorique et Philosophie*, pp. 132–141.

word argumentation being taken to mean a "proof" that fails to satisfy the requirements of formal logic, yet is appropriate to the audience to which it is presented.[1]

Given the general tenor of Perelman's intentions, it is not surprising that he sees little hope of encompassing all the forms of human reasoning within a calculus of probability. Quite the contrary, he is of the opinion that much of the difficulties to which philosophy has become accustomed are due to an overly rigorous requirement that a proof in any domain of thought imitate as much as possible the mathematical and/or scientific proof. Rejecting this legacy from the classical rationalists, Perelman simply distinguishes two kinds of proof, recognizing not only the scientific type but also the "dialectical" or "argumentative" type, that is to say, "any argument which diminishes our doubt, which suppresses our hesitations." [2] The larger implications of this distinction as an approach to what Perelman calls regressive philosophy (not unlike Gonseth's "open philosophy") need not detain us here except to note that Perelman restricts philosophical argument to rhetorical persuasion. Be that as it may, it is on the basis of this same distinction that Perelman asserts the impossibility of formulating the vast scope of argumentation in mathematical fashion.[3]

In Polanyi and even more so in Perelman, then, we see at work the same reaction against rationalistic "objectivity" as has been characteristic of existentialist phenomenology. And one effect of this reaction is that they make it more possible to see the calculus of probability within the larger context of nondemonstrative reasoning as such.

---

[1] Perelman, *Rhétorique et Philosophie*, pp. 16-18, 121-131; *Traité de l'Argumentation*, Vol. I, pp. 1-5.

[2] Perelman, *Rhétorique et Philosophie*, pp. 122 and 123, where he notes that, since the audience may accept an argument in spite of its logical deficiencies, "Nous considérerions comme preuve, dans ce cas, tout argument qui diminue notre doute, qui supprime nos hésitations." By thus broadening the notion of proof and emphasizing the aspect of subjective adherence Perelman rejoins not only the ancient rhetorical tradition but the accepted viewpoint of medieval disputation as expressed in the notions of *probabilis* and *opinio*. This affinity to medieval thought, however, is apparently unknown or at least unimportant to Perelman, who goes from Cicero to the Renaissance in his historical survey of rhetoric. See *Rhétorique et Philosophie*, p. 40.

[3] Perelman, *Traité de l'Argumentation*, Vol. I, pp. 1, 5; *Rhétorique et Philosophie*, p. 33. Leo Apostel, for one, is not entirely in agreement with Perelman's distaste for formalization. Insisting that argumentation is present within as well as outside of science, he urges that the new rhetoric be a hypothetico-deductive science, tending towards axiomatization on the basis of the calculus of relations. In fact, he envisages both logic and rhetoric subsumed under a "super-rhetoric" which would be as extensive as a theory of argumentation and as rigorous as formal logic. See his article, "Rhétorique, Psycho-Sociologie et Logique," in *La Théorie de l'Argumentation*, pp. 263-314 and especially 304, 309-310, 314 fn. 45.

Though neither questions the restriction of "probability" to a mathematical sense, the very tenor of their work favors an enlargement of meaning. All that is lacking is the freedom of a Bertrand Russell.

PROBABILITY MODERN AND MEDIEVAL

Needless to say, our survey of modern ideas about probability is by no means exhaustive. Yet we have considered a sufficient variety of authors to allow us to make a few generalizations. These we may state as follows, by letting P stand for "meaning of probability" and P_i for a particular meaning of probability.

1. There is more than one P. (This is generally admitted.)

2. In the set of P, there are at least two members: the general, or common sense, P and the scientific P (P_s).

3. Taking "scientific" in a broad sense, one might speak of not only a mathemathical P (P_m) but also a psychological P, a sociological P, or even an epistemological P.

4. But if "scientific" is taken in a strict sense, then P_s has reference to the calculus of probability and hence is mathematical.

5. For most authors, in fact, P_s is roughly equivalent to P_m.

6. P_s may be understood either as an explanation or as an interpretation of P_m.

7. If P_s is considered to be interpretative of P_m, then the interpretation which is P_s may be taken either to be conventional or to be exclusive:

7.1. P_s *conventional:* There is more than one member of P_s, the choice of which is determined by factors extrinsic to mathematics;

7.2. P_s *exclusive:* There is one and only one P_s acceptable as an interpretation of P_m:

7.2.1. This exclusive P_s may be either a statistical frequency (P_f) or a logical relationship (P_r) but not both: $P_f \neq P_r$;

7.2.2. This exclusive P_s is, as seen from different points of view, either P_f or P_r.

The preceding is, of course, nothing more than a skeleton outline of extremely complex and diversified analyses of the notion of probability. Nonetheless, it is our contention that the restriction of meaning thus indicated does in fact represent an almost universal feature of the current discussions. It is also our contention, however, that *this restriction is decidedly more verbal than real.* This point should by now be abundantly clear; but to be sure we shall here gather together some of the reasons for the failure of modern writers to effect the restriction to which they most certainly aspire.

1. *The mathematics of probability is not the same as the probability of knowledge nor is it the same as the knowledge of probability.* Bertrand Russell calls our attention to the fact that those who would limit P to a statistical meaning are the least entitled to say, as they sometimes do, that all knowledge is probable; for, there are no statistics, no frequencies, that show anything of the kind. If, on the other hand, one would rather limit P to a logical meaning, he is faced not only with the obstacle of Gödel's theorem but also with the fact, stressed by Popper, that logic is deprived of content and is ultimately tautological.

2. *The mathematics of probability is not the same as the probability of mathematics.* Thus we find Polya compelled to speak about mathematical reasoning as "plausible," Borel appealing to the numerical criterion of general acceptance, and Russell, quite willingly, distinguishing the personal conviction of the mathematician from the proposition of which he is convinced.

3. *The logic of probability is not the same as the probability of logic.* Thus we find the strongest defender of a formalized nondemonstrative logic, Rudolf Carnap, speaking about his dream by means of statements which he refers to as "plausible." The full significance of this fact is well brought out by the strictly logical theorems demonstrated by Craig, Tarski, and Gödel.

4. *The calculus of probability is not the same as the probability of a calculation.* Here we are involved in the whole vast problem of the relationship between mathematics and the world, more specifically the problem of induction (or confirmation, or corroboration). Once again Russell's observation that even data may not be certain is much to the point, and it is not without reason that he appeals to a nonmathematical credibility to found so-called inductions of probable propositions.

5. *The mathematics of probability is not the same as the probability of an event.* The arguments of Servien are not easily gainsaid, and at least Russell would be willing to agree with them. However much Popper might try to establish an inherent connection by speaking of "propensity," the mathematical calculus of probability cannot predict the outcome of an individual event. Here Gendre would have to agree with Servien that the calculus describes "dice in the air" and with Russell that the individual die is, for the mathematical formulation, no more than an instance, that is to say, a logical fiction. In short, the certitudes of mathematics as such have nothing to do with chance or randomness

or uncertainty in nature. That they are used, and successfully, is a fact of a different order, and the attempt to explain this fact is at least as old as the Pythagoreans.

6. *In particular, the mathematics of probability is not the same as the probability of a proposition.* That propositions (all of them, if you will) may well be probable and that, perchance, one might be able to devise a formal system expressive of the probability involved is not here in question. The point is simply that mathematics cannot exhaust the layers and depths of meaning which accrue to the observation that a given proposition is probable. With good reason, then, does Carnap admit, however reluctantly, that there is a "psychological" meaning of probability, and with equal reason does Popper appeal to *doxa* or verisimilitude to express the uncertainties of human knowledge. They both have much to learn from what Polanyi tells us about "personal knowledge" and about the role of the calculus as "a maxim like other maxims." We therefore watch with great interest Perelman's efforts to build up a "new rhetoric," a logic of argumentation, a dialectic of "the preferable."

By way of summary, then, there is today a general tendency to restrict the notion of probability to a mathematical meaning; but this tendency is in fact ineffective because the notion of probability transcends the bounds of mathematics. From various points of view, one sees attempts to deal in other terms with what was formerly spoken of as one or another aspect of probability. Credibility, verisimilitude, *doxa*, personal or superior knowledge, argumentation, open or regressive philosophy, the preferable, the plausible, inductive logic and the non-demonstrable – all these and other terms refer each in its own way to some aspect of knowledge which is not "scientific," which is not demonstratively certain.

It might even be the case, as some maintain, that *all* knowledge is probable – though not in the sense of the mathematically probable. But even if this is the case, what in fact does it mean to say that all knowledge is probable, or "only" probable? Probable as opposed to what? If someone should reply to the latter question that all knowledge is probable as opposed to being certain, then we must ask him whether or not he is certain about this sweeping generalization about knowledge. Moreover, we must ask him to explain the rather obvious fact that many people seem to be certain about all kinds of things. If our objector adds the rejoinder that their certitude is unfounded, then we must in turn ask him upon what he founds his judgment as to the unfoundedness of other people's certainty. What, in other words, are the criteria for certainty which he presupposes when he declares that man is not justified in having certitude? If he declares that there are no criteria, then we are led to suspect that we are free to reject his position. But, more to the point, our dialogue has simply caused us to fall back to that even more fundamental question as to what we mean by knowledge.

The foundational questions thus brought into the open are certainly (or, at least, probably!) deserving of attention even if they are not capable of being definitively resolved. On the other hand, even if such questions could be resolved there would still remain an even more troubling question which is of more immediate interest to contemporary philosophers of science. The question is this. If *all* knowledge is probable, then what if anything is unique about the probability that is determined by utilization of the calculus of probability? Why, in other words, should Bertrand Russell feel justified in speaking of "probable probability" with regard to empirical data fed into the calculus?

To these questions we shall return in our concluding section, where we distinguish between the systematic and the non-systematic and show how the calculus of probability had been viewed until recently as an instrument directed to the non-systematic. The historical perspective thus provided will by no means "solve" the contemporary problem of probability, neither as this applies to the calculus of probability nor as this applies to broader epistemological considerations. But it will help considerably, we think, to clarify some ideological presuppositions behind the problems themselves. It is to this end, then, that we direct our attention to a medieval theory of probability.

Why a *medieval* theory? As should be obvious from what has been said since our opening remarks, we would no longer hesitate for fear that a medieval theory might not have been mathematical. But even granting this *carte blanche*, is there any good reason to go back quite so far? We think that there is.

That the contemporary confusion over the notion and extension of "probability" should lead us back to the days before Pascal and Fermat, before Cardano, and even before Copernicus and Galileo might be justified in the light of the following considerations. J.-L. Gendre, to begin with, comes to the conclusion that a solution of the contemporary problem must be sought among the philosophers of the sixteenth and seventeenth centuries. But, as Servien points out, *it is precisely because of the mingling of philosophical and even theological ideas in the mathe-*

matical foundations that the problem has been presented to us in the insoluble form in which we know it. To take just one example, Pascal himself was by no means merely a mathematician, nor was he even, in his own mind, primarily a mathematician. He was a soul seeking God, without, if possible, the help of the Jesuits. Thus perhaps did he see in his "geometry of chance" a way around the then heated controversy over grace and free will in which the Molinist theory supported by the Jesuits played such an important role. This accomplished, he could make his famous bet on the afterlife and devote the remainder of his days on earth to the Jansenist vision of Port-Royal. Granting, then, as Gendre intimates, that a study of ideas of the past can help us in our understanding of the crisis of probability, we nevertheless dare not restrict ourselves to the ideas of the probabilists themselves. We must go beyond their ideas on probability to the sources of these ideas – in philosophy and even in theology.

However, as John Henry Randall so eloquently demonstrates, the roots of Renaissance and Enlightenment thought are to be found in the Middle Ages – that is to say, in a time relatively innocent of any mathematical concept of probability. According to Randall, there are three principal medieval currents of thought which, separately or in various combinations, go to make up Renaissance and eventually Enlightenment philosophies. These are: (1) Augustinianism; (2) Thomism; (3) Occamism.[1] It would be be very well worth while to study the notion of probability in each of these separate medieval currents. But the enormity of the task defies the capacities of one single book if not of one single lifetime. Consequently, we have singled out for our own investigations just one of Randall's three currents, that of Aristotelian-Thomism, as found specifically in the writings of Thomas Aquinas himself.

In Thomas Aquinas we have access to a theory – and, as we shall see, a rather elaborate theory – of probability relatively untrammeled by mathematical considerations. More than this, in Thomas's theory of probability we shall find an important correlative notion which the ideal of "objectivity" has since quite killed off. This notion is one which expresses, in all the depth which a Polanyi or a Perelman could want, the aspect of personal commitment. The notion in question is that of *opinion*.

Neutral as far as mathematicians are concerned, and slanted for the

---

[1] For the views of Randall see *The Career of Philosophy: From the Middle Ages to the Enlightenment* (New York-London, 1962), especially pp. 13–43.

modern mind only with respect to social studies (which tell us about "public opinion" on the basis of "public opinion surveys"), opinion is of fundamental importance in medieval evaluations of knowledge. In its Latin form, *opinio*, this term is a direct translation of the Greek *doxa*, which Popper has found so fortuitous for his non-mathematical observations about human knowledge.

This *doxa* of which Perelman's Sophists made so much, and from which Socrates and Plato sought to escape, and which Aristotle sought (not altogether successfully) to embrace into his vision of the universe – this *doxa* the early medieval dialecticians and rhetoricians sought to exploit under the heading of *opinio*. It was this same *doxa*, now under the guise of a *sententia*, which generations of medieval theologians sought to surmount in their commentaries on Peter Lombard. It was this same *doxa* which reappeared in full dress in the thirteenth century when European Christians found themselves in possession of the entire corpus of Aristotle's works complete with the elaborate Mohammedan interpretations of the Arabs. And, finally, it was this same *doxa* which had to be distinguished from the irrefrageable conviction of faith, the uniqueness of which seemed in dire jeopardy of annihilation in the face of so much "pagan" knowledge the source of which was reason alone. Of all the efforts to preserve both the autonomy of "the philosophers" and the uniqueness of what had been handed down by the "holy doctors," none was more intense or more perspicacious than that of Thomas Aquinas.

It is with all this in mind, then, that we turn to Aquinas to study not only the medieval notion of probability but also that of opinion. The latter, in fact, will serve as a kind of focal point for our study of the former: in all that we say, we shall ever have in mind as our goal to elucidate the relationship or relationships which obtain, in Thomas's mind, between *opinion* and *probability*. As the analysis of this chapter has attempted to make clear, our findings in this regard can well be of considerable historical interest.

PART TWO

A MEDIEVAL NOTION
OF PROBABILITY

CHAPTER II

OPINION, ERROR, AND HUMAN IMPERFECTION

"All that I have written is as straw." With these words, it is said, Thomas of Aquino laid down his pen, leaving unfinished his most famous work, the *Summa Theologica*. Shortly thereafter, while on his way to the Second Council of Lyons (1274), he became ill and died.[1] Just three years after his death, his work would be called in question by others – an event of no little historical importance. With the Condemnation of 1277, however, we are not concerned.[2] There is for our purposes more than enough to wonder about in that seemingly pejorative evaluation which Thomas himself is said to have made of his own work.

What ever could have prompted this man – recognized even by his greatest enemies as at least one of the outstanding thinkers of his century – to utter such a devastating criticism, such a sweeping disavoval of what had been, at least in human terms, his whole life, his very reason for being on this earth? Explanations, to be sure, have often been suggested, some of which would see the event as a physical attack of one kind or another, others as some overwhelming mystical experience. For those who prefer to close out the great scholar's life on a mystical plane, Thomas at that moment was filled with a vision of ultimate reality so illuminating that all other, ordinary, human knowledge was by comparison insignificant and irrelevant. However one wishes to interpret the event in depth, there is this much to be said on the surface: somewhere towards the end of an extremely prolific

.

---

[1] See Joseph Pieper, *The Silence of St. Thomas* (New York, 1957); A. Walz, "De St Thomae Aquinatis e vita discessu," *Xenia Thomistica* (Rome, 1925), t. III, pp. 41–45; H. Petitot, "La mort de S. Thomas d'Aquin," *Vie Spirituelle* 10 (1924): 312–336.

[2] For the significance of the Condemnation of 1277, see Fernand Van Steenberghen, *The Philosophical Movement in the Thirteenth Century* (London-New York, 1955), pp. 94–106; Etienne Gilson, *History of Christian Philosophy in the Middle Ages* (New York, 1955), pp. 385–427; Joseph Pieper, *Scholasticism* (New York, 1960), pp. 126–135.

career as teacher and writer, the man Aquinas expressed the conviction that all the fruits of his labors were marked with the effects of human frailty.

We could no doubt strive for a kind of hermeneutic erudition by asking ourselves if the purported event ever really happened. We shall not, however, for its historicity is quite unimportant. The event in question, though probably legendary, has an advantage over many so-called brute facts in that it was amazingly fitting and appropriate. For, it makes a story which in the telling summarizes one of the most significant aspects of the thought of the man involved; and thus, in brief, if it did not happen, it should have.

To put this all somewhat differently, whatever that eleventh hour experience might have been, it was certainly not a sudden revelation which undid everything that Thomas had ever thought before. For, his writings are filled to overflowing with observations and reflections upon the limitations of human knowledge in general, the feebleness of philosophy, the humble stammerings of theology, the lack of vision which afflicts the man of faith. Nor are his statements along these lines to be taken merely as tongue-in-cheek humility of the man who knows all things. Thomas Aquinas does not know all things, and in many ways he is the first to admit it. To go even farther than that, there is ample reason to wonder what, if anything, he really felt that he knew with absolute assurance. A strong statement, to be sure, but one which will take on various nuances of meaning in the course of the study which we now undertake.

We are not, of course, directly interested in Thomas's testimonies to his own ignorance or to that of man in general. We are interested rather in what he means by the notion of probability. But, as has already been suggested, Thomas's usage of the term "probability" is closely connected (how closely remains to be seen) with the term "opinion." But the notion which Thomas wishes to express by the term "opinion" has its roots deep in the fact of human ignorance. Accordingly, since it is of the utmost importance that we place the notion of probability within its proper context in Thomas's thought, we must first come to grips with the notion of opinion; and the latter, in turn, can only be understood within the larger context of man's cognitional inadequacies.

It is, therefore, with human ignorance that we must begin in our quest for the notion of probability. But, inasmuch as a beginning already implies motion towards a goal, it is perhaps useful to indicate at the outset where our discussion will ultimately lead us. Disconcerting though it may be to those of a more empirical bent, Thomas's dialectic of opinion and probability can only come to a halt when the inquiring mind finds its fulfillment in the unending sight of God. Nor is this ultimate intellectual fulfillment in God merely incidental to what Aquinas has to say about human knowledge in general and probability in particular. It is nothing less than the very heart and soul of his dialectic of human thought. For Thomas, probability is a qualificative of opinion, opinion is the object of dialectical argumentation, dialectical argumentation is man's means of transcending his own ignorance, and the transcendence of ignorance is accomplished only in the beatific vision of the life beyond. For Thomas, in other words, it is by applying argumentative method to human opinions that one establishes or destroys their probability, and thus slowly moves beyond the merely probable towards that ultimate vantage point at which man participates according to his capacity in the divine omniscience. Thus, in effect, every thought expressed by Thomas Aquinas is fundamentally dialectical, and the dialectic itself is theotropic.

The glorious finality of this quest for knowledge is all the more awesome from man's point of view in that he rather literally begins from a cognitional zero. This, so to speak, puts man in his epistemological place; for, the knowledge of God, as it were at the opposite extreme, is of infinite plenitude. For man alone, as Kant will later emphasize, this infinite distance cannot be traversed in finite time. Nonetheless, the movement of reason from total ignorance towards total vision is not affected by Zeno's paradoxes; and thus, with the help of God, it is ultimately possible for the mind of man to achieve that which it naturally desires. This is, of course, as it should be, since (as Aristotle had insisted) nature does nothing in vain.

A. THE LIMITATIONS OF HUMAN KNOWLEDGE

1. The Fact of Human Ignorance

Thomas, then, admits a kind of epistemological optimism when viewing man *sub specie aeternitatis*. But from the strictly human point of view, he generally sees the acquisition of knowledge as a difficult task indeed. That knowledge must be acquired, and is so hard to come by, is itself an indication that it is not, as Plato asserted, innate.[1] Quite

---

[1] In III *De An.* 1. 4, n. 624.

the contrary, man's knowledge in this world is ever dark and shadowy afflicted with doubt and uncertainty.[2] Starting out as an Aristotelian *tabula rasa* potentially capable of knowing all things, the human mind nonetheless is doomed to frustration if it should expect to exhaust that potentiality in this life.[2] Man's knowledge is simply characterized by imperfection, and there are no accoutrements, natural or supernatural, which would permit him to escape these limitations so long as he remains a regular inhabitant of our planet.[3] As Thomas notes in one place, it is apparently the will of God that many things be simply unknown to us.[4] Indeed, even that which we know is permeated with the finitude of our capacities:

> So defective is our knowledge that no philosopher can ever exhaust what there is to know about one fly. Thus we read that one philosopher spent thirty years in solitude that he might know the nature of the bee.[5]

Though the highest of all material beings because of his intellect, man is the least perfect of all intellectual beings. Infinitely inferior to God in intelligence, man is no less inferior to angels.[6] Indeed, greater is the distance between the knowledge of an angel and that of the greatest philosopher than is the distance between that philosopher's knowledge and the knowledge of a country bumpkin.[7] For Thomas, in other words, there are three major forms of intellection, divine, angelic, and human, and the latter is in every respect the most imperfect. Indeed, so inferior is the human way of knowing to that of angels and *a fortiori* to that of God, that Thomas will even refer to man's mind as a kind of prime matter of the intellectual universe.[8]

The root of man's intellectual imperfection is not, however, in the fact that he is intellectual but in the fact that he is rational. The difference between intellectuality and rationality is all the difference between rest and motion, between possession and privation, between fulfillment and desire, between the knowing and the seeking of knowledge.[9] Thus, whereas God *is* intellection in this sense, and the angel *has*

---

[1] *Q.D. de ver.* 24, 3c.

[2] *Q.D. de spir. cr.* q. un., a. 10c.

[3] *S.T.* I–II, 68, 2 ad 3. See also II–II, 8, 1.

[4] *Quodl.* 3, q. 9, a. 2 *in contr.*

[5] "Cognitio nostra est adeo debiles quod nullus philosophus potuit unquam perfecte investigare naturam unius muscae: unde legitur, quod unus philosophus fuit triginta annis in solitudine ut cognosceret naturam apis." *In Symb.* Prol., n. 864.

[6] *Q.D. de ver.* 5, 8c.

[7] *In Symb.*, Prol., n. 865.

[8] *In I Met.* l. 1, n. 2.

[9] See *S.T.* I, 58, 3c; *De rat. fidei* c. 3, n. 963; *C.G.* III 108; *Quodl.* II, q. 2, a. un., c and ad 1; *Comp. theol.* c. 105, n. 210.

intellection, man must *acquire* intellection. In other words, man must proceed step by step, on his own level, to approach some semblance of that intuitive knowledge which is essentially divine and innately angelic.[1]

This properly human process of rational inquiry might be spoken of as a movement from imperfect to perfect knowledge, but even this must be understood relatively to man. More accurately, the movement in question is from the less perfect to the more perfect, from the more imperfect to the less imperfect. Thus from many imperfect concepts we form a concept which is more perfect; knowledge which is vague is gradually made more precise, more distinct, more accurate. In order to know any given object we try to distinguish it from other things by finding out in what way it is the same, in what way it is different.[2] More often than not, we must content ourselves with a knowledge of accidental differences because essential differences are unknown: even our distinction between men and beasts on the basis of rationality and irrationality is an expression of accidental rather than essential differences.[3] Moreover, we are often compelled to satisfy ourselves with a knowledge of the effects of things rather than with the things themselves, or, more generally, of the relationship of one thing to another rather than of the thing itself.[4] So also the weakness of our intellect requires us to deal with things one by one because we do not see the relationship between them, the common ingredient that is universality.[5] A piecemeal process, to be sure, made necessary for man due to the fact that unlike God and unlike the angel he cannot see in the principles of knowledge all that those principles imply.[6]

Man generalizes about things, of course, and his generalizations are true manifestations of what is thus known. But though true and truly manifestative, man's generalizations are only partial; seldom, if ever, are they exhaustive of the content of a thing. For, things are ever richer in detail than man's partial cognitive glimpses. It is, in fact, the very detailedness of things which points out to us the imperfection of what

---

[1] *S.T.* I, 14, 4; 55, 1; 84, 87, and 88. See also *S.T.* I, 14, 7; 17, 8; 55, 2c.
[2] See Edmund F. Byrne, *The Thomistic Metaphysics of Unity and Multiplicity and its Role as a Foundation for the Doctrine of Distinction* (unpublished Master's Thesis, Loyola University, Chicago, 1956), pp. 135–158.
[3] *S.T.* I, 77, 1 ad 7. See *Q.D. de ver.* 10, 1 ad 6; 4, 1 ad 8; *In VII Met.* l. 12, nn. 1551–52; *S.T.* I, 29, 1 ad 3, I–II, 18, 7c; 49, 2 ad 3 (ad finem); *In De Trin.* 6, 1 c; *De ente* c. 5, nn. 25 and 31; *In I De Generat.* l. 8, n. 5.
[4] *In De Trin.* Proem. II, 2 ad 2; *In I Post. Anal.* l. 4, n. 16; *Quodl.* 11, 2, a. un. ad 1.
[5] *In De div. nom.* c. 3, l. un., n. 251.
[6] *Q.D. de ver.* 15, 1; *S.T.* I, 79, 8. See also *Q.D. de ver.* 12, 1; 14, 9–11.

we know; for, implicit in all our knowledge is the realization that there is yet more to be known. Man is more at home, more at ease with general ideas about things. Thus does he ever attempt to reduce the complex to the simple, the variable to the invariable, the relative to the absolute. To the extent that things resist such reduction, to the extent that they suggest to the mind a multiplicity of aspects yet unordered and unexpressed, man is kept aware of the incompleteness of what he has already discovered. The more there is to say about a thing, if you will, the less can a man be certain about the accuracy of all that he says.

Thus, in terms of the objects of our knowledge, we know perfectly neither beings superior to man nor beings inferior to man. Though our classifications of things do tell us something about those things, still they over-simplify the complexity of material beings and they overly complicate the simplicity of immaterial beings.[1] Many of the properties of material things are unknown to us, and even when we know the properties of things we are not often able to explain perfectly why things have the properties we find in them.[2] Still less are we able to know all that is to be known about "separate substances," that is, about angels and especially about God. These higher beings we know more by comparison, or rather by contrast, to material things.[3] We have neither definitions nor demonstrations about angels, and we believe far more about God than we know, even though in himself God is infinitely knowable. Similarly, we do not have direct scientific knowledge even of the human soul, but know it rather in function of the body.[4] In short, what man knows about anything is feeble and imperfect by comparison to what there is to know about that thing.

2. Human Error and Its Causes

Granting, then, that it is difficult for man to acquire knowledge, how explain this difficulty? Thomas addresses himself to this question especially in his early and somewhat more Platonic work, the *De Veritate* (1259), but the answers he there gives are implicit in all his later writings.[5] The difficulty, he says, can be due either to the knower

---

[1] *S.T.* I, 50, 2c; *In De Trin.* q. 6, a. 1 ad q. 2c; *S.T.* I, 108, 3c. See also *S.T.* I, 3, 3; 12, 7c; 14, 3c; 56, 1 ad 2; 86, 1 ad 3; III, 2, 2; *C.G.* I. 65; *De ente* c. 4, *Q.D. de pot.* 9, 1c.

[2] *C.G.* I, 3.

[3] *De ente* c. 6; *In III De. An.* l. 8, n. 710; *C.G.* IV, 1; *In I Post. Analyt.* l. 41, n. 363.

[4] *Q.D. de an.* q. un., a. 7 ad 16; *Q.D. de ver.* 5, 2 ad 11; *C. G.* I, 11.

[5] *Q.D. de ver.* 9, 5 c; 12, 2 c; 13, 3; 18, 5 ad 4. See also *II Met.* l. 1. It would be more in

or to the object of knowledge. However, his manner of explaining this distinction makes it apparent that for him it is essentially the knower who is, if you will, at fault. For, an object is difficult to know insofar as it is "remote" or "distant" from us. An object may be "distant" either in itself or simply from our point of view. Thus, future contingents are in themselves "distant," whereas spiritual things, especially those that are eternal, are in themselves most knowable and thus are unknown to us only because of our cognitional deficiencies. As will be pointed out later, however, even future contingents are perfectly known by God, and hence even in this case it is our deficiency which makes them unknown to us. The fault, in short, is in us; for we are intellectual underlings.

Thus far, however, we have really said no more than that the limitations of human knowledge are due to human limitations: a statement perhaps not totally devoid of interest, but hardly very enlightening. For, what is really involved here is the thorny problem of error; what error is, where error is located (figuratively speaking, of course), and what is the cause or causes of error.[1]

(a) The Phantasm as the Source of Error

On various occasions Thomas declares that passion or love for pleasure is responsible for diverting men from what is reasonable, especially though not exclusively in their actions.[2] Lust, in particular, is a cause of "blindness of mind" and "dullness of the senses."[3] All feelings and emotions are, moreover, functions of knowledge; thus, since all human knowledge is somehow founded upon the senses, whatever affects the senses can indirectly disturb man's knowledge. Often impressed by the fact that the great mass of men follow passion rather than reason, Thomas likes to trace this unfortunate fact of human

keeping with the state of the evidence to date the *De Veritate* as 1256–1259. For the sake of simplicity, however, we give here and throughout our study only the date which most authorities would recognize as a satisfactory *terminus ad quem* for the work in question. For the most part, this method of chronology is quite sufficient for our purposes; but we shall not hesitate to give dates for both *terminus a quo* and *terminus ad quem* where it is relevant to do so. We base our chronology on the very useful survey by I. T. Eschmann, "A Catalogue of St. Thomas's Works: Bibliographical Notes," in Etienne Gilson's *The Christian Philosophy of St. Thomas Aquinas* (New York, 1961), pp. 381–437. Also useful for this purpose is the brief summary given by Fernand Van Steenberghen, *Histoire de la Philosophie: Période Chrétienne* (Louvain-Paris, 1964), pp. 100–101.

[1] For a detailed history of the problem of error see L. W. Keeler, *The Problem of Error from Plato to Kant: A Historical and Critical Study*, Rome, 1934.

[2] See, for example, *S.T.* I–II, 10, 3 ad 2; *In VI Polit.* l. 5, n. 996; VII, l. 10, n. 1191; l. 4, n. 1103.

[3] *S.T.* II–II, 15.

behavior to bodily changes. In accord with the common medieval view, he attributes such bodily changes to the influence of the celestial bodies, that is, the planets. Indeed, the vast majority of men succumb to these superterrestrial forces; the wise who resist are comparatively few in number.[1] Be that as it may, this astronomical alternative to the theological doctrine of original sin is intended more as an explanation of moral turpitude than of error as such. Besides, the influence of the planets in this regard would seem to be conditional rather than causal.[2] In any event, Thomas elsewhere mentions faulty reasoning as well as passion as a cause of error in action.[3] Moreover, he also asserts that even sin as such affects one's desire for the good more than his knowledge of the true.[4]

None of the foregoing, however – neither sin nor passion nor planets – is more than a factor or a condition leading to error. The real culprit, the immediate source of error, is the work of the imagination: the phantasm. The reasons which lead Thomas to this position are too complex for our purposes, but they will be somewhat in evidence when we take up the distinction between the scientific and the opinionative parts of the soul. For the present, it is enough to note that Thomas is committed to the essential accuracy of both senses and intellect. Thus he finds himself compelled to trace not only errors of sensation but also errors of the intellect to deviations of imagination.[5] Error, in other words, is due to a misreading of the senses on the one hand or a misguiding of the intellect on the other. So also, from this narrow psychological point of view, he can speak of men following their phantasms rather than their reason.[6] The value of using the phantasm as the scapegoat for error lies, of course, in the fact that it preserves the operational integrity of both senses and intellect, neither of which, according to Aristotelian teaching, can in general be frustrated in the attainment of its natural end. Thus, it is not the senses which fail but the phantasm, it is not the intellect which fails but the phantasm. Properly speaking, in other words, error is due neither to the senses nor to the intellect, but to the phantasm.[7]

---

[1] *Comp. theol.* c. 128, n. 255; *C.G.* III, 85 and 154; *Q.D. de ver.* 22, 9 ad 2.

[2] For a rather thorough collection of texts relevant to this question, see Thomas Litt, *Les Corps célestes dans l'univers de saint Thomas d'Aquin* (Louvain-Paris, 1963), pp. 200–214.

[3] *In III De An.* l. 15, nn. 820–826.

[4] *S.T.* I–II, 109, 2 ad 3.

[5] *Q.D. de ver.* 1, 11; *S.T.*, I, 94, 4c.

[6] *In III De An.* l. 6, n. 670; l. 15, n. 819.

[7] *In IV Met.* l. 12, n. 673; l. 14, nn. 692–707; *S.T.* I, 54, 5 ad objectiones; *Q.D. de malo* 7, 5 ad 6.

The advantages of this position are, however, more apparent than real. For, Thomas is committed to the position that the phantasm is the basis, or object, of all human thought. Whatever man knows, whatever man thinks, must be founded somehow upon a phantasm, either because the phantasm represents the reality or because that which the phantasm represents is negated of the reality.[1] As a corollary of this position, man's knowledge can never go beyond what is seminally expressed either positively or negatively in phantasms.[2] To put this in another way, human knowledge is based upon and limited by a psychic representation of space and time. Thus, if we now recall what was said above about the phantasm as the source of error, we must conclude that the phantasm is both the source of truth and the source of error. We are not very far from the Cartesian notion of an evil genie, nor, for that matter, from what Karl Popper calls a conspiracy theory of error.

Our purpose at this point, however, is by no means to initiate a critique of Thomas's theory of knowledge. We merely wish to note that there is a certain inconsistency in the role which that theory gives to the phantasm, and to suggest that there is a fundamental problem of a far more serious nature which leads him to this theoretical impasse. It is precisely in uncovering this problem that we bring into our discussion the notion of opinion.

(b) Opinion as the Locus of Error

In order to put this notion of opinion in its proper context right at the outset, we must point out that, though Thomas considers the phantasm to be the principal source of error, he does not locate error precisely in the phantasm. The phantasm is indeed the psychic focal point of all the various internal and external factors that lead one into error. But to say that error as such is *in* the phantasm would be tantamount to denying that human cognition is intellectual. Accordingly, granted that phantasmal disturbances are the principal *source* of error, and that these disturbances may be due to any of a number of factors internal or external, an error as such, if it is to be genuinely human, must somehow be intellectual. That is to say, error is *in* the intellect, and consequently nothing external or internal to man is properly speaking false except insofar as the intellect is thereby led to assent to the misrepresentation. Thus it is only by way of

---

[1] See especially *In De Trin.* 6, 2 ad 2 and ad 5; also, *In De Mem.* l. 2, nn. 311–319; *Q.D. de an.* q. un., a. 15c ad fin.

[2] *C.G. III, 41.*

analogy that an object of cognition or a psychic image of that object could be called "false." Falsity, or error, is properly speaking in the intellect.[1]

But, as Aristotle insists, the intellect cannot be frustrated in its natural desire or capacity for truth; how, then, can the intellect be subject to error? To say without qualification that the intellect is capable of error would destroy the very foundations of intellectual certitude – not only certitude about principles but also certitude about conclusions founded upon those principles. Thus would be destroyed in one fell swoop the very possibility of demonstrative science. To allow this to happen, however, is as unpalatable to Thomas as it was to Aristotle.

For the sake of clarity, we might state Thomas's problem in the form of a dilemma. If error is not in the intellect, then its opposite, truth, is not in the intellect either. But if error is in the intellect, then the intellect can be frustrated in its natural desire for truth, which amounts to saying that truth is not in the intellect (or, at least, that it cannot be known as truth). But error is either in the intellect or it is not in the intellect. Therefore, in either case, truth is not in the intellect, and thus the intellect is frustrated in its natural desire for truth.

It was perhaps in order to resolve this grave dilemma that Aristotle was compelled on the one hand to elevate opinion (*doxa*) beyond the level of sensation and at the same time mark it off sharply from intellectual certitude (*episteme*). Whether Aristotle's *doxa* is strictly intellectual knowledge or not is beyond the scope of our investigations.[2] In any event, for Thomas Aquinas *opinio* is intellectual and, though intellectual, lacks the perfection of science. More immediately to the point, precisely because opinion is in the intellect and yet is distinct from science, the aforementioned dilemma is at least theoretically capable of solution. The details of the solution, which involve the distinction between the scientific and opinionative parts of the soul, will be taken up a bit later. For now let it merely be noted that, thanks to opinion, error may safely be admitted into the intellect without endangering the security of certitude and science.

---

[1] *Q.D. de ver.* 1, 2c; 1, 10; *S.T.* I, 17, 1c; 4 ad 3.

[2] For a thorough study of this question, and one to which we are greatly indebted, see L.–M. Regis, *L'Opinion selon Aristote* (Ottawa-Paris, 1935).

B. OPINIONATIVE KNOWLEDGE

Opinion, then, has an extremely important role to play in Thomas's theory of knowledge – a role, in fact, which (because of the problem of faith) is far more extensive than in the thought of Aristotle himself.[1] This, however, will gradually become clear in the course of our study. For the moment, we must try to pinpoint somewhat more precisely just what Thomas means by opinion.

1. *The Notion of Opinion*

To begin with it is necessary to introduce some important lexico-graphical observations the justification of which must be left to the gradual development of our subject. For, what we have been calling and shall continue to call "opinion" involves several different aspects of cognition, some of which Thomas identifies by means of more than one term. Fittingly enough to the English-speaking reader, the generic term which Thomas uses to refer to opinionative knowledge is the etymologically obvious, *opinio*. This term, as Thomas uses it, is as wide in scope as the Greek *doxa*. For that very reason, however, *opinio* is in fact an extremely complex term, involving at least three distinguishable aspects of cognition. The three aspects of *opinio* here in question are: (1) psychological; (2) logical; and (3) epistemological.

From a *psychological* point of view, *opinio* may refer either to a habit or to an act flowing from that habit. Taken as a habit of opinionative knowledge, *opinio* refers to the set or ensemble of all non-demonstrative but properly intellectual knowledge. Taken as an act flowing from that habit, *opinio* means more specifically a member of the set of opinionative knowledge, namely, some one opinionative judgment.

From a *logical* point of view, *opinio* involves aspects both positive and negative. Taken positively, *opinio* denotes not only what modern logicians would call a sentence or proposition (or a set of propositions) but also the positing of a proposition as a statement or assertion.[2]

---

[1] The relationship between opinion and faith will be considered in some detail in Chapter 6, where we consider all human knowledge as it were from the viewpoint of eternity.

[2] This double role of *opinio* as signifying both a proposition and an assertion, together with the psychological aspect of *opinio* as either a habitus or an act of the intellect, is of some importance with regard to what Thomas has to say about falsity and error. *Error* is for Thomas a psychological term for the act of making a false assertion. *Falsum*, on the other hand, is an epistemological term which in its most proper sense expresses the lack of agreement between thought and reality. Thus, "false" may be applied to any aspect of cognition

Taken negatively, *opinio* also connotes "non-demonstrative," or, perhaps better, "not demonstrated." What we here call the positive and negative aspects of *opinio* might also be called absolute and relative. For, taken in itself, an *opinio* is an assertion; but taken with respect to demonstration, *opinio* is non-demonstrative.

From an *epistemological* point of view, the negative aspect of *opinio* as non-demonstrative is seen to involve a particular kind of *adherence* on the part of the subject. Whether this adherence may be characterized as certitude or not (Thomas is not always consistent on this point), what is important is that it is an adherence based on criteria other than strict demonstration. Accordingly, though the adherence in question is "reasonable," it is not unqualifiedly "rational." It is reasonable in the light of authority behind the opinion and in the light of arguments in its favor. But precisely because this adherence is not based on demonstration, it is not unqualifiedly rational; rather does it involve subjective factors of volition and consent to the truth of what is asserted.

As will be seen in the course of our study, these various aspects of *opinio* are of the greatest importance in understanding Thomas's theory of probability. For, the complexity of the former term is such as to make the latter equally complex.

For the moment, however, we prefer to remain within our lexicographical context by calling attention to a variety of other terms which Thomas utilizes to refer to one or another aspect of opinionative knowledge. In particular, we here have in mind the terms *aestimatio*, *existimatio*, and *sententia*. None of these terms has the same scope of meaning as does *opinio*, but each refers to one or several of the aspects of cognition covered by *opinio*. Logically speaking, all three of the terms are used to refer to a non-demonstrative assertion. Accordingly, all three convey the same epistemological note of imperfect cognition as does *opinio*. From a psychological point of view, however, the difference of these terms from *opinio* is more pronounced. In accordance with the logical aspects, all three terms are used to refer to an act flowing from a habit. But only *aestimatio* is used to refer to a habit of knowledge as such; and since this term often suggests a kind of sense-judgment, it cannot readily be equated with *opinio*, which is taken to be properly intellectual. *Sententia*, on the other hand, is used especially to signify the judgment which culminates a process of deliberation and decision; hence this term has more volitional overtones than do the others. None of these terms, finally, is used as is *opinio* to refer to the ensemble of all opinionative knowledge. *Opinio*, in other words, may be either universal or particular, abstract or concrete. The other terms, are usually particular and, with the exception of *aestimatio*, concrete.[1]

In view of these lexicographical considerations, then, we have elected to follow Thomas's lead by referring to any aspect of non-demonstrative knowledge by the English word *opinion*. By so doing, we accept the etymologically obvious, in spite of the fact that the English word as currently used does not have all the nuances of Thomas's *opinio*. Since, on the other hand, certain nuances of *aestimatio, existimatio,* or *sententia* are only occasionally of importance to our study of the notion of probability, we shall not in general hesitate to translate these terms as well by the English *opinion*.[2] Having made these clarifications as to translation, we further warn the reader in advance that we shall make no consistent effort to express stylistically which of the various cognitive aspects of *opinion* is meant when we use this term. If not discernible from the context, this may well be due to the fact that it is no more clear from Thomas's usage.

Resuming now the main thread of our discussion, we recall that the source of error is the phantasm and that the expression of error is an opinion (though neither, it must be noted, is always or even usually erroneous). Thus, by clarifying the similarities and differences between a phantasm and an opinion we shall come to a better understanding of what Thomas means by the latter. In particular, we shall thus be able to insist that opinion is properly intellectual.

In his comparatively early commentary on the *De Divinis Nominibus* (1258–1267) Thomas is called upon to say little more than that an opinion is distinct from a phantasm. Although on one occasion he

---

to which the term *opinio* is applicable. "Error," however, is restricted in application to the psychological aspect of *opinio*, especially to the intellectual act of making a false assertion. See especially *Q.D. de malo* 3, 7c, a text which we shall have occasion to discuss shortly in connection with Thomas's usage there of the term *sententia*.

[1] Another term which deserves to be mentioned here is *judicium*. In spite of its heavy legalistic overtones, this term has been rather universally accepted by interpreters of Thomas Aquinas to express the intellectual act of combining or separating concepts in the way indicated by an affirmative or negative proposition. This term, to be sure, is often used by Thomas himself, but not nearly so often as his commentators might lead one to believe. Where they would say "*judicium*" Thomas himself might well say instead "*opinio*" or some variant thereof. The discrepancy is, unfortunately, far from being merely semantic. By this impoverishment of Thomas's terminology one tends to overlook a subtle nuance of his thought which is of some importance. For, where Thomas uses the term *opinio*, as he often does, to signify in a general way the mind's adherence to a given position, he thereby leaves room for the possibility that the mental act in question might be merely tentative.

[2] For some indication of the similarities and differences between *opinio, aestimatio, existimatio, sententia,* and *judicium,* see the references given under these headings in Ludwig Schütz, *Thomas-Lexikon* (New York, 1957), and in Roy J. Deferrari and others, *A Lexicon of St. Thomas Aquinas* (Washington, D.C., 1948).

speaks of brute animals as having *opinio*, he shortly thereafter identifies *opinio* as *aestimatio,* a function of sensation.[1] This is interesting; for, in the *De Veritate* of the same period (1256–1259) he refers to *imaginatio, opinio,* and *aestimatio* as three distinct habits or powers which are subject to falsity (contrary to *sensus, scientia,* and *intellectus principiorum,* which are not).[2] Again in his commentary on "Dionysius" he places opinion between "reason having science of truth" and "the irrational parts of the soul." Both opinion and *phantasia* are referred to as deficient knowledge, the former falling short of science and the latter falling short of the certitude of sense.[3]

It is on the basis of Aristotle's *De Anima* that Thomas most clearly distinguishes *phantasia* from *opinio*. His commentary on this work (1267–1271) requires him to note the distinction between the "sensitive" and "opinionative" parts of the soul, the one being that by which we sense (*sentire*), the other that by which we have an opinion (*opinari*). Even here, however, Thomas feels called upon to point out that by opinionative is meant *intellectual: opinativo, id est intellectivo.*[4] Further on, in announcing that Aristotle will show these two to be distinct, he notes more explicitly that *phantasia* pertains to sense and *opinio* pertains to the intellect.[5] Shortly thereafter he is called upon to distinguish three ways of thinking (*intelligere*): (1) by way of science, which has to do with things speculative and necessary; (2) by way of prudence, which has to do with contingent actions; and (3) *by way of true opinion,* which seems to stand between the first and the second and to be related to both.[6] In subsequent passages of interest to us, Thomas simply follows Aristotle's arguments for the distinction between *doxa* and *phantasia,* that is, opinion and imagination. Imagination can be influenced by free will, opinion cannot. Emotion can result from opinion, not from imagination as such. Opinion involves faith (*fides*), which is the result of persuasion; but it is reason, and not sense, that is persuaded. Finally, and this is the most telling argument, since one can have a true opinion concomitant with a "false" image or phantasm, either opinion is distinct from image or the same thing

---

[1] *In De div. nom.* c. 1, l. 3, n. 77: "Neque potest (Deus) comprehendi sensu neque phantasia sive imaginatione, neque opinione, in quibus bruta communicant; neque etiam comprehendi potest per ea quae sunt propria rationalium." See n. 84.

[2] *Q.D. de ver.* 2, 12 c.

[3] *In De div. nom.* c. 7, l. 4, n. 731; c. 9, l. 2, n. 826.

[4] *In II De An.* l. 4, n. 269.

[5] *In III De An.* l. 4, n. 615.

[6] *In III De An.* l. 4, n. 630.

may be both true and false at the same time.[1] In short, Aristotle's *De Anima* provides Thomas with sufficient justification for distinguishing an opinion from a sense image and locating opinion in the intellect as such.[2]

That an opinion is properly speaking intellectual is, as we have already noted, of the utmost importance for Thomas, as it was for Aristotle. For, it is by virtue of opinion that the intellect may be said to err without jeopardizing the integrity of both principles and conclusions of science. Thomas often says that error occurs when the intellect unites what is not in reality somehow united or divides what is not in reality somehow divisible. Even more, error in the strict sense can occur *only* in the judgment – or, from the viewpoint of logic, in the proposition.[3] With all of this we need not have any quarrel. Our concern is not with the epistemological position, but with its theoretical justification, with the manner in which Thomas integrates the position into his theory of knowledge. For, it is on this level that we find him face to face with the crucial problem to which we have already alluded and which he averts, as did Aristotle, by means of the notion of opinion. For all that Thomas says about the intellect judging falsely, he never characterizes such a judgment as being in any way "science" or "scientific." If identified at all, it is always *opinio* or one of its variants that must endure such fallibility.[4] Thus, in answer to the question as to whether there can be falsity in the intellect (*intellectus*), he states his customary view that *intellectus*, in the sense of the formation of concepts, is susceptible to error only insofar as a judgment enters in. Then, with regard to judgment as such, he says that if *intellectus* be taken in a wide sense so as to include such operations (of the mind) as opinion and reasoning, then there can be falsity in the intellect so understood; but, he at once insists, this in no way implicates science: *numquam tamen si recte fiat resolutio in prima principia.*[5]

---

[1] *In III De An.* l. 4, nn. 632–636; l. 5, nn. 649–654.

[2] We are by no means here implying that Aristotle analyzes the nature of opinion, that is, of *doxa*, only in the *De Anima* or that Thomas's acquaintance with Aristotle's views on this subject is limited to the *De Anima*. We use this work and Thomas's commentary on it solely as illustrative of the fact that Thomas, like Aristotle, considers opinion to be specifically intellectual and not merely an aspect of sense knowledge. For an analysis of the place of opinion in Aristotle's psychology of knowledge, see L.-M. Regis, *L'Opinion selon Aristote* (Paris-Ottawa, 1935), Ch. 2.

[3] See *Q.D. de ver.* 1 in toto; 1, 2; 1, 3; 1, 10; *In III De An.* l. 9, n. 763.

[4] This precision of terminology is especially noticeable in discussions on truth in the Commentary on the *Metaphysics*. See, for example, *In IX Met.* l. 11.

[5] *Q.D. de ver.* 1, 12. See also *In III De An.* l. 7, n. 683; *In de Mem.* l. 2, n. 323; *In VII Polit.* l. 4, n. 1103.

Similarly, in discussing the perennial problem of knowing or saying something true about what is subject to change (a problem later exploited by Hegel), Thomas appeals again to opinion. As stated by Thomas, the problem is one of catching Socrates just at the moment when he is seated and before he spoils everything by standing up. So long as the slippery fellow holds still, a judgment or proposition to that effect is as accurate as a photograph; but the epistemic fragility of any intellectual commitment in such a case is too obvious to require further elaboration. Thus, when speaking of the mind's involvement with contingent events of this sort, Thomas carefully identifies that mental act as an opinion.[1] To say it once again, the mind can err insofar as it has opinions; for, it is a characteristic of opinion that it can be false as well as true.

Since, accordingly, opinion is conveniently ambivalent, it is in terms of opinion that Thomas expresses his realist doctrine that the existence or non-existence of a thing is the criterion of intellectual truth or falsity.[2] For, if such is the criterion, then not every opinion need be true. Moreover, since an opinion need not be true, it is, as it was for the Greeks, "knowledge of those things about which we do not have certain judgment." [3] Stating the same thing according to the more precise Aristotelian formulation, "opinion signifies an act of the intellect inclined to one alternative while retaining respect for the other." [4] It is a kind of commitment or consent to what seems to be the case whereby one recognizes that the truth of the matter might be just the opposite.[5]

Thus, as Thomas is led to point out in his commentary on the *De Divinis Nominibus*, opinion somehow stands midway between truth and error. This suggests, within the context of that work, mediation between multiplicity and unity and between evil and good.[6] It will require all the rest of our study to bring out fully what these two

---

[1] See, for example. *In III Met.* l. 7, n. 414; IX, l. 3, n. 1798; l. 11, nn. 1917–1919; *S.T* I, 16, 8 c and ad 3; 85, 2 c; I–II, 64, 3 c.

[2] *Q.D. de ver.* 1, 2 obj. 3 and ad 3.

[3] "Opinio (accipitur) autem pro cognitione eorum de quibus certum iudicium non habemus." – *In III De An.* l. 5, n. 639.

[4] "Opinio enim significat actum intellectus qui fertur in unam partem contradictionis cum formidine alterius" *S.T.* I, 79, 9 ad 4. See also II–II, 1, 4 c; 5 ad 4; 2, 1 c.

[5] *In I Post. Analyt.* l. 44, nn. 400–401. As we shall see when we begin to consider opinion with respect to probability, Thomas's view of the nature of opinion is by no means as simple as the few texts here cited might seem to indicate. We have, however, said enough for present purposes and thus for the time being prefer to leave well enough alone.

[6] See *In De div. nom.* c. 4, l. 4, nn. 327–329, 332; l. 5, n. 349; l. 7, n. 379; l. 11, n. 450; l. 22, nn. 572, 579.

parallelisms are meant to reveal. For the moment, we must concentrate a bit upon opinion in its relationship to good and evil, especially insofar as it leans more to the latter than to the former.

2. False Opinion as the Evil of the Intellect

Without going too deeply into Thomas's theory of evil, relevant though it is at this point, let us merely note that for him evil has a kind of reality only insofar as it is in something good. That is to say, evil is a defect in something otherwise good, resulting not from the natural tendencies of that thing but in spite of those tendencies, or from a failure of those tendencies to accomplish their natural end. Thus, according to the well-known Aristotelian example, a monster, qua monster, is evil as a result of defective semen.[1] Similarly, for Thomas, sin is a kind of moral monster, resulting not from reason as such but from a defective exercise of reason.[2]

In this vein of thought, not altogether unfamiliar to Plato, Thomas likes to say that, since the intellect is naturally directed to truth, error is as it were the monster of the mind.[3] Not surprisingly, this mental monster is identified as an opinion – not just any opinion, of course, but a false opinion. Harking back to Aristotle's reference to the false as the evil of the intellect, Thomas speaks of a false opinion as a kind of defective operation of the intellect. Not unlike a monster brought forth out of defective semen, a false opinion is often the result of a defect in the process of reasoning.[4]

Now, to say that error, or a false opinion, is a kind of monster produced by the intellect is little more than a metaphor. But it is an extremely interesting metaphor which needs to be considered rather carefully. For, by means of this metaphor Thomas wishes to say that a defective assertion is due in some way to an anterior defect in the mental furniture upon which that assertion is based. Some cases of error can, of course, be explained by appealing as Thomas does to defective reasoning. But this does not suffice for those cases of error in which the reasoning which generates the assertion is flawless. In such cases

---

[1] *Q.D. de malo* 1, 3 c.
[2] *Q.D. de ver.* 24, 8 c; *In De div. nom.* c. 4, l. 22, n. 589.
[3] *C.G.* III, 107. This image of error as a kind of mental monster Thomas borrows from Averroes. See *Q.D. de ver.* 18, 6 c.
[4] *Q.D. de malo* 16, 6 c. See also *In VI Met.* l. 4, nn. 1230–1240. Given this association of false opinion with evil, it is not surprising that false opinion, at least about God, is prohibited by divine law. See *C.G.* III, 118.

the roots of error are sunk more deeply into the intellectual ground from which it springs. To put this in terms of Thomas's psychology, the *act* of making a false assertion must flow from a *habit* of false presuppositions.

These psychological roots of error are laid bare rather clearly in the *De Malo,* in a passage in which Thomas is laying the groundwork for a kind of epistemology of heresy. Noting on the basis of Aristotle's *De Anima* that *nescience* implies merely the negation of knowledge, i.e. non-knowledge, and that *ignorance* implies a lack or privation of knowledge of which one is capable, he goes on from these observations to characterize *perverse ignorance* and *error* in the strict sense. Perverse ignorance (*ignorantia perversae dispositionis*) is a "habit of false principles and false opinions (*opinionum*) which impedes knowledge (*scientia*) of the truth." Perverse ignorance, then, is a *habit.* Error, however, is an *act* flowing from such a habit, and involves the explicit positing of a false proposition: *falsam sententiam.*[1]

Apart from some interesting subtleties of terminology, this passage is particularly important in that it causes us to seek the roots of false opinion taken as an assertion in a habit of false opinion. And thus we bring clearly to light the problem of the presence of falsity in an intellect naturally directed to truth.

As we have already noted, intellectual fallibility is restricted to the domain of opinionative knowledge, and this restriction is of the utmost importance to Aristotle's theory of science. It should come as no

---

[1] *Q.D. de malo* 3, 7 c. It will be noted from the Latin phrases here given in parentheses that in this passage Thomas distinguishes between *opinio* and *sententia* from a psychological point of view. In this context, *opinio* is considered as an intellectual habit, whereas *sententia*, in the sense of "assertion," is taken as the product of an act flowing from that habit. This usage is more or less in accord with Thomas's use of *sententia* for the decision which culminates a process of deliberation (to be discussed in Chapter 5). But in *Q.D. de ver.* 14, 1 c, Thomas puts both terms on the same logical level and distinguishes between them on the basis of epistemological considerations. There he relates *sententia* to *assentire* and thus is able to say that *sententia* implies firm assent to one part of a contradiction whereas such firm assent is lacking in the case of *opinio.* This usage he traces, as also at *In* I *Sent.*, Prol. div. and III, d. 23, q. 2, a. 2, 1 c, to Avicenna and Isaac Israeli. (For Avicenna, see *Metaph.* I, 9; 74r; *De Anima* V, 6; 26r. For Isaac, see *De definicionibus*, MK 307; 28, 321: 7.) As we shall see in many different contexts, however, Thomas does not hesitate to attribute firm assent to *opinio.* That Thomas accepts such a basis for distinction in the *De Veritate* is due rather to the fact that he is in the process of showing that faith (*credere*) is a unique intellectual act, and therefore he must dispose of any other intellectual acts which have been distinguished by the philosophers. He subsequently finds other ways of isolating faith and thus makes no further use of the distinction between *opinio* and *sententia.* Here as elsewhere, if we may put it somewhat facetiously, Thomas has more terms than he knows what to do with. For the dependence of *De malo* 3, 7 c upon the *De Anima* see *In* I *De An.* l. 4, n. 51; II, l. 11, nn. 363 and 370. For the application of *De malo* 3, 7c to the notion of heresy, see *Q.D. de malo* 8, 1 ad 7, a text which will be considered in Chapter 3.

surprise, then, that Aristotle very carefully maintained a sharp and clear distinction between fallible opinion and infallible science, lest the latter be tainted by the former. To this end, he (1) refused to grant opinionative knowledge as such the status of a virtue and (2) posited separate parts of the soul for opinion on the one hand and science on the other.[1] Thomas, for the most part, is inclined to accept this theoretical defense of the infallibility of science. But, as we shall see, in the course of his life he weakens the defense by modifying his interpretation of Aristotle. The modification in question would scarcely arouse the curiosity of a non-scholastic; but, within the context of Thomas's own thought, this modification has implications of far greater importance than Thomas himself realizes. For, after all, what difference does it make to say that "scientific" and "opinionative" refer to distinct powers or to say that they refer only to distinct habits? But we are getting a bit ahead of ourselves.

(a) Opinionative Knowledge Not a Virtue

To begin with, Thomas agrees that opinionative thought does not constitute a virtue. For, as he learns from Augustine as much as from Aristotle, actions which are an expression of virtue cannot but be good, by the very definition of virtue.[2] The rigorous idealization which such a view of virtue implies might well be discussed for its own sake, but this is not to our purpose. It is enough for us to note that Thomas so conceives virtue. Strictly speaking, only those virtues which make a man good as man (namely, the moral and theological virtues) can fulfill the strict meaning of the definition. In a secondary sense, however, any habitual exercise of the intellect which, as it were, produces only good fruit may also be considered a virtue, an intellectual

---

[1] Aristotle, VI *Ethics Nich.* cc. 3, 6, 7 and especially c. 2: 1139, a, 26–31. See Regis, *L'Opinion selon Aristote* (Ottawa-Paris, 1935), pp. 58–62 and 67. It is outside the scope of our study to determine precisely in what manner Aristotle conceived his division of τὸ λογὸν ἔχον (or διάνοια) into ἐπιστημονικόν and λογιστικόν. Regis perhaps finds too much order in Aristotle's thought when he divides τὸ λογιστικόν into two neatly distinct parts, one theoretical (τὸ δοξαστικόν) and the other operational (τὸ βουλευτικον). Be that as it may, he does have reason for saying that τὸ ἐπιστημονικόν and τὸ λογιστικόν are better seen as different aspects of διάνοια rather than as different powers. It is doubtful, however, if Aristotle really directed himself to the nature of the distinction, at least not in the clear manner in which the question presented itself to the Scholastics. Thomas, for example, is very much concerned as to whether the "*pars scientifica*" and the "*pars opinionativa*" or "*ratiocinativa*" are distinct powers or merely distinct habits of the soul. As we shall see, he at first maintains that they are distinct powers, but then later in his career satisfies himself that, according to the better interpretation of Aristotle, they are merely distinct habits of one and the same power. For Regis's objection against a stronger interpretation see *op. cit.*, p. 58 and fn. 2.

[2] *Q.D. de virt. in comm.* q. un., a. 2c.

virtue. Qualifying for the title of virtue in this secondary sense is the Aristotelian triumvirate, wisdom (*sapientia*), science, and understanding of first principles (*intellectus* in a special sense). Opinionative knowledge, however, does not qualify.[1]

Thomas explains with considerable precision why opinion cannot constitute a virtue. To be a virtue, it would have to produce nothing but good acts. This follows from the fact that virtue by definition is the perfection of a capacity so as to make that capacity the source of good acts. But good and evil as far as the intellect is concerned are very simply truth and falsity. Thus, an intellectual virtue must infallibly produce truth, as does science (by definition). Unfortunately, an opinion may be either true or false; so, consequently, opinionative knowledge is not a virtue.[2]

It must be added, however, that opinion fails to qualify as a virtue precisely insofar as it is intellectual, that is, insofar as it is concerned primarily with truth and falsity. More precisely, the failure of opinion to qualify is due to the fact that it is taken to be located in the speculative intellect, the object of which is the necessary, that which cannot be other than it is. There are intellectual virtues concerned with the contingent, namely, art and prudence, but they are practical rather than speculative in orientation; that is, they are directed respectively to human production and human action. Thus, the criterion of their perfection is not conformity with reality but rather conformity with what one seeks in the right way to accomplish.[3]

In all the foregoing, it will be noticed, the reasoning is quite flawless,

---

[1] *S.T.* I–II, 57, 2. See also Aristotle, VI *Ethic. Nich.* c. 3: 1139, b, 17–18; Thomas, l. 3, n. 1143; *S.T.* I–II, 64, 3 ad 3; *Q.D. de ver.* 18, 6c.

[2] *Q.D. de ver.* 14, 8c. See also *Q.D. de ver.* 14, 3c and ad 5; *S.T.* I–II, 56, 3 ad 2; 57, 2 ad 3; 55, 4c; II–II, 1, 3c.

[3] *S.T.* I–II, 57, 2 ad 3; 4 ad 2; 5, obj. 3 and ad 3; 64, 3. As we shall have occasion to see in various contexts, there are more problems suggested in this brief paragraph than we care to broach at this point. Of particular importance here is the fact that Thomas eventually comes to associate the speculative intellect with the necessary and the practical intellect with the contingent. Thus, as we shall now see, the opinionative "part" of the soul becomes hardly distinguishable from the practical intellect. Be that as it may, it is quite clear from other texts that Thomas wants to allow for opinions with regard to *speculabilia*. That he has difficulty arranging the various aspects of human knowledge in neat compartments is due at least in part to the fact that he is trying to make sense out of Aristotle's not always consistent distinctions. As a result, the task of interpreting Thomas as to just what he would like to do with opinion and where he would like to put it is no easy one and has by no means been satisfactorily completed. For a thorough introduction to the problems here mentioned and to the relevant literature, see John E. Naus, *The Nature of the Practical Intellect according to Saint Thomas Aquinas*, Rome, 1959. For a fairly recent attempt to explain these problems of distinction together with the basic texts from Thomas's writings, see Jean Pétrin, *Connaissance Spéculative et Connaissance Pratique; Fondements de leur distinction*, Ottawa, 1948.

provided only that one grant the hidden presuppositions. The most important of these presuppositions, however, is that science and the other intellectual virtues are in fact as rigorously infallible as Aristotle has defined them to be. Once this is granted, the rest is simply a matter of qualifying and distinguishing with enough subtlety to delimit the scope of any intellectual activity which might, if left to itself, impinge upon the austere and awesome perfection of the intellect at its theoretical best.

(b) The Opinionative "Part" of the Soul

This process of subsidiary second-guessing is seen in its clearest light with regard to Aristotle's distinction between the scientific and opinionative, or ratiocinative, parts of the soul. As taken up by Thomas, this distinction gradually assumes a variety of interesting nuances and eventually, as noted above, a significant modification. Involved here is the question, much discussed during the Middle Ages, as to whether the soul is the direct and immediate source of its diverse activities or whether it carries out these activities through the mediation of different powers, which in turn would be more directly concerned with the various operations. As for Thomas himself, not only is the soul endowed with powers, but these powers become perfectly operative only insofar as they are molded and formed by habits.[1] At stake, then, in the question before us is the precise manner in which science on the one hand and opinion on the other fit into the scheme of powers and habits.

In his earlier formulation of the relationship between the scientific and the opinionative, Thomas sees them as clearly distinct powers, diverse one from the other precisely insofar as the object of one is the necessary, which is known with certitude, and the object of the other is the contingent, which is known only by way of a kind of conjecture. This, for example, is the view of the *De Veritate* (1259).[2] The same position still appears in the *Quaestio Disputata de Anima*, where he simply declares that for Aristotle in **VI** *Ethics* the scientific and the ratiocinative are diverse powers, "because necessary and contingent differ in genus." [3]

---

[1] *S.T.* I, 77; 78, 1; *In* I *Sent.* d. 3, q. 4, a. 2; *Q.D. de spir. creat.* q. un., a. 11; *Quodl.* 10, q. 3, a. 1; *Q.D. de an.* q. un., a. 12. See Charles A. Hart, *The Thomistic Concept of Mental Faculty*, Washington, D.C., 1930.

[2] *Q.D. de ver.* 15, 2 ad 3. See also 2 ad 12 and ad 14.

[3] *Q.D. de an.* q. un., a. 12c. The problem of chronology is of unusual importance for under-

Once faced with the actual text of the *Ethics*, however, Thomas's thoughts about this distinction become considerably more subtle and, one might almost say, troubled. In his commentary on VI *Ethics* (1271–1272) Thomas correlates the scientific with the speculative intellect and the opinionative with the practical intellect. For, his major contention here is that contingents are known in particular only by the practical intellect but the universal aspects of contingents are known by the speculative intellect.[1] The relationship thus suggested is interesting enough, to be sure; but hardly has Thomas made it than he is forced to turn a dialectical somersault to square the interpretation with III *De Anima*, where Aristotle intimates that the speculative and the practical are not diverse parts of the soul.[2]

In any event, the subtle distinctions which Thomas is compelled to make in order to harmonize the *De Anima* and the *Ethics* appear as a rather neat synthesis in the Prima Pars of his *Summa Theologica* (1266–1268).[3] There he begins by denying that the scientific and the opinionative are distinct powers; both the necessary and the contingent, he says, are known by the same power. The one can be known perfectly because it has perfect being and truth, the other can be known only imperfectly because it has only imperfect being and truth. In other words, the fault is somewhat less in the mind and more in things; for, it is now the same intellectual power knowing things according as the things themselves are knowable. To account for the difference in cognitive results, Thomas posits different habits in the place of different powers: the same power has "diverse aptitudes for receiving diverse

standing the development of Thomas's thought on the scientific-opinionative distinction. Van Steenberghen gives 1269 as the date of this *Q.D. de anima*. But, as Eschmann points out, it is very difficult to mark off precisely the date of an actual disputation, of the literary composition, and of the edition of such a work. There is rather general agreement, however, that both the commentary on the *De Anima* and that on the *Nichomachean Ethics* belong to Thomas's second Paris sojourn (1269–1272). Prior to his own commentary on the *Ethics* (1271–1272) Thomas apparently depended upon his own transcript of lectures given on this work by Albert the Great. This might explain the stronger view as to separate powers which we find in the *De Veritate* and in the *Q.D. de anima*. It does not explain, however, the presence of Thomas's most mature statement on this question in the Prima Pars, which was probably completed by 1268. It at least seems clear from all this that a. 12 of the disputation *de anima* received its final form before 1268. At the other end, one wonders if perhaps the relevant passage in the Prima Pars (79, 9 ad 3) might not have been introduced after the commentary on the *Ethics*. For a summary of relevant problems of dating, see Eschmann in Gilson, *The Christian Philosophy of St. Thomas Aquinas* (New York, 1961), pp. 387, 389–391, 404–405.

[1] *In VI Ethic.* l. 1, esp. nn. 1119–1123. See also l. 3, n. 1152.

[2] *In VI Ethic.* l. 2, n. 1132. See Aristotle, III *De Anima* c. 10: 433, a, 12–20; 433, b, 1–5; Thomas, l. 15, nn. 820–828.

[3] *S.T.* I, 79, 9 ad 3.

habits." In fact, says Thomas, this is really what Aristotle was getting at all along.[1]

Whether in fact Thomas did at last interpret Aristotle aright on this point is beyond our interests here. What is important for us is the fact that Thomas never really figured out even to his own satisfaction just why Aristotle made the troublesome distinction in the first place. And the more he tried to explain it, the more he tended to eliminate it.[2] His effort to associate the scientific-opinionative pair with the speculative-practical in his commentary on the *Ethics* manifests, in other words, a new realization of the need for more critical evaluation of the Aristotelian distinctions. For, by trying to base the distinction between speculative and practical on a distinction between necessary and contingent, he is practically equating speculative with scientific and practical with opinionative. For this reason, perhaps, the speculative-practical pair came to assume much more importance in Thomas's thought, while the scientific-opinionative was reduced to a somewhat synonymous expression of the same thing.[3]

[1] *S.T.* I, 79, 9 ad 3: "Philosophus posuit duos particulas animae, scientificum et ratiocinativum, non quia sunt duae potentiae, sed quia distinguuntur secundum diversam aptitudinem ad recipiendum diversos habitus, quorum diversitatem ibi inquirere intendit." See Aristotle, VI *Ethics Nich.* c. 2: 1139, a, 5–15; Thomas, l. 4, n. 1174. For a complete discussion, on a textual basis, of the change in position that is here involved see Naus, *The Nature of the Practical Intellect according to Saint Thomas Aquinas* (Rome, 1959), Ch. I.

[2] A good illustration of Thomas's difficulties in this regard can be drawn from the I–II of his *Summa Theologica*, which is attributed to his second sojourn at Paris, hence simultaneous with or perhaps even prior to his commentary on the *Ethics*. In 56, 3c, Thomas explains at some length how both the "practical intellect" and the "speculative intellect" can be the *subjects* of good habits, that is, of virtues. Shortly thereafter, at 57, 4 ad 2, he is faced with the assertion of VI *Ethics* (c. 6: 1140, b, 35–1141, a, 8) that art and prudence are concerned with contingents. This leads him to say that art and prudence are alike in that they both have the "opinionative *part*" of the soul as their *subject* and contingents as their object ("*materiam*"). In this context, he does not mention either "speculative intellect" or "practical intellect." But, interestingly enough, he does speak of "speculative *habits*." In his commentary on the relevant section of VI *Ethics* (l. 5, nn. 1175–1179), he again in effect equates speculative with scientific and practical with opinionative. The problem here in evidence is that Thomas takes both distinctions to be psychological, whereas in fact the speculative-practical is essentially teleological and the scientific-opinionative is logical or, better, epistemological.

[3] It is rather unfortunate that analysts of Thomas are little interested in the distinction between scientific and opinionative. Even when concerned with the speculative-practical relationship, they make little of Thomas's tendency to correlate the former with the latter. Naus, for example, alludes to the fact and gives a number of references (*The Nature of the Practical Intellect*, pp. 18–19) and then shows how Thomas tends to make the necessary the object of the speculative and the contingent the object of the practical (Ch 4). He apparently feels, however, that whatever significance this parallelism may have is more or less outside the scope of his study. On the other hand, the whole tendency of his study and of many of the texts which he brings forth is in support of our contention that Thomas bases the distinction between speculative and practical upon differences in end or purpose as much as if not more than upon any objective difference between necessary and contingent. Thus his major conclusion, which is quite in accord with the point we are here trying to make, that

What is more, not only did Thomas diminish the importance of the scientific-opinionative distinction, but he also tended to soften the distinction between the speculative and the practical. For, in a variety of late texts he prefers to distinguish speculative and practical not so much in terms of formally diverse objects as in terms of different ends or purposes. Since it is, after all, the person who chooses to think for one or another purpose, a distinction based on finality makes it very difficult to consider "speculative" and "practical" – or, for that matter, "scientific" and "opinionative" – to be different "parts" and still less different "powers" of the soul.[1]

These brief considerations lead us to wonder if Thomas really saw all that was implied in the direction in which his thought was taking him on this question. In particular, it does not seem to have occurred to him that the distinction between the scientific and the opinionative parts of the soul might be a necessary corollary of Aristotle's rigorous conception of the nature of science. Of course, the distinction itself was for Thomas simply a given. But to the extent that he reflected upon and attempted to appreciate that given, his explicit attempts at interpretation betray an implicit criticism.[2] As a matter of fact, Thomas modifies Aristotle's rigorous conception of science in a variety of ways. But, as we shall see at length in our study, the modifications in question are due not so much to reflection upon the nature of science as to what Thomas considers to be exigencies of the Christian faith.[3]

Thomas eventually does away with any real distinction between speculative and practical intellect. The only thing that Naus lacks in this regard, as did Thomas himself, is a clear realization of how dangerous such a position is to Aristotle's theoretical protection of the infallibility of science.

[1] We say here that to base these distinctions upon finality involves difficulties, but we do not say that it would be impossible for Thomas to do so. He can very well use in this regard his distinction between *finis operis* (the intrinsic finality of a thing) and *finis operantis* (an extrinsic finality imposed upon a thing by an agent). But this latter distinction is applicable only on the assumption that speculative and practical (or scientific and opinionative) are already distinct (in terms of *finis operis*) and hence that the use of, say, the scientific with regard to matters opinionative involves an extrinsic imposition of finality (*finis operantis*). In other words, this distinction between ends or purposes is, as applied to the "parts" of the soul, no more than a corollary of the thesis that there are "parts." To use the distinction in defense of that thesis involves one in a *petitio principii*; for, it is only on the assumption that there are parts, each with its own "nature," that the notion of *finis operis* is relevant.

[2] For other discussions of the distinction between the opinionative and scientific parts (or powers) of the soul, see *In II Sent.* d. 24, q. 2, a. 2 ad 2 and ad 3; *In III Sent.* d. 17, a. 1 q. 1 a. 3 diff. 3; *In De Trin.* 6, 1 ad 4; *In I Met.* l. 1, n. 34; *In III De An.* l. 14, 15, 16, esp. n. 828; *In VI Ethic.* l. 1, 2, 4; *S.T.* I, 32, 1 ad 2; *In II De Caelo* l. 17, n. 2.

[3] The exigencies here in question involve, above all, the need to defend the superiority of divine over human knowledge, and hence of revelation over reason. The various forms which this defense takes in the writings of Thomas will be brought out by a number of considerations to which we shall direct our attention. In this chapter we shall discuss the superior knowledge of those closer to God. In Chapter 3 we shall discuss the superiority of the tra-

3. Transcendence over Opinion: The Way to Happiness

We have now seen that error, which is expressed as a false assertion, is the evil of the intellect. As a first consequence of this fact, we have seen that, since opinionative thought may be productive of (intellectual) evil, such thought cannot constitute a virtue, as does science, but must be more or less rigorously distinct therefrom.

A second consequence of the fact that falsity is an evil is that, as evil, it is to be avoided at all costs. By all the means at his disposal, man must seek to escape, to overcome, to transcend his proneness to evil, in this instance the evil of ignorance, of error, of the false opinion. It is this very aversion to the evil of the intellect which constitutes, as it were, the point of departure and the driving force of all man's efforts to acquire definitive truth. As Thomas expresses this familiar Aristotelian idea in his commentary on the *Metaphysics*, doubt and wonder arise from ignorance, and it is wonder that leads to the quest for scientific truth (*philosophia*). For, when one is in a state of wonder about anything, he is by that very fact seeking an escape from ignorance. This dialectic of privation and possession applies not only to the individual but to the human race as a whole. For, just as the wonders of the child are no longer the wonders of the man, so also the problems which first led men to wonder are gradually resolved and thus give way to deeper and greater problems.[1]

(a) Happiness as Knowledge of Truth

Since there is no *thing* that is totally, essentially evil, but only things good in themselves which are more or less evil, the very notion of "more" or "less" evil, that is, of a graduation of evils, implies not an absolute evil but an absolute good. In other words, to say that something is "less evil" means that it is "more good," or, if you will, "closer to being altogether good"; to say that something is "more evil" means that it is "less good," that is, "farther from being altogether good." Accordingly, since error is the evil of the intellect, Thomas can main-

dition of "the saints" over that of "the philosophers." We shall see how faith escapes the pitfalls of merely human knowledge, especially in connection with dialectical disputation (Chapter 4) but also in connection with doubt and opinion (Chapters 3, 4, and especially 6). Finally, in Chapter 6, we shall see how the beatific vision, so to speak, puts all terrestrial knowledge in its place.

[1] *In* I *Met.* l. 3, nn. 53–55. See *Comp. Theol.* c. 136, n. 275; *S.T.* I, 110, 4 ad 2. See also Guy Godin, *L'admiration, principe de recherche philosophique d'après Saint Thomas d'Aquin,* Paris, 1960.

tain on the basis of this theory of evil that to say "more" or "less" false implies not that there is something totally or absolutely false but rather that there is something simply true.[1] This means that not all opinions have equal status; they are not all equally true or untrue – some are more false, or more true, than others. Moreover, this very gradation of truth and falsity suggests to man the possibility of attaining to what is definitively true. Thus, to be content with just any opinion on the grounds that one is as good as another is to be intellectually sick without desire to be cured. Such despair would be justified only if there were no cure, that is, no truth to be attained; but since there are degrees of truth, therefore there is truth.[2] Alas, then, for the man who would not cure his intellect, who would not rise from his ignorance, who would not overcome his false opinions. Such a man is oblivious of his very destiny.

For, the destiny of man is nothing less than wisdom. Wisdom, that great human dream whereby, for Aristotle, one knows all things, even the difficult, with certitude and in terms of their causes.[3] Again for Aristotle and "the philosophers," this wisdom involves knowing the "separate substances." Desire for such knowledge is natural to man, and a natural desire cannot be in vain.[4] Thus, all reasoning in all the sciences is ultimately directed to such knowledge, which is the special goal of the highest of all the sciences, *scientia divina*, knowledge about God, who is "the most noble of all things knowable." [5] Since, furthermore, man is destined, at least supernaturally, for such ultimate knowledge, he can achieve happiness only to the extent that he does in fact acquire such knowledge.[6] Accordingly, in seeking ultimate knowledge man is really seeking his happiness: it is to achieve happiness that man seeks knowledge. Happiness, then, is the ultimate goal of all philosophizing, and this happiness consists in knowledge of (one or more) "separate substances." This, says Thomas, is the view both of "the philosophers" and of "the saints." [7]

---

1 *Q.D. de malo* 2, 9 ad 7.
2 *In* IV *Met.* l. 8, n. 658.
3 *In* I *Met.* l. 2, n. 43.
4 *In* I *Met.* l. 1, nn. 3–4.
5 *In De Trin.* 6, 1 ad 3; *C. G.* III, 25, where God is described as "nobillissimum scibile."
6 *In* VII *Polit.* l. 10, nn. 1184–1188; l. 11, n. 1216; VIII, l. 1, nn. 1267–1268; *In De Trin.* 6, 4 obj. 5 and ad 5.
7 *In De Trin.* 5, 1 ad 4; see also 6, 4 obj. 5 and ad 5; *S.T.* I–II, 66, 5 ad 2.

(b) Truth Perfected in God

From a slightly different point of view, man's efforts to acquire knowledge, implying as they do a desire for ultimate knowledge, are in effect aimed at God's own knowledge, which is thus the model, the standard of excellence and the goal of all that man knows or seeks to know. As Thomas puts this point in his *Compendium Theologiae*, rationality (i.e. intellectuality) involves infinity either potentially, in creatures, or actually, in God. Thus, the "intellectual end" of the creature is to become like God by actualizing in himself that knowledge always possessed by God but possessed by man only potentially.[1] Accordingly, just as circular motion is the most perfect because the terminus is joined to the starting point, so also that motion of reason is most perfect which proceeds as it were circularly from unity to multiplicity and back to unity.[2] That there exists such an ultimate unification of all knowledge, and that this ultimate unification is not merely a sort of Kantian transcendental ideal but an independent entity seems clear to Thomas precisely because of the limitations of human knowledge. In his *De spiritualibus creaturibus* (1268) he offers three arguments in support of this contention, which say, in effect: (1) our imperfect intellect is but a participation in a (substantial) perfect intellect; (2) the changeableness of our human intellect requires that there exist an intellect (*intelligere*) which is fixed and at rest, without the need for discourse to which we are subject; (3) that there is an intellect in potentiality to knowledge presupposes the existence of an intellect which is always in actuality.[3]

Whether one agree with Thomas that he is in fact talking about a supreme entity or whether one prefer to see in all this simply an hypostatisation of man's dream of perfect knowledge, Thomas's ultimate cognitional aim remains clear enough. That this ultimate aim is commendable enough in itself many will also readily allow. But, living as we do with painful memories of the tragic consequences which may flow from totalitarian thought once it is allowed room to maneuvre outside of purely academic speculation, we tend to be somewhat wary of any steps, however long ago taken, in that same direction. That such wariness is in some ways justified with regard to Thomas's thought remains for us to show. However, we may say at once in his favor that his displacement of interest away from the human and towards the

---

[1] *Comp. theol.* c. 103, n. 206.
[2] *Q.D. de ver.* 8, 15 ad 3; *In De div. nom.* c. 5, l. 1, n. 645; c. 7, l. 2 nn. 711–714.
[3] *Q.D. de spirit. creat.* q. un., a. 10c.

divine, away from this world and towards the next, manifests its weaknesses more in what does not concern him than in what does, more in what he does not say than in what he does say.

Such comments, no doubt, may strike the reader as being rather irrelevant to what is supposedly a discussion of opinion and probability. Without pausing at this point to allay such understandable misgivings, permit us merely to suggest the relevance, leaving a more detailed justification for later. To this end, let us admit at once that Thomas is a theologian and thus, not surprisingly, would be most interested in learning about God; if nothing else, this is at least etymologically obvious. Nevertheless, within the framework of his primordial interest he does have much to say about opinion and probability, as well as about various related questions with which a theory of probability must sooner or later become involved. If, therefore, even in the discussion of such questions he is primarily interested in God, then one might expect this interest to have some effect upon the manner in which and the extent to which he directs himself to those questions for their own sakes. This, we maintain, is often the case, and it is especially relevant to his treatment of probability and what has since been associated with probability. For, with the support of various texts from Aristotle, if he must be content with knowledge that lacks certitude, he would rather that that knowledge be about nobler objects, and the noblest of all is God. To put his view in the form of a maxim, among objects equally good and noble, concentrate on the more certain; among objects about which one is less certain, concentrate on the more noble.[1] The problem of the value judgments here required is, of course, considerable and deserving of discussion; but our interests lead us elsewhere.

C. IDEAL MODELS OF PERFECT KNOWLEDGE

We have noted that for Thomas man's knowledge is quite limited but the goal of that knowledge exceeds all bounds; for, this goal is nothing less than the knowledge of God himself. The ambiguity of this statement is intentional, but for now we take it to mean than man seeks to match in himself the perfect knowledge possessed by God alone. If, therefore, the divine knowledge is what Thomas seeks for man, then this view of human knowledge is best seen in contrast to God's. To establish this

---

[1] S.T. I–II, 66, 5 ad 3. See Aristotle I De Anima c. 1: 402, a, 2–4; II De Caelo c. 12:291 b, 27–29; I De Partibus Animal. c. 5; 644, b. 31–35; I Metaphysics c. 2: 982, b, 28–30.

contrast is, fortunately, a comparatively simple task; for, Thomas does it all for us, and frequently. In fact, he consistently delights in pointing out how God is better off cognitionally than we are.

Nor is it only God who surpasses us in knowledge, but all who are closer to God than we. One may be closer to God either by nature or by grace; that is, if we may put it somewhat coarsely, some creatures are created better, others are helped more by God – hence, they are either intrinsically or extrinsically superior to us in knowledge. Angelic knowledge is by nature superior to ours. However, there are also certain men who are superiorly endowed with knowledge: Adam, who got his start before original sin; the prophets; and the greatest of the prophets, Jesus.

Hence, *to put the limitations of ordinary human knowledge in context, it is well for us to consider briefly how Thomas visualizes the cognitional abilities of these superior beings.* For this purpose, we have no better guide than Thomas himself. For, when he asks in the *Summa Theologica* what the human intellect can know about material things, he breaks this down into a discussion of the singular, the infinite, the contingent, and the future.[1]

1. God's Knowledge

In general, Thomas can even go so far as to say that all human knowledge is error in contrast to divine knowledge, that every created intellect is in darkness if compared to the radiant light of the divine intellect.[2] Expanding upon this neo-Platonic image of darkness and light, he finds day and night, dawn and dusk in various intellects human or angelic according as they participate in or imitate the divine radiance.[3] On a somewhat less metaphorical plane, Thomas insists that human science does have some perfection inasmuch as what we really know we know with certitude; but there is something imperfect even in the certitude of science, for it depends for its existence upon a discourse, a kind of movement of reason, from principles to conclusions.[4] All such reasoning processes, then, pertain to the imperfection of our intellect, and are in no way characteristic of divine knowledge, which for Thomas is perfect and total vision of all truth.

[1] *S.T.* I, 86.
[2] *In de div. nom.* c. 7, l. 1, n. 701; *Q.D. de ver.* 8, 16 ad 1. See also *Q.D. de pot.* 9, 5c; *Q.D. de ver.* 2, 11.
[3] *Q.D. de pot.* 4, 2 ad 14.
[4] *Q.D. de ver.* 2, 1 ad 4. See also *S.T.* II–II, 49, 5 ad 3.

In a way, we have said all when we say that for Thomas God knows everything. The rest is just a matter of spelling out what "everything" includes: all beings, actual and possible, necessary and contingent, universal and singular, substantial and accidental, finite or infinite, present, past or future. Whatever is or can be, was or might have been, will be or could be – all is known by God in one simple intuitive glance which transcends all time and is ultimately identical with God himself. The divine knowledge is perfect, infinite, infinitely perfect, total, absolute, and utterly comprehensive. Moreover, there is no critical problem for God, since God's knowledge is creative: man has knowledge of things because things exist, but the ultimate reason why those things exist in the first place is because God knows them. Here we have all the difference between logical and ontological truth: things are the criterion or measure of truth for us, but the measure or standard of the things themselves is God's knowledge of them. In short, if anything is, or was, or will be, might have been, can be, or could be, this is in every instance due to the fact that it is so known by God as actually or possibly existing.[1]

That the attribution of such absolutely comprehensive knowledge to God raises serious and difficult problems – the problems of free will and of evil, to mention just two examples – is by no means unrecognized by Thomas. But he would far rather face such problems head-on than detract in any way from the absolute totality of divine knowledge. How he does in fact deal with such problems is, for the most part, outside the scope of our study, impressive though his solutions often are.[2] It is enough for us merely to have remarked that such is, for Thomas, God's knowledge.

2. Angelic Knowledge

As we have already noted, the knowledge possessed by any creature, however exalted, is but meager in comparison to that of God; but some creatures do fare better than every-day run-of-the-mill mortals. Of first importance among superior beings are the angels, the existence of

---

[1] The absolute perfection of God's knowledge is a constantly recurring subject in the writings of Thomas, precisely inasmuch as he likes to compare less perfect types of knowledge to the divine. He directs himself specifically to the question, however, in S.T. I, 15; C.G. 44–71; Q.D. de ver. 2; Comp. theol. cc. 28–31. For a summary of Thomas's position on God's knowledge, see Etienne Gilson, The Christian Philosophy of St. Thomas Aquinas (New York, 1956), pp. 110–114.
[2] See in this regard Fernand Van [Steenberghen, Ontologie, 3e éd. (Louvain, 1961) pp. 204–231; Gerard Smith, Natural Theology (New York, 1951), Ch. XIII and Appendix.

whom is obvious to Thomas both from the authority of Scripture and from the authority of philosophers who posited some such beings to explain planetary motion.[1] The position of angels in Thomas's intellectual hierarchy is perhaps seen most quickly by recalling the Aristotelian triumvirate of intellectual virtues, namely, wisdom, understanding of principles, and science. If we now map these three intellectual virtues onto the three levels of intellectual beings – the divine, the angelic, and the human – we thus construct for ourselves a fairly accurate picture of Thomas's intellectual universe. Proper to God in the fullest sense of the word is wisdom; proper to angels in a rather full sense of the word is understanding of principles; proper to man, but by no means in the full sense of the word, is science. Wisdom, it will be recalled, is certain and causal knowledge of all things however difficult they may be to know; and this, to be sure, is God's prerogative. A knowledge of reasoned conclusions, on the other hand, can only be human, for only man is afflicted with the task of learning one thing on the basis of another. The reasoning which leads to science would be unnecessary if man could see intuitively all that is included in the principles: science would be telescoped into the understanding of principles and the reasoning process would fall away like the last stage of a rocket whose payload is now in orbit.[2]

This, in summary fashion, is how Thomas understands angelic knowledge. Starting off their existence with a full supply of principles together with all the knowledge implied therein, angels ever contemplate what man methodically seeks with his plodding reasoning processes.[3] Unlike men, angels do not have to overcome dispositions which hinder clear thinking, nor do they have errors to dispel. If they do learn anything new (and they can, since they are not God) the new knowledge just pops in, like a *deus ex machina*, from God himself or from some other angel.[4] Thus blessed with a goodly abundance of all that they need to know, angels are not burdened with the well-known human problem of planning, deliberating, and arriving at a decision as to what is to be done and what to do.[5]

[1] See Thomas Litt, *Les corps célestes dans l'univers de saint Thomas d'Aquin* (Louvain-Paris, 1963), Ch. 5. For a thorough treatment of Thomas's theories about angels, including the question of angelic knowledge, see James D. Collins, *The Thomistic Philosophy of the Angels* (Washington, D.C., 1946).

[2] Since Thomas also likes to compare angelic and human knowledge, he is led to discuss angels' knowledge on numerous occasions. For a more orderly treatment of the subject, however, see *S.T.* I, 54–58; *Q.D. de ver.* 8–9.

[3] See, for example, *Q.D. de ver.* 8, 15c; *S.T.* I, 55, 2; 58, 3.

[4] *Q.D. de ver.* 9, 3c. See also 9, aa. 1, 2 and 5.

[5] *Q.D. de malo* 16, 4c.

Having thus indicated the superiority of angelic over human knowledge, we need only add a few words about its inferiority to the divine. The basic difference is at least roughly the difference between perfect wisdom and a good solid understanding of principles and what they imply. A further difference consists in the fact that though angels transcend time as we know it, they do not have God's simultaneous intuition of all things at once and as one.[1] Moreover, angels are finite and not infinite, and their knowledge is essentially by means of species, or ideas, and hence universal.[2] From these various limitations it follows that, unlike God, angels do not know the infinite except in a finite way, they do not know the singular except insofar as it participates in a species known, and they do not know the future except insofar as it is somehow revealed in things existing at present.[3] Because of the intrinsic superiority of their knowledge over ours, however, angels both good and bad are much better than we at knowing singulars and conjecturing the future.[4]

Combining now the virtues and the limitations of angelic knowledge, we are driven to the conclusion that angels must have opinionative knowledge. And, as a matter of fact, Thomas tells us as much himself, in an important passage in which he builds his discussion around the term *opinio*.[5] Note at once, however, that the "psychological" fact of having opinionative knowledge does not have the same epistemological import for bad angels, or devils, as it does for the good angels. Within the limits of its natural intellectual capacities, Thomas tells us, no angel ever assents to a false opinion. But in the case of knowledge which surpasses the natural capacity of angels, there is a sharp difference based on moral considerations. Good angels, because good, remain immune from false opinion even with regard to the supernatural; but it is precisely in this area that the bad angels, because bad, can and do contract that worst of all diseases. This significant difference Thomas explains with

---

[1] See *S.T.* I, 58, 2; *Q.D. de ver.* 8, 14.

[2] *S.T.* I, 55; 2; 57, 1; *Q.D. de ver.* 8, 8 and 9.

[3] *S.T.* I, 57; *Q.D. de an.*, q. un., a. 20 ad 4; *Q.D. de pot.* 4, 2 ad 17; *Q.D. de ver.* 8, 11 and 12. It must be noted in this connection that, as far as we know, Thomas does not explicitly raise the question as to whether angels know the infinite. This is rather curious, since he discusses knowledge of the infinite both with regard to God and with regard to man (see *S.T.* I, 14, 12; 86, 2; *C.G.* I, 69). In saying, then, that angels know the infinite in a finite way we are in fact reading something into what Thomas says about the way in which angels know many things simultaneously (see *S.T.* I, 58, 2; *C.G.* II, 101). In any event, the point is not essential to us, since all we really wish to show here is that angels have knowledge which is inferior to that of God but superior to that of men.

[4] *Q.D. de ver.* 8, 12c; *S.T.* I, 57, 3c; *Q.D. de malo* 16, 7c.

[5] *Q.D. de malo* 16, 6c.

the help of "Dionysius." The intellectual humility of the good angels, says Thomas, is so perfect that they never "go out on a limb" about things which are beyond them. The devils, however, are tripped up both speculatively and practically because of false pride with regard to their intellectual capabilities. The moral, of course, can hardly be lost on the man who would strive towards angelic perfection.

The extent to which this somewhat grandiose picture of angelic cognition can be attributed to a theological need to explain how God could condemn the angels who "fell" in one swift instant is not for us to evaluate. Still less would we wish to deprive theologians and exegetes of the ticklish question as to the very existence of angels. These woes of sophistication never crossed the medieval mind; and it is with the latter that we are concerned.

3. Adam's Knowledge

Turning now from angels on high to man in the state of innocence, let us now gaze with envy at Thomas's picture of what might have been if Adam had only looked ahead. From this consideration, as a matter of fact, we will not only gain further insight into Thomas's idealization of our intellectual ambitions but will also have occasion to notice an interesting change both of position and of terminology with regard to opinion. Our remarks deal with Adam's knowledge first as presented in an early work, the *De Veritate* (1256–1268), then in a work written some ten years later, the Prima Pars of the *Summa Theologica* (1266–1268).[1]

Asking in the *De Veritate* whether Adam could err or be deceived, Thomas declares that the difference of opinion on this question is more verbal than real; for, however one cares to state it, Adam in the state of innocence neither erred nor succumbed to any kind of false opinion (*qualiscumque falsa opinio*). In fact, not only was he free of false opinion, but he hardly had any opinions at all (*penitus nulla opinio*); whatever he knew, he knew with certitude.[2] The underlying reason for which Thomas takes this remarkable position is basically the same problem which brings forth his glowing report on angelic cognition: how explain the disconcerting fact that Adam as well as his descendants are reduced to the human condition as we know it as a result of just one sin. To suppose that God should exact such a punishment upon one whose

---

[1] *Q.D. de ver.* 18; *S.T.* I, 94. See also *In* II *Sent.* d. 23, q. 2, a. 3.
[2] *Q.D. de ver.* 18, 6c.

moral decisions are based upon knowledge no more enlightened than ours would be unthinkable. Thus the theoretical need to endow Adam with such astounding intellectual gifts that his rebellion could as a consequence only be due to sheer malice and not, as is often the case with us, due to the frailty of passion or ignorance.[1] In any event, it is fortunate for us that Thomas sees himself faced with such a problem, since it leads him to portray the human mind at its cognitional best.

Still with reference to the *De Veritate*, then, Thomas takes Augustine's dictum that every false opinion (*aestimatio*) is error as sufficient reason to absolve Adam of that.[2] So doing, he undercuts the efforts of some to allow Adam to "opine lightly" (*leviter opinando*) about something false without precisely giving his assent, the absence of assent thus exonerating him from formal error.[3] Not good enough that; for, as Augustine says, the false proposition as such (*aestimatio*) is error, and error is an evil not consonant with the state of innocence. To show this, Thomas gives three arguments, the first two of which support his weaker position (exclusion of *false* opinion) and the third of which leads him to his stronger position (exclusion of *all* opinion). These arguments assume, respectively, that in the state of innocence there is: (1) absence of corruption or evil; (2) absence of "*monstruositas*"; (3) absence of any disorientation (*inordinatio*). As for the first two arguments, the minors are (1) that the false is the evil of the intellect (after Aristotle) and (2) that a false opinion is a kind of monster (after Avicenna). In the third argument, Thomas jumps from truth taken simply to infallible truth: *verum id quod habet infallibilem veritatem*. The latter being properly speaking the goal of the intellect, any commitment of the intellect, whether perfect or imperfect, on the basis of "some fallible sign" thus amounts to a disorientation of the intellect. Since commitment on the basis of the fallible is precisely characteristic of opinion as such, all opinion must be excluded from Adam's intellectual paradise.

Dealing with other aspects of Adam's knowledge in the same work, Thomas does not allow Adam to see God in his essence but does grant him a preternatural participation in God's wisdom. He grants him

---

[1] See *Q.D. de malo* 7, 7.

[2] Strictly speaking, as noted above, Thomas declares that the difference of opinion on this question is more verbal than real; but *de facto* his own position is more in support of those who would deny opinion to Adam than of those who would not. Thus he is in fact accepting the assertion of Augustine (*Enchiridion* 17: PG 40: 240) in agreement with Hugh of St. Victor (*De sacramentis* I, 6, 13; PL 176: 270), Peter Lombard (*Sententiae* II, 23, 3; QR I: 417–418) and Albert the Great (*In II Sent.* d. 23, a. I: BO 27: 391).

[3] Here he is perhaps referring to the view of Alexander of Hales (*Summa Theol.* I–II, n. 520: QR II: 773–774) and Bonaventure (*In II Sent.* d. 23, a. 2, q. 2; QR II: 540).

quasi-angelic knowledge of all that is implied in the principles of human knowledge but does not grant him either natural or supernatural knowledge of angels as such.[1] Pacifying those who would not even let Adam sleep for fear that he would err by granting reality to his dreams, Thomas says it is all right for Adam to sleep because dreams pertain to sensation and not to the intellect as such.[2] As for whatever children Adam might have had in the state of innocence, Thomas grants them equivalent cognitive excellence; but, preferring Aristotle to Plato, he considers their knowledge acquired rather than innate, on the presupposition that the feebleness of an infant is natural rather than an effect of original sin.[3]

Thomas's later treatment of Adam's knowledge in his *Summa Theologica* is in its general lines little different from that of the *De Veritate*. There are, however, numerous subtle changes which are most relevant to our subject. Though interesting enough in themselves, we disregard the greater clarity and economy of language, the more knowledgeable dependance upon Pseudo-Dionysius, the more relaxed *savoir-faire* of the professional in dealing with the views of others. What concerns us directly is rather the following: (1) two specific references to the firmness or certitude of knowledge; (2) a change of terminology from *opinio* to *existimatio*; (3) explicit reference only to his weaker position with regard to Adam's knowledge, namely, the exclusion of *false* opinions.

Repeating his views from the *De Veritate* that Adam saw neither God nor angels in their essences, Thomas nevertheless insists that with regard to each Adam's knowledge was much superior to ours. His knowledge of God, intermediate between ours and that of the blessed in heaven, enjoyed a "radiation of the First Truth" unimpeded by external things, thus making possible "a clear and firm contemplation of intelligible effects."[4] Somewhat similarly, because of a greater ability to pass through Pseudo-Dionysius's stages from external things to the soul to angels and thence to God, Adam had "a more certain and fixed knowledge of interior intelligibilia" than do we.[5] Also in accord with the earlier presentation, Adam had all the knowledge which man could naturally acquire from the principles of knowledge, and knew as well whatever supernatural truths he needed to order his life well. But

[1] *Q.D. de ver.* 18, arts. 1, 2, 4 and 5.
[2] *Q.D. de ver.* 18, 6 ad 14.
[3] *Q.D. de ver.* 18, 7 and 8.
[4] *S.T.* I, 94, 1.
[5] *S.T.* I, 94, 2.

he did not know "men's thoughts, future contingents, or some singulars, such as how many pebbles are lying in a river, and the like." [1]

Secondly, the possibility of Adam's having been deceived is no longer concerned with *opinio* nor even with *aestimatio*, but solely with *existimatio*.[2] Thus, the view that Adam could "lightly opine" a *"falsa aestimatio"* is now said to refer to *"qualiscumque existimatio levis . . . sine assensu credulitatis."* In keeping with this revised terminology, Thomas even switches from Augustine's reference to *"falsam aestimationem"* to a neutral statement from the same authority as to the absence of evil in the state of innocence.[3] Taking this together with Aristotle's bare statement that the false is the evil of the intellect, Thomas concludes, without the slightest reference to *"opinio,"* that before the fall the intellect of man did not accept (*acquiesceret*) the false as true.[4] It will also be noted in the brief phrases quoted above that Thomas now speaks not simply of *"assensus"* but of *"assensus credulitatis."* In keeping with this modification, where he would otherwise speak of opinion about something, he now refers to *believing*. For example, with regard to false propositions about future contingents or about men's thoughts, Adam would not estimate falsely (*existimare falsum*) but would merely believe such a proposition to be possible: *credidisset quod hoc esset possibile.*

So thoroughgoing, in short, is the change of terminology from the *De Veritate* to the *Summa Theologica* that one must presume there are important theoretical considerations at stake. What these considerations might be, however, is difficult to say; for, Thomas often utilizes the term *opinio* both in the *Summa* and in other late works.[5] We suggest, therefore, that his extreme caution in this instance has to do with the problem of Adam as such rather than with the term *opinio* itself.

In the third place, then, that Thomas makes no explicit reference here to his stronger position, that Adam had no opinions at all, is quite

---

[1] *S.T.* I, 94, 3. Adam's knowledge of supernatural truths included faith with regard to the divine mysteries, including both the Trinity and the Incarnation. See *S.T.* II–II, 2, aa. 7 and 8; 5, 1; *Q.D. de ver.* 18, 3.

[2] *S.T. I*, 94, 4.

[3] The sources in Augustine are, respectively, *Enchiridion* c. 17; PL 40; 240 and XIV *de Civitate Dei* c. 10; ML 41: 417.

[4] Aristotle's dictum is taken from VI *Ethics Nich.* c. 2: 1139, a, 27–31: Thomas l. 2, nn. 1130–1132.

[5] See, for example, *S.T.* I, 79, 9 ad 4; I–II 55, 4c; 57, 2 ad 3; II–II, 1, 5 ad 4; 4, lc; 24, 10c; 29, 3 ad 2; 129, 6c; III, 9, 3 ad 2; *Q.D. de an.* q. un. a. 12, a. 6c; *In De Causis* passim and esp. VI, l. 6, n. 173; *Q.D. de malo* 1, 1 ad 11; 12, 1 ad 13; 16, 6c; *Q.D. de virt. in comm.* q. un., a. 2c.

clear. In view of what we have just said above, however, it is not at all clear what significance is to be given to this modification. Merely by changing his terminology, of course, Thomas does avoid attributing *opinio* to Adam. But in effect, and in spite of the revised terminology, Thomas is surely admitting that there was in Adam something quite equivalent to opinionative knowledge. What he will not admit is that such knowledge, whatever it be called, was in any way false. Thus, for example, Thomas allows that Adam did not know the number of pebbles in a river, but he says nothing as to whether he made a guess or not, and whether or not that guess had to be accurate.

Whatever historians of theology wish to make of all this, we have said quite enough for our more limited purposes. After all, we are not concerned with the fine points of Thomas's theory of pristine human knowledge. What does concern us is the light this sheds on what Thomas would consider the ideal state of human knowledge; and for this purpose, at least, the foregoing should admirably suffice.

4. Superior Human Knowledge

Though it hardly seems necessary in a world that has seen Hiroshima and Nagasaki, Dachau and Bergen-Belsen, we mention for the sake of completeness that man is not in a state of original innocence. For reasons of his own, to be sure, Thomas was also aware of this fact; and, as we are now in the process of showing, he found one expression of the fact in the limitations of human knowledge. There is, accordingly, something deeply moving in Thomas's efforts to depict what it must have been like *before*. For, what he says with regard to Adam is, after all, an expectation of what it will be like *after*. Between the before and the after, however, is the long interval of *now*, of man's halting struggles for grandeur, for truth, for understanding. Thus the importance – from our limited epistemological point of view, be it noted – of those mortals divinely endowed who, sharing our failings, yet have surpassed us by far in the excellence of what they knew. Chief among these, in the eyes of Thomas, are the prophets, the greatest of the prophets, Christ, and those whom Christ teaches from within for the sake of special missions.

(a) Prophetic Knowledge

Since we shall have more to say about prophecy later on when we take up the question of knowing, or predicting, the future, we here limit ourselves to a few brief remarks.[1] First of all, it seems safe to say that Thomas is extremely interested in prophecy. He is a theologian, of course, and the prophets of the Old Testament as of the New are an important part of his heritage. But this fact alone is not enough to explain, for example, that one of his very first works is a commentary on Isaiah (1256–1259).[2] Moreover, if we disregard the more properly psychological considerations of the mind in the *Summa Theologica*, we find that, while 35 articles are devoted to human knowledge as such, almost as many (28) deal with prophecy and mystical visions. These latter subjects occupy 44 pages in the Marietti edition of the *De Veritate*, as compared, for example, to 26 pages dealing with faith.

How account for this interest in prophecy? To be sure, the subject is closely related to what is now more frequently discussed under the heading of revelation, a properly theological concern. But another reason, we think, and one which is even closer to the interests of the medievals and of Thomas in particular, is that the prophet has special intellectual contact with the divine knowledge itself. God imprints his knowledge upon the mind of the prophet, thereby enabling him to know things of which ordinary mortals are incapable – a brief reminder of paradise and a pledge of beatitude to come.

From this epistemological point of view, Thomas says that prophecy can be knowledge of anything, but it is especially concerned with things which are remote (*procul*) from the knowledge of man. This may mean (1) remote from the knowledge of the prophet himself, though not from all men (as when a prophet sees a distant land); (2) exceeding the knowledge of all men universally because of the deficiency of human knowledge (as the mystery of the Trinity); or (3) remote from our knowledge because unknowable, and unknowable because still undetermined, namely future contingents. It is with the latter, says Thomas,

---

[1] The notion of prophecy will be implicit in just about everything we have to say, in Chapter 5, with regard to man's knowledge of the future contingent event. For, while it would today be more appropriate to discuss knowledge of the future in connection with scientific prediction, for Thomas the very idea of scientific prediction needs to be discussed primarily in order to clarify what is meant by prophecy, or prediction, in the strict sense.

[2] In positing an early date for the *Expositio in Isaiam prophetam*, we are here following the opinion of De Guibert and Mandonnet as opposed to that of Roy and Glorieux, who propose instead 1269–1272. Be that as it may, there is an even stronger argument for the point we are here trying to make. Apart from a lost exposition of the Canticle of Canticles and some eleventh-hour lectures on the first 54 Psalms (1272–1273), Thomas's only writings on books of the Old Testament are expositions of the prophets, namely, Isaiah, Jeremiah, and Job (the latter having been considered a prophet during the Middle Ages). For a summary of arguments for different dating of the exposition of Isaiah, see Eschmann in Gilson, *The Christian Philosophy of St. Thomas Aquinas* (New York, 1961), pp. 395–396.

that prophecy is most properly concerned.[1] Leaving, then, the proper concern of prophecy for later, we turn to the greatest of all the prophets, Jesus of Nazareth.

(b) *Christ's Knowledge*

In view of the profound religious significance of Jesus, it is well to clarify in advance the viewpoint and intention of the following observations. We are concerned with the notion of opinion in the thought of Thomas Aquinas, more specifically with opinion as the immediate bearer of intellectual error. This has led us to a consideration of various ideal intellects, angelic and human, in Thomas's thought. That he, as a Christian, should find in Christ such an ideal is readily understandable. It by no means follows, however, that the man Jesus was in fact intellectually endowed as Thomas imagines him to have been. As a matter of fact, Thomas's idealization of the Man of Sorrows tends to make of the latter a rather unapproachable God-machine. Faithfully grinding out the conclusions of his rigid Christological presuppositions, Thomas produces the apocryphal gospel of the intellectual – not a baby Jesus who turns clay into pigeons, but a fully turned out Aristotelian wise man superendowed with layers of supernatural cognition to fill in the gaps. But we are here in no way concerned with the historical Christ or the Christ of Christianity, or whatever. We are specifically and solely concerned with Thomas's theoretical picture of Christ's intellect insofar as this picture sheds light on what he, Thomas, would consider ideal human knowledge.

Fortunately, then, for our purposes, Thomas's fundamental presupposition with regard to Christ as man is not merely that Christ was really or fully human but that Christ was *perfectly* human, that is, *human to perfection*. This presupposition, whether stated explicitly or not, serves him repeatedly as a kind of automatic minor premiss. His reasoning runs somewhat as follows: man perfected to his fullest capacity has *x*; Christ is man perfected to his fullest capacity; therefore Christ has *x*. Disregarding the possible validity of such reasoning with regard to Christ's love, we find that as Thomas applies it to Christ's knowledge it is pure rationalism, with little relationship and little reference to Scripture except for dialectical illustrations. Thus, for example, the following from the *De Veritate*. After noting that our intellect knows all things potentially and is perfected by knowing, Thomas concludes:

[1] *S.T.* II–II, 171, 3c.

And therefore some philosophers visualize the natural perfection of man by saying that man's ultimate happiness consists in the fact that in man's soul is described the order of the whole universe. Christ *therefore* had this perfection, so that by means of science divinely infused in him he might know the precise nature of things (*res in propria natura*), much more perfectly (*multo fortius*) than man in the state of innocence or angels using only knowledge natural to them.[1]

In spite of later reevaluations as to *how* Christ knew, about which we shall soon speak, the passage here quoted contains in germ the rationale for Thomas's idealization of *what* he knew. For, Christ surpassed not only the prophets, not only Adam and the angels, but *a fortiori* all the philosophers and all their intellectual aspirations.

Thomas consistently held to the totality of Christ's knowledge, changing his mind only as to the manner or mode in which such cognitive perfection was available to him. At the time when he wrote the above passage, he was still sufficiently Platonist to allow such knowledge to be merely infused. In time, however, his ideas as to what is properly *human* about human perfection became more definitively Aristotelian. Since, therefore, it is of the very essence of Christian doctrine that Christ was fully human, and the human is more accurately described by Aristotle than by the Platonists, Thomas's Christ simply became more Aristotelian.

In effect, this meant that Thomas came to ascribe experiential knowledge, that is, knowledge acquired by sense experience, to Christ. For, as he came to realize, his earlier view would have Christ more or less "checking" to verify that things are in fact as he has known them all along.[2] But in reality this slight modification does little to palliate his cognitional caricature of Christ; rather is it simply the addition of something which, in the light of Aristotle, the Lord had to have to be intellectually perfect. Thus, to save something of the intrinsic superiority of Christ even with regard to experiential knowledge, Thomas insists that he was not taught, as we are, but learned all by himself.[3] More telling is the fact that, even while adding experiential knowledge to Christ, Thomas holds on to the intuitive as well, attributing this to him

---

[1] *Q.D. de ver.* 20, 3c: "Et ideo quidam philosophi attendentes naturalem perfectionem hominis, dixerunt ultimam felicitatem hominis in hoc consistere quod in anima hominis describatur ordo totius universi. Habuit ergo Christus hanc perfectionem, ut per scientiam sibi divinitus infusam res in propria natura cognosceret, multo fortius quam homo in statu innocentiae, vel angeli secundum cognitionem naturalem."

[2] See *In* III *Sent.* d. 14, a. 3, q. 1 a 5 ad 3; d. 18, a. 3 ad 5; *S.T.* III, 9, 4c; 12, 2c; 10, 2 ad 2.

[3] *S.T.* III, 9, 4 ad 1; 12 in toto.

from the first moment of his prenatal existence.[1] Moreover, to the experiential and the infused he also adds prophetic knowledge, which is higher than either because directly from God; and we have not even mentioned the rather substantial fund of truth available to Christ from the fact that he was also divine.[2]

To spell out, then, what we have here been implying, the question for Thomas was never *whether* Christ as man knew everything of which man is theoretically capable; his only question was *how*. Thus, for example, he must say that Christ knew the infinite, even if only in a finite way, namely, by means of conceptualization.[3] Learning by himself, Christ *acquired* knowledge of all things on the basis of those which he personally experienced. In this way, however, Thomas admits, Christ did not know absolutely everything – just everything of which the unaided light of reason is capable.[4] This limitation would keep Christ from knowing past and future singulars; but, no matter, Christ had "the fullness of prudence, by way of the gift of counsel [supernatural, infused knowledge], in virtue of which he knew all singulars, past, present, and future." [5]

Lest there be any misunderstanding, this reference to counsel should not be taken to imply that Christ had to take counsel, or deliberate, before deciding what to do. Christ was spared this imperfection of ordinary mortals, because from the first instant of his conception he was, in the words of John, "full of grace and truth." This means for Thomas that from the very beginning Christ had not only the plenitude of justifying grace but also of truth known. Having, as it were, certitude about all things, he could choose immediately, instantaneously.[6]

By virtue of this same all-inclusive certitude, Christ was incapable of fear, since fear implies uncertainty as to whether an anticipated evil can or cannot be avoided.[7] He did have a kind of anguish, however, inasmuch as his senses did not always go along with what he knew by reason was to be done. But this is in no way the anguish of imperfect

---

[1] *S.T.* III, 11; 9, 3; 34, 2 ad 2. It is illustrative of Thomas's bent of mind that even in attributing instantaneous humanity to the embryo that was Jesus, he makes a singular exception; for in his view the embryo ordinarily evolves through the stages of plant and animal before becoming human. See *S.T.* I, 76, 3 ad 3; 118, 2 ad 2; III, 33, 2 ad 3.

[2] *Comp. theol.* c. 216; *S.T.* III, 7, 8; 9, 1 and 2; 10 in toto.

[3] *S.T.* III, 10, 3.

[4] *S.T.* III, 12 and esp. 12, 1 ad 1 and ad 3.

[5] *S.T.* III, 11, 1 ad 3: "Quia igitur Christus habuit plenitudinem prudentiae, secundum donum consilii, consequens est quod cognovit omnia singularia, praeterita, praesentia et futura."

[6] *S.T.* III, 34, 2 ad 2.

[7] *S.T.* III, 15, 7c.

mortals, who see good reasons for alternative choices, and thus suffer from their inability to decide which is simply better.[1]

In short, though we are not aware of Thomas's saying so in so many words, Jesus never had anything so characteristic of limited intelligence as an opinion. Whatever the cognitive source or sources of his knowledge about any given thing, what he knew – and he knew all – he knew with a certitude so pervading that he was never called upon to reflect, to deliberate, to ponder possibilities, to suffer the excruciating pain of even momentary indecisiveness. What better intellectual excellence could any man desire for his days on this inscrutable planet? If there be better, well, then, it just never came to Thomas's attention.

(c) Charismatic Knowledge

Before closing our survey of superior intellectual gifts as portrayed by Thomas, we should for the sake of completeness add a word about those Christians who by special privilege share some of the intellectual superiority of Christ so that they might teach others. The various supernatural "gifts" which they receive (gratiae gratis datae) are aimed at persuading others of the truth of divine revelation. Thus, as Thomas explains, they must have the knowledge themselves, they must be able to "confirm" or "prove" what they say (otherwise their teaching would be inefficacious), and they must be able to present their teaching in a manner appropriate to their listeners. On the basis of these three requirements, obviously borrowed from rhetoric, Thomas finds a place for each of the variety of gifts spoken of in Christian tradition.[2]

D. THE DIALECTICAL ROAD TO TRUTH

As should be clear from the discussion just concluded, *it is in looking to the ideal that Thomas tells us, in reverse, of man's cognitional imperfections as they appear to him.* The natural man both in himself and even more in contrast to superior intellects is woefully afflicted with opinionative knowledge, which often enough is erroneous. Man's very method of learning, by a process of reasoning, is itself a mark of his inferior and imperfect status in the intellectual hierarchy. Nonetheless, this very process of reasoning is man's one and only natural means of glimping what is seen by his intellectual betters. Thus, for man, the

---

[1] S.T. III, 18, 6 ad 3.
[2] S.T. I–II, 111, 4c; C.G. III, 154.

crucial importance of reasoning and reasoning well: enter, then, those basic liberal arts of rhetoric and, especially for Thomas, dialectic.

As already suggested by Thomas's application of the rhetorician's prerequisites to supernatural gifts, he seldom if ever refers to rhetoric for its own sake but only in connection with the serious business of faith or morals.[1] Thus he compares the way in which the rhetorician and the prudent man make conjectures (the latter, unlike the former, seeks truth); he discusses how devils can persuade us to evil; and he outlines various degrees of suspicion about others on the basis of light conjectures.[2] Otherwise, he is silent on this subject, except when commenting on Aristotle. Writing on the latter's *Politics*, for example, he has to say a few words about the role of rhetoric in governing.[3] Similarly, the *Posterior Analytics* gives him occasion to mention that non-demonstrative processes of reasoning are studied expressly in the *Topics* and by extension in the *Rhetoric* (suspicion of truth) and the *Poetics* (representation of truth).[4] On none of the latter three works, however, did Thomas write a commentary; his concern is with higher things.

What these higher things are for Thomas should by now be fairly clear. Yet it should be noted that it is the lot of man to proceed towards ultimate intellectual blessedness by way of natural means, as much as this is possible. And to this extent at least Thomas is willing to follow the route of the philosophers, which one enters by way of the seven liberal arts, of which the most important is logic.[5] This rational methodology which is logic is therefore a valuable discipline in its own right (*logica docens*) and an indispensable instrument of procedure in sciences which deal not with reasoning but with reality (*logica utens*).[6] But inasmuch as logic is an instrument, and thus at man's disposition, it may like any instrument be either abused for personal motives or used responsibly for the attainment of truth. The perversion of logic, as seen through Aristotle's eyes, is sophistry: the sophist, whose reason-

---

[1] See especially *Contra Impugn.* III, sect. 1, c. 5 (12), nn. 408–418.

[2] *S.T.* II–II, 49, 4 ad 3; 60, 2c and 3c.

[3] *In IV Polit.* l. 4, n. 580; V, l. 4, nn. 772 and 774; l. 7, n. 810.

[4] *In Post. Analyt.* Proemium, n. 6.

[5] *In De Trin.* 5, 1 ad 3; 6, 1 ad 3. With regard to the medieval notion of seven liberal arts, Paul Abelson's *The Seven Liberal Arts: A Study in Medieval Culture* (New York, 1906) is still valuable. For an excellent summary of theoretical and practical efforts to relate the Aristotelian sciences to this arts curriculum, see Fernand Van Steenberghen, *The Philosophical Movement in the Thirteenth Century* (London-New York, 1955), Ch. 2. For the preparatory role of early medieval rhetoric and dialectic in the development of speculative theology, see M.-D. Chenu, *La Théologie comme Science au XIIIe Siècle*, 3e éd. revue et augmentée (Paris, 1957), especially Chapters 1 and 2.

[6] *In De Trin.* 5, 1 ad 2; 6, 1c; *In IV Met.* l. 4, nn. 576–577.

ing has only the appearance of rationality, seeks to confuse rather than to confirm, to confound rather than to convince. The high purpose of truth demands that one transcend the motivations of the sophist to seek at least the probable and, where possible, demonstrative truth. Thus, as Aristotle explains in his *Metaphysics*, it is in the purpose of his quest that the philosopher is set apart in dignity from the sophist and even from the dialectician. Dealing with all things, as does the sophist, his dealings differ in that they are directed to truth. Arguing with the tools of logic, as does the dialectician, he thus acquires opinion on the basis of the probable; but he transcends the dialectician in that for him the dialectical is but a tentative means of closing in on definitive truth.[1]

Presupposing, then, this rectitude of philosophical intention, Thomas is able to correct the prejudice of Aristotle by attributing scientific status both to rhetoric (*sophistica*) and to dialectic.[2] For, considered in themselves they are branches of demonstrative logic (*logica docens*), dealing respectively with methods of arguing on the basis of the apparent and on the basis of the probable. It is only as applied (*logica utens*) that these argumentative methodologies are limited by the uncertainty of their object. This limitation, however, is of little concern to the philosopher; for, to him the apparent and the probable are but stepping stones to the certain. His destination is nothing less than demonstration. Yet he remains but a man, and hence must use the stepping stones: he must pass by way of the apparent, by way of the probable. This means, in effect, that he must apply the methods of argumentation to the opinions of men. For, on the level of tradition, what men think to be the case is in fact "the apparent"; and the best of what men think, still more, the best of what the best men think, is "the probable."

---

[1] *In* III *Met.* l. 2, nn. 352–354; l. 4, n. 371; IV, l. 4, nn. 572–575.
[2] *In IV Met.* l. 4, nn. 576–577.

CHAPTER III

TRADITION AS A SOURCE
OF OPINION AND PROBABILITY

If it is true that the probable is the best of what the best men think, then it is important that we determine as clearly as possible which men Thomas himself considers to be intellectually "the best." For, it goes without saying that Thomas's value judgments in this regard will have a considerable bearing upon the way in which he evaluates opinions and determines probability. In other words, we are here interested in what might be called the hereditary presuppositions of Thomas's theory of probability. These presuppositions, as we shall see at some length, center around the fact that Thomas is the conscious heir of two fairly distinct traditions which, in his eyes, are not of equal profundity. For, not surprisingly, Thomas sees in the Judaeo-Christian tradition something so uniquely transcendent that by comparison the views of "the philosophers," however interesting and informative, could only be ancillary to and confirmatory of the higher truth of the former.

To bring out, then, the role of tradition in Thomas's theory of probability, we shall here consider: (1) his views as to the nature of the two traditions which constitute his intellectual heritage; (2) the relative authority which he attributes to these two traditions; (3) the importance which he gives to orthodox as opposed to heterodox opinion; and (4) the limitations implicit in this authoritarian criterion of probability.

A. THE TWO TRADITIONS: "PHILOSOPHY" AND "THE FAITH"

To begin with, Thomas is consciously aware of his being the heir of two fairly distinct traditions, namely, that of "the philosophers" and that of "the saints." In order, then, that we might know whereof we speak with regard to the role of tradition in Thomas's thought, it is well that we provide a description, through Thomas's eyes, of each of these two traditions. This means in effect showing that for Thomas "the philosophers" represent the heritage of unaided reason and "the saints" that of revelation. Taken as separate branches of knowledge, the former constitutes "philosophy" and the latter "the teachings of the faith," especially as developed by "*sacra doctrina*" or "theology."

According to Thomas, it was *the ancient Greeks* who first introduced rational speculation into human culture. The knowledge thus attained was first referred to as *sophia* (wisdom) and those who sought it came to call themselves *philosophoi* (lovers of wisdom). Thus this quest for rational knowledge of the world, as well as the body of knowledge attained, came to be known as *philosophia*. In the beginning restricted to a search for the fundamental sources of change (*physica*), philosophy in time came to include the unchanging quantitative objects of *mathematica* and then even the unchanging and unchangeable Source of all changing things. Because of the exalted object of its investigation, the last mentioned branch of philosophy was referred to as *first philosophy;* because it was thought possible only after a prolonged study of changing things, it was called *meta-physica* (after physics); because it involved a rational refinement of poetic and popular ideas about the gods, it was known as *theology*.[1]

Quite important for Thomas's purposes, the Greek *philosophers* made a sharp distinction between *episteme* ("scientific certitude"), certain knowledge "apodictically" demonstrated by reasoning, and *doxa* ("opinion"), an assertion for which favoring arguments can be given but which nevertheless is not thereby demonstrated and the truth of which, therefore, remains open to question. All sciences, including that which was called *theology*, were contained within the scope of *philosophy*. Yet, since not all the assertions defended by the philosophers were demonstrably necessary and certain, philosophy in this large sense had to include much that one could consider to be not *episteme* but only *doxa*, not science but only *opinion*.

Now, throughout the same period of time, and indeed commencing even earlier, another people, *the descendants of Abraham*, were gradually and haltingly acquiring profound insights of their own – not only about the God whom Greek arguments were approaching, but about their own relationship to this God. Like the Greeks, they too resorted to

---

[1] See *In Met.* Proemium and Commentary on Book I, esp. l. 3; *In De Trin.* 5 and 6. The latter is available in an English translation by Armand Maurer under the title, *The Division and Methods of the Sciences*, 3rd rev. ed., Toronto, 1963. See also Anton-Hermann Chroust "Some Reflections on the Origin of the Term 'Philosopher'," *The New Scholasticism* 38 (1964) 423–434.

poetical descriptions of God and even engaged in considerable reasoning about his role in their lives. But, in marked contrast to the critical rationalism of the Greeks, the primary and ultimate source of the Hebrews' knowledge of God was not their own powers of reasoning but God's own revelation of himself. The Hebrews, in short, though dependent instrumentally upon the word of man for their knowledge of God (a knowledge that could only have been *doxa* for the Greeks), nonetheless achieved ineluctable certitude (without benefit of rational *episteme*) through faith in that God as the authoritative source of those words.

Then, in the fullness of time, *the Word of God,* henceforth to be known as a divine person, took on human nature and brought to fulfillment the preparatory revelations to the Hebrews. This ultimate truth, revealed in and through Christ, both constituted and was contained in the New Testament, the writings of which thus transcend without replacing those of the Old. For, what else was the message of Christ but the divine announcement of the "good news," the *evangelium,* that his promises to the Hebrews were now fulfilled? And, coming as it did from God himself, this message was pre-eminently true, for God could neither deceive nor be deceived.

Oblivious of hermeneutical nuances now taken more or less for granted, Thomas, like his predecessors in the faith, was so taken by the thought of direct contact with the divine that he saw without seeing that even the biblical writers were as human as the Greeks. Instruments of the divine they were, but merely instruments. God, quite simply, wrote the Bible; and therefore the Bible from beginning to end was but a concrete manifestation of the longed-for divine omniscience. No question here, then, of false opinion or even of true opinion: whatever is said is said with a certitude divine, in which man shares by accepting the unquestionable authority of the Speaker.

Comparing now these two foundational sources of Thomas's intellectual heritage, we find here all that is essential for his distinction between divine teachings accepted on faith and human teachings defended or if possible demonstrated by reason. The latter are accepted only to the extent that they can be defended; the former are defended because they have been accepted. The latter are or are not true independently of the teacher or teachers; the former are and can only be true precisely on account of the Teacher. For, the latter are but human, whereas the former are divine.

Perfectly obvious, all of this, so long as one is in fact distinguishing between God and man. If, however, that sharp distinction should become somewhat blurred certain interesting consequences might well result. For, to the extent that one is in fact distinguishing between human authorities who qualify as "the children of God" and those who are but "the children of men," there will be a tendency to evaluate the former according to criteria not entirely applicable to the latter. As we shall see, Thomas is not altogeher immune from this tendency. In spite of his perfectly honorable intentions, he is so committed to the truth of Christian teachings that he cannot help but look to "the saints" for a clearer expression of the truth than would be possible for the mere "philosopher." The result is a subtle weighting of authorities in favor of the followers of Christ, in such a way that Thomas involves himself in a general presupposition at times productive of the well-known fallacy, *post hoc ergo propter hoc.*

This somewhat negative aspect of Thomas's approach to "the philosophers" had, of course, already had a long and varied history in Christian thinking. To be sure, Thomas's own attitude in this regard is a long way from that of some early Christian thinkers who felt that all pagan wisdom was simply stolen from the Old Testament. Yet, as we shall see, there are still clear traces of this early "triumphalism" in Thomas's thought. But what there is of triumphalism in Thomas's thought must be recognized as having a considerably different significance than did the triumphalism of Thomas's predecessors in the faith.

For one thing, the basic distinction here in question had in the course of time taken on some important nuances. The early Christians had tended to view the distinction somewhat simply as that between "faith" and "reason." Later on, it had come to be seen more as a distinction between "revelation" (or, better, "revealed truths") and "philosophy." By the time of Thomas, however, the basic distinction had shifted more to that between "theology" or divine science on the one hand and "philosophy" or human science on the other.[1]

Implied in the foregoing shift of emphasis, secondly, is a development in Christian speculation of such vast proportions that it can almost be

---

[1] For a thorough presentation of this whole development, together with an abundance of bibliographical data, see Yves Congar, *La Foi et la Théologie* (Tournai, Belgium, 1962); "Théologie," *Dictionnaire de Théologie Catholique*, Vol. 15, cols. 342–502. It should perhaps be noted in passing that since the time of Thomas Aquinas the basic cultural distinction between human disciplines has shifted still further, so that today there is a general tendency to place science (that is, mathematical and empirical science) on one side and other disciplines, including both philosophy and theology, on the other. For some interesting reflections on this development, especially in terms of its later consequences, see Pierre Conway and George Q. Friel, "Farewell, Philosophy," *The New Scholasticism* 24 (1950): 363–397.

said that Thomas is faced with a completely different intellectual milieu than had been the early Christian thinkers.

The first Christian believers, quite unconcerned with the teachings of "the philosophers," took as their primordial task simply to make clear and explicit the internal contents of the message which had been handed on to them from Christ. But human limitations before such an immense responsibility soon became apparent. An ever changing variety of diverse interpretations arose, and the all-important word of God was in imminent danger of being forever beclouded by the words of men. Throughout the ensuing controversies, the criterion of truth remained what God had in fact revealed: the word of God handed down by word of man. Nonetheless, the word of God, as contained in Sacred Scripture, was evidently not accepted by all, and even if accepted was not easily formulated in accessible human terms. Whence the need not so much for rational demonstration, which was not thought possible, but for rational elaboration and presentation. In this way, defenders of Revelation learned to utilize the procedures and even the findings of "the philosophers" for the purpose of explicitating the Christian message. Philosophical theology was both adopted by and incorporated into a new theology of revelation. As it happened, this revelation-theology came to depend more and more upon rational methodology, to such an extent that some Christian observers were of the opinion that the method was overshadowing its object. Be that as it may, the high point of this development was reached in the thirteenth century, after many previously unavailable writings of "the philosophers," especially those of Aristotle, had become available to Western Christians.

The Christians themselves, however, were by no means in agreement as to the value which their faith allowed them to attribute to these newly available "philosophical" writings. The positions which they did in fact adopt were based upon a number of factors too complex to detail here; but of the greatest importance in this regard was the extent to which they felt that the Moslems had correctly interpreted the thought of Aristotle. Since opinions on this subject differed considerably if not violently, the contrast between philosophy-science and revelation-theology came to assume truly critical proportions in the latter part of the thirteenth century. Some Christian thinkers wished in effect to transfer practically all *episteme* from philosophy to revelation-theology. Others tended rather in the opposite direction, placing unlimited confidence in the power of philosophy-science to attain whatever truth it is possible for man to know. The resulting controversy was centered in the then preeminent University of Paris, where Thomas Aquinas spent the greater part of his active teaching career.

Convinced as he surely was of the value of all knowledge, both reasoned and revealed, it was yet Thomas's duty as a Master of Theology to preserve and defend the integrity of his faith without detriment to what had been learned by the philosophers. Thus there fell to him, at this unique moment in the history of thought, the task of sorting out from among the multi-varied opinions of men those which most faithfully expressed the one Truth to whom all are subject and upon whom all depend for what they know.[1]

B. THE RELATIVE AUTHORITY OF THE TWO TRADITIONS

That the progress of human knowledge is and must be a common or community enterprise is a fundamental presupposition of the method and procedure of Thomas Aquinas. He explicitly states as much on various occasions throughout his life.[2] Far more important than what he says, however, is what he does. After fulfilling the requirements for the doctorate in theology with the usual commentary on Lombard's collection of opinions (*Sententiae*) of the Fathers, he goes on to comment upon one ancient authority after another: various books of the Bible, the writings of such Christian authors as Boethius and "Dionysius," and especially those of the *corpus Aristotelicum*. Even those writings of Thomas which are not directed specifically to some one document from the past are nonetheless filled with references to the opinions of others, who are sometimes identified by name and sometimes not. Among those who are named, Augustine and "Dionysius" loom large among "the saints"; but in addition to these, Thomas's sources more or less run the gamut of Christian writers from both East and West. As for those authors who are not Christian, Thomas is well acquainted with the "modern philosophers," most of whom are adherents of Islam; but his sympathies are more with the

---

[1] The question as to when and under what circumstances Thomas became consciously aware of the ideological drama in which he was involved has been the subject of much discussion by historians. Inasmuch as the details of this question are outside the scope of our investigation, we have here deliberately avoided any explicit reference to Thomas's earlier and later periods at Paris. See in this regard Van Steenberghen, *Aristotle in the West*, pp. 181–208; Josef Pieper, *Scholasticism* (New York, 1960), pp. 111, 118–126.

[2] See *In* II *Met.* l. 1, nn. 275–276, 287–288; *S.T.* I, 44, 2c; II–II, 1, 7 ad 2; *Contra Impugn.* c. 2 [3], n. 53; *In* III *Polit.* l. 8, n. 424; *Q.D. de pot.* 3, 5.

ancients, of whom the greatest is, simply, the Philosopher.[1] It is, then, to this intellectual heritage that Thomas directs his own thought. The content of this heritage nourishes his reflections and provides the material out of which he forms and formulates his own "personal" opinions.

It must be noted at once, however, that though Thomas recognizes his dependence upon the thought of his predecessors, he places definite limits both upon the extent and upon the significance of this dependence. This fact is well brought out by a passage in which Thomas is considering Averroes's view as to the metahistorical import of man's collective attainment of knowledge. This view Thomas summarizes as follows:

> The more we come to an actual understanding of things, so much the more perfectly is the agent intellect extended to us. But this progress and movement towards extension is brought about by study of speculative sciences, through which we come to understand truths and eliminate false opinions, the latter being extraneous to this development as are monsters extraneous to normal organic activity. Whence also men help one another towards this progress as they mutually assist one another in the speculative sciences. When therefore we have come to know in fact all that can be known, then the agent intellect will be united to us organically (*ut forma*), and through it we shall understand perfectly, just as we now understand perfectly those things the knowledge of which we already possess.[2]

It is not to our purpose to investigate how accurately Thomas has presented the thought of Averroes, though this is by no means irrelevant. Even as given his thought suggests to the contemporary mind an almost Teilhardian vision. This vision, however, Thomas rather summarily dismisses on the basis of Aristotle's authority together with some independent counter-arguments. Most important for our purposes, Thomas gives not the slightest indication that there might be some small grain of truth in that which he is attacking. He does not, for example, look for any similarity, however remote, between Paul's

---

[1] For a fairly good idea of the scope of Thomas's literary heritage, at least by way of tradition, see the list of authors and works cited by Thomas in his *Summa Theologica* and *Summa Contra Gentiles: Indices in Summa Theologiae et in Summa Contra Gentiles S. Thomae Aquinatis* (Turin-Rome, n.d.), Indices Primus and Tertius, pp. 1-137, 154-162.

[2] *C.G.* III, 43: ". . . Quanta plura intellecta in actu fuerint in nobis facta, perfectius intellectus agens continuatur nobis. Hic autem profectus et motus ad continuationem fit per studium in scientiis speculativis, per quas vera intellecta acquirimus, et falsae opiniones excluduntur, quae sunt extra ordinem huius motus, sicut monstruosa extra ordinem naturalis operationis. Unde et ad hunc profectum iuvant se homines, sicut iuvant se invicem in scientiis speculativis. Quando ergo omnia intellecta in potentia fuerint in nobis facta in actu, tunc intellectus agens perfecte copulabitur nobis ut forma, et intelligimus per ipsum perfecte, sicut nunc perfecte intelligimus per intellectum in habitu." This last expression, "per intellectum in habitu," might also be understood more technically as referring to *intellectus* in the special sense of knowledge of first principles.

admonitions to "be of one mind in Christ Jesus" and the Arab's
suggestion that through learning and mutual understanding men come
to participate more and more in what Thomas himself would prefer
to call the light or reflection of the First Truth. Nor does Thomas admit
to seeing any relationship between Averroes's view and the Christian
doctrine of the solidarity of mankind as the Body of Christ.

Why, then, we may legitimately ask, does Thomas adopt in this
instance such a negative attitude towards the thought of a philosopher
who in numerous other ways has taught him so much? The answer
to this question lies partly in the manner in which Thomas integrates
the view of Averroes into his own thinking and partly, we suggest,
in Thomas's presuppositions as to the irrelevance of an unbeliever's
thought to properly Christian teachings.

First, then, a few words as to the manner in which Thomas focusses
upon what Averroes says about the progress of human knowledge.
For Thomas, what is at issue here is not at all the fact that science
represents a cumulative effort of the human community. What he sees
in Averroes's words is simply one more aspect of the great medieval
problem of the agent intellect. As Thomas considers this problem, it is
largely a question of guarding the Christian doctrine of personal immortality against what he takes to be Arabian misinterpretations of
Aristotle. In practice, then, this means showing that neither the
possible nor the agent intellect of Aristotle's teachings need be understood in a collective sense as common to all men. Having thus posed
the problem before the Christian community, Thomas is not so much
interested in understanding as in disproving what is unacceptable to
the Christian. Accordingly, it is personal immortality and the integrity
of Aristotle which are at stake, and not the possible avenues of
rapprochement between Muslim and Christian ideas.

This suggests, in the second place, that there are certain presuppositions involved in the way Thomas evaluates the Arab's thought.
These presuppositions, quite simply, have to do with the relative
profundity of Christian and non-Christian speculation. In the eyes of
Thomas, though it was once commendable to be a "philosopher," to
be *merely* a philosopher after one has been called to be a "saint" is
indicative of intellectual pride that cannot but lead to error.[1] But the
Moslem, unlike Aristotle, has been called to be a "saint," to be a
follower of Christ – and yet he has neglected this call. Accordingly,

---

[1] *Contra Impugn.* III Pars, cc. 4 [11] and 5 [12], nn. 398–418; *In Symb.* Prologus, nn.
864–865. Other references will be given in the course of this chapter.

the Moslem's thought cannot be judged on the same level with Christian teaching but only on the level of philosophy, which was unseated from its throne with the coming of Christ.[1]

All this amounts to saying, in brief, that though Thomas does perforce consider the opinions of others, not all opinions are equal or equally received. On the contrary, each opinion is weighted according to its author or authors, and these in their turn are weighted according to the specific tradition, saintly or philosophical, to which they appertain. In general, Thomas is interested only in the thought of the wise. But he attributes greater wisdom to "the saints" than to "the philosophers," and among the philosophers the wisest is Aristotle.

1. Reason and the Opinions of the Philosophers

Though Thomas takes as his point of departure the opinions of men, this does not mean, not even in theory, that all opinions are equally deserving of attention. What is of interest for Thomas is the opinions of the wise, the learned. Opinions held by the unlearned and ignorant masses are of such little worth in his eyes that, like Parmenides, he usually opposes such opinions to the truth of the matter in question. According to the opinion of the foolish, clothes make the man, not according to the truth of the matter.[2] According to the opinion of men, the shame and disgrace of sin are inversely proportional to its frequency, but not according to the very nature of the vices in question.[3] The ignorant are amazed about many things which to the learned are naturally explicable: *secundum opinionem admirantis* as opposed to *secundum rei veritatem*.[4] Accordingly, it is of the utmost importance to evaluate the character of a person on the basis of what he really is (*in ipso*) rather than on the basis of what others think of him (*in opinione aliorum*).[5] In short, though truth is to be found in the opinions of men, the possession of such truth is largely the prerogative of the wise,

---

[1] See *C.G.* I, 1–8, and especially c. 6, where Thomas paints a not very ecumenical picture of Muslim teaching and practice in order to show the inferiority of Muslim to Christianity. The latter, of course, is portrayed in the ideal, without any reference to un-christlike activities of Christians vis-à-vis their Moslem brethren. This leads Thomas to conclude, in c. 7, that he must proceed on the level of reason alone, that is to say, of "philosophy." For a broader perspective on the problem here suggested, see R. W. Southern, *Western Views of Islam in the Middle Ages* (New York, 1962).

[2] *S.T.* II–II, 130, 2 ad 3.

[3] *S.T.* II–II, 143, 4 ad 2; 1–4, 2 ad 2 and ad 3; 3 ad 4. See also *Quodl.* 6, q. 4, a. un., ad 2.

[4] *Q.D. de pot.* 6, 2c. See also *S.T.* I, 110, 4 ad 2; *Comp. theol.* c. 136, n. 275.

[5] *S.T.* II–II, 112, 1c; *In De Trin.* I, c. 1, n. 4.

whose opinions are clearly distinguished from those of the masses.[1]
It is, therefore, with the opinions of the wise that one must begin if
he would find the truth.[2]

(a) Philosophers and The Philosopher

This interest in the opinions of the wise is, of course, well exemplified
for Thomas in the works of the Philosopher, who, as he says, proceeds
first according to the tradition of others and then according to his
own opinion.[3] Among the various opinions of the ancients as recorded
by Aristotle, some are said to be common to all or at least common to
a particular school, others are taken as proper to one or another thinker.
Thus, for example, there was the "widespread" (*famosa*) opinion that
every soul is incorruptible; there was a "common" opinion that the
happiness of the individual is equivalent to the happiness of the state.[4]
So also, Aristotle bases his definition of the wise man on what is
commonly accepted, what is the general opinion.[5] Among the natural
philosophers, it was practically a "common dogma" or, as Thomas also
expresses it, a "common conception of the mind" that from nothing
nothing comes.[6] The opinion that earth is a principle was "ancient"
and "public, *because many agreed to it*." [7] Even the important Aristotelian assertion that "anyone is of the opinion that he knows
something when he knows all its causes from first to last" is the
expression of a common opinion.[8]

The importance of these common opinions consists in the fact that
because they are widely accepted (*famosae*) they are taken to be
probable. Accordingly, arguments which proceed on the basis of what
is commonly held are taken to be probable: if the premises are
"probable and widely accepted" in this sense, then the argument is
probable whether those premises are granted by an opponent or not.[9]

---

[1] *In* III *Polit.* l. 3, n. 376; l. 7, n. 401; I, l. 4, n. 76; *In* II *Phys.* l. 9, n. 217; *In* I *Polit.*
l. 4, n. 87; VII, l. 2, n. 1070; *S.T.* I, 13, 9 and 10.
[2] *In* II *Polit.* l. 1, n. 169; *In* I *Met.* l. 11, n. 180; *Q.D. de pot.* 7, 6c.
[3] *In* III *Polit.* l. 1, n. 348.
[4] *In* I *De An.* l. 10, n. 163; *In* VII *Polit.* l. 2, n. 1060.
[5] *In* I *Met.* l. 2, nn. 36–42.
[6] *In* XI *Met.* l. 6, n. 2227; *Q.D. de pot.* 3, 1 ad 1.
[7] *In* I *Met.* l. 12, n. 186.
[8] *In* I *Phys.* 1. l, n. 5. It is not to be supposed, however, that this or any similar expression
is for Aristotle nothing more than a common opinion. Aristotle is not interested in merely
recording what men think but in uncovering the deeper implications of their thoughts. See
Gerard Verbeke, "Démarches de la réflexion métaphysique," in *Aristote et les Problèmes de
Méthode* (Louvain-Paris, 1961), pp. 120–121.
[9] *In* III *Phys.* l. 8, n. 352.

Thus in the *Physics* Aristotle argues "disputatively on the basis of probable propositions which were widely accepted among the ancients."[1] An argument of this kind, which elsewhere in his commentary on the *Physics* Thomas calls "a probable argument based on the authority of the wise," is considered a "sign," that is, a kind of pointer towards the truth.[2] In view, then, of this association of the probable with what is commonly accepted, Thomas will even use a kind of shorthand by referring to an opinion as "probable among all" or as "probably held (*existimatur*) by many."[3]

It is important to note that Thomas's usage of both *probable* and *opinion* fluctuates in these texts between an objective and a subjective pole. In some instances *opinion* refers to a proposition as such; in other instances it refers rather to the adherence to that proposition. Similarly, it is sometimes the opinion taken as a proposition that is said to be "probable," while at other times it is the adherence to a proposition that is so characterized. In one and the same passage, for example, he says first that a particular opinion (*proposition*) is being "used (by Aristotle) as probable" and that it is "probable on the basis of the opinion (*adherence thereto*) of other philosophers."[4]

The association of probability with the very adherence to or acceptance of a proposition takes on a special nuance when it is a question of a restricted group or even of a single individual that accepts the proposition. For, in this case the proposition is said to be

---

[1] *In* I *Phys.* l. 11, n. 91: "Hic autem procedit disputative ex propositionibus quae erant apud antiquos famosae."

[2] *In* III *Phys.* l. 6, n. 328: "Ex quo colligitur probabile argumentum ab auctoritate sapientum, quod ad philosophiam naturalem pertineat determinare de infinito."

[3] *In* VIII *Phys.* l. 9, n. 1049; IV, l. 2, n. 421.

[4] *In* VIII *Phys.* l. 14, n. 1089. If we may abstract from polemical concerns of the time, it is largely because of a failure to distinguish between the objective and the subjective poles of *opinio* that T. Richard could claim the authority of Thomas Aquinas for his view that opinion excludes doubt and that therefore there are no degrees of probability. We may grant Richard and others of his persuasion that for Thomas *opinio* (taken as subjective adherence) may exclude doubt and hence involve even (subjective) certitude. As we shall soon see, this is precisely the problem of the heretic in Thomas's view. If, however, *opinio* be taken objectively to mean an assertion as such, then Thomas would determine its probability – even its degree of probability – on the basis of the authority of those who adhere to it (*opinio* taken subjectively) and even more so on the basis of the arguments brought forth in its favor. Opinion as adherence implies a psychological relationship between subject and a given assertion. Probability implies a logical relationship between a proposition (*opinio* taken objectively) and arguments (including that from authority) in its favor. See T. Richard, *Le Probabilisme moral et la Philosophie*, Paris, 1922; reviewed by M. R. Cathala, *Revue Thomiste* 6 (1923): 102–112. See also the following articles by Richard in defense of his contention that if an opinion is probable it is by that very fact certain: *Revue Thomiste* 6 (1923): 155–178; 7 (1924): 174–191; 404–415; 8 (1925): 452–473; 10 (1927): 165–195; 14 (1931): 131–156. Richard's position in this regard is essentially the same as that of A. Gardeil, "La Certitude Probable," *Revue des Sciences Philosophiques et Théologiques* 5 (1911): 237–266, 441–485.

probable not in itself or to many but according to the opinion of that group or individual. Thus, in discussing a disagreement among commentators on Aristotle as to whether one of his arguments is in fact demonstrative, Thomas rejects Alexander's analysis because it involves an assumption which goes against (literally, destroys) "a certain (opinion which was) probable and widely accepted by Aristotle and all the Peripatetics." [1] In much the same way, Thomas sometimes saves Aristotle embarrassment by noting that much that is said in his logical works is said "not according to his own opinion but according to the opinion of others." In particular, this is his explanation for the assertions that virtue consists in suffering nothing and that evil is a genus or category. He attributes the former opinion to the Stoics, the latter to Pythagoras. And in each case he says that the assertion is not true according to Aristotle's own opinion, but is probable (or, probable in his time) according to the opinion of the other philosophers in question.[2]

The value of these opinions which seem true to many or to some and are thus from that point of view (or perhaps better, from *their* point of view) probable is, according to Thomas, that they cannot be totally false but must be at least partly true. So, at least, he puts it in commenting on Aristotle.[3] But when on his own, and "against the Gentiles," he qualifies this maxim, admitting somewhat more reluctantly that there is some truth to it.[4] This qualification, we think, is not at all insignificant. However, we shall come to that soon enough. For the moment we will be doing well just to point out a problem which this investigation of the opinions of others entails.

The problem, rather obviously, is this: granting that every opinion which is probable at least to some of the wise contains some element of truth, that is, is "partly true," how in the world decide which part is the true part and which part is not? For Thomas, commenting rather closely on Aristotle's own words in the *Metaphysics*, the solution to this problem is at least in principle simple enough. At issue in the passage in question are the different views about the motions of the planets. Aristotle introduces his discussion of these views by noting that one is to love both parties of a dispute but is to be persuaded

---

[1] *In* VI *Phys.* l. 5, n. 798: "In hoc destruitur quoddam probabile et famosum apud Aristotelem et omnes peripateticos."

[2] *S.T.* I–II, 59, 2 obj. 1 and ad 1; 48, 1 ad 1; *Q.D. de malo* 1, 1 ad 11; 12, 1 ad 13; *C.G.* III, 9; *Comp. theol.* c. 116, nn. 227–228.

[3] *In* I *Phys.* l. 11, n. 88.

[4] *C.G.* III, 9.

by the position which is more certain. That Aristotle should say such a thing, Thomas explains, is

because in accepting or repudiating opinions, man must not be led by love or hate for the one introducing the opinion but rather by the certitude of truth . . . For, those on either side (of a dispute) have searched diligently for the truth, and by so doing have helped us. However, we must "be persuaded by the more certain," that is, (we must) follow the opinion of those who have arrived more certainly at the truth.[1]

The point is well taken, and would no doubt be acceptable to all men of good will. The only trouble is that it really tells us nothing about how to decide which opinion is the more certain; and this is, after all, the root of the problem, as Thomas realizes quite well enough himself.

The solution to the problem just posed obviously does not reside in anything so simple as a choice. But to the extent that choice does enter in, Thomas, for his part, chooses Aristotle, at least as far as the philosophers are concerned. For Thomas, in other words, what was above referred to as *Aristotle's own opinion* is, to the extent that the Christian faith will allow, equivalent to *the truth*. Thus in general the difference between the opinions of other philosophers and the opinion of Aristotle is the difference between what is probable and what is simply true. Accordingly, when Aristotle passes from a discussion of the opinions of others to the defense of his own, he is not simply presenting another opinion; he is determining the truth.[2] To what extent Thomas is himself convinced of this is perhaps impossible to decide. But it is certainly worth noting that Thomas rarely if ever speaks of an Aristotelian position as being merely probable except in those few instances when that position (as, for example, that the world is eternal) is directly opposed to what for Thomas is an essential tenet of his faith.[3]

Having thus cast his philosophical lot with the opinion of Aristotle, at least to the extent that his Christian faith will allow, Thomas often finds himself faced with the not altogether facile task of determining just what is the opinion of Aristotle. In the preceding chapter, we had occasion to show how Thomas wrestles with the Aristotelian dis-

---

[1] *In XII Met.* l. 9, n. 2566: ". . . quia in eligendis opinionibus vel repudiandis, non debet duci homo amore vel odio introducentis opinionem, sed magis ex certitudine veritatis, ideo dicit: 'Amare quidem utrosque, persuaderi vero a certioribus.' Utrique enim studuerunt ad inquirendum veritatem, et nos in hoc adjuverunt. Sed tamen oportet nos 'persuaderi a certioribus,' idest sequi opinionem eorum, qui certius ad veritatem pervenerunt."

[2] *In II De An.* l. 1, n. 211; *In I Phys.* l. 12, n. 98; III, l. 10, n. 370; IV, l. 11, n. 520; *In II Met.* l. 1, n. 273; III, l. 1, n. 338; IV, l. 1, n. 529.

[3] Aristotle's position on the eternity of the world and Thomas's reaction to that position will be discussed in Chapter 6.

tinction between the scientific and the opinionative parts of the soul. Now, just above we have seen that he attributes to other philosophers opinions which do not square with basic Aristotelian tenets, and that he argues strenuously against any interpretation of the philosopher's psychology which would make impossible personal immortality. Numerous other examples of this same quest for the pure untainted position of Aristotle might be mentioned, and some of them will come up in subsequent discussions.[1] But no one seriously questions Thomas's enthusiasm for Aristotle, except perhaps to insist that there is more Platonism, or better neo-Platonism, in Thomas's thinking than he himself realizes or admits.[2] The latter contention we do not contest as to the fact but only as to the significance of the fact. As far as Thomas is concerned, it is Aristotle and not Plato who offers "the true principles of philosophy"; and, as he tells us in his commentary on the *Politics*, the opinions of Plato are known only by way of Aristotle.[3] As we shall have occasion to note further on, he recognizes "Platonic" views in the thought of both Augustine and "Dionysius." But to the extent that he follows or utilizes such views, and this is not at all inconsiderable, he does so not because they are the views of Plato but because they are the views of "the saints." For, to his way of thinking there is just one philosopher, and that is *the* Philosopher.

(b) The Saints and Secular Learning

Neither philosophers nor the Philosopher, however, is for Thomas the richest source of truth. That prerogative belongs to Christ, whose teachings have introduced into the mainstream of thought a whole new dimension of truth which reduces all of philosophy, as Paul says of the Old Testament, to the role of pedagogue. Not that the Christian may therefore disregard philosophy: though it is pedagogue only, it is still pedagogue. Thus in his early diatribe against opponents of religious orders (1256), Thomas notes at considerable length the example of Jerome and other Fathers of the Church before him in support of his contention that to disregard worldly learning would make one like a blind man envying those who can see.[4] Immediately after this passionate defense of worldly learning, however, he points out that it is and

---

[1] In particular, we will be called upon to give a variety of examples in Chapter 6, where we take up the question as to what Thomas considers demonstratively true.

[2] See R. J. Henle, *Saint Thomas and Platonism: A Study of the Plato and Platonici Texts in the Writings of Saint Thomas* (The Hague, 1956).

[3] *Q.D. de spir. creat.* q. un. a. 3c.

[4] *Contra Impugn.* III, sect. 1, c. 5 (12), nn. 408–413.

must be secondary in importance to Sacred Scripture.[1] This, he says, can be seen from the fact that at first fishermen were converted to Christ and they in turn converted orators and philosophers. Accordingly, "our faith does not consist in the wisdom of men but in the power of God." [2] Having thus clarified his scale of intellectual values, Thomas can then say that it is only when "the teachings of worldly philosophy" are made primary that there arise "heresies contrary to Christ." [3] And thus does he establish the point really at issue, namely that the religious (such as himself, of course) can pursue "secular" studies so long as he removes the errors contained therein by means of "sacred" studies. Indeed, his commitment to abstinence and to chastity is an asset to the attainment of such learning, which will not make him proud provided that he have charity.[4]

In commenting on the Apostles' Creed, Thomas notes, somewhat hyperbolically, that the whole world believes in and has been converted to Christ.[5] Whatever the statistical accuracy of the observation, its importance as a value judgment cannot be lightly dismissed. For, even if we qualify this observation by referring to the obvious fact that Thomas is often intellectually engaged with the thought of those who are not Christian, this in no way changes his evaluation of the way things should be. Accordingly, in his approach to those who are not of his own persuasion, Thomas rarely deals with persons but with their ideas, and his approach to ideas in such cases is apologetical rather than ecumenical. He does not, for example, write *about* the ideas of "the Gentiles," he writes simply *against* the errors of the Gentiles. Similarly, even within the confines of Christianity, he does not write *about* the ideas of the Orthodox but *Against the Errors of the Greeks*. He does not write *about* the ideas of those who are opposed to the religious life but

---

[1] *Contra Impugn.* III, sect. 1, c. 5 (12), nn. 414–418.

[2] *Contra Impugn.* n. 414: "Sed tamen posteriores doctores magis adhuc usi sunt sapientia et eloquentia saeculari propter eandem rationem qua non prius philosophi et rhetores sunt electi ad praedicandum, sed plebeii et piscatores, qui postmodum philosophos et oratores converterunt; ut scilicet fides nostra non consistat in sapientia hominum, sed in virtute Dei."

[3] *Contra Impugn.* n. 417: "Glossa illa loquitur de sapientia saeculari quae adversa est Deo: quod contingit quando sapientia saecularis ponitur principalis: tunc enim sequitur quod aliquis velit regulare fidem secundum documenta sapientiae saecularis; et exinde sequuntur haereses contrariae Christo."

[4] *Contra Impugn.* III, sect. 1, c. 4 [11], nn. 400, 404. The attitudes which Thomas is here rejecting, and which nevertheless his own outlook only partially transcends, are deeply indebted to centuries of Christian reflection upon the value of human learning to the believer. For a particularly fascinating and richly documented study of this aspect of Thomas's heritage, see Jean Leclercq's study of monastic culture entitled *The Love of Learning and the Desire for God* (New York, 1962), esp. chs. 5–7 and ch. 9.

[5] *In Symb.* Prol., n. 867.

Against Those who Attack the Worship of God and Religion: a passionate treatise, at times almost vitriolic, which identifies the opposition as destroyers of the New Israel (on the basis of Psalm 82) and Antichrist.[1] One can hardly overlook the apologetical character of these works, nor, at least with regard to the last mentioned, the vehemence of the conflict involved.[2] And precisely insofar as these works are apologetical, if not polemical, Thomas addresses himself to opponents as opponents and as opponents only.[3]

That this disputative procedure was the accepted style of the times in no way alters the simple fact that Thomas follows that style, not only in his obviously apologetical works but in most of his others as well.[4] Accordingly, to read Thomas without taking into account the disputative mentality which pervades so much of his thought is in some ways not to read Thomas at all. This is by no means meant to imply that Thomas is not in fact committed to anything, but rather that if one takes at face value his arguments for that to which he is committed, one does so at his own peril. As we have already had occasion to note, the probable, even the probable which one does not himself accept as true, is a recognized instrument of dialectic provided that the ultimate goal is truth. The full implications of this usage will become clear only in the following chapter, where we take up the dialectical procedure as such. For the time being, it is enough just to point out that Thomas is by profession a theologian; and thus when he says, as he does at the

---

[1] *Contra Impugnentes Dei Cultum et Religionem*, Proemium.

[2] For a brief summary of the not entirely academic controversy between seculars and religious at the University of Paris, together with Thomas's role in that controversy, see Frederick Copleston, *A History of Philosophy*, Vol. II (Westminster, Md., 1952), pp. 215–216.

[3] We are grateful to Joseph Pieper for reminding us that the title of the *Summa Contra Gentiles* is not Thomas's but is rather a later addition. Indeed, we are even prepared to accept, if need be, that Thomas is not responsible for the title of any of his works. In any event, Van Steenberghen's summary of critical problems with regard to the *Contra Gentiles* (see his *Aristotle in the West*, pp. 193–196) has led us to refer to this work as "apologetical" rather than "polemical." We are not, however, thereby accepting Pieper's contention that the *Contra Gentiles* (or any other of Thomas's works) is inappropriately titled. For, as we have already suggested, Thomas nowhere shows as much sympathy for the thought of medieval non-Roman Catholics as he does for that of Aristotle. In view of Thomas's prolific literary output, it simply is not enough to say that he was too involved in the controversy over Aristotle to write an objective appreciation of, say, some Arabian text, many of which were available to him in Latin translations. There is, in short, a lacuna here, and the lacuna demands an explanation. It is our contention that the explanation consists in the fact that Thomas's attitude, as a Catholic theologian, towards non-Catholic thought is, if not polemical, at least apologetical. Or, to put this somewhat differently, he could not understand a De Lubac writing *about* atheistic humanism or a De Waelhens writing *about* the thought of Martin Heidegger. Thomas does not write *about* the thought of "infidels," he writes *against* their errors. For Pieper's observation, see his *Scholasticism* (New York, 1960), p. 160.

[4] See M.-D. Chenu, *Introduction à l'Etude de Saint Thomas d'Aquin*, 2ième éd. (Paris-Montreal, 1954), Ch. II.

beginning of his *De Articulis Fidei*, that the whole concern of theologians has to do with doubts about articles of faith, the implications of this dialectical point of view cannot be lightly dismissed.[1]

2. *Revelation and the Opinions of the Saints*

We can only conclude from the foregoing that Thomas's principal authority is certainly not any of the philosophers, not even Aristotle, but rather Sacred Scripture. Thus he clearly distinguishes, after Boethius, between "philosophical theology" and "theology of Sacred Scripture," or, according to another formulation, "divine science which the philosophers transmit" and "divine science which is accepted by divine inspiration."[2] Whereas an argument from authority is the weakest of all arguments for the former, since the authorities involved are only human, an argument from authority for the latter is the best possible argument, since the authority is God himself. Thus, from the viewpoint of the theologian (which is, after all, the viewpoint of Thomas), arguments based on the authority of canonical Scripture produce necessarily true conclusions. The authoritative statements of Scripture are the proper concern of the theologian. But also the proper concern of the theologian are the authoritative statements of other doctors of the Church, although arguments based on such authorities are only probable. The statements of other, *merely* human authorities, that is to say, "the philosophers," also provide probable arguments, but such arguments are, as it were, extraneous to theology.[3] The full meaning of this subtle division must wait till the next chapter. What is important at the moment is that there is a weighting of authorities, if ever so slight, in favor of those who are in the tradition of Sacred Scripture and whose views, therefore, are just a bit more than merely human: only probable, as is true of other authorities, but proper to theology, whereas the views of others are extraneous. To be sure, as Thomas notes, such authorities have no argumentative value if one

---

[1] *De articulis fidei et Ecclesiae sacramentis*, Proemium: "Verum cum omne Theologorum studium versetur circa dubietates contingentes articulos fidei et Ecclesiae sacramenta, si ad plenum vestrae petitioni satisfacere vellem, oporteret totius Theologiae comprehendere summatim difficultates." See also *S.T.* I, 1, 8; *C.G.* I, 9; *Quodl.* 4, q. 9, a. 3.

[2] *In De Trin.* 5, 4c: "theologia philosophica" and "theologia sacrae Scripturae"; ad 3: "scientia divina, quae est per inspirationem divinam accepta" and "scientia divina, quam philosophi tradunt." See also Proemium II, 2c; *S.T.* I, 1, 1 ad 2.

[3] *S.T.* I, 1, 8 ad 2: "Sed tamen sacra doctrina hujusmodi auctoritatibus [philosophorum] utitur quasi extraneis argumentis, et probabilibus. Auctoritatibus autem canonicae Scripturae utitur proprie, ex necessitate argumentando. Auctoritatibus autem aliorum doctorum ecclesiae, quasi arguendo ex propriis, sed probabiliter." See also *S.T.* II–II, 1, 5 ad 2.

does not accept them as authoritative; but Thomas himself is inclined to accept them, and it is this that is here of interest to us.[1]

Generally speaking, with the exception of Sacred Scripture, Thomas would admit only papal statements of doctrine as being safe from error.[2] When the "holy Doctors" interpret Scripture, they are guided by the Holy Spirit, but their expositions do not necessarily require belief.[3] Nor is everything that is said by or attributed to "the saints" to be considered as enjoying the authority of the saints. For example, Thomas rejects the authority of Origen insofar as the latter follows erroneous opinions of ancient philosophers.[4] He rejects an argument based on a certain book entitled *De Spiritu et Anima* on the grounds that this work is not that of Augustine, nor does the anonymous author manifest any familiarity with "the sayings of the saints." [5] Similarly, he deprecates an argument based upon Costa ben Luca's *De Differentia Spiritus et Animae* because "that book does not have great authority."[6] On yet another occasion, he indicates that it is beneath the dignity of a theologian to use a mere canonist, that is, a canon lawyer, as an authority.[7]

Allowing, then, for these and other similar qualifications, faith enjoys in Thomas's view the authority *par excellence*, because it rests ultimately upon the authority of God himself. The believer, unlike Adam, might very well have a false opinion (*falsum aliquid aestimare*) about matters which require merely human conjecture, as for example with regard to the precise time of Christ's birth; but that he should have a false opinion about what is "of faith" is impossible. In other words, within a carefully prescribed area, namely, that of the defined doctrines of the Church, the believer shares in the knowledge of God himself and to just that extent is immune from error.[8]

Though limited, this immunity from error which comes with faith can be developed and extended by reflecting upon and drawing out the consequences of what God has revealed. This, in short, is the awesome prerogative of theology, or *sacra doctrina*, which Thomas speaks of as

---

[1] *In De div. nom.* c. 2, l. 1, nn. 124–125.

[2] *Quodl.* 9, q. 8, a. un. c. See also *S.T.* II–II, 1, 10.

[3] *Quodl.* 12, q. 17, a. un. ad 1. Accordingly, the authority of the saints is never to be given priority over that of Sacred Scripture. See *Quodl.* 3, q. 4, a. 2c.

[4] *Q.D. de spir. creat.* q. un., a. 5 ad 1.

[5] *Q.D. de spir. creat.* q. un., a. 3 ad 6; a. 11 ad 2.

[6] *Q.D. de spir. creat.* q. un., a. 3 ad 9: ". . . tamen etiam ille liber non est magnae auctoritatis."

[7] *Contra Retrahent.* c. 13, n. 829: "quamvis inconsonum et de risibile videatur quod sacrae doctrinae professores, Juristarum glossulas in auctoritatem inducant, vel de eis disceptent."

[8] *S.T.* II–II, 1, 3c and ad 3. See also 11, 2c; 4, 6c.

a kind of derivative or extension of the science of God and of the blessed in heaven.[1] To put this in more contemporary terms, for Thomas the foundations of theology are not in reason but in God. Theology derives its certitudes not from the light of human reason, as is the fallible lot of other sciences, but from the light of the divine knowledge itself.[2]

This being the exalted state of theology, Thomas is compelled to point out that doubts about the principles of theology, namely, about articles of faith, in no way indicate that the matter in question is uncertain; such doubts simply manifest the weakness of the human intellect.[3] Thus does his longing for God's own certitude lead him to dehumanize theology by removing from the notion of certitude any relationship to the subject and transferring that relationship – analogically, if you will – to the object sought. Moreover, as a corollary of this concept of what might be called theocentric certitude, Thomas attributes to weakness of intellect the theologian's dependence upon merely human knowledge (*philosophia*).[4]

To view this theoretical glorification of theology merely as a humanly understandable manifestation of Thomas's love for his own field of specialization is to miss the point entirely. Thomas is little concerned with encomia of a human science, even be it his own, but rather with the ineluctable prerogatives of divine truth itself. It is of

---

[1] *S.T.* I, 1, 2c. The passage here in question has had a long and controversial history among commentators on Thomas Aquinas. In our opinion, however, the controversy has been misdirected. For, the commentators have taken the article at face value as declaring that *sacra doctrina* is a science, and thus have dedicated themselves to the task of elucidating what Thomas here means either by *sacra doctrina* or by *scientia*. Thus, with the help of a brief observation in *In Sent.* Prologus, q. 1, a. 3, these commentators have developed the idea that theology is a "subalternate" or at least a "quasi-subalternate" science, in that it borrows its principles from a higher science, namely, in Thomas's own words, "scientia Dei et beatorum." The resulting controversy over the best way to characterize the scientific status of theology has simply disregarded as obvious Thomas's truly startling declaration that there is a kind of human knowledge which proceeds in a seemingly human way and yet is related to God's own knowledge somewhat as is applied to pure mathematics. As the present study is attempting to show, however, Thomas's position in this regard can hardly be taken as obvious; for, it is simply one more illustration, although an extremely important one, of what we have already referred to as Thomas's theotropic bent of mind. Be that as it may, a good view of the traditional statement of the problem can be gained from the following: M.-D. Chenu, *La Théologie comme Science au XIIIe Siècle* (Paris, 1957), ch. 5; Victor White, *Holy Teaching: The Idea of Theology according to St. Thomas Aquinas* (London, 1958), esp. pp. 12–14; Gerald F. Van Ackeren, *Sacra Doctrina: The Subject of the First Question of the Summa Theologica of St. Thomas Aquinas* (Rome, 1952), esp. pp. 90–100; Etienne Gilson, *The Elements of Christian Philosophy* (New York, 1963), Ch. 2. We especially call attention to Gilson's Note 21 on the chapter cited, in which he criticizes the notion of subalternation so thoroughly as to take all meaning out of Thomas's explicit words in the *Summa* about "scientia Dei et beatorum."

[2] *S.T.* I, 1, 5c. See also 1, 8c.

[3] *S.T.* I, 1, 5 ad 1. See *Q.D. de ver.* 14, 1; *S.T.* II–II, 2, 1c; 7, 2 ad 2.

[4] *S.T.* I, 1, 5 ad 2.

this that he is really speaking, regretting all the while how little of it he, as mere man, possesses. Of this much, however, he is certain: man's longing for that infinite wisdom which has touched the angels, Adam, the prophets and above all Christ can be satisfied only by clinging to that which has already been revealed here below and which will become fully manifest in beatitude hereafter.[1] It is, in short, God's own knowledge which is in question; and, since it is clearly a question of God, that knowledge cannot but be certain. If our feeble intellects are hesitant before what is Truth itself, this can only be because we are, as it were, turning our own weak eyes directly into the sun. But weak though they may be, they can hardly help but noticing that it is in fact the sun.

C. THE INTELLECTUAL EVIL OF UNBELIEF

In the light of the foregoing, there is already some reason for suggesting that Thomas's concern for divine truth leads him to minimize the role of the human recipient of such truth. Taking too little account of his own basic distinctions in this regard, he idealizes – one might even say divinizes – propositions which he takes to have been revealed by God; and, as a result, he tends to overlook the rather relevant fact that it is still man who conceptualizes and formulates divine revelation.[2] One far-reaching consequence of this telescoping of the divine into the human is that Thomas Aquinas cannot easily understand how a regularly functioning mind, once exposed to the light of faith, could fail to see the light or even fail to see that it comes from God. As a result, Thomas's theory of unbelief in general and of heresy in particular is so unrealistic that it is perhaps best understood as one more manifestation of his theotropic bent of mind.

[1] See S.T. II–II, 2, 3.

[2] We have in mind here two texts in particular, one of which is directly relevant and the other somewhat more indirectly. In S.T. II–II, 1, 2c, first of all, Thomas notes that the object of faith is incomplex from the viewpoint of God; but for men who know conceptually, the object is complex. He then goes on to point out (ad 2) that the act of faith terminates not in propositions but in the realities expressed thereby: "Actus autem credentis non terminatur ad enuntiabilia, sed ad rem: non enim formamus enuntiabilia, nisi ut per ea de rebus cognitionem habeamus, sicut in scientia, ita et in fide." The second observation, only indirectly relevant, is to the effect that Sacred Scripture expresses truths about God metaphorically, in keeping with the level of ordinary men (S.T. I, 1, 9c). Having noted this, Thomas goes on to show from various points of view (answers to objections) that this manner of presentation is most fitting to human nature. We only wish to say here that it is a pity Thomas did not apply similar reasoning in formulating his attitude towards heresy and towards the religious beliefs and the expressions thereof of non-Christians. Compare, for example, what Thomas says about the fittingness of Scripture with what he says about the erroneous notions which pagans have about God (S.T. II–II, 10, 3c). See also S.T. II–II, 4, 6; 5, 4.

As Thomas sees it, unbelief is the chief cause of immoral conduct, and is more serious than all other sins with the single exception of hating God.[1] His reasoning is more or less as follows. Sin being a turning away from God, the more directly and explicitly one turns away from God, the greater is the sin involved. But if a man's opinion about God is false, then his opinion is not about God but about something that is not God. Accordingly, a false opinion about God is not a partial approach to God but rather an intellectual cause of estrangement, and the more false the opinion the greater the estrangement. Thus, not to accept what God has revealed about himself is the most direct and explicit rejection of God of which man is capable with the exception of actually hating God.

It is not surprising, then, that, as Thomas asserts in the *Contra Gentiles*, man is obligated by divine law to believe correctly.[2] This assertion he defends with a series of arguments which can only be described as sophistical (and which he surely recognizes as merely disputative). The last of these arguments, for example, says in effect that, since false opinion is the evil (or vice) of the intellect and the job of divine law is to prohibit vice, therefore divine law prohibits false opinions about God and the things that pertain to God.

Up to this point, Thomas's views about the importance of correct belief might perhaps be acceptable to anyone willing to admit the existence of God and man's dependence upon him. But Thomas is considerably more specific as to what he means by correct belief and its opposite, unbelief. To put it simply, unbelief is for Thomas the failure, if not the refusal, to accept the teachings of Christ as expressed in the Catholic faith.[3] To be sure, Thomas makes room for alleviating circumstances, as in the case of the Apostle Paul, who at first persecuted the early Christians; but on the basic principle he stands firm.[4] Thus for him the only real question in this regard is whether and to what extent the individual is responsible for his lack of belief.

Without any doubt, the worst of all unbelievers is the formal heretic, that is, the onetime Catholic who has explicitly rejected one or more

---

[1] In *Q.D. de malo* 3, 8 ad 1, Thomas says simply: "Ignorantia infidelitatis . . . in se quidem est gravissimum peccatum." However, in *S.T.* II–II, 10, 3, he considers unbelief only the greatest of sins with regard to good morals, declaring explicitly in *S.T.* II–II, 34, 2, that hating God is simply speaking the greatest of all sins. See also 20, 3; 39, 2 ad 3; III, 80, 5; *In IV Sent.* d. 13, q. 2, a. 2. That unbelief is the chief cause of immoral conduct is implicit in *S.T.* II–II, 10, 3c and especially in 10, 6.

[2] *C.G.* III, 118.

[3] *S.T.* II–II, 1, 10; 2, 5–8; 5, 3; 11, 1c.

[4] *S.T.* II–II, 10, 3 ad 1 and ad 2.

of the doctrines of the Church. For, as Thomas sees it, responsibility for unbelief is determined according to the extent to which the individual has been exposed to the truth about Christ. Speaking in generalities, Thomas assumes that the moral conduct of the heretic will be better than that of the Jew, and that the moral conduct of the Jew will be better than that of the pagan, because of the varying degree of proximity of each to Christ, the fount of truth. But for precisely the same reason, the unbelief of the pagan is less culpable than that of the Jew, and the unbelief of the Jew is less culpable than that of the heretic. Unbelief, in short, is the greatest of moral faults, and of all unbelief heresy is the most heinous.[1]

1. The Nature and Scope of Heresy

That Thomas should consider heresy such a grievous affront to God is a direct consequence of his tendency to identify man's knowledge of revelation with the divine knowledge itself. For, as he sees it, once one has come to have faith in the truths of revelation, he thereby and thereafter draws upon not merely human but truly divine knowledge. To think momentarily that God is not both three and one is only a venial sin, because this can be explained as due to merely human reason. Should one, however, go on to reflect upon the doctrine of the Trinity and decide that it is opposed to God's revelation of himself as one, then one commits a mortal sin. The reason for this seems to be that in Thomas's view such reflection could be engaged in only with knowledge from God or, in his own words, with "divine knowledge." To oppose one's merely human thoughts to such knowledge is somewhat like defending a proposition which a *reductio ad absurdum* has shown to be contrary to an established truth.[2] Thus, if we may put this somewhat facetiously, once a man has come to believe, his thoughts are no longer his own, or at least not only his own; for, some of his thoughts are from God.

It is important to note, however, that the area of knowledge within which man's thought is aided and perfected by faith is rather precisely delimited. Accordingly, the kinds of false opinion which Thomas would consider to be heretical are also limited. As we have already pointed

---

[1] *S.T.* II–II, 10, 6. See also 10, 3 ad 3; 10, 5. In *S.T.* II–II, 12, 1c, Thomas identifies one meaning of apostasy as having to do with a total rejection of the faith. In ad 3, however, he points out that this does not constitute a separate species of unbelief but is simply an aggravating circumstance.

[2] *Q.D. de malo* 7, 5 ad 11.

out above, he certainly recognizes that the Christian can adhere to a false opinion about what is not essential to his faith. Moreover, even this notion of what is essential to faith is rather precisely delimited in scope. As Thomas points out on various occasions, a proposition may pertain to faith in one of two ways: (1) directly and principally pertinent to faith are the very articles of faith transmitted by God himself; (2) indirectly and secondarily pertinent to faith is any proposition which necessarily implies a conclusion contrary to an article of faith.

The very denial of an article of faith constitutes heresy, especially if the denial is pertinacious. As for the other propositions, however, the factor of historical development enters in. Before the Church has clearly determined that a given proposition implies something contradictory to a teaching of faith, the believer might well accept it as true and thereby adhere to a false opinion which is in fact contrary to his faith. But once the heretical implication has been made manifest, one can no longer adhere to the proposition in question without being guilty of heresy. In other words, in the course of time more and more propositions are found to be intrinsically relevant to the teachings of faith, and by that very fact more and more propositions are added to the category of what is heretical.[1] This is not to say that the Church manufactures new articles of faith, but simply that the original revelation from God comes to be seen more clearly in its implications and expressed more precisely, in which process heresies themselves play as it were the role of catalysts.[2]

In view, then, of the extreme complexity of the factors which go into the determination of what pertains to faith, the individual should not make the foolish mistake of identifying his own opinion as a truth of faith; for, in so doing, he may unduly characterize as requiring faith an assertion which can be clearly disproved by reason.[3] Accordingly, wherever one cannot rely upon the supernatural authority of divine revelation, he must follow the nature of things in whatever assertions he has to make.[4]

A rather interesting illustration of an opinion which Thomas does not relate to faith, and which, therefore, he discusses according to "the nature of things," can be drawn from the question about angels and bodies. The question arises from two different points of departure: (1) whether angels (and/or demons) have bodies; (2) whether the

---

[1] S.T. I, 32, 4c; II–II, 1, 7; 11, 2c. See also II–II, 2, 5–8.
[2] Contra Errores Graecorum Proemium, n. 1029.
[3] Q.D. de pot. 4, 1c.
[4] S.T. I, 99, 1c.

heavenly bodies, i.e. the planets and stars are animated or, if you prefer, living. Since we are not here interested in subtleties of the hylemorphic theory, we might simply state the conjoined question as follows: whether the stars and planets are living.

At first Thomas rejects the possibility as an "error of the philosophers."[1] Then, still taking the negative himself, he agrees with Augustine that it is an open question and does not pertain to the faith one way or the other.[2] In the *De Potentia* (1259–1268) he notes that Jerome and Origen take the affirmative along with Plato and Aristotle and that the modern (theologians) tend to take the negative; he himself still follows Augustine's view as "more reasonable" and leaves the question open.[3] In the Prima Pars (1266–1268) he again notes the diversity of opinion both among philosophers and among Doctors of the faith, then asserts on his own that the planets are animated but in an entirely different manner from that of "lower animals"; moreover, because of the equivocity involved, the traditional difference of opinion is more verbal than real.[4] In the *De Spiritualibus Creaturibus* (1268) he adds that there are probable arguments favoring either side of the question; but, though Augustine leaves it in doubt, there are spirits moving (*rectores spiritus*) the heavenly bodies, though the latter are not animated as are lower animals by their souls.[5] In his *De Anima* (1267–1271) he mentions John Damascene as forerunner of the view which is "more common among modern theologians" that the heavenly bodies are inanimate. Because of the arguments on both sides, he posits as certain (*pro firmo tenentes*) only that the heavenly bodies are moved by some intellectual being; but, as for himself, he goes along with Aristotle in holding that an intellectual substance without sensitive powers is the form of a heavenly body – that is, that heavenly bodies are living.[6] Thus, the opinion which Thomas at first rejected as an error of the philosophers and then, under the influence of Augustine, came to consider an open question, he finally seems to have favored against the common view of theologians and on the authority of the Philosopher.[7]

---

[1] *In II Sent.* d. 8, 1c.

[2] *C.G.* II, 70; *Q.D. de ver.* 5, 9 ad 14.

[3] *Q.D. de pot.* 6, 6c.

[4] *S.T.* I, 70, 3c.

[5] *Q.D. de spir. creat.* q. un., a. 6c.

[6] *Q.D. de an.* q. un., a. 8 ad 3.

[7] By here attempting at least a rough estimate of the historical development of Thomas's thought on this question, we come to a different conclusion than that of Litt, who maintains that Thomas simply remained in doubt as to the animation of the celestical bodies. See his *Les Corps Célestes dans l'Univers de S. Thomas* (Paris-Louvain, 1963), pp. 108–109.

From the foregoing example, to which others could readily be added, it is clear that Thomas recognizes a certain freedom for the "sons of God" with regard to whatever is not a doctrine of faith. In fact, his sense of freedom goes even so far as to encourage discussion of matters of doctrine. As we shall see in the next chapter, however, matters of doctrine are not subjected to dialectical disputation in order to determine whether they are true but merely to clarify the fact that they are true. Since the "sons of men" would be reluctant to admit such a restriction of their "academic freedom," they cannot be considered as having the same right to discuss matters of doctrine. Lacking faith, they thus lack the necessary prerequisite to discussing what pertains to faith. Needless to say, then, their opinions with regard to doctrines of faith cannot be regarded as having the same authority as do the opinions of believers. Faith, in short, entails a certain intellectual competence not available to one who lacks faith.

2. *The Psychology of Heresy*

If in fact the doctrines of faith can be stated in intelligible propositions, it is by no means obvious why the non-believer and *a fortiori* the heretic should be incapable of discussing these doctrines intelligently. To explain this intellectual incompetence of the heretic, Thomas suggests that there is some sort of moral disorder at the root of heretical thought.

In our discussion of the relationship between opinion and error we had occasion to refer to a passage from the *De Malo* in which, we noted, Thomas is laying the groundwork for a kind of epistemology of heresy.[1] In this passage, it will be recalled, Thomas speaks of *nescience* as the simple non-possession of knowledge and of *ignorance* as the privation of knowledge of which one is capable. To these he then adds *perverse ignorance*, which is a habit of false principles and false opinions as a result of which one is impeded from knowing the truth, and *error*, which is the actual expression of perverse ignorance in a false proposition. Now, in a subsequent passage in the same work, he repeats these distinctions and identifies heresy as error in the sense indicated.[2] The specificity of heresy, he says, consists materially in the fact that the error is about something which pertains to the faith and formally in the fact that the person (knowing, of course, that the faith is involved)

---

[1] The passage in question is *Q.D. de malo* 3, 7c. See above, ch. 2, p. 70 and fn.
[2] *Q.D. de malo* 8, 1 ad 7.

remains pertinaceous in his error. "This pertinacity," Thomas suggests, "arises from pride. For there is great pride in that a man prefer his own insight (*sensum suum*) to truth divinely revealed." [1]

This, of course, is the heresy of the informed, the educated, the man who knows enough to know better. His heresy, which is explained as intellectual pride, is not to be confused with that of the uninformed. The latter's heresy is due rather to vice and concern for bodily well-being:

> Therefore that heresy which is due to simple ignorance, if in fact it is a sin, springs from some one of the aforementioned vices [the seven capital sins]. For, it is imputed to a man as sin if he does not bother to learn what he is bound to know. But (such indifference) is apparently the result of materialistic self-interest (*accidia*), which has to do with an aversion to one's spiritual good insofar as this is a hindrance to bodily well-being. [2]

Implied in this simplistic analysis of heresy are, of course, a host of hidden presuppositions, all of which boil down to the obviousness of Catholic doctrine both as divine and as revelation. In view of Thomas's constant and clear insistence upon the supernatural character of divine revelation on the one hand and of faith on the other, this narrow-minded evaluation of the motives of the non-believer must be understood in function of his teachings on the influence of divine grace upon man's intellectual processes; but this latter we leave to the consideration of theologians. From our more restricted point of view, it is enough to note that, although Thomas insists that the object of faith is not propositions about God but God himself, he makes little use of this richly suggestive observation in his considerations of heresy. [3]

Thomas is, of course, aware of the fact that the so-called heretic may be just as convinced of the truth of his convictions as is the orthodox Christian of the truth of his. This, however, does not complicate matters for Thomas; it only confounds the woes of the heretic. Having explained away the doubts of the orthodox faithful by transferring certitude to God, Thomas explains the certitude of the heretic – *which, in this instance, he calls "certitude of adherence"* – simply as a formally unjustifiable fact. From this point of view, certitude is not the

---

[1] *Q.D. de malo* 8, 1 ad 7: "... quae quidem pertinacia ex superbia oritur; magna enim superbia est ut homo sensum suum praeferat veritati divinitus revelatae." For the notion of pertinacity see *S.T.* II–II, 138, 2. See also II–II, 11, 1 ad 2.

[2] *Q.D. de malo* 8, 1 ad 7: "Haeresis ergo ex simplici ignorantia proveniens, si sit peccatum, ex aliquo praedictorum vitiorum exoritur. Imputatur enim homini ad peccatum, si non curat addiscere ea quae scire tenetur. Videtur autem hoc ex accidia provenire, ad quam pertinet refugere spirituale bonum, in quantum est impeditivum boni corporalis." See also *S.T.* II–II, 11, 1 ad 3.

[3] *S.T.* II–II, 1, 1c; 1, 2 ad 2; 6 ad 2; qq. 10 and 11.

prerogative of faith but can be the effect of any of Aristotle's intellectual virtues as well as of "false faith." But "false faith" is not a virtue; and hence, appearances to the contrary, the firm adherence of the heretic to his own religious convictions is not an act of virtue but merely the result of his own arbitrary choice.[1] In other words, the "faith" of a heretic is not a virtue in fact (*secundum veritatem*), however much it may be considered such by men (*secundum opinionem hominum*). That is to say, his faith is not "true" but only "apparent." [2]

This, then, being Thomas's theoretical attitude towards unbelief in general and heresy in particular, it can almost be presupposed that, in his eyes, the thought of those afflicted with this particular vice could hardly be placed on a par with that of "the saints." The limitations of our study prevent us from entering into a detailed analysis of Thomas's attitude towards the thought of the Arabs in terms of its being viewed as that of infidels.[3] In any event, as we have already suggested, Thomas's preference for Aristotle over his Arabian commentators is to some extent due to the fact that the Philosopher had not been called to explicit faith in Christ, whereas the Arabs had been so called. Thus the notion of unbelief is applicable to the Arabs but not to Aristotle. The latter, accordingly, is looked to for the pure essence of what can be known by reason alone. The Arabs, on the other hand, must be approached with great caution. For, their thought derives not from pure reason alone but from reason tainted by unbelief.[4]

---

[1] *Quodl.* 6, q. 4, a. un. c.

[2] *Quodl.* 6, q. 4, a. un. ad 2; *In De Trin.* I, c. 1, n. 4. For a more detailed consideration of Thomas's attitude towards heresy, especially with regard to practical consequences, see Jacques Leclercq, *La Liberté d'Opinion et les Catholiques* (Paris, 1963), pp. 120–139.

[3] We have referred to Thomas's somewhat cavalier treatment of Averroes's views on the progress of human knowledge, and are also aware of at least one occasion on which Thomas refers to one of the same writer's views as "ridiculous" – neither of which approaches would he be likely to use with regard to the opinions of "the saints." On the other hand, the aspect of antiquity enters into the latter category, with the result that Thomas can direct himself to his contemporary Christians with all the vehemence of his *Contra Impugnantes Dei Cultum et Religionem*. Accordingly, much further study would be required before anything substantial could be said on the relationship between Thomas's theory of unbelief and his approach to non-Christian thinkers, in particular the Arabs.

[4] This attitude of confidence in the ancients for the purity of their thought coupled with mistrust of more contemporary non-Christian thinkers is by no means confined to the thirteenth century. It has lived on right down to our own day, and is found at times in the most unexpected places. For an interesting example of what we have in mind, see Yves Congar, *La Foi et la Théologie* (Tournai, Belgium, 1962), pp. 177–179.

3. Moses Maimonides and the Jews

That there may be something to this conjecture with regard to the Arabs is at least indicated by Thomas's attitude towards the great Jewish scholar, Rabbi Moses Maimonides, who is known to Thomas, whether directly or indirectly, as Rabbi Moyses. To state the matter simply and bluntly, Thomas usually has nothing but scorn for anything which comes forth from the mouth of Maimonides.

If the Rabbi would suggest from Scripture (a device not unknown to Thomas) that the heavens are animated, Thomas treats this as a "proof" and says that it is "frivolous." [1] If the Rabbi would say that we know God neither as he is in himself nor by demonstration but only by faith, Thomas says that this opinion is "manifestly false" because the opposite has been proven by the philosophers with "irrefragible arguments." [2] If the Rabbi would hold that human language signifies God only insofar as there is a similarity of effects to God and thus by way of negation, Thomas gives the impression that he is simply rejecting this in favor of the view of "Dionysius." [3] If the Rabbi would suggest that the vision of angels to men was visionary rather than real, Thomas simply notes that "this position does not preserve the truth of Scripture." [4] If (somewhat dubiously) the Rabbi is said to hold that God moves bodies and bodies have no power to move themselves, Thomas says the position is "stupid" and that it is "contradicted by the sayings of philosophers and saints." [5]

In general, then, Thomas's approach to the Rabbi tends to be somewhat negative, especially by comparison to his conciliatory efforts to see "the saints" always in the best possible light. The fact of the matter is that for Thomas Moses Maimonides is of little worth in interpreting Scripture and of less worth in matters of philosophy.[6] More generally speaking, the works of Thomas as a whole are marked

---

[1] Q.D. de an. q. un, a. 8 ad 19.

[2] Q.D. de ver. 10, 12.

[3] Q.D. de pot. 7, 5c; see ad 2 and 7, 7c.

[4] Q.D. de pot. 6, 7c: "haec positio veritatem Scripturae non salvat."

[5] Q.D. de ver. 5, 9 ad 4: "haec positio stulta est cum auferat rebus omnibus naturales operationes; et contrariatur dictis philosophorum et sanctorum."

[6] It must be admitted, however, that Thomas is pleased with Maimonides' rejection of an eternal world. See In II Sent. d. 1, q. 2, a. 3, quaest. 1; Resp. de Art. CVIII q. 97, n. 924. Etienne Gilson also likes to point out that Maimonides is the source of Thomas's ideas on the need for revelation: The Elements of Christian Philosophy (New York, 1963), p. 312: Note 4 to Chapter 2. Thomas, to be sure, admits this dependence in Q.D. de ver. 14, 10c, but not in S.T. I, 1, 1c nor in C.G. I, 4. See, however, S.T. I–II, 101, 3 ad 3.

by a complete absence of any reference to the vast literature of Talmudic and halakhic interpretation.

It is perhaps not irrelevant to this consideration that, while recognizing a canon law against forcing anyone to accept the faith, Thomas is so taken with the excellence of belonging to the fold that he rather likes the idea of "inducing the Jews of their own free will to obligate themselves by oath or by vow to receive baptism." For, as he facilely reasons, there is no force involved in getting someone to promise what is, after all, for his own good. Thus, he says, "no one in his right mind" would say that such a procedure is illicit.[1]

An attitude of this kind is perhaps best seen within its immediate historical context. For, it was not too many years before, in the year 1240, and in the same university city of Paris, that a most significant debate took place between Christian and Jewish scholars, to the subsequent detriment of the Jewish community as a whole. Through the instigation of a Jewish apostate working through the Inquisition, Rabbis Yehiel of Paris and Moses of Coucy, together with two other colleagues, were forced to show that their teachings did not in fact encourage hatred of and crimes against Christians. Questions posed to the Jews were based not upon the actual attitudes and practices of the Jews, but (with shrewd disputational skill) upon talmudic dicta which the Jewish halakhists themselves (especially Rabbi Moses of Coucy) had been striving to modify in accordance with traditional methods of casuistry. The whole debate is a marvelous illustration of medieval verbal dialectic, complete with *ad hoc* arguments based not on the proponents's convictions but upon the assumptions of the opponent. As might be imagined, the encounter pushed the halakhists to seek still further justifications for tolerating Christians. But, more important to our purpose, it also seems to have turned the Christians from an attitude of comparative tolerance and towards more critical investigations of Jewish customs and tenets.[2] To what extent this

---

[1] *Contra Retrah.* c. 13, n. 822: "Per votum autem aut iuramentum non infertur homini vis, sed ex eis voluntas hominis confirmatur in bonum: unde per hoc non redditur homo invitus, sed magis firmiter volens; et iam incipit homo quodammodo facere, inquantum se obligat ad faciendum. Et per hunc etiam modum nullus sanae mentis diceret esse illicitum inducere Judaeos ut se propria voluntate obligarent vel iuramento vel voto ad accipiendum baptismum." See also *S.T.* II–II, 10, 8c; 12.

[2] For a thorough discussion of this incident in the general context of Jewish-Christian relations during the Middle Ages, see J. Katz, *Exclusiveness and Tolerance: Studies in Jewish-Gentile Relations in Medieval and Modern Times*, Scripta Judaica III (New York, 1961). Katz also provides ample bibliography for more detailed study of the question. To Katz's bibliography, however, must be added in particular B. Blumenkranz, *Les Auteurs chrétiens latins du Moyen-Age sur les Juifs et le Judaïsme* (London, 1963).

historical change had an influence upon the attitude of Thomas himself can only be judged, of course, by what little he says in his writings.

D. INADEQUACY OF AUTHORITY AS A CRITERION OF PROBABILITY

The foregoing considerations suggest quite a number of difficult problems, and to some of these we have made allusion in passing. The scope of these problems is so vast, however, that it is necessary to bring back into focus our purpose in undertaking these considerations. We are concerned with Thomas's notion of probability, which is intimately related to that of opinion. Having seen in the preceding chapter that man must strive to go beyond the limitations of opinion, we then pointed out that he can do this only by taking opinions themselves as his point of departure. This being the case, we were then led to investigate the question as to which opinions Thomas would consider most valuable to the search for truth. For, as we noted at the conclusion of Chapter Two, what is needed is the best of what the best men think. We are now able to say that for Thomas "the saints" are of more help in this regard than are "the philosophers," and of all the philosophers Aristotle is the chief source of truth.

Now, should it be necessary to point this out, what we are here involved in are to a large extent nothing more than socio-historical categories. And however important these categories may be to Thomas, they are not of themselves an adequate criterion for the attainment of probability, to say nothing of definitive truth. In other words, they do not of themselves provide an adequate basis for a permanently valid theory of probability. For, what we have here been considering is in effect the background for Thomas's argument from authority; and, even allowing for prerogatives of faith, man's evaluation of what is authoritative does change.[1]

To close this chapter, then, we propose to point out from a consideration of Thomas himself the weaknesses inherent in a notion of probability that is based primarily upon an extrinsic attribution of authority to the opinion or opinions in question. In Thomas's case, such extrinsic attribution of authority involves two general presuppositions: (1) that

---

[1] As we shall see at length in the following chapter, Thomas is well aware of the limitations of authority in this regard. His awareness, however, is not so great as to prevent him from thinking in terms of what he himself considers authoritative. And this is the issue for the moment.

there are two distinct traditions; (2) that one of these is of greater authority than the other. We shall, then, direct our observations to these two presuppositions.

1. Flaws in the Distinction between Traditions

To begin with, there are for Thomas two distinct traditions, two distinct sources of authority, to which he may appeal for support of his own opinions, namely, the authority of the philosophers and the authority of the saints. And thus it is, as we have already had occasion to note, that one so often finds in Thomas's writings the familiar two-pronged argument from authority, used either affirmatively or negatively: both the saints and the philosophers agree with this position; this position is against the opinion of both saints and philosophers.[1] This basic formulation undergoes various modulations or modifications, usually by reducing one or the other tradition to its principal authority: that is, "the philosophers" may be reduced simply to "Aristotle," and "the saints" may be reduced simply to "the teaching of faith" or to "Sacred Scripture."[2] But the basic idea remains the same: Thomas presupposes that he is drawing upon two distinct traditions for argumentative support.

As evidence for the distinction between these two traditions Thomas likes to point to the fact that the position of "the philosophers" and that of "the saints" differs on a variety of questions. Consider, for example, the following. For the philosopher, notes Thomas, wisdom is speculative, whereas for the believer it is not only speculative but practical.[3] Similarly, the believer considers creatures differently than does the philosopher.[4] Again, the views of the philosophers as to what angels know is different from the views of theologians.[5] Both saints and philosophers agree that angels help God govern corporeal creatures; but, whereas some philosophers posit that angels can create, the opinion of the saints is rather that angels have an effect upon lower creatures only mediately, by moving the heavenly bodies.[6] Related to the latter difference about creation is the fact that since the philosophers believe

---

[1] *C.G.* II, 4; III, 85; *Q.D. de ver.* 5, 8c; 9 ad 4; 18, 5 ad 8; *In de Trin.* 6, 4 obj. 5; *Q.D. de an. q. un. a.* 8 ad 3; *Quodl.* 4, q. 2, a. 2; 9, q. 5, a. 1c; *Contra Retrah.* c. 3, n. 748; c. 5, n. 756; 9, n. 799; *S.T.* I–II, 61, 3c; *Q.D. de pot'* 6, 3c; *In De div. nom.,* c. 2, l. 2, n. 151.
[2] *Quodl.* 3, q. 5, a. 3 *in contr.;* *Q.D. de ver.* 18, 5 ad 8.
[3] *S.T.* II–II, 19, 7c. See also I, 1, 4 and 6; II–II, 45, 6 ad 3.
[4] *C.G.* II, 4.
[5] *Q.D. de ver.* 16, 1c.
[6] *Q.D. de ver.* 5, 8c. See also *Q.D. de pot.* 1, 4c, ad 1 and ad 4; and compare 6, 3c.

higher intelligences create lower, they can explain how angels know one another on the basis of an argument not available to the saints.[1] So also, philosophers and saints do not mean the same thing when they say that angels know material things.[2] With regard to the respective analyses of man, the theological notion of grace is unknown to philosophers, who consider only those things in the soul which are proportionate to human nature.[3] Similarly, virtues are considered differently by philosophers and by theologians, and the two groups of thinkers also understand man's ultimate good differently (according as it is proportionate to or exceeding human powers).[4] Philosophers do not posit any habits in the will, whereas theologians say that charity is in the will.[5] Finally, for the moral philosophers sin is considered insofar as it is contrary to reason, whereas the theologian views sin especially insofar as it is an offense against God.[6]

Now, however accurate Thomas's historical judgment might have been at the time in question as to the division of opinion between "saints" and "philosophers," that judgment simply is no longer applicable. The socio-historical categories in terms of which he divides the opinions of men are no longer meaningful; or, if in some way still meaningful, they are by no means adequate to categorize all the differences of opinion that stem from a variety of traditions unknown to Thomas. Moreover, if we leave aside the factor of historical conditions, we can find absolutely no reason, from a logical point of view, for the fact that a "philosopher" holds one opinion and a "saint" another. Given different historical circumstances, the position attributed to either might well have been just the reverse. In short, the distinction between "saints" and "philosophers" is of no value for determining the intrinsic probability of a proposition. This distinction has only extrinsic value, insofar as the audience addressed accepts the socio-historical categorization involved and considers it significant in the determination of probability.

That the categories of "saint" and "philosopher" provide no more than an extrinsic criterion of probability can further be shown from the fact that, logically speaking, the way in which Thomas attributes probability to the opinion of a "saint" is in no way different from the

---

[1] Q.D. de ver. 8, 7c.
[2] Q.D. de ver. 8, 8c.
[3] Q.D. de ver. 27, 2 ad 7.
[4] Q.D. de ver. 14, 3c; 6 ad 5.
[5] Q.D. de ver. 24, 4 ad 9. See, however, S.T. II–II, 58, 4.
[6] S.T. I–II, 71, 6 ad 5.

way in which he would attribute probability to the opinion of a philosopher. In other words, even though he presupposes that the tradition of "the saints" is more probable than that of "the philosophers," he is constrained by the exigencies of language and logic to make some opinions of the saints more probable than others. Thus, in dealing with the question as to whether the *caelum empyreum* has an influence upon lower bodies, he has to admit that the negative opinion of some is "rather probable" (*satis probabile*), but feels that, in the light of "Dionysius's" theory of hierarchy, it is "more probable" (*probabilius*) that there is some influence.[1] He expresses the view that the teachings of faith favor admitting that men's souls after death know "separate substances"; for, he says, since it does not seem probable that the souls of the damned have no knowledge of demons, it therefore seems "much less probable" (*multo minus probabile*) that the good souls would not know the angels.[2] In arguing for the doctrine of original sin, he rejects the opinion that human defects are merely natural; for, if one presupposes divine providence, it is "rather probable" that God would remove such defects were it not for original sin.[3] He also feels that one can say "probably" that the guardian angel of a pregnant woman also looks after the infant in her womb.[4] And when he evaluates three different opinions as to what happens to the drop of water added to the wine at Mass, he takes to be "more probable" the opinion of those who say that the water is converted first into wine and then into the blood of Christ.[5] As a final example, when faced with various opinions as to the location of Paradise, Thomas rejects the view of those who "opine" that it is along the equator, because Aristotle says, and this is "more probable," that such a place would be too hot. Thomas does not commit himself as to the precise locality, but says it must be believed that Paradise is in the most temperate locality, wherever that might be.[6]

Now, anyone not impressed by the distinction between "saints" and "philosophers" would have great difficulty recognizing a difference, from the point of view of formal logic, between probability as used above and probability as used with regard to opinions of "the philosophers." That the content of the propositions might not be found in

[1] *S.T.* I, 66, 3 ad 2. See I, 10, 6; 47, 2; 50, 4.
[2] *Q.D. de an.* q. un., a. 17c.
[3] *C.G.* IV, 52.
[4] *S.T.* I, 113, 5 ad 3. See also 114, 5c.
[5] *S.T.* III, 74, 8c.
[6] *S.T.* I, 102, 2 ad 4.

propositions put forth by the philosophers is perfectly true; but, as already suggested, this fact is of secondary importance and can be quite well explained on the basis of socio-historical factors irrelevant to logical structure as such. The difficulty of maintaining any such distinction is further complicated by the fact that in the discussion of Paradise (and Thomas's writings are filled with similar cases) the authority of Aristotle, a philosopher, is introduced to determine the probability of a proposition which is supposedly proper to the tradition of the saints. But we shall have more to say about this in connection with the presupposed superiority of the saintly tradition.

2. Flaws in the Superiority of the Saintly Tradition

As the discussion about Paradise well illustrates, Thomas does make use of and interests himself in the tradition of the philosophers; but he identifies himself with that of the saints. The manner in which he considers many questions often involves a curious mingling of the two traditions, but never in such a way that the sacred tradition comes out second best. To keep the same example, Thomas does call upon Aristotle for support in his contention that Paradise is not around the equator; but the whole discussion is based upon Augustine's assertion to the effect that Paradise is a real place and that it is "in the most noble locality in the whole world." [1] In other words, even where the two traditions are mingled, that of the saints enjoys a certain priority.

The priority of the saintly tradition is, in turn, based upon the assumption that it has attained a deeper understanding of truth than has that of the philosophers. This is well illustrated by the following example. After noting Augustine's warning about human frailty when it comes to questions about what angels can or cannot do, Thomas points out (thus guarding the prerogatives of the saintly tradition) that philosophers also disagree in their views about such things. To the extent that philosophers recognize that angels can move the celestial bodies they are in accord with the outlook of faith (*fidei sententia*); faith simply goes farther in saying that angels – subject, of course, to God – can also move other bodies.[2]

Thomas's hierarchy of authorities is, however, even more amply illustrated by his analysis of the *Liber de Causis*, which in this regard is a kind of Exhibit A. Here we have Thomas faced with a work which

[1] S.T. I, 102, 2 ad 4; 1c.
[2] Q.D. de pot. 6, 3c.

had long been attributed to Aristotle but which contains opinions unacceptable to the medieval Christian. The task of the theologian committed to the compatibility of Aristotle with Christian faith (at least for the most part) is therefore clear, and Thomas does a fine piece of textual criticism to show that the work is in fact neo-Platonic and heavily dependent upon Proclus. But what really shines through Thomas's study of this work is his evaluation of the traditions: that of faith over that of the philosophers; and, among the philosophers, that of Aristotle over all others. To show this in detail it is almost necessary to give the whole commentary as a reference. However, in lieu of that, it is perhaps sufficient for us to indicate a few twists and turns of Thomas's critique. In the work he finds now a position which is repugnant to the truth and to the opinion (*sententia*) of Aristotle, now places where the author seems to follow the views of Platonists or of "Dionysius" in particular, now an opinion contrary to that of Aristotle.[1] Now the author discusses a matter in regard to which the opinion of Aristotle is more in accord with Christian faith, or with Catholic doctrine; and now the author gives a proof which, though conceded by some philosophers (including, in fact, Aristotle), is not necessary, namely, the argument to the effect that the world is eternal.[2] In the process of this critique, Thomas succeeds rather well in making his point about the neo-Platonic roots of the *De Causis*. But, what is of interest to us, he also reveals implicitly his scale of values with regard to the traditions with which he deals; and that of the saints, that of faith, is given clear priority.

Granting, then, for the sake of discussion that the tradition of "the saints" is superior to that of "the philosophers," we now propose to show that to base an argument upon this superior authority, as Thomas often does either explicitly or implicitly, presents serious difficulties. For, this assumption of superiority: (1) can lead to unwarranted justifications of what is objectively evil; (2) cannot explain the fact that "saints" at times fall into the same errors as do "philosophers"; (3) cannot explain except on the most tenuous grounds how a "philosopher" might know something apparently not known or not known as well by "the saints." At the very least, these difficulties are so great as to make the assumption of superiority valueless for what the moderns would call an objective theory of probability.

---

[1] *In De Causis* II, l. 2, nn. 53–56; III, l. 3, n. 83; IV, l. 4, nn. 102 and 121; V, l. 5, nn. 35 and 141.

[2] *In De Causis* X, l. 10, n. 241; XI, l. 11, n. 264; XIII, l. 13, n. 289; XVIII, l. 18, nn. 344–345.

(a) Superiority as a Justification of Evil

With regard to the justification of evil, take for example the question of the liceity of war, in dealing with which Thomas involves himself in an utterly dismaying abuse of the authority of "the saints." Says Thomas on the subject, if good men could not keep their peace of heart in war, then all wars would be illicit.[1] Since, however, "the saints" wage war, and the saints are good men, one need not doubt that men can fight a war and keep their peace of heart. In particular, such violence is justified against "sinners," since, after all, "the saints" engage in such activities (obviously, since they are saints) for the sinners' own good. When the saints wage war, they act not out of hate, but out of love.[2] Without involving ourselves in unnecessary comment, let us merely note that the best part of this whole discussion is the beautiful objections so handily demolished by Thomas's dialectics.

(b) Error in the Superior Tradition

In the second place, on the assumption of superiority it is extremely difficult to explain how "the saints" could fall into the same errors as "the philosophers." Indeed, it is difficult enough to explain, on this assumption, why the saints should even need to have recourse to the opinions of philosophers, as apparently they do. For, not only does this suggest that one tradition is not superior to the other but that in fact the two traditions are not even neatly distinct.

Thomas realizes full well, of course, that the two traditions with which he deals are not absolutely autonomous and independent entities. He certainly recognizes, for example, the "Platonism" in the thought of the Fathers, in particular in that of Augustine, of Boethius, and of "Dionysius."[3] But this is not in itself an insurmountable problem, so long as one avoid the implication that the saints are subordinate to the philosophers. In other words, similarity of opinion in some regards is not in itself an argument against the over-all superiority of the saintly tradition. It is only when the saints involve themselves in an error of the philosophers that the assumption of superiority is endangered.

If such be the case, Thomas will sometimes save a saint from embarrassment by pointing out, as he also does for Aristotle, that the

---

[1] *Contra Impugn.* c. 3 (15), n. 462. See also *S.T.* II–II, 10, 9c.

[2] *Contra Impugn.* c. 4 (16), n. 473.

[3] See, for example, *Q.D. de ver.* 21, 4 ad 3; *In De div. nom.* c. 5, l. 1, n. 634; *In De Trin* Proemium I, 1 ad 4.

saint in question is giving not his own view but the view of others.[1] Or, as he sometimes expresses it, this or that saint is merely recounting a less true, less probable opinion from the philosophical tradition without himself believing it.[2] In some instances, of course, this could very well be the case; but it is worth noting that, with the exception of Aristotle, Thomas does not make similar observations about the less felicitous opinions of the non-baptized.

Be that as it may, it is not always so easy, however much one may desire it, to exonerate a saint from an error found in the philosophers. In such cases Thomas seems to feel that, cost what it may, honesty is the best policy. For example, in his commentary on the *De Divinis Nominibus* Thomas clearly recognizes that "Dionysius" follows the Platonists in many things; but he will not admit that the saint might have been taken in to such an extent as to hold that demons have sense faculties. In a later work, however, he concedes that, since "Dionysius" followed Platonic opinion (*sententiae Platonicae*) in many things, it is "rather probable" that he did in fact go along with the animality of demons.[3]

Such weakness on the part of a saint is, of course, somewhat unpleasant for Thomas, especially inasmuch as for him Aristotle is the Philosopher and therefore it were better for the saints not to have involved themselves in Platonic thought. For, to use an expression which we find only once in Thomas (and in an objection at that) some philosophers are "more probable" than others.[4] As the expression is used, it suggests greater *probity* and hence, on the part of the saints, stronger *approbation*, insofar as these philosophers have opinions more in keeping with the teachings (as then understood, of course) of faith. That any philosopher could be more probable, in this sense, than Aristotle is for Thomas rather unthinkable – or, to use a term which will be developed in the next chapter, *inopinabile*.

(c) Superior Knowledge in the Inferior Tradition

In any event, there is, in the third place, a still greater difficulty with regard to the assumption that the saintly tradition is superior to that of the philosophers. It is, of course, bad enough that saints sometimes

---

[1] See *Q.D. de an.* q. un., a. 7 ad 1; a. 9 ad 5 and ad 12; *Q.D. de pot.* 5, 4c; 10, 5 ad 2.
[2] See *In De div. nom.* c. 2, l. 2, n. 151. Note also how deeply Thomas digs for some element of truth in an opinion of Peter Lombard which, taken as it stands, Thomas does not wish to accept: *Q.D. de pot.* 9, 7c.
[3] *In De div. nom.* c. 4, l. 19, n. 538; *Q.D. de malo* 16, 1 ad 3.
[4] *S.T.* I, 46, 2 obj. 1.

adhere to the same erroneous opinion as do philosophers. But even worse is the fact that the knowledge of the philosophers seems in some respects to be vastly superior to that of the saints. In fact, the philosophers sometimes manifest a knowledge even more profound than that of God's chosen spokesmen who have written the canonical Scriptures. To suppose that this apparent superiority might in fact be real is unthinkable for Thomas, especially in view of his conviction that these sacred writers, these prophets, were somehow in direct contact with the divine knowledge itself.

The problem thus posed, of course, is that of faith versus science; and throughout the period of nascent Christianity, up to and including the time of Thomas, the chief mathematical science was astronomy.[1] How, then, account for the fact that the philosophers seem to have a superior knowledge of astronomy than did, for example, Moses?

One way, of course, is to say that astronomy is, after all, just a hypothetical system which saves the appearances, thus making of astronomy a practical instrument rather than a statement about the universe as such. This convenient and most common approach, which Thomas himself uses on occasion, enables one to avoid a direct confrontation with the problem – so long, at least, as there is no Galileo to claim epistemic truth for astronomy.[2] But Thomas is by no means restricted to this one explanation. Sometimes, instead of questioning the knowledge of the philosophers, he simply attributes the difficulty to hermeneutical failure to comprehend what is certainly contained in Scripture; at other times, he admits that truths known by the philosophers are not recorded in Scripture – not because of any ignorance on the part of the sacred writer, but because of his pastoral concern for the limited intellectual capacity of his audience. We shall say a few words about each of the two latter approaches.[3]

---

[1] For an account of medieval astronomy and Thomas's knowledge thereof see Thomas Litt, *Les corps célestes dans l'univers de saint Thomas* (Paris-Louvain, 1963), pp. 293–372. See also J. G. E. Dreyer, "Medieval Cosmology," in *Theories of the Universe* (ed. Milton K. Munitz: New York, 1957), pp. 115–138.

[2] See Litt, *Les corps célestes*, pp. 361–366.

[3] For a general consideration of problems involved in the evaluation of astronomical hypotheses see A. Sesmat, "Controverses médiévales sur la valeur des hypothèses astronomiques," *Revue de Philosophie* 38 (1938): 381–409. A more detailed consideration of Thomas's attitude towards astronomical hypotheses will be found in Litt, *Les corps célestes*, Ch. 18. Litt's collection of texts and knowledgeable evaluation of what they signify is remarkable. His treatment of the subject suffers, however, from a failure to take into consideration Thomas's disputational attitude towards these hypotheses. Whatever their scientific importance, they were only indirectly of interest to Thomas; for, his first concern was simply the defense of his faith.

The first approach, which lays the blame on human incompetence, takes as its point of departure Augustine's dictum to the effect that the authority of Scripture is greater than the capacity of all human talent combined. Said specifically with regard to the problem of waters above the firmament, this hermeneutical principle reduces all efforts at interpretation to the level of opinion. And thus we find Thomas, in dealing with the question himself, rummaging through all sorts of different opinions, saintly and philosophical, ancient and modern. In the Prima Pars (1268), he agrees with Basil against Origen that the waters above the firmament are something corporeal, and accordingly devotes his attention to which of the four elements, if not Aristotle's fifth element, is involved.[1] In his fourth *Quodlibetal Question* (1269–1272) the question centers around what is meant by *above* the firmament; for, as he notes, the "modern philosophers" posit a ninth sphere, which is starless, above the eighth sphere of the stars. This modern view, he feels, is compatible with Augustine's opinion that "the waters" refers simply to corporeal matter of whatever kind. He then adds another interpretation, without identifying its proponent (since Augustine's authority is involved), to the effect that "the waters" simply means that there is *"diaphaneitas"* (reflection of light?) in the heavens. He then justifies this gentle divergence from Augustine by noting that any opinion is permissible so long as it "saves the truth of Sacred Scripture." [2]

The second approach, which attributes the silence of Scripture about a truth known by the philosopher to pastoral concern on the part of the biblical writer, is, of course, the more necessary the more obvious is the discrepancy and the more compelling the philosopher's authority. Take as an excellent example, the astronomical relationship between the stars and their sphere, which must be squared with Moses' assertion: "God said, 'Let there be lights in the firmament.'" [3] John Chrysostom had had to deal with Ptolemy's theory that the stars move independently of their sphere, and thus are not "fixed"; so he understood Moses as saying *where* the stars are but not *how* they are there. Thomas, however, has it on Aristotle's authority that the stars are fixed and move only insofar as the sphere revolves. This appears to Thomas to go beyond what Moses said, so Thomas posits that Moses was writing for

[1] *S.T.* I, 68, 2.
[2] *Quodl.* 4, q. 2, a. 2. Note especially the following: "Sic ergo secundum quamcumque opinionem potest veritas sacrae Scripturae salvari diversimodi. Unde non est coarctandus sensus sacrae Scripturae ad aliquid horum." .
[3] *Gen.* I: 14.

ordinary folk who see the movement not of spheres but of stars.[1] It is this same concern for the uneducated masses which kept Moses from mentioning air, angels, planets, and prime matter in his account of creation; for, though he knew about these things as well as any mere philosopher, his audience would not have understood.[2]

That these are *ad hoc* solutions to the basic problem is not too difficult to see, nor should it be supposed that Thomas is himself unaware of this fact. Even a lesser mind than his can recognize that the two positions are in fact mutually contradictory if expanded into general principles of interpretation. For, on the one hand he is saying that the truth (as known by the philosophers) *is* contained in Scripture, only we fail to see it; on the other hand, he is saying that the truth *is not* contained in Scripture, because the sacred writer (in particular, Moses) did not wish to confuse the unlearned with what they would not understand. We have here, then, another example of medieval dialectic at its best. Each particular question is answered to the extent required by the opponent and on the basis of presuppositions acceptable to the opponent. Fundamental to either of the foregoing hermeneutical approaches, of course, is the assumption that Moses did in fact know whatever any philosopher could ever discover.

Thus once again we are faced with a problem which is annoying and perhaps even inconceivable from the viewpoint of today's more matter-of-fact procedures. We have, namely, followed attentively what Thomas has to say on several questions which involve Scripture and the philosophers; and yet nothing he has said entitles us to conclude any more than that he is determined to defend the integrity of Scripture. What, then, does he really think? Does he even have what we like to call "an ultimate view" on this frequent object of his disputational skill? In the face of the obstacles, it would be hazardous to answer with a simple affirmative.

However, there is one text in the *De Potentia Dei* which more than any other appears to be a straightforward statement of Thomas's position – what we might call his "metadialectical" position.[3] The problem this time is to square the philosophers' teachings about matter with the account in Genesis of creation. Thomas opens with a review of certain warnings from Augustine apropos to such questions: (1) as to the truth of Scripture; (2) as to the literal sense.[4] The first

1 *S.T.* I, 70, 1 ad 3.
2 *S.T.* I, 68, 3c; *Q.D. de pot.* 3, 18c; 4, 2 ad 30, ad 31 and ad 34. See also *S.T.* I, 1, 9.
3 *Q.D. de pot.* 4, 1c.
4 *XII Confess.*

amounts to the familiar admonition not to ascribe to the faith what is only a personal opinion. The second refers the first specifically to Scripture, in that the latter must not be unnecessarily tied to one interpretation, false or even true. It is what Thomas says with regard to the latter, that is, "true" interpretations, that is of interest to us.

Noting that a variety of valid interpretations are possible, and acknowledging the great wisdom of the philosophers, he stresses the apologetic value of leaving the way open for still other interpretations. This he justifies on the grounds that Scripture has many different meanings, or "senses" – a position difficult to maintain, perhaps, from a merely human point of view, but not so difficult if one grant that God, who knows all things, is the principal author of the sacred writings. Presupposing divine authorship, then, Thomas is even willing to admit that the philosophers might know things unknown to the sacred writers. For, with God on his side, what can he lose? By virtue of a multiplicity of meanings, one simply ties Scripture to the omniscience of God (in this instance, the Holy Spirit). And show us a philosopher who can stand up to divine omniscience! Behold, then, the ultimate justification of the superiority of "our" tradition over "theirs."

The text in question is, as should be apparent, so important that we must break the continuity of our discussion to make room here for at least the key section thereof:

... For, the dignity of divine Scripture is such that in one expression (*sub una littera*) many meanings are contained. As a result, so suited is Scripture to diverse intellectual milieux that any given individual is surprised to find the truth which he knows contained therein. This makes our defense against non-believers easier. For, if the manner in which someone interprets Sacred Scripture appears false to him, he can have recourse to some other meaning thereof. Whence the following is believable: God granted it to Moses and to the other authors of Sacred Scripture that whatever truths men might be able to learn they themselves knew, and that these (truths) they would express in one writing (*sub una serie litterae*). Thus, any one of (these truths) *is* the meaning of the author. Whence even if the interpreters of Sacred Scripture relate to the letter some truths which the (human) author did not know, those truths were surely known to the Holy Spirit, who is the principal author of divine Scripture. Accordingly, any truth which, taking into account the context, can be related to divine Scripture is the meaning thereof.[1]

---

[1] *Q.D. de pot.* 4, 1c: ... Hoc enim ad dignitatem divinae Scripturae pertinet, ut sub una littera multos sensus contineat, ut sic et diversis intellectibus hominum conveniat, ut unusquisque miretur se in divina Scriptura posse invenire veritatem quam mente conceperit; et per hoc etiam contra infideles facilius defendatur, dum si aliquid, quod quisque ex sacra Scriptura velit intelligere, falsum apparuerit, ad alium eius sensum possit haberi recursus. Unde non est incredibile, Moysi et aliis sacrae Scripturae auctoribus hoc divinitus esse concessum ut diversa vera, quae homines possent intelligere, ipsi cognoscerent, et ea sub una serie litterae designarent, ut sic quilibet eorum sit sensus auctoris. Unde si etiam aliqua vera ab expositoribus sacrae Scripturae litterae optentur, quae auctor non intelligit, non est

Thus does Thomas go beyond the *ad hoc* measures which suffice for dialectical disputation, especially that based upon the wisdom of Moses, to plead his case before the divine tribunal. From the viewpoint of dialectics as such, this is nothing more than an appeal to the highest authority. It is a good tactical maneuvre, and cannot but guarantee a successful case – providing, of course, that one is pleading before a Christian jury.

Thomas, in short, finds himself heir to two traditions. And, with regard to these two traditions, he more or less takes it for granted (1) that the two traditions are essentially distinct and (2) that the tradition of the saints is superior to that of the philosophers. There are, however, great difficulties connected with these presuppositions. For, (1) the presupposed distinction is by no means neat and clearcut and (2) the presupposed superiority is not easily defended.

Be that as it may, we do not wish to leave even a momentary impression that Thomas's theory of probability is nothing more than an evaluation and choice of opinions. As we have already noted and will presently be discussing in detail, his dialectical methodology goes much deeper than that. Nonetheless, it cannot be denied that the manner in which Thomas weights opinions according to the tradition to which they appertain does play a role, however secondary, in his decisions as to what is or is not probable. Accordingly, since probability is a function of opinion, it has been necessary for us to consider how Thomas weights opinions. In the light of these considerations we might now observe that this weighting of opinion is far more on the level of implicit presupposition than on the level of explicit declaration. For, involved in Thomas's every thought is the whole framework of medieval dialectic, which serves in his hands to defend the superiority of the divine over the human, of the saints over the philosophers. In short, Thomas is by profession a theologian; and, as he sees it, the task of the theologian is a dialectical defense of Christian faith.

dubium quin Spiritus sanctus intellexerit, qui est principalis auctor divinae Scripturae. Unde omnis veritas quae, salva litterae circumstantia, potest divinae Scripturae aptari, est eius sensus." See also *S.T.* I, 1, 10; *Quodl.* 3, q. 14, a. 1; 7, q. 6; *In* I *Sent.* Prol., a. 5; IV, d. 21, q. 1, a. 2, q. 1a 1 ad 3.

CHAPTER IV

PROBABILITY IN DISPUTATION
AND DEMONSTRATION

From our consideration of tradition as a source of opinion and probability, we have seen that Thomas weights different opinions differently according to the probability – or, if you will, the probity – of the authority or authorities who support the opinion in question. In effect, the previous chapter amounted to a consideration of the argument from authority as found in Thomas Aquinas; and, in the light of this consideration, it should be clear that authority plays an important role in Thomas's thought and methodology. But this is in no way meant to imply that Thomas would consider authority (his own or others') a sufficient criterion for the determination of truth. Authority, even multiple authority, is but a sign, a pointer towards the truth. The establishment of truth cannot be accomplished except by means of argumentation which results in demonstration.

A. OPINION, PROBABILITY AND DISPUTATION

That an argument from authority as such cannot of itself be determinative of the truth Thomas points out in a variety of ways. For one thing, authority (*auctoritates*) is useless in arguing against those who do not accept the authority in question.[1] And, as Thomas has occasion to note in his commentary on the *Politics*, teachers do not readily yield to authority.[2] What is directly in question here, of course, is political authority; yet the reason for such reluctance on the part of teachers is surely their insistence on appropriate proof. In the second place, even if one accepts the authority in question, be that authority God himself (as in the case of faith), an argument or proof based on such authority is not a demonstration; it simply makes an

---

[1] *De rat. fidei* c. 1 (Proemium), n. 955.
[2] *In* IV *Polit.* l. 10, n. 631.

opinion credible.[1] Thirdly, even the fact that an opinion is widely accepted, and hence probable because so widely accepted, does not guarantee the truth of the opinion; for, it sometimes happens that what is acceptable to many (*pluribus opinabile*) is not true as it stands (*simpliciter verum*).[2] In other words, truth and falsity cannot be determined on the basis of common acceptance. Putting all this together, we are left with the conclusion that one must go deeper than mere authority. The means of going deeper is dialectic, and the motive in the conviction that there is truth to be discovered.

1. Contradiction, Truth and Disputation

This resource to dialectic, that is, to dialectical disputation, as a means to the discovery of truth is not a wholly artificial procedure but has its roots in man's disagreement with his fellow man. It is a matter of common experience that men disagree with one another, that some hold one opinion and some hold the contrary, that what is affirmed by some is denied by others. The question, then, is not whether men disagree with one another but rather, what is one to think about this disagreement and what is one to do about it.

One might, of course, adopt the view which Thomas (after Aristotle) attributes to Pythagoras (but which did not die with him) that truth is whatever seems true to me, and falsity is whatever seems false to me.[3] This amounts to saying that definitive truth is unattainable and that, accordingly, I must make do with what seems to be the case according to my own lights, however bright or dim they may be. That such a view has been entertained from time to time in the history of thought, not excluding our own day, need hardly be defended here. What is important is that for Thomas such a view entails the very death of the intellect, the anullment of reason, the reduction of man to the level of the beasts. For, to say that the opinion which I hold is true (for me) and the opposite opinion held by another is true (for him) is to say ultimately that all opinions are equally true or, what comes to the same thing, equally false. Not only does this drain the notion of truth of all significance; but, what is even more disastrous, it throws out of the

---

[1] *Quodl.* 3, q. 14, a. 2 ad 1: "Probare autem per auctoritatem, non est demonstrative probare, sed fide rei opinionem facere." See also a. 2 c.

[2] *In* IV *Met.* ll. 11–14 and esp. l. 11, n. 671: ". . . judicium certum de veritate non convenienter potest sumi ex multitudine et paucitate, ut scilicet dicatur esse verum quod multis videtur, falsum autem quod videtur paucis; cum quandoque illud quod est pluribus opinabile, non sit simpliciter verum."

[3] *In* IV *Met.* l. 9, nn. 661–662.

court of human discourse the foundational principle of non-contradiction. For, if the proposition which states my opinion and the contradictory proposition which states a contrary opinion are both true, then contradictories are simultaneously true and discussion is at an end.[1]

Unwilling to content himself with the intellectual despair that is implied in unmitigated relativism, Thomas turns to dialectic as man's ordinary means of transcending the claims of opposite opinions. For, as he notes in an ambiguous statement, love of truth must take precedence over love of self; and patience with (or, as we might say, toleration for) the views of others is no excuse for not having a zealous concern for truth.[2] Accordingly, if opposite opinions are held with regard to one and the same matter, then these opinions must be submitted to dialectical disputation, in order that the truth of the matter might be discovered for the greater benefit of all concerned. Needless to say, if the goal of dialectic were merely to raise difficulties and thus call everything into doubt, no one would be the gainer. But questions are not raised for the sake of doubt; they are raised for the sake of truth.[3] From this point of view, even the uneducated know how to settle their disagreements by means of a certain informal dialectic; and it is this informal method of argumentation which the learned must use to perfection by following the rules of formal logic.[4]

Dialectical disputation, in other words, takes as its very point of departure the question that is raised by opposite opinions.[5] Each of the opposed opinions constitutes one side of the dispute, and the disputation itself consists in the presentation and consideration of the arguments in favor of either side. The arguments thus presented in favor of one side or the other are "probable" in the sense indicated in the preceding chapter, that is, probable inasmuch as they draw their conclusions from premises which are probable.[6] The propositions which serve as premises are, in their turn, probable on the basis of

[1] Thomas's understanding of the principle of contradiction is based upon, in particular, Aristotle's analysis of the principle and of its foundational importance in Book IV of the *Metaphysics*. See Thomas's commentary, ll. 5–17.

[2] *Contra Impugn.* c. 2 (14), nn. 435–448.

[3] *In De div. nom.* c. 4, l. 14, n. 473.

[4] *Quodl.* 4, q. 12, a. 2 ad 12.

[5] *In I Post Analyt.* l. 21, n. 179: "Ex interrogatione et responsione fit disputatio." It is to be emphasized that in speaking here of disputation we are referring only to dialectical disputation; for, Thomas also speaks of demonstrative disputation, that is to say, a disputation whose purpose is demonstration. See below, p. 142 fn. 2.

[6] *In Post. Analyt* Proemium, n. 6: "Syllogismus dialecticus ex probabilibus est." An even clearer statement of what is here involved is provided by Albert the Great, *Soph. Elench.* Libr. I, tr. I, c. 4: "Dialecticae disputationes sunt ex probabilibus collectivae contradictionum, hoc est ad utramque partem contradictionis opponentes."

widespread acceptance, or acceptance by some particular authority (whether an individual or a group), or, especially, acceptance by the opposition. In a certain sense, then, the whole purpose of the disputation is to build up the authoritative probability of one side or the other – or, what is even more desirable, of both sides.[1]

Indeed, this very concern for the strength of opposite claims is, as it were, the essence of dialectical disputation. For, the purpose of disputation as such is not the determination of truth; this is the function of demonstration, which, if possible, follows upon the preparatory consideration of dialectic.[2] The purpose of disputation is rather to present as well as humanly possible the reasons for adhering to either of the two opposite opinions. For, as we have already had occasion to point out, it is presupposed that no opinion can be totally devoid of truth, especially if it is in some way probable.[3] It is therefore of the utmost importance to one seeking definitive truth that he be able to see each of the opposed opinions in its full strength, with all of its supporting arguments. Having this information at his disposal, he can then judge objectively as to what element of truth is contained in either opinion.

As should already be clear, then, Thomas has no objection against disputation on religious grounds. At first sight, no doubt, this observation might seem a bit irrelevant. But it must not be forgotten that Thomas is a Christian and a rather good one at that. And for him the essence of Christian morality consists in charity, or mutual love.[4] How, then, it may be asked, can one preserve charity among men and yet engage in disputation – especially in view of the fact that peace, or concord, among men is a necessary concomitant of mutual love?

That this love for others can be violated in disputation Thomas grants, especially if one is arguing against the truth, but to some extent even if one is arguing against what is false but "in an inordinate manner." Such abuses of disputation he calls, after Cicero, "contra-

---

[1] *In I Phys.* l. 11, n. 93; l. 13, n. 114.

[2] *In I Phys.* l. 10, n. 75; IV, l. 17, n. 571; l. 4, n. 434; *In IV Met.* l. 1, n. 529; *In De Trin.* 6, 1 c. It is to be noted that Thomas makes a distinction, based on Aristotle, between *disputatio dialectica* and *disputatio demonstrativa* (*In I Post. Analyt.* l. 1, n. 9; l. 28, n. 227). But the English "disputation" is not broad enough in meaning to allow us to speak of "demonstrative disputation." Accordingly, we use "disputation" only in the sense of dialectical disputation. As a substitute for *disputatio* in the generic sense, we speak of "argumentation." See below, p. 145 fn. 5.

[3] *In I Phys.* l. 11, n. 93; l. 13, n. 114.

[4] See Gérard Gilleman, *The Primacy of Charity in Moral Theology* (Westminster, Md., 1961).

riness in speech" (*contrarietas locutionis*).[1] This being said, however, he still insists that disputation need not be incompatible with charity. For, he says, the peace among men which charity must effect requires not an agreement of opinions but an agreement of wills. That is to say, somewhat as Aristotle says about friendship, peace among men depends not upon intellectual acceptance of the same opinions but upon volitional accord as to what goods are to be sought by men. Providing, then, that men are in accord as to the good, then they may very well disagree, without serious detriment to mutual love, about which particular things pertain to that good and which do not. Such peace among men is, to be sure, imperfect, marred as it is by at least a certain minimum of dissension; but perfect peace is possible only when truth is known completely and every desire is fulfilled, that is to say, in heaven. Lacking such bliss, men must with all honor agree to disagree, that they might learn the truth through argumentation with one another.[2] By so doing, one might even give up an opinion which he finds agreeable, precisely because of arguments brought forward against such an opinion.[3] On the other hand, there is no man more unfortunate than a certain Elymas, mentioned in the *De Divinis Nominibus*, for he subscribed to erroneous opinions only because there was no one to show him the weakness of the arguments upon which he based his position.[4]

Reading between the lines, we detect here a note of sadness that the limitations of the human condition require recourse to argumentation. But, at the same time, one notices a confidence that truth will out in the process of disputation. The refusal to submit to this process would, accordingly, amount to a bestial willingness to remain ignorant or, worse yet, the victim of error. Thus, in answer to those who would hinder religious vocations, Thomas urges his opponents to present their objections before the learned, who are capable of replying, so that truth may be the authority.[5] In other words, an opinion as such is of little worth taken by itself; what gives value to an opinion are the arguments in its favor; and the value of these arguments can only be determined

---

[1] *S.T.* II–II, 38, 1 c; Cicero, *De Rhet. ad Herenn.* l. IV, c. 14.
[2] *S.T.* II–II, 29, 3 ad 2; Aristotle, *Ethics Nich.* IX, c. 6: 1167, a, 21–1167, b, 4. Thomas summarizes this position in *S.T.* II–II, 37, 1 c: "concordia quae est caritatis effectus est unio voluntatum, non unio opinionum." See also *S.T.* II–II, 10, 7; *Contra Impugn.* c. 2 (14), nn. 443–448.
[3] *Q.D. de ver.* 22, 5 ad 3.
[4] *In De div. nom.* c. 4, l. 3, nn. 766–768.
[5] *Contra Retrah.* c. 16, n. 859.

by submitting them to disputational attack.[1] In this way and in this way only can man ploddingly approach that perfect possession of truth which is the prerogative of the divine and of those divinely favored.

2. Theoretical Foundations of Disputation

In the light of the preceding chapter it should be mentioned at this point that there is something rather simplistic about Thomas's esteem for dialectic. For, confident as he is that truth will out, he tends in spite of himself to disregard the vital role which personal motives and prejudices might play both in the manner of disputing and in the evaluation of opposing arguments. The disputational procedure as he sees it is at least superficially that utilized by Aristotle as well as by earlier medieval masters.[2] Thus it is possible to draw a comparison between, say, Book I of the *Physics* and a typical Thomist "article": (1) presentation of doubts and errors; (2) determination of the truth; (3) solution of doubts. This amounts to a stylized version of a genuine face-to-face debate as it would appear to one interested party convinced of the truth of his own position and thus able to characterize the opposite position as an error the arguments for which must therefore be "solved." But enough has already been said about the weighting of opinions so that we may here restrict our attention to the abstract theory as such. The resulting idealization is accordingly to be modified in the light of human factors with which we have already dealt.

(a) Argument as Distinguished from Demonstration

The first aspect of argumentation which must be made clear to the modern reader is that an argument as such – or, if you will, even a "proof" – is not for Thomas equivalent to a demonstration. This point must be stressed since, after all, the very heart of a disputation is the arguments therein presented, which arguments, precisely as used in this way, are said to be "disputative." [3]

Thomas uses a variety of terms for what we would usually call an argument, among them *ratio* (in this usage, a "reasoning") and *probatio* (a "proof," but not necessarily demonstrative). The Latin word *argu-*

---

[1] A clear distinction between an opinion and arguments in its favor is suggested in the following passages: *In* I *Met.* l. 5, n. 97; l. 9, n. 137; l. 10, n. 166; *In* II *Phys.* l. 2, n. 150; l. 13, n. 255.

[2] See M.-D. Chenu, *Introduction à l'Etude de Saint Thomas d'Aquin* (Montreal-Paris, 1945); *La théologie comme Science au XIIIe Siècle* (Paris, 1957). See also Thomas, *In* I *De An.* l. 10, n. 147.

[3] *In De Mem.* l. 4, n. 350; *In* I *Phys.* l. 11, n. 93.

mentum is rarely if ever used in the etymological sense from which our English word is derived. Quite to the contrary, in one place, where Thomas is dealing with Paul's definition of faith as given in the Vulgate, he gives four meanings of *argumentum* only one of which approaches the English *argument*, namely, "the very act of discursive reasoning." [1] He is similarly led to consider the term *argumentum* in connection with the manner in which Christ manifested himself to his disciples after his resurrection.[2] In this instance, he goes beyond the Vulgate's use of *argumentum* to show that the Greek *tekmerion* should rather be translated as *"signum evidens ad probandum."* that is to say, "a sign evident to the senses whereby some truth is manifested." This meaning of *argumentum* he traces even to Aristotle. But he also notes that there is another meaning of *argumentum* which comes from Cicero, who defines the term as *"ratio rei dubiae faciens fidem."* [3] In discussing this other, apparently archaic, meaning of *argumentum*, Thomas uses the circumlocution, *probatio argumentativa,* to express the original meaning.

For this reason, together with the fact that *probatio* is for Thomas the basic and generic term for the statement of a reasoning process, we take *probatio* to be more or less equivalent to the English *argument.*[4] The English derivative, *proof,* would also be roughly applicable except for the fact that this term is quite generally taken to be synonymous with *demonstration,* a synonymy which, as we shall see, is completely incompatible with Thomas's usage of the corresponding Latin terms. We therefore prefer to translate *probatio* (or *ratio,* when used in an equivalent sense) by the English *argument;* but we do not exclude *proof* as an acceptable translation. What is important is that *demonstration* be kept in a class by itself as the perfect or apodictic argument (or proof). *Argument,* then, shall be taken in a generic sense for any rational defense of a proposition. This rational defense may, in turn, be merely *dialectical* (or disputative, or probable, or opinionative) or it may be *demonstrative.*[5] So much, then, for terminology.

---

[1] *Q.D. de ver.* 14, 2 ad 9. The meaning in question is, in the original, "ipsum actum rationis discurrentis."

[2] *Acts* 1: 3; *S.T.* III, 55, 5 c.

[3] *Topicorum* c. 2, n. 6; Ed. Teubner.

[4] It is important to note here that we are referring to the common sense meaning of *argument,* which is roughly equivalent to *argumentation,* or rational defense of a proposition, and not to the technical sense of the logic of truth functions, where *argument* refers rather to a propositional expression.

[5] This precision of terminology is based upon a wide variety of texts utilized in this chapter, but in particular it is an expression of the very pointed distinction made at *In I Post. Analyt.* l. 21, n. 175 and l. 28, n. 227. We might also call attention to *Q.D. de ver.* 2, 4 ad 5: '. . . demonstratio est species argumentationis, quae quodam discursu intellectus perficitur." See above, p. 142 fn. 2.

(b) Linguistic Presuppositions of Disputation

Turning now to a more direct consideration of argumentation, we begin by stating explicitly some of the presuppositions to disputation already implicit in what has been said by way of introduction. For, Thomas's confidence in the ability of man to argue his way to truth does involve, to be sure, a certain number of presuppositions. Not the least important of these, perhaps, is what might be called a willingness to disregard the influence of human factors, about which enough has already been said. But it should also be noted that Thomas's view of disputation suffers to some extent from the historically understandable defect of a rather absolutist conception of language. To be sure, Thomas's so-called moderate realism is such as to preserve him from the gross excesses of word-analysis that will characterize much of later scholasticism; but foreshadowings of this tendency are not entirely absent from his writings. It must be admitted, in short, that by contemporary standards Thomas's confidence in the natural language as revelatory of reality is at the very least uncritical.[1] This qualification aside, however, Thomas has much of value to say about the role of language in disputation. And to begin with we may distinguish three general prerequisites which more or less interpret Aristotle's method of *aporia*.

A first prerequisite to disputation is a common vocabulary. As Thomas observes, whether one is simply arguing against the views of someone else or is arguing for the sake of determining the truth, it is an essential condition for disputation that terms have finite significations. If a question is raised about "man," one must reply with regard to man and not with regard to non-man; for, to take the latter alternative destroys the very possibility of disputation by opening the discussion to an infinite series.[2] It is perhaps for this reason that Thomas, in spite of his own rather flexible hermeneutics of the Bible, goes along with

---

[1] We take this position notwithstanding Thomas's wise cautions against word-for-word translations from one language to another, in *Contra Errores Graecorum* Proemium, n. 1030. For, though Thomas at times involves himself in what might be called the problem of a translator, even then he tends to see this problem as basically one of finding the correct Latin word upon which he will then comment. Even more characteristic of his methodology is the tendency to determine realities on the basis of words, a tendency particularly noticeable, for example, in his treatment of virtues and the various adjuncts of virtue. In effect, one would say, Thomas often takes as his task as theologian to justify analytically an enumeration of distinct realities provided by traditional authority, whether scriptural (e.g. the number of commandments) or patristic (e.g. "the daughters of lust") or philosophical (e.g. the number of intellectual virtues). See, as just a few examples of this procedure, S.T. I, 108; I–II, 61; 68, 4; 69, 3; 7, 3; 25, 4; 57, 2 and 6; 70, 3; 72, 2 and 7; 100, 3–7, II–II, 1, 8; 24, 9; 25, 12; 48, 1; 148, 4 and 6; 153, 5; 154, 1.

[2] *In IV Met.* 1. 7, nn. 615, 623. See also *In I Post Analyt.* ll, 21–26.

Aristotle's method of dealing with Plato's metaphorical language strictly on the basis of *what* Plato says.[1]

A second prerequisite to disputation is a common starting point. At the very least, each side must accept some statement which can serve as the basis of disputation. In addition, each side must be willing to present its arguments either for or against the statement thus put in question. If either of the two sides refuses either to accept a base statement or to present arguments for or against that statement, then a disputation is impossible.[2] Obvious, perhaps, but not at all trivial: it takes two sides to argue, and strictly speaking there can be "sides" only with respect to one and the same question. By way of corollary, then, neither opinion about the question may be self-contradictory; for, this would automatically remove one side from consideration, and thus again make disputation impossible.[3]

A third prerequisite to disputation is a common goal. Each side must admit at least implicitly that truth is attainable and that it is truth one seeks to attain. After all, to engage in argumentation in all seriousness without the desire for truth as one's motive is either meaningless or malicious. For, as we have just seen, argumentation is possible only if each side defend a proposition which is somehow contradictory to that defended by the other side. If, then, one denies the possibility of knowing or at least approaching truth, what reason could he have for wishing to oppose his opinion to that of someone else? At the very least, he must recognize that the affirmation and the negation of one and the same proposition cannot both be perfectly true. For, if contradictories are both admitted as true, then any argument presented for one can be shown to be equally favorable to the other.[4] In short, disputation presupposes that the opinion of one side is at least more true than that of the other side; and this in turn presupposes that these opposite opinions are expressed as meaningful propositions.[5] By way of corollary, if a person is simply unwilling to submit his opinion to the test of disputation, he cannot easily be dissuaded from error should that be his plight.[6]

---

[1] *In I De An.* l. 8, nn. 107-108.

[2] See *In I Post. Analyt.* l. 5, n. 46.

[3] Struggling with a textual problem, Thomas is led to observe, according to one reading: "Tunc enim opinio est bene contemperata, quando praedicatum non repugnat subjecto: cum autem opinio implicat opposita, tunc non bene contemperatur." – *In IV Met.* l. 9, n. 659.

[4] *Quodl.* 8, q. 6, a. 3; *In IV Met.* ll. 15-17.

[5] *In IV Met.* l. 6, nn. 602-606; l. 8, nn. 642-644 and 659.

[6] *In XI Met.* l. 6, n. 2241.

In the light of all the foregoing, it is perhaps safe to consider as the principal requirement of disputation that it be truly bilateral – that there be in the fullest sense of the expression two sides to the question. Without two sides, there is in fact really no question, no recognizable difficulty or problem; and it is precisely the problem, the *dubitatio*, which makes the disputation a worthwhile enterprise. For, the very purpose of disputative argumentation is to clarify wherein lies the difficulty of the question.[1]

This is more or less Aristotle's method of *aporia*, that is, of starting an inquiry into a subject by pointing out the difficulties which must be resolved. According to Aristotle, this method is intended to bring out the difficulties of a given question, and this for four reasons: (1) subsequent investigation of truth is simply the solution of doubts previously raised; (2) the pinpointing of the doubt shows the way to go to find the truth; (3) awareness of the difficulty is a prerequisite to knowing when one has attained the truth; (4) one can better judge the truth after having heard all arguments on both sides.[2] To these ends, then, one deliberately seeks probable arguments for both sides, so that one's doubt about the question will be well founded – or, as later scholastics would say, so that one's doubt will be positive rather than negative.

This, says Thomas, is Aristotle's usual method of procedure. He even quotes Averroes to the effect that dialectical disputation is as it were the principal part of metaphysics.[3] Though he does not commit himself as to the truth of Averroes' assertion, Thomas's own procedure, especially in his theological works, differs only as to its presuppositions. Thus, for example, in trying to establish that the soul after death is capable of knowing intellectually, Thomas refuses to settle for an easy solution. He admits that the question would present little difficulty if one followed Plato's view that sensation is merely an incidental stimulus to intellection or Avicenna's view that sensation is dispositive to intellection. But, preferring as he does Aristotle's contention that the senses are necessary for human intellection, he must take the question to be "more difficult." [4]

In short, for Thomas as for Aristotle, it is only by seeking and surmounting difficulties that one can come to the truth; and to this end it is necessary to see both sides of a question.

---

[1] See *In* I *Phys.* l. 2, nn. 17 and 19; l. 14, n. 128; III, l. 5, n. 309; IV, l. 2, n. 415; *In* III *Met.* l. 3, n. 368.

[2] *In* III *Met.* l. 1.

[3] *In* III *Met.* l. 1, nn. 343–345.

[4] *Q.D. de an.* q. un., a. 15.

(c) The Metascientific Role of Disputation

Granted, then, that to attain the best answer to a given question both sides of that question should be considered. But who, it may be legitimately asked, has the competence to consider both sides of a given question? This problem of competence, as real today as it was for Thomas, is by no means trivial. For, to solve this problem one must be able to delineate the boundaries between science and metascience, between what is said *in* a science and what is said *about* a science. It is of considerable interest, then, to see how Thomas resolves this problem with regard to disputative argumentation. As we shall now see, his solution amounts to a distinction between disputation appropriate to a special science and disputation appropriate only to a general science, namely, either logic or metaphysics.

(i) The Extraneous Opinion. The first point to be made in this regard is the rather obvious one that a disputation might very well deal with any subject matter or, if you will, with the subject matter of any branch of studies. Thus, the disputants might be concerned about matters pertaining to theology, to psychology, to cosmology, to political theory, or whatever – or they might even be concerned about problems pertaining to logic as such.

A second point is somewhat more subtle and, what is more important, contains the key to Thomas's position. Whenever a proposition is subjected to dialectical inquiry, that proposition is evaluated in terms of its consistency, or compatibility, with other propositions which for one reason or another are accepted as true. In the case of rhetorical argumentation, the truth of propositions which serve as criteria of judgment is presumed by the audience, and hence need not be defended. Similarly the principles and the established conclusions of a given science are also presumed true by the audience and need not be defended. There is, in short, an undercurrent of "dogma" which determines for any group of disputants what may or may not be disputed.[1]

It is for this reason that Thomas can refer to some propositions as being *"inopinabile."* This term cannot be accurately translated into English; but it suggests both "unacceptable" and even "unthinkable."

---

[1] This usage of the word "dogma," though perhaps irreverent to some, is nonetheless a most effective expression for the unquestioned base of any domain of thought. We are here indebted to Thomas S. Kuhn, "The Function of Dogma in Scientific Research," *Scientific Change* (ed. A. C. Crombie: London, 1963), pp. 347–369. Compare the notion of a "tacit component" of knowledge in Michael Polanyi, *Personal Knowledge* (Chicago, Ill., 1958), Part Two, pp. 69–245.

If we may speak in terms of the latter, a proposition is unthinkable because it contradicts basic principles of thought or basic principles of a special science, or because to accept it one would have to accept other propositions which are felt to be absurd. Thus those who deny the principle of excluded middle fall into *"positiones inopinabiles."* [1] Similarly, the assertion that grammatical science is numerically identical in all men is *inopinabile*. [2] A stronger judgment is expressed by calling an opinion impossible. [3] Somewhat more cautiously, Thomas rejects the proposition that light moves with finite velocity by saying that this is extremely questionable, "as it were, difficult or entirely impossible." [4]

Arguments presented in favor of such propositions are, in Aristotle's terminology, "movable," which for Thomas means "destructible." For, such arguments can easily be shown to be based upon impossible presuppositions. [5] To manifest such impossibility is to *disprove* the proposition: *improbare* or *reprobare*. [6] An opinion the arguments for which are thus disproved is accordingly said to be "destroyed" and is thus "improbable" in the sense that it lacks proof or is unproven. [7] Indeed, for the purpose of thus "destroying" an opinion Thomas will even appeal to "experience" as being contradictory to the given opinion, as, for example, that of Plato with regard to reminiscence. On the other hand, if an opinion is not somehow destroyed in disputation it is said to have been "saved." [8]

Now, of all these "unthinkable thoughts" about which we have been speaking some are of particular interest. These are what Thomas calls "extraneous opinions." An extraneous opinion is one which is incompatible with the established structure of a given science or, more rarely, of all science in general. As distinguished from a heretical opinion, which in one way or another subverts some tenet of faith, an extraneous opinion subverts the principles of some particular branch of knowledge which is based entirely on reason. Thus the opinion that nothing moves would destroy physical science, since the latter presupposes motion;

---

[1] *In* IV *Met.* l. 16, nn. 731–732. See also l. 16, n. 720.

[2] *C.G.* II, 73.

[3] *In* I *Met.* l. 9, n. 134; *Q.D. de spir. creat.* q. un., a. 2 c.

[4] *In* II *De An.* l. 14, n. 412: "Sed quod lateat nos successio in motu luminis, ab oriente, usque ad occidentem horizontis nostri, hoc habet magnam quaestionem, tamquam difficile aut omnino impossibile."

[5] *In* I *Met.* l. 15, n. 229; *In* I *Post. Analyt.* l. 22, n. 181.

[6] See, for example, *In* II *Phys.* l. 13, n. 255; *In* I *Met.* l. 12, n. 181; *Quodl.* 6, q. 2, a. 2 c; *Q.D. de ver.* 3, 1 c; 5, 3 c.

[7] See *In* VIII *Phys.* l. 13, n. 1078.

[8] *Q.D. de ver.* 19, 1 c.

the opinion that the will is not free would destroy ethics, since the latter presupposes freedom of the will; the opinion that parallel lines can intersect would destroy geometry, since the latter presupposes the opposite.[1]

By its very nature, then, an extraneous opinion is in a way "meta-scientific." Even if an opinion of this kind seems to refer to the subject matter of some particular science, it is never the task of that science as such to deal with it. Indeed, there is no consistent way in which the science could deal with such an opinion, for the latter contradicts its very principles. Accordingly, such opinions must be dealt with on the level of "logic" as such or of metaphysics.[2]

Unfortunately, this seems to mean only that the more general science is to disprove the extraneous opinion and thus defend the integrity of the special science which has been brought under attack.[3] It does not seem to have occurred to Thomas that an extraneous opinion might itself constitute a new insight or even a new science. As far as he is concerned, Aristotle is correct in saying that such maverick opinions arise either from an inability to solve sophistical arguments in their favor or simply from intellectual belligerence (*protervia*).[4] More specifically, by defending an opinion of this kind one reveals his inability to distinguish between what is credible and what is incredible (in logic), between what is better and what is worse (in ethics), and between what is a principle and what is not (in demonstrative sciences).[5]

In short, the very notion of an extraneous opinion is at least implicitly metascientific. For one thing, it puts a limitation upon what might be disputed with a view to possible inclusion within a given science. Very simply, a special science is not to dispute about any proposition which is contradictory to the very principles of that science. Secondly, the notion of an extraneous opinion presupposes a meta-scientific discipline capable of dealing with it. In the light of these considerations, it is of only secondary importance that Thomas's manner of dealing with an extraneous opinion implies an overly rigid conception of the internal and, if you will, eternal integrity of a science.

---

[1] *Q.D. de malo* 6, a. un. c; *In* I *Post. Analyt.* l. 22, esp. n. 183.

[2] See *S.T.* I, 1, 8 c; *In De div. nom.* c. 2, l. 1, n. 124; *In* I *Post. Analyt.* l. 21; *In* I *Phys.* l. 2; II, l. 7, n. 206; VIII, l. 5, n. 1006; *In* IV *Met.* l. 5, esp. nn. 592–593.

[3] See, for example, *S.T.* I, 1, 8 c; I–II, 14, 6 c; and esp. *In* IV *Met.*

[4] *Q.D. de malo* 6, a. un. c.

[5] *In* VIII *Phys.* l. 6, n. 1018.

(ii) Logica Utens as a Metalanguage. Be that as it may, there is an even more important sense in which disputation is metascientific. This consists in the fact that it is, with respect to the language of any special science, metalinguistic.

To begin with, whatever the subject matter and whatever the particular problem which is under discussion, the disputational procedure is essentially the same.[1] For, the immediate purpose of disputation is not to incorporate a given proposition within the formal structure of a particular science but rather to clarify for the disputants themselves just what it is that the proposition is saying, what its contradictory is saying, and what are the implications of each. In other words, disputation is merely preparatory to structural incorporation, inasmuch as it helps the disputants to "get their bearings" with regard to the alternative propositions in question.[2]

For this purpose, however, one is not dependent upon the principles and conclusions (today we might prefer to say, the axioms and theorems) of a particular science but may utilize propositions which are extrinsic to the structural complex of the sciences.[3] Thus the language available for disputation is free by comparison to the language of the particular science, which is bound. The disputational language is at least as rich as the spoken language of the disputants, whereas the specialized language of the particular science is restricted by its principles, or axioms, to a determinate subset of that language.[4] From this point of view, then, the natural language constitutes a metalanguage with respect to the language of the special science, and disputational procedure as such is to that extent metascientific.

In some respects, then, disputation may truly be described as metascientific. But at the same time it must be stressed that disputation is also prescientific. Hence the point of departure for disputational

---

[1] *S.T.* I–II, 57, 6 ad 3: "Inquisitio autem nondum est per propria principia; quia his habitis, non esset opus inquisitione, sed iam res esset inventa . . . Unde et in speculativis una est dialectica inquisitiva de omnibus: scientiae autem demonstrativae, quae sunt judicativae, sunt diversae de diversis." See also II–II, 51, 4 ad 2. It is of the utmost importance to recall at this point that we are still speaking of *dialectical* argumentation. For, as this text indicates, Thomas would insist that each particular science has its own proper way of *demonstrating* insofar as it deals with a specific subject matter on the basis of proper principles. See *In* I *Post. Analyt.* ll. 17–21; l. 20, nn, 171–172; 1. 21, nn. 174 and 178–179.

[2] *In* I *Post. Analyt.*l . 20, n. 172: "Dialecticus enim non procedit ex aliquibus principiis demonstrativis, neque assumit alteram partem contradictionis tantum, sed se habet ad utramque (contingit enim utramque quandoque vel probabilem esse, vel ex probabilibus ostendi, quae accepit dialecticus). Et propter hoc interrogat." See also *In* I *Post. Analyt.* l. 33, nn. 278–279.

[3] *In* I *Post. Analyt.* l. 21, n. 175; l. 20, n. 171.

[4] See *In* I *Post. Analyt.* l. 17. nn. 154–157.

arguments is probability rather than what Thomas calls the nature of things; and the immediate goal is not demonstration but the justification of an opinion as probable.[1] The disputation is a help towards the eventual determination of things, but mainly insofar as probability is taken to be a sign of or pointer towards truth.[2] Accordingly, disputation looks for logical consistency or inconsistency of a proposition taken by itself, or with respect to what men generally consider to be true, or with respect to the particular science in question. For the most part, however, what is sought is a consistency of probable opinions with one another. For, we repeat, the aim of dialectical disputation is analysis rather than demonstration; it is more a logical unfolding of implications than a definitive pronouncement of science.[3] It is extra-scientific and pre-scientific rather than scientific in the strict sense. It is, in short, preliminary and preparatory – the ground-clearing operation which must precede construction of the building.[4]

It will be seen, then, that this view of disputation implies a close connection between what is "logical" and what is "reasonable" on the one hand and what is "probable" on the other. This, in turn, raises an interesting problem with regard to the relation of probability to the real. The problem, however, is not too pressing for Thomas. As we shall see, he simply takes the bull by the horns and opts for a golden mean as a kind of practical criterion of probability.

We note first of all the relationship between the logical and the reasonable within the context of disputational procedure. In commenting upon Aristotle's disputational procedure in the *Physics*, Thomas says that the Philosopher is proceeding *"rationabiliter"* rather than *"naturaliter,"* that is, according to principles of logic (*rationalis philosophia*) rather than according to principles of natural science.[5] As he elsewhere notes, an argument (*probatio*) on this level is concerned

[1] *In I Post. Analyt.* 1. 31, n. 258: "Quia enim syllogismus dialecticus ad hoc tendit, ut *opinionem* faciat, hoc solum est de intentione dialectici, ut procedat ex his, quae sunt maxime opinabilia, et haec sunt ea, quae videntur vel pluribus, vel maxime sapientibus." See the remainder of this extremely important passage, in which dialectical procedure is contrasted with demonstrative and probability is shown to be a sufficient culmination to the former. See also *In Post. Analyt.* Proemium, n. 6, and *In De Trin.* 6, 1 c. See below, p. 185 fn. 1.

[2] *In De Trin.* 6, 1 c: "Et hoc modo rationabiliter procedi potest in qualibet scientia, ut ex probabilibus paretur via ad necessarias probationes."

[3] By a quirk of usage, the term which for Aristotle refers to demonstration (namely, *analysis*) is now used much more loosely —and thus we use it here – for rational inquiry as such. (We abstract, of course, form special meanings such as that given the term by Kant.) See *In I Post. Analyt.* 1. 33, n. 278.

[4] For a quite similar view of the relationship between dialectical argumentation and probability, see William A. Wallace, *The Scientific Methodology of Theodoric of Freiberg* (Friburg, Switzerland, 1959), pp. 73–76.

[5] *In III Phys.* 1. 8, nn. 350 and 353.

with predicates (*per viam praedicationis*) rather than with motion as such (*per viam motus*), and thus is properly logical rather than physical.[1] Accordingly, he says (again on the *Physics*), propositions thus defended are not usually qualified as "necessary" or "impossible" but as "reasonable" (*rationabile*) or "unreasonable" (*irrationabile*).[2] On occasion Thomas uses these latter notions in the comparative. Thus in his commentary on the *De Anima* he refers to one particular opinion as being "more unreasonable than the opinions of other philosophers"; and in the *De Veritate* he says that a particular opinion about how angels teach one another is "more reasonable" than two other opinions.[3] In much the same way, Avicenna's view about the agent intellect is introduced as being "not reasonable." [4]

This mode of speaking, says Thomas, Aristotle was wont to adopt when dealing with the probable.[5] And thus is suggested a terminological similarity between "reasonable" (*rationabile*) and "probable" (*probabilis*). For, both terms refer in different ways to what we have chosen to call an *argument*, that is, a "*ratio*" or a "*probatio*." Nor is the connection entirely interpretative on our part; for, Thomas suggests it himself, in his commentary on the *De Anima*. In one place, where he notes that a given opinion goes against the evidence of the senses (*ad sensum apparet falsum*) and is incompatible with known truths (*inconveniens*), he states that that opinion is also "*irrationabile*," meaning that it is held by those not having "reason": *dictum non habentium rationem.*[6] This is somewhat ambiguous, to be sure; but shortly before, he takes "more reasonable" (*rationabilius*) to mean "more probable" (*probabilius*). In this latter case, although the opinion in question involves a doubt (*dubitatio*), it can be supported by probable arguments (*poterit probabiliter ostendi*) – and yet, it is subsequently rejected.[7] It is in this tentative sense of "proof" that Thomas elsewhere concedes that some arguments (*rationes*) prove their point (*probant*) and yet are susceptible to correction: *quamvis ad eas possit responderi aliquo modo.*[8]

---

[1] *In* VII *Met.* 1. 2, n. 1287. See also 1. 3, n. 1308, where Thomas makes basically the same observation with regard to "*quod quid erat esse.*"

[2] *In* VIII *Phys.* 1. 7, n. 1027.

[3] *In* I *De An.* 1. 11, n. 168; *Q.D. de ver.* 9, 2 c.

[4] *Q.D. de ver.* 10, 2 c; also 10, 6 c.

[5] *In* VIII *Phys.* 1. 7, n. 1027.

[6] *In* I *De An.* 1. 13, n. 195.

[7] *In* I *De An.* 1. 10.

[8] *Q.D. de ver.* 8, 7 c.

In any event, this lumping together of the logical, the reasonable and the probable further suggests a concern for the real, for "the nature of things," which would be inadmissable in formal logic as such. For, here it is not a question of pure logic but of logic in action, *logica utens*. In other words, we are here involved with logic in the medieval sense of dialectics: an instrument in the hands of the special scientist, or of the philosopher or theologian, who seeks ultimately to demonstrate new truths within the structural context of his particular science.[1] To do this, he begins, tentatively, by arguing on the basis of propositions held commonly or at least in certain quarters with regard to the subject matter of interest to him. These propositions, inasmuch as they have not been shown to be logically implicated by the principles, or axioms, of the science, are not known as necessary but only as probable. The arguments presented in favor of such propositions are not intrinsic to the science, that is, are not *proper* to that science, but are extrinsic, or *common* to many sciences, since they are based more upon what men generally hold to be true than upon what is demonstrated to be true within the given science.[2]

In the light of these considerations, we can see more clearly what is involved in Thomas's linking of the probable with the "logical" in the sense of "rational" or "reasonable." What is involved is nothing less than a theoretically unjustified linking of logic with reality. As a result of this marriage of convenience, when Thomas says of a proposition that it is more probable or less probable he means that it is "more true" or "less true," that is to say, at the very least, that in the light of current knowledge it is a better (or worse) expression of the true state of affairs than is the opposing opinion. Thus, in spite of the epistemic limitations of opinion, he is not adverse to saying of an opinion that it is "true" or "more true." [3] Nonetheless, precisely because in such cases he is referring to an opinion, the qualificative "true" must be under-

---

[1] To be absolutely faithful to Thomas's words we would here have to say that it is the dialectician (*dialecticus*) who performs this function. There is, of course, no such profession in the modern world. But this, we think, in no way prevents us from saying, without detriment to Thomas's intention, that the special scientist, *qua* dialectician, carries out this task of preliminary disputation. With regard to the role of logic as *logica utens* in the special sciences see *In De Trin.* 6, 1 c.

[2] Thomas's distinctions between proper and common, intrinsic and extrinsic propositions are of considerable metascientific importance. They are, in fact, basic to the preceding analysis and will take on still further significance when we treat of the special case of foundational propositions, or principles. For a thorough view of these distinctions, see the following: *In I Met.* l. 10, n. 164; II, l. 5; IV, l. 4; XI, l. 3, n. 2204; l. 10, n. 2329; *In III Phys.* l. 8, n. 349; VIII, l. 18, n. 1123; l. 20, n. 1136; *In De Trin.* 6, 1; *In I Post. Analyt.* l. 20, n. 5; *In I De An.* l. 1, n. 15; l. 2, nn. 24–25.

[3] *Quodl.* 6, q. 2, a. 2 c; 10, q. 5, a. 2 c.

stood to mean "probably true" or "true on the basis of what is probable." Indeed, he is likely to add "probable" when he calls an opinion "true." [1] But he is even more likely to leave out the "true" and simply say that the opinion is "probable" or "sufficiently probable" or something of the kind. [2]

An important consequence of this marriage of convenience between logic and reality is that Thomas never explicitly refers to a proposition as being true and at the same time improbable, or false and at the same time probable. Generally speaking, the false is ultimately "improbable," that is, incapable of defensible proof; the true, on the other hand, is ultimately "probable," that is, susceptible of defensible proof. [3] Thus in his commentary on the *Politics* Thomas notes that there is no need to bother with what is obviously false; it is enough, he says, to concentrate on the probable. [4] By implication, then, probability for Thomas would seem to involve only a logical relationship between a given opinion, or proposition, and the proofs which can be given for that opinion. His usage of "probable" and "improbable" has nothing to do with the statistical likelihood or unlikelihood of what is so characterized. That God should become man, for example, is most unlikely; but for Thomas it is true that God has become man, and therefore he would never say that it is improbable. Quite the contrary, because it is true it is probable, that is, capable of proof – not of demonstration, in this case, but of defending or supporting arguments.

(*iii*) *Probability as a Golden Mean.* All this having been noted, we are now in a position to pinpoint the central difficulty of Thomas's view of probability. As we have already mentioned, Thomas does not provide a theoretical justification of his tendency to relate the probable with the true and the improbable with the false. This does not mean, however, that no theoretical justification is possible. Indeed, it seems clear that at least in principle the true is probable (that is, defensible)

---

[1] *In* I *Phys.* l. 6, n. 38.

[2] See, for example, *Q.D. de malo* 7, 11 c. *Q.D. de pot.* 5, 7 c.

[3] *In* I *Phys.* l. 6, nn. 16–17; *Q.D. de spir. creat.* q. un., a. 9 ad 9. As we shall see in Chapter 6, Thomas does speak of Aristotle's arguments for the eternity of the world as being "probable", even though he himself considers that opinion to be false. What we are here saying, however, is that we are not aware of a single instance in which Thomas explicitly combines "true" with "improbable" or "false" with "probable". Thus, even when speaking of Aristotle's (false) opinion as being "probable", he does not in fact say that it is both false and probable. That this is implied and thus suggests some interesting problems does not seem to have occurred to him.

[4] *In* II *Polit.* l. 1, n. 170: ". . . ad inveniendum veritatem, non multum prodest consideratio eorum quae sunt manifeste falsa, sed eorum quae probabiliter dicunt."

and the false improbable (that is, indefensible). But a justification of this kind, however beautiful in theory, is of little practical value. For, the very nature of matters deemed only probable is such that Thomas's pairings amount to a begging of the question. To say, in other words, that the true is probable and the false improbable is one thing; but it is quite another thing to say that what is probable is true and what is improbable is false. As the history of science can amply demonstrate, what seems rationally defensible today might not seem rationally defensible tomorrow, and vice versa. The human condition is such that one looks through the probable towards the true; he seldom has the privilege of looking at the true in order to judge what else might be probable. Thus, when Thomas says, as he does on occasion, "this opinion seems to me to be more probable," he perhaps indicates more clearly what is in fact involved in the attribution of probability than when he simply declares an opinion to be probable or improbable.[1]

It is, we think, precisely because of these inevitable difficulties that, theory aside, Thomas tends to be quite human when evaluating the two sides of a question. In short, he seldom makes a clear-cut choice of one over the other. In typical scholastic fashion, he is more inclined to make distinctions or qualifications which limit the scope of a statement so as to manifest some truth which it seeks to express.[2] This modification of statements which say too much is in part a manifestation of the Aristotelian conviction, previously mentioned, that no opinion is totally false. Of course, as Thomas points out, "when two opinions are contrary to one another with regard to the same thing, one must be true and the other false." [3] Since contrary opinions are expressed in contradictory propositions, this observation is theoretically sound provided it be added that each term is in fact being used in the same sense in each proposition. For, as noted above, equivalence of signification is a necessary prerequisite to disputation. But Thomas's concern about the incompatibility of opposition is far more theoretical than methodological. In practice, he has a tendency to find some aspect of truth in either side of an argument.

In other words, with Thomas the outcome of disputational procedure is more often than not a kind of compromise solution which takes into account the merit of each opposing opinion. For Thomas, at any rate,

---

[1] See, for example, *Quodl.* 8, q. 3, a. un. c.

[2] See M.-D. Chenu, *Introduction à l'Etude de Saint Thomas d'Aquin* (Paris-Montreal, 1954), p. 80.

[3] *Quodl.* 8, q. 6, a. 3 c: "Quando duae sunt opiniones contrariae de eodem, oportet esse alteram veram et alteram falsam."

harmonization of opposing viewpoints is frequently made necessary because of his role as a kind of intermediary between two traditions; and, as we have seen, this sometimes leads him to emphasize what is at best superficial agreement. It would be wrong to suppose, however, that he is interested in agreement for the sake of agreement. This is clearly belied by his vigorous attacks against positions which he is convinced are false. The search for harmony, then, is more precisely a search for complementarity, and dialectical disputation is considered the ideal instrument for the manifestation thereof.

What is implied here, of course, is that *truth, like virtue (and, Thomas would add, like faith), is a kind of golden mean between the extremes of opposite errors.*[1] Thus, commenting on the *Politics*, Thomas says that by attacking both sides of a question one learns "something of the truth" from each side.[2] And writing on the *De Anima* he has occasion to speak about opinions which "in some way state the matter correctly, and in some way do not state it correctly."[3] It is perhaps also with this notion of a mean in mind that Thomas likes to place Aristotle's opinion (on one occasion called an *opinio media*) between opposed opinions of other philosophers.[4] Similarly, in his independent writings he not infrequently contents himself with pointing out advantages and disadvantages of either of two opposed opinions. Thus, for example, in discussing the Catholic doctrine of the Virgin Birth, he considers the advantages of viewing this doctrine first in the light of Aristotle's opinion that only the mother provides matter for an infant, then in the light of the opposite view that the body of an infant derives matter from the father as well as from the mother.[5]

This notion of truth as a mean must not, however, be taken as a kind of *a priori* principle in terms of which all opposing opinions are judged. In actual practice, the nature of the question and the weight of the arguments on either side are the major factors in terms of which a solution is stated. Sometimes Thomas might say that if an opinion is understood in one way it can be upheld, but understood in another way it is impossible.[6] At other times he sees some truth in each of two opposing opinions and therefore deals with the arguments on both

---

[1] *Contra Impugn.* c. 3 (4), n. 75; c. 1 (2), n. 16; c. 4 (3), n. 168.

[2] *In* III *Polit.* l. 11, n. 459. See also *Q.D. de malo* 2, 1 c.

[3] *In* II *De An.* l. 9, n. 339: "Et sic patet quod utrique praedictorum opinantium, aliquo modo dicunt recte, et aliquo modo non dicunt recte."

[4] See, for example, *In De Sensu*, l. 10, n. 138; *Q.D. de virtut. in comm.* q. un., a. 8 c; *Q.D. de ver.* 10, 6 c.

[5] *C.G.* IV, 45.

[6] *Q.D. de spir. creat.* q. un., a. 11 c.

sides.[1] Again, among a number of different opinions he might find that one of them "contains more truth" than the others and yet admit that the others in some way are also true.[2] Finally, he might simply reject both sides of a controversy and state a different opinion as a solution.[3]

In short, we do not wish to imply that Thomas's concept of probability is nothing more than that of a golden mean between extremes. This being said, however, it is nonetheless inescapable that the golden mean remains for him something of an ideal in this regard. Just as virtue is a mean between extremes in the practical order, so also Aristotle's opinion is a mean between philosophical extremes and the teaching of faith is a mean between theological extremes.

These criteria of speculative truth, by now quite familiar to us, are well in evidence in a passage of the *De Veritate,* where Thomas is asking if the mind acquires knowledge from sense objects.[4] He sorts out two opposite opinions: (1) science is derived entirely from external causes; (2) science is derived entirely from internal causes. On each side of the question he distinguishes two different explanations of the opinion thus upheld. With regard to the first, Plato appeals to separate forms, a theory which, Thomas says, has been sufficiently disproved (*reprobata*) by Aristotle; Avicenna appeals to a separate intellect, but, says Thomas, this opinion does not seem reasonable (*rationabilis*). With regard to the second, he mentions first the view that all knowledge is innate and declares that this too does not seem reasonable; moreover, he adds, it should be considered disproved (*reprobanda*) both because of the teachings of faith and because of the views of philosophers. Accordingly, the opinion that the soul causes its own knowledge does not seem entirely reasonable, says Thomas, for this opinion implies innate ideas.[5] Having made this somewhat artificial division of opposite opinions, he then declares that the view of Aristotle, which is *intermediate between the two extremes* in that it attributes the development of knowledge to both internal and external causes, is *"more reasonable."* Finally, he goes on to explain how each of the other opinions is at least partly true.

---

[1] *Q.D. de malo* 2, 1 c.

[2] *Q.D. de malo* 2, 2 c; *Quodl.* 8, q. 3, a. un; 9, q. 3, a. un. ad 3; 10, q. 5, a. 1 c; a. 2 c; *Q.D. de ver.* 8, 9; 10, 6.

[3] *Q.D. de ver.* 6, 2 c.

[4] *Q.D. de ver.* 10, 6 c.

[5] In spite of oversimplifications required by the condensed treatment, it seems that Thomas is again speaking of Avicenna's theory of the agent intellect, more elaborately developed in *Q.D. de an.* q. un., a. 15 c.

There is in this early statement more respect for non-Aristotelian views than is the case in Thomas's later writings, but with this fact we are not here concerned. What is of interest to us is simply the manner in which Thomas sets up the question along disputational lines, draws upon authority – especially the authority of faith – to reject one or another opinion, takes the Aristotelian view as a kind of golden mean closer to the truth, then finally points out the partial truth of each of the other opinions. The text is, in short, a miniaturization of Thomas's lifelong dialectical approach to the views of others: as respectful as possible towards all but duly weighted in the direction of Aristotle and even more towards the Christian faith.

(d) Faith, Probability and Disputation

This reference to faith as an arbiter of probability brings us to the final point to be considered with regard to the theory of dialectical argumentation. As should be clear from our previous chapter, the truths of faith taken more or less strictly are exempt from the hazards of disputation. Based as they are not upon human but upon divine authority, they are not susceptible to being disproven by any counter-arguments however forceful the latter may be. The defense of an article of faith may, to be sure, be extremely difficult in view of man's inability to see clearly all that is implied in God's revelation; but that it can be defended rationally against any human objection is an *a priori* certitude for the believer.

This assurance of being in the way of truth at least with regard to some propositions does not, however, make the task of defending them any less arduous. In fact, as we have already noted, Thomas sees the whole of theology to be a kind of elaborate defense of the Christian faith against "doubts" raised about it.[1] He indicates in his somewhat exegetical introduction to the *Contra Gentiles* that divine truth is truth in the strictest sense of the word (*antonomasice*), and thus any objection against divine truth is bound to be false.[2] Nonetheless, such truth escapes man's capacity for demonstration; the best he can hope to do is to show the error of assertions made against it. These heretical assertions, he says in writing on the *De Divinis Nominibus*, are based on sophistical arguments.[3] But, on the other hand, arguments pre-sented by the saints to prove a teaching of faith are not demon-

[1] *De art. fidei* Proemium, n. 597.
[2] *C.G.* I, 1.
[3] *In De div. nom.* c. 4, l. 23, n. 604.

strations; they have only persuasive value (*persuasiones quaedam*) insofar as they show that the teaching in question is not impossible.[1] To take a well-known example, Thomas insists that the doctrine of the Trinity cannot be demonstratively proven; arguments brought forth in its favor are not necessary nor are they even probable except to the believer. To attempt a demonstration of doctrines such as this, he says, is derogatory to faith, for it gives the non-believer the impression that one's belief is based on such flimsy arguments. Before believers, who accept the authority of Scripture, one may well argue on the basis of that authority. But before the non-believer one must be content to show the non-impossibility of such doctrines.[2] Thus in the *Contra Gentiles* Thomas argues on the basis of natural reason, and accordingly even speaks of "demonstrative truth" with regard to his arguments; but he admits that this manner of proceeding is deficient when it comes to what pertains to God.[3]

As he notes in writing on the *De Trinitate*, the findings of philosophy are always useful for the theologian; but where there is disagreement between the two, faith must be the arbiter. This primacy of faith is defended on the grounds that the light of reason can never be genuinely opposed to that of faith, and hence apparent conflicts are at least in principle soluble.[4] Such theological utilization of knowledge naturally acquired does not, says Thomas, involve a vicious circle; for, as is true with regard to any science which borrows propositions from an inferior science, theology does not content itself with proofs given for those propositions in the inferior sciences, but provides proofs of its own on the basis of self-evident principles.[5] These self-evident principles, no doubt, must here be understood to be what has been infallibly revealed by God, in particular as this is found in Sacred Scripture.

The articles of faith, then, impose a certain limitation upon the scope of disputation, precisely insofar as the propositions in question are not susceptible to being disproven. Indeed, if a proposition is an article of faith, the contradictory of that proposition is heretical; hence no one is free to defend the latter except for the purpose of clarifying its opposite.[6] Thus, the relationship of a proposition to the faith plays an important role in deciding whether or not that proposition is available

---

[1] *S.T.* II–II, 1, 5 ad 2.
[2] *S.T.* I, 32, 1. See also *In De Trin.* Proem. I, 4 c.
[3] *C.G.* I, 2.
[4] *In De Trin.* Proem. II, 3.
[5] *In De Trin.* 5, 1 ad 9.
[6] See *S.T.* II–II, 10, 7; *Resp. de Art.* XXXVI art. 22, n. 751.

for disputation, or, if available, the manner in which it is to be used. Now, it will be recalled that a proposition is "unthinkable" if it is either self-contradictory or contradictory to the principles, or axioms, of whatever science would deal with that proposition. Such a proposition is an "extraneous opinion." Thus, if we include under "science" that science whose principles are the articles of faith, then we must add that a heretical proposition is "extraneous" and thus "unthinkable" for disputation in the ordinary way.[1]

As Thomas himself notes, the doctrine of the Trinity and other articles of faith are dealt with disputatively every day in the schools; but the purpose of such disputation is not the establishment of a *dubitatio* but simply "the understanding and manifestation and confirmation of truth." [2] The only reason he can see for avoiding such disputation in the schools would be to avoid giving scandal to those who might think the disputation implies doubt about the truths of faith. On the other hand, he adds, one can readily prevent such misunderstanding by simply pointing out publicly that one is not disputing in the sense of building up doubt but only as a means of finding arguments in favor of the truth.[3]

These latter points about disputation in the context of faith are made in connection with responses to a series of questions put to him rather late in his turbulent academic career (1271), apparently by a religious superior who had cause to doubt Thomas's orthodoxy on various matters. The questions themselves are more often than not much more superficial than is characteristic of Thomas's own thought. Nonetheless, Thomas's replies to these questions provide us with some interesting insights into the way in which he visualizes the extent to which "the faith" can intervene as a brake on disputation.

For example, in dealing with various questions about the location of hell, which others wanted to put in the center of the earth, Thomas insists that the question has nothing to do with theology and cannot be answered anyway. He says one can determine the distance to the center of the earth by astronomical arguments, if that makes any difference; and, moreover, gravity seems to imply that the earth is solid all the way to the center. In view of the latter, Thomas himself doubts that hell is there, although he does not think it would be

---

[1] *Q.D. de malo* 4, 6 obj. 2 and ad 2.
[2] *Resp. de Art.* XLII art 32, n. 805: "Quoditie in scholis Magistrorum disputetur et de Trinitate et de aliis articulis fidei, non propter dubitationem, sed propter veritatis intellectum et manifestationem et confirmationem."
[3] *Resp. de Art.* XXXVI art. 22, n. 751.

temerarious to hold that it is. As for him, he simply does not know where hell is located.[1]

On the other hand, Thomas is inclined to grant demonstrative status to philosophers' arguments that the celestial bodies are moved by some intellectual being or beings, which, to follow the general consensus of both philosophers and saints, are better understood to be angels. But this whole question, he says, has little if anything to do with faith; it is rather a question of physics.[2] Along the same lines, he notes his inability to see what the exposition of philosophical texts has to do with the teachings of faith.[3]

In short, the general tenor of these responses amounts to a downplay on the relevance to faith of the questions asked. Accordingly, he notes that the questions raised would have to be treated much more extensively "outside the limits of theology." [4] His principal complaint, however, which he presents ever so politely, is that he was not informed of any arguments in favor of or opposed to the positions on which he has been asked to comment.[5]

Also contained in these responses is Thomas's familiar repetition of Augustine's warning against ascribing to faith what is simply a matter of human opinion.[6] A practical consequence of this attitude finds expression in a rather touching letter to an apparently unlearned man who has asked for guidance as to how he may use opinions of biblical exegetes in his preaching.[7] After mentioning such things as the star which appeared to the Magi, Thomas simply concludes that what is uncertain is not necessarily erroneous, yet should not be preached.

Much more could be and has been said about the structure of articles and questions especially but not exclusively in the *Summa Theologica*. Valuable as would be such a study, it is not directly of interest to us.[8]

---

[1] *Resp. de Art.* XXXVI art. 24, n. 755; art. 25, n. 757; *Resp. de Art* XLII, art. 31, n. 804; art. 42, n. 815.

[2] *Resp. de Art.* XLII arts. 3–7, nn. 775–780.

[3] *Resp. de Art.* XLII art. 33, n. 806.

[4] *Resp. de Art.* XLII n. 815: "Haec sunt, Pater reverende, quae pro nunc occurrunt, licet plura sint extra Theologiae limites requisita." See also Proemium, n. 772.

[5] *Resp. de Art.* XXXVI n. 770: ". . . non enim absolute responderi poterat ad ea diversum sensum poterant continere; praesertim cum non scripseritis quid contra hujusmodi articulos objiceretur. Sic enim potuisset, et absolutius et certius responderi." *Resp. de Art.* XLII Proemium, n. 772: "Fuisset tamen mihi facilius respondere, si vobis scribere placuisset rationes, quibus dicti articuli vel asseruntur vel impugnantur."

[6] *Resp. de Art.* XLII Proemium, n. 772.

[7] *Resp. ad Lectorem Bisuntinum de Art.* VI.

[8] See Ghislain Lafond, *Structure et Méthode dans La Somme Théologique de Saint Thomas d'Aquin* (Paris, 1961); Per Erik Persson, *Le plan de la Somme théologique et le rapport Ratio-Revelatio* (Paris, 1958); P. Suerdmont, *Tabulae schematicae cum introductione de principiis et compositione comparatis Summae theologicae et Summa contra Gentiles Sancti Thomae* (Turin 1943).

For, we are here referring to Thomas's theological methodology only insofar as it helps clarify his view of disputation as an instrument for dealing with opinions and evaluating their probability.

As we have seen, then, certain qualifications must be made in Thomas's theory of disputation if theology or, more specifically, faith is involved. For, because of faith the category of "unthinkable thoughts" must be said to include not only the rationally *inopinabile*, the extraneous opinion, but also the heretical, the proposition which contradicts a tenet of faith. With regard to the latter, the prerequisites for genuine disputation are not fulfilled; for, very simply, there are not two sides to the question but only one – the side of truth. In this domain, then, the side of probability is predetermined. In principle, at least, the only valid arguments here are arguments in favor of the teachings of faith.

3. *The Human Element in Disputation*

Making allowances, then, for the modified character of disputation when teachings of faith are involved, disputation has as its general purpose the establishment and clarification of a positive theoretical doubt as to the truth of a given proposition. This disputative purpose is, in turn, of a preliminary character in that it is aimed towards a particular science within which the doubt thus established is to be resolved and, if possible, the truth of the question demonstrated. Accordingly, disputative argumentation is not to be confused with demonstration. The former is, as it were, extrinsic to the structure of a science; the latter, by its very nature, can only be intrinsic to that structure. Thus the arguments brought forth in disputation are said to be extrinsic, in that they proceed not strictly on the basis of the principles of a science but on the basis of the probable, on the basis of common opinion or on the basis of opinions acceptable to the adversary.[1]

Unlike demonstration, then, disputative argumentation is not concerned with definitive determination of truth but with defense of one side of a question against obstacles brought to light by the other side.[2] From the subjective point of view, in other words, the burden of argumentation has to do with what the other side can bring against one's position. This in itself makes the value of a disputation a function

---

[1] *In* IV *Phys.* l. 1, n. 407; l. 15, n. 558; VI, l. 7, n. 823.

[2] *In* VI *Phys.* l. 4, n. 779; *in* I *De An.* l. 6, n. 74; l. 10, nn. 147 and 157; *In De Trin.* 6, 1 c; *S.T.* II–II, 51, 2 ad 3.

of the skill and insight of each of the adversaries; that is to say, a disputation can be no better than the arguments for either side. For, it is largely what one side says that determines what the other side can or need reply. Disputation, if you will, is a dialogue with a difference: it is a dialogue in which each party need give no more than is required by what the other side says. It is not, therefore, so much a confrontation of persons as it is a confrontation of ideas which men choose to defend for the sake of mutual clarification. Each learns better what he really holds or can hold by discovering what others can bring against his position; for, intellectual honesty demands that he be able to answer, or "obviate," objections to his position if he is to continue holding it.[1] It is in this sense that such defensive arguments are somewhat unfortunately described as *"ad hominem"* or even "personal," in that they proceed on the basis of what other men say.[2]

Now, so long as truth remains the sole motive of dispute, disputation is an admirable instrument for the attainment thereof, and is, no doubt, the ordinary way in which men learn from one another. The hazards clearly lie in the fact that opposing ideas inhabit not a world of their own but rather the minds of living men. And thus the task of distinguishing not only in theory but also in practice between the opinion to which one is opposed and the man who defends that opinion is forever a delicate one indeed. Should it be necessary to illustrate this point, one need only allude to the unfortunate practical consequences which have found their way into history as a result of the theoretically admirable conviction that "error has no rights."[3]

From the human point of view, then, the possibility of abusing disputative procedure is ever present. And, as we have seen, Thomas is consciously aware of that possibility. *Sub specie aeternitatis*, he is no more pleased by the fallible instrument in his hands than would be the staunchest critic of scholasticism in general. But, as he sees it, the alternative to engaging in disputation is to remain in ignorance. For, in this vale of tears, truth may be determined only by way of demon-

---

[1] *In* I *De An.* l. 10, n. 157: "Notandum tamen quod haec solutio praedictae dubitationis non est distinctiva et definitiva veritatis, *sed obviata.*" See also *In* I *Met.* l. 1, n. 23.

[2] *In* VI *Phys.* l. 4, n. 779; *In* XI *Met.* l. 5, esp. n. 2220; *Quodl.* 5, q. 5, a. 1; 3, q. 11, a. un. in contrarium. Such arguments are also said to be *rationalis* (*In De Trin.* 6, 1 c), *persuasoria* (*In De Trin.* Proem. II, 1 ad 5) or *dialectica* (*S.T.* II–II, 51, 2 ad 3). Similarly, an argument of this type is sometimes said to be a *demonstratio* in a wide sense of the term – not *"simpliciter"* or *"absolute"* but in reply to an adversary. See *In* I *Phys.* l. 3, n. 24; *In* III *Met.* l. 5, n. 392; V, l. 6, n. 838.

[3] See Jacques Leclercq, *La Liberté d'Opinion et les Catholiques* (Paris, 1963), pp. 246–250.

stration; and one can arrive at demonstration only by way of the preparatory clash of opposing opinions.

Thus, disputational procedure implies a kind of dialectic even in the Hegelian sense. For, it is out of the very opposition of the opposing views that a new and more adequate statement of the truth – a synthesis, if you will – is sought. And from this point of view each particular opinion is but a stage in the growth of men's knowledge – not taken by itself but precisely insofar as it is opposed to another opinion. To this extent, dialectical disputation implies intolerance of differing opinions. For, this very difference of opinion is itself an indication that there is a higher truth to be attained which will incorporate the relative merits of these lesser, more partial statements of truth. That this intolerance of partial truth is all too easily concretized by identifying "others" as the victims of partiality is not due to disputation as such but to the fact that disputation ceases to be truly dialectical. For, as we have seen, genuine disputation is possible only so long as it is recognized that there are two sides to a question.

At least in theory, then, there is no doubt in Thomas's mind but that an opinion as such has only a "probable" grasp on truth, however well it might have been defended in disputation. For, whether one or one thousand arguments are brought forth in its favor, the opinion remains no more than probable so long as it has not been tied to ineluctable principles – and this can be accomplished only by way of demonstration.

Demonstration, therefore, is the ultimate aim of argumentation; and as a result, knowledge that is based only on probability, the fruit of disputation, is by comparison imperfect. Accordingly, this notion of probability, which is so favorably applied to an opinion that is supported by reliable authority or that is well defended in disputation, takes on a pejorative signification when seen in comparison to demonstrative truth. It is to this less attractive aspect of probability that we now turn.

B. OPINION, PROBABILITY AND DEMONSTRATION

The probable, which characterizes and marks the limit attainable by disputation as such, is transcended to the extent that one is able to demonstrate a necessary connection between a proposition and principles. A demonstration having been found for a given proposition, that proposition is henceforth free of the vicissitudes of disputative pro and con; it is no longer probable or improbable, but necessary, and its contradictory is impossible. Such, in brief, is how Thomas sees the difference between the probable and the demonstrated. To see this difference in detail would require a thorough investigation of Thomas's Aristotelian theory of science. The latter, however, has long been a rather popular subject for students of Thomas Aquinas, so it would be somewhat superfluous for us to retrace here steps already taken often enough.[1] Nonetheless, Thomas's notion of probability is such that we cannot entirely bypass a consideration of his theory of science. For, as he sees it, the very notion of probability connotes, among other things already discussed, the non-attainment of scientific certitude. With a view, then, to further clarification of what Thomas means by the probable, we must here undertake at least a cursory presentation of what he means by the scientific, the demonstrated.

1. Thomas's Theory of Science

For Thomas, the term *scientia* has both a singular and a collective referendum. Taken in the singular sense *scientia* refers to a particular proposition which has been demonstrated.[2] Taken collectively, *scientia* refers to an ensemble of propositions which have been demonstrated. The ensemble of propositions referred to as *scientia* might, in turn, be either generic or specific. In other words, *scientia* taken collectively might refer to the set of all demonstrated propositions or only to a subset of those propositions demonstrated in some special branch of studies. In the latter case, however, Thomas will often delimit his object with some qualificative, as, for example, *scientia grammatica* or

---

[1] See in this regard the following: O. Bennett, *The Nature of Demonstrative Proof according to the Principles of Aristotle and St. Thomas Aquinas* (Washington, D.C., 1943); K. Dougherty, *The Subject, Object and Method of the Philosophy of Nature according to Thomas Aquinas* (Washington, D.C., 1951); Melvin A. Glutz, *The Manner of Demonstrating in Natural Philosophy* (River Forest, Ill., 1956). Also of interest, especially as an alternative interpretation of Aristotle's teaching, is Damascene Webering, *Theory of Demonstration according to William Ockham* (Louvain-Paderborn-St. Bonaventure, N.Y., 1953).

[2] To use more scholastic terms, *scientia* in this sense refers materially to a given proposition or propositions, formally to the demonstration which links it to principles (*S.T.* II–II, 1, 1 c). In other words, *scientia* is not a proposition as such but a known relationship of that proposition to principles. For this usage, see for example *S.T.* III, 9, 3 ad 2; *C.G.* I, 94; *Q.D. de ver.* 11, 1 c; *Q.D. de virt in comm.* q. un., a. 9 ad 11. It should be noted that students of Thomas Aquinas pay little attention to this most important usage – and not surprisingly, since Thomas himself is not very explicit about it. About the closest he comes to being explicit is, in fact, his distinction between *scientia* as a habit and *scientia* as an act (see, for example, *S.T.* I, 13, 7 ad 6). Be that as it may, if this usage is not recognized many passages in which he speaks about *scientia* are simply unintelligible; and this, as we shall see, is particularly the case when he is comparing *scientia* to opinion or probable knowledge of a proposition.

scientia divina.[1] In whatever way *scientia* is used, though, it always implies a strict relationship of logical necessity between at least two propositions, one of which founds and justifies the other.[2] Propositions which fulfill this role of founding other propositions are called principles.

From the preceding, then, we can see that our brief metascientific inquiry must take account of propositions deemed scientific and, even more, of the relationship of all such propositions to their founding principles.

(a) The Scientific Proposition

Strictly speaking, the proposition deemed scientific must be: (1) universal; (2) necessary; and hence (3) certain.[3] All three of these traits will be subjected to more careful scrutiny in the following chapters.[4] We here limit ourselves to a few brief observations which will permit us to pass directly to a consideration of the logical structure of science as seen by Thomas. For it is this, in the final analysis, that distinguishes the "scientific" from the merely "probable."

In other words, science for Thomas is structural. No proposition merits the appellation "scientific" all by itself, without reference to other propositions. For Thomas, the very notion of science is relational, in that it connotes a structural link between a given proposition and some foundational proposition.[5] Thus when we say that a scientific proposition is universal, necessary and certain we are saying implicitly "within a given structure built upon principles known (or assumed) to be universal, necessary, and certain." Accordingly, there is ample

---

[1] This collective sense of *scientia*, as well as the division into generic and specific, is too obvious to require defense. For an abundance of illustrations together with a vast variety of adjectival modifiers, see Ludwig Schütz, *Thomas-Lexikon* (New York, 1957), pp. 724–732: *scientia*. For examples of *scientia* modified by an adjective, see *S.T.* I, 1, 2 c; II–II, 47, 11 c; *C.G.* II, 73. See also *S.T.* I, 14, 1 obj. 3 and ad 3; I–II, 76, 1 c; 77, 2 c; *Q.D. de malo* 3, 6 c; *In* I *Post Analyt.* l, 43, n. 387.

[2] Strictly speaking, Thomas would have to say three propositions are involved, since the proposition deemed scientific is linked to a principle by the mediation of at least one other proposition, in accordance with good syllogistic theory.

[3] See *In* I *Post. Analyt.* l. 4, nn. 32–34; l. 9; l. 13, n. 109; ll. 16 and 39; l. 42, nn. 376–381; l. 44, nn. 396–397; II, l. 20, nn. 584, 592; *S.T.* I, 86, 3 c; I–II, 67, 3 c; II–II, 47, 5 c. To be complete, we would have to add as a further trait, causal, or based on causes. But our whole discussion of the three traits indicated has as its very purpose to show just that. For, it is precisely by knowing a proposition in and through the principles of the relevant science that proposition is known causally. Thus the absolutely essential role of principles in Thomas's theory of science.

[4] Qualifications of the traits of necessity and universality will be discussed especially in Chapter 5. The trait of certainty and to some extent that of necessity will be qualified by considerations in Chapter 6.

[5] *Q.D. de virt. card.* q. un., a. 2 c; *Q.D. de malo* 7, 7 c. *S.T.* I, 14, 1 obj. 2; 60, 2 c; I–II, 65, 1 c; 67, 3 c; II–II, 1, 1 c; 23, 7 ad 2; 51, 2 c; *In* I *Post. Analyt.* l. 42, n. 380.

reason for saying that the traits of a scientific proposition are not so much prerequisites as they are consequences of that proposition's being deemed scientific.

Take, in the first place, the trait of universality. This implies that for a proposition to be scientific in the strict sense it must be true of every member of the class represented by the grammatical subject of that proposition.[1] This class, moreover, is taken to be not merely logical but real, implying at the very least that the class is not empty. Thus the scientific proposition is assumed to have content; but, precisely insofar as it is "scientific," it transcends the limitations of that content. In other words, Thomas's concept of a scientific proposition is more than that of a protocol statement of inductive findings. He likes to explain the passage from sense particulars to the universal assertion in terms of Aristotle's theory of abstraction; for he is empiricist enough to demand that any scientific proposition be somehow tied to sense experience. As he notes in commenting on Aristotle, there are two ways of acquiring science: (1) by induction from sense particulars; (2) by demonstration from universals. He adds, however, that the deduction of one universal proposition from another is of scientific value only if founded upon a proposition that is induced from sense experience.[2] But a founding proposition is a principle. Thus, the universality of a scientific proposition depends upon the universality of principles to which it is structurally related. This, in turn, allows us to transpose the problem of universality – or, if you will, of induction – to the level of founding principles.

The seond trait of a scientific proposition is that it is necessary. This means, at least in theory, that what is asserted by means of that proposition cannot be other than it is. Moreover, since the scientific proposition is assumed to have content, the necessity in question is thought to be not merely logical but real. But, as we shall see at length in the next chapter, Thomas follows Aristotle in allowing that there can be demonstration of necessary aspects of what is otherwise contingent and, even more, demonstration with regard to what happens only for the most part (*ut frequenter*).[3] This admission alone is enough to take the teeth out of the trait of necessity if necessity is to be understood simply as a real necessity expressed by a given isolated proposition. It further diminishes the import of the trait of universality;

---

[1] *In* II *Post. Analyt.* l. 12, nn. 524–525; I, l. 9, esp. n. 79.
[2] *In* I *Post. Analyt.* 1. 30, nn. 251–253. See also *In* II *Post. Analyt.* l. 20; *In* I *Met.* l. 1.
[3] See *In* I *Post. Analyt.* l. 42, esp. nn. 373–374.

for, a proposition is strictly speaking universally applicable to all members of a class only if it is always true of each member of that class. But, leaving the full implications of all this for later, we need only conclude here that a scientific proposition cannot be considered as "necessary" without any reference to the system within which and thanks to which it is considered necessary.[1] Accordingly, the necessity of a scientific proposition, qua scientific, is logical, in that it derives from principles deemed necessary. How this logical relationship is to be referred to the real depends ultimately upon the relationship of the principles to the real. Thus the question of necessity as a trait of a scientific proposition may also be transposed to the level of principles.

The third trait of a scientific proposition, we recall, is that of certainty. But, as with the other traits, that of certainty is not independent of the certainty of principles. A "conclusion" that is recognized as being necessarily true and hence certain can only be derived from premises that are themselves deemed necessary and hence certain.[2] If one is able to arrive at such a conclusion, he is said to have science in the strict sense of the word, and the syllogism which causes this certain knowledge of a conclusion is, strictly speaking, a demonstration.[3] Science, in short, implies demonstration, and demonstration implies the linking of one proposition to another as its justification. Thus a premiss must at the very least be more known and more certain than the conclusion or conclusions derived therefrom.[4] Since, however, not every proposition can be derived from still another proposition, one must assume as a foundation one or more propositions the certainty of which is not demonstrated but is rather presupposed.[5] Such foundational propositions are, of course, the principles upon which the certainty of deduced propositions depends. Thus the question of certainty in science can also be transposed to that of the certainty of principles.

We see, then, that the whole weight of science rests upon the principles of science. For, the necessity (and thus the universality and the certainty) of any given scientific proposition derives from the

---

[1] Thomas makes a similar observation, directly with regard to truth and certainty, at *In* II *Post. Analyt.* l. 12, n. 525.

[2] See *S.T.* I, 85, 6 c; I–II, 67, 3 c; *In* I *Post. Analyt.* l. 42, n. 380; *In* IV *Met.* l. 6, n. 596; *Q.D. de ver.* 16, 2 c.

[3] *S.T.* I–II, 54, 2 ad 2; *C.G.* I, 57; *In* I *Post. Analyt.* ll. 13–14; *In* VI *Ethic.* l. 4, nn. 1164–1165.

[4] *In* I *Post. Analyt.* l. 4, nn. 42–43; l. 6; l. 7, n. 61; l. 8, nn. 61, 71 and 71 bis; II, l. 20, n. 585.

[5] *In* I *Post. Analyt.* l. 7, nn. 62 and 64; l. 18, n. 151; l. 19, n. 162; l. 20, n. 171; l. 21, n. 177; l. 35, n. 307; l. 41, n. 368; II, l. 2, n. 426.

necessity of premises upon which it depends, and the latter must ultimately be founded upon what are considered self-evident principles. These "first principles" are, accordingly, both the foundation and the justification of any strictly scientific demonstration. Thus the concern of Thomas as an Aristotelian is to manifest a necessary connection between proposition and principles, that is, to show that a given proposition follows necessarily from principles taken to be ineluctable. Only when this strict relationship of implication has been manifested can one rightfully speak of having scientific knowledge of the proposition in question. Thus, for example, not every proposition about changing bodies is part of physics but only those propositions which can be reduced to the principles of physics.[1] In other words, a proposition may well be learned without recourse to principles; but insofar as that proposition is incorporated into the structure of science it is manifestly dependent upon the principles of science as effect upon cause.[2]

Assuming the truth of the principles, a proposition necessarily deduced therefrom cannot be false. Strictly speaking, then, science is incapable of falsity.[3] Falsity comes rather from assuming as a principle what is false, or from incorrectly relating a proposition to the principles.[4] Similarly, one who does not know or does not accept the principle that the whole is greater than any of its parts cannot acquire the science of geometry but will fall into many errors.[5]

In short, structural dependence upon correct principles is the basic requirement for qualifying a given proposition as truly scientific. So long as one is unable to establish such structural dependence, he can claim no more than probability for the proposition in question. Thus our study of probability in Thomas Aquinas leads us to consider more carefully what he has to say about the principles of science.

(b) The Principles of Science

The first thing that must be noted in our discussion about principles of science is that we are now speaking of science in the collective sense. As noted above, the ensemble of propositions referred to as science

---

[1] See In V Phys. l. 5, n. 684; Q.D. de ver. 14, 8 ad 16; In De Trin. Proemium I, 3 c and ad 1.

[2] S.T. I, 85, 8 ad 1: ". . . In accipiendo scientiam, non semper principia et elementa sunt priora . . . Sed in complemento scientiae, semper scientia effectuum dependet ex cognitione principiorum et elementorum." See also Aristotle, I Physics c. 1; 184, a, 10–16; Thomas l. 1; l. 3, n. 22; S.T. I, 14, 1 obj. 2; 60, 2 c; I–II, 51, 2 c; Q.D. de ver. 3, 3 ad 7.

[3] S.T. I, 85, 6 c; In I Ethic. l. 4, n. 40; l. 44, n. 405; II, l. 20, n. 596.

[4] S.T. II–II, 55, 3 c; Q.D. de ver. 16, 2 ad 1; 22, 6 c; Q.D. de malo 7, 7 c.

[5] S.T. I–II, 65, 1 ad 4.

might be the set of all scientific propositions or some subset of those propositions which constitutes a special science. Accordingly, when we speak about the principles of science we are in fact referring to two different levels of principles: (1) those common to all scientific knowledge; (2) those which are proper to any one of the special sciences.[1]

Secondly, we must emphasize something already suggested by our remarks about the traits of a scientific proposition, namely that there is a certain ambivalence in Thomas's view of the foundations of science. For, his view of a scientific proposition is, as it were, both empiricist and deductivist at the same time. This same ambivalence, which is by no means peculiar to Thomas's philosophy of science, is carried over into his metascientific views about the principles of science.

The two aspects of science here indicated might be entitled, first, the logical structure of science and, secondly, the foundations of science. Both aspects are relevant to the notion of probability, the first explicitly and the second implicitly. We shall, therefore, take both into consideration in what follows.

With regard to the logical structure of science, we must bear in mind that a given proposition, deemed scientific, depends for its value as scientific both upon special principles of the science in which it is incorporated and upon common principles that are the foundation of all intellectual knowledge.[2] The special principles are often called simply principles or, more technically, *positiones* or *elementa*. The common principles are often called first principles or *dignitates* or *maximae propositiones*.[3]

Thomas distinguishes two kinds of *first principles*, those which are the basis of definitions and those which are the basis of demonstrations. The former are the so-called transcendentals: being, one, good, and so on. The latter are fundamental propositions, such as that of non-contradiction, that of the whole and its parts, and so on. In either case, he insists, these principles are somehow discovered in the objects of sensation; and thus, whatever man is capable of knowing is and must be ultimately founded in sense experience.[4] The totality of all propositions which go to make up man's scientific knowledge is, accordingly, contained at least virtually in what is known through sense experience.

---

[1] See *In* I *Post. Analyt.* l. 15; l. 18, esp. nn. 151–158; ll. 20 and 21; l. 36, n. 314; l. 43, esp. nn. 387 and 394; *In* IV *Met.* l. 5, esp. n. 595.

[2] See *In* I *Post. Analyt.* ll. 20 and 21.

[3] See *In* I *Post. Analyt.* l. 5, nn. 49–52; l. 36, n. 314; *S.T.* I, 85, 8 ad 1.

[4] *In De Trin.* 6, 4 c. See also *Q.D. de ver.* 11, 1 c; *In* I *Post. Analyt.* l. 5, nn. 50–52; l. 20.

On the other hand, whatever is not somehow knowable through principles based on sense experience cannot be known by human reason.[1] This explains, for example, why the doctrine of the Trinity is unknowable to reason, namely because that doctrine is not based upon knowledge acquired through the senses.[2] The first or common principles, in other words, are as it were the seeds or roots of human knowledge, in such a way that one knowing the principles is potentially capable of learning all the conclusions implied therein.[3]

According to the commentary on the *Posterior Analytics*, these common or first principles are known immediately and even quasi-automatically once the meaning of their terms is understood. Thus these principles are known by the educated and the uneducated alike. Of all these self-evident principles known to all the principle of non-contradiction is absolutely fundamental; but also given as an example of this type of principle is the assertion that the whole is greater than any of its parts.[4] In any event, acceptance of these principles, here referred to as *dignitates*, is prerequisite to any demonstration in any science. But neither is a *dignitas* itself demonstrated nor does it enter formally into any demonstration; what is required is rather that it be presupposed and accepted. For this reason, plus the fact that every science has its own proper subject matter, a *dignitas* cannot possibly serve as the basis for an *a priori* deductive system of all conclusions of all the sciences.[5] The *dignitates*, in short, are necessary but not sufficient for science; they are a *sine qua non* condition for scientific demonstration.

The *special principles* proper to each of the special sciences enter more directly into the demonstrations of the special sciences. For, each science deals with a special class of things, and hence must deal with these things, as it were, on their own terms, with principles proper to the kinds of things with which it deals.[6] A special principle, then, is very simply a definition of the subject matter to be developed by the special science. By means of a distinction remotely equivalent to that now current between *explicandum* and *explicatum*, Thomas is able to make Aristotle say that a founding definition may be considered either

[1] *Q.D. de ver.* 12, 3 ad 2; *S.T.* I–II, 3, 6 c.
[2] *Q.D. de ver.* 10, 13 c. Compare *S.T.* I, 32, 1.
[3] *Q.D. de ver.* 12, 1 ad 3; 16, 1 c. See also 14, 11 c; *In* I *Post. Analyt.* l. 7, n. 67.
[4] *In* I *Post. Analyt.* l. 5, nn. 49–50; l. 36, n. 314; *In* IV *Met.* l. 5, n. 595.
[5] *In* I *Post. Analyt.* l. 15, n. 130; l. 20; l. 43, nn. 387 and 394.
[6] *In* I *Post. Analyt.* l. 15; l. 21, nn. 174 and 178; l. 41, n. 367; l. 43, n. 394.

as a predicate (*positio* in a narrower sense) or as a complete proposition (*positio* also, or *suppositio*).[1]

Considered *as a complete proposition*, a special principle is in itself as self-evident as are the *dignitates*, inasmuch as the grammatical subject implies the predicate or, if you will, the predicate is included in the grammatical subject. However, the recognition of this self-evidence demands a certain amount of explanation; hence, such principles are not known by all men but only by the wise, that is to say, perhaps, by the specialists. As an example of such a principle we are given the proposition that all right angles are equal.[2]

Considered simply *as a predicate*, a special principle is the *explicatum* of the concept deemed primordial. Not every explicatum, of course, is a principle in this sense, but only such *explicata* as can serve as the foundation of a science.[3] For example, the arithmetician founds his science by giving, as the *explicatum* of unity, "that which is indivisible with respect to quantity." [4]

Each particular science, then, presupposes not only the *dignitates*, or principles common to all sciences, but also *positiones*, which are special principles proper to the subject matter of that science.[5] Armed with the metascientific support of the *dignitates*, the special scientist develops his subject matter upon the foundation of *positiones*. The latter, taken as definitions, are used as *media* (middle terms) in order to show that various *passiones* (attributes or, in logical terminology, predicates) are predicable of that subject taken as a class.[6] The ideal, of course, is to achieve certitude that a given *passio* is predicable of the whole

---

[1] This terminological refinement is te be found at *In I Post. Analyt.* l. 5, nn. 49–52, where Thomas is faced with a difficult text. Elsewhere, Thomas tends to be much freer in his use of *positio* and *suppositio*, either of which may refer to a complete proposition or, as we would say, an assertion. As will be noted shortly, *suppositio* (even in the passage just cited) also suggests "presupposition," in that the given science does not demonstrate its founding proposition but borrows it from some other science in which it is demonstrated. For a more detailed consideration of what is "presupposed" in a science, see *In I Post. Analyt.* l. 18, nn. 157–158. See also Schütz, *Thomas-Lexikon* (New York, 1957) under *positio* and *suppositio*. It should finally be noted that *suppositio* as here used should not be confused with the *suppositio* of terms, so much discussed by medieval logicians. Regarding the latter usage, see William and Martha Kneale, *The Development of Logic* (Oxford, 1962), pp. 246–274; I. M. Bochenski, *A History of Formal Logic* (Notre Dame, Ind., 1961), n. 27: Supposition, pp. 162–173.

[2] See *In I Post. Analyt.* l. 2, n. 19; l. 5, n. 458; l. 7, n. 67; l. 20, n. 170; *In IV Met.* l. 5, esp. nn. 592–595; *In De Hebdom.* 1. 1, nn, 13–18.

[3] See *In I Post. Analyt.* l. 16, nn. 138–139; l. 26, n. 215; II, l. 8, n. 488.

[4] *In I Post. Analyt.* l. 5, n. 51.

[5] In addition to references cited above, see also *In I Post. Analyt.* l. 18, nn. 151–152; l. 20, n. 170.

[6] See *In I Post. Analyt.* ll. 2–3; l. 15, n. 129; 1. 18, nn. 153–158; *In V Met.* l. 1, n. 749; *In De Trin.* 2, 2 ad 3.

class. For such certitude, it must be shown that that *passio* is necessarily inherent in any member of the class. In other words, the proposition in which the given *passio* functions as predicate must be true of every individual endowed with the attribute signified by the subject of the proposition: applicable always and for all individuals contained in the class under consideration.

We note here a kind of hierarchical relationship between the common foundational principles (*dignitates* or first principles) and the special principles (*positiones*) which found the special sciences. This hierarchical structure Thomas completes by positing a similar relationship between the various special sciences. The very idea of a principle, of course, suggests that it is a starting point, that is, that there is nothing logically prior to it upon which it depends.[1] But, as Aristotle had already pointed out, one may determine rationally what are to be the principles of a given science. This, according to Aristotle, might be done on the basis of induction or by *presupposing* a given proposition which has been demonstrated in another science.[2] A science whose principles are presupposed in the science itself but are proven in a more fundamental science Thomas calls a subalternate science. Thus, for example, the theory of measurement (*geodaesia* or *geosophia*) is subalternate to arithmetic, medicine is subalternate to physical science.[3] One possessing knowledge of a subalternate science is said to have scientific knowledge not because of the principles assumed but because of conclusions drawn from those principles. As for the principles themselves, if one is unable to demonstrate them, then for him they are only probable. It is, in other words, precisely insofar as a special principle is known only probably that it is called a *suppositio*.[4]

This theory of subalternation, then, implies as a corollary that the certainty which is characteristic of science is subject to gradation. For, according to this theory the very notion of a principle is relative or, if you will, analogical.[5] Generally speaking, a given proposition serves

[1] See *S.T.* I, 33, 1 c and ad 3; *In* I *Sent.* d. 29, q. 1, a. 1 ad 1 *In* I *Phys.* l. 10; *In* V *Met.* l. 1. From these passages it will be seen that *principium* has a wider range of meanings than the logical meaning which is of interest to us. Be that as it may, the logical meaning further suggests that a principle is not demonstrated: *In* I *Post. Analyt.* l. 7, nn. 62 and 64; l. 18, n. 151; l. 19, n. 162; l. 20, n. 171; l. 21, n. 177; l. 35, n. 307; l. 41, n. 368; II, l. 2, n. 426.
[2] See *In* I *Post. Analyt.* l. 5, n. 50; l. 18; *In* VIII *Phys.* l. 3, nn. 993–994; *In* VI *Met.* l. 1, nn. 1149–1150.
[3] See *S.T.* I, 1, 8 c; *C.G.* III, 79; *Q.D. de ver.* 9, 1 ad 3; *In De Trin.* Proemium 2, 2 ad 5; 2, 1, 1 ad 5; *In* III *Met.* l. 6, n. 396; l. 7, nn. 413–414; *In* I *Post. Analyt.* l. 15; l. 25, nn. 208–211; l. 41, n. 357.
[4] *Q.D. de ver.* 14, 10 ad 3; *In* I *Post. Analyt.* l. 19 and esp. n. 162; l. 39, n. 341.
[5] This is stated explicitly with regard to common principles at *In* I *Post Analyt.* l. 18, n. 154. See also *In* IV *Met.* l. 5, n. 591.

as the principle, or foundation, of other propositions because of its greater universality, that is, because it has wider applicability.[1] This criterion of universality, however, tends to be explained in terms of simplicity. It is on the basis of simplicity, for example, that some types of argumentation, and above all the Barbara syllogism, are said to be more efficacious than others.[2] Similarly, sciences which start from fewer principles are more certain than those which add on other principles. Accordingly, in the Aristotelian conception geometry follows upon and is less certain than arithmetic.[3] Again, the more closely a science deals with material things the less certain it is, because of the changeableness of matter. Thus applied mathematics is considerably less certain than is pure mathematics.[4] The non-intelligibility of matter which is here implied is further explained as deriving from the impossibility of knowing the infinite, since in dealing with concrete individuals one approaches the infinite.[5]

At this point the astute reader will note that our discussion of Thomas's theory of science has turned a complete circle and that, as a result, Thomas's desire to make science both deductive and empirical remains theoretically unjustified. For, on the one hand, Thomas insists that all scientific propositions are somehow based upon sense experience. The certainty of science, he continues, depends upon the certainty of its principles; and the principles and the first principles *par excellence* are also based upon sense experience. On the other hand, the more a science is involved with the concrete the less certain it is; the more a science abstracts from the concrete the more certain it is. Thus we have what might be called a polarity of certitude: certitude in human knowledge must be founded upon induction from sense particulars; but the degree of certitude attainable is directly proportional to the extent to which a given proposition abstracts from concrete individuals as such. In short, in Thomas's theory of science the material objects of sense experience constitute both the foundation and the limit of all scientific endeavor.

It is, of course, easy to say that Thomas's theory of abstraction resolves the apparent antinomy. But, however valuable that theory may be from a psychological point of view, it is epistemologically weak.

---

[1] *In* I *Post. Analyt.* l. 4, nn. 43 and 43 bis; l. 19, esp. n. 166; l. 36, n. 314; l. 40, n. 354; *Q.D. de ver.* 9, 1 ad 3.
[2] *In* I *Post. Analyt.* ll. 36–40 and esp. l. 36, n. 318.
[3] *In* I *Post. Analyt.* l. 41, nn. 357–360; *In* I *De An.* l. 1, nn. 3–6; *S.T.* I, 1, 5 c.
[4] *In* I *Post. Analyt.* l. 41, n. 358. See also I, l. 25, nn. 208–210.
[5] *In* I *Post. Analyt.* l. 38, n. 335.

Epistemologically speaking, the theory of abstraction amounts to a begging of the question. For, what Thomas is saying in effect is that our thoughts mirror reality because reality is reflected in our thoughts.[1] He may, of course, be absolutely right; but he does not thereby provide an adequate justification for what he chooses to consider the principles, or axioms, of all science in general and of the special sciences in particular. Still less does he thereby justify the traits of necessity, universality and certainty which he likes to attribute to science. What is here at stake, of course, is nothing less than the still pressing problem of induction.

This is well brought out by the way in which Thomas tries to found the principles of science in sense experience. As he notes in one place, the very fact that men disagree about conclusions is sufficient indication that conclusions are not, as Plato had suggested, "naturally known." But, Thomas adds, men are in agreement about principles, and thus principles are "naturally known," that is to say, known without recourse to reasoning.[2] This position, of course, is somewhat modified by the distinction between first principles known to all and special principles known only to the wise. As for a first principle, however, Thomas agrees with Aristotle (1) that one cannot be deceived or in error about it; (2) that it cannot be suppositional but must be absolute; and that (3) it must be known naturally and not acquired by reasoning.[3] Just how a man comes to know these principles "naturally" is, of course, somewhat difficult to explain. Thomas, at any rate, seems to go from an early tendency to consider them as Platonically given to a later agreement with Aristotle that they too are acquired through sense experience. Especially on the basis of the *Posterior Analytics* he can say quite simply that man acquires experience of many individuals, or events, of the same kind and that from this experience he is able to make an "induction" of both the general and the special principles of science.[4]

---

[1] Here we are, of course, considerably oversimplifying a rather elaborate theory of knowledge. If, however, we are to believe Etienne Gilson, this is just about what Thomas is saying – in fact, all that he need to say. See Gilson's *The Christian Philosophy of St. Thomas Aquinas* (New York, 1956), pp. 207–235. For an excellent study of the many and varied attempts to develop an epistemology on the basis of Thomas's views, see Georges Van Riet, *L'Epistémologie Thomiste: Recherches sur le problème de la connaissance dans l'Ecole Thomiste Contemporaine*, Louvain, 1946. Our approach to Thomas's thought has been considerably influenced by that of Van Riet, especially as expressed in his *Problèmes d'Epistémologie* (Louvain-Paris, 1960).

[2] *C.G.* II, 83.

[3] *In IV Met.* l. 6, nn. 597–599.

[4] See *Q.D. de ver.* 22, 7 c; *In De Trin.* 6, 4 c; *In I Post. Analyt.* l. 30, nn. 252–253; l. 42, n. 378; II, l. 20; *In I Met.* l. 1.

Needless to say, the mere assertion of empiricism does not in itself provide an adequate foundation for the principles of science. Yet at the same time one can well agree with Thomas that the principles do in fact constitute the foundation of science. The only problem that remains in this regard, then, is to explain why the principles are in fact foundational. For Thomas, it might seem, the answer would lie in the fact that the principles are more necessary, more universal, and more certain than conclusions derived from them. From this it would surely follow that one cannot acquire knowledge of a given science unless he has correct knowledge of the principles of that science.[1] It is interesting to note, however, that to express this notion of "correct knowledge" of principles, Thomas uses terms which usually mean opinionative knowledge: *recta existimatio* or *aestimatio recta*.[2] This suggests some interesting problems as to the solidity of the principles themselves, but to this we shall return in a later chapter.[3] A not altogether unrelated problem will quite sufficiently occupy us for the time being, namely, that of the cogency of a demonstration founded upon such principles. As Thomas puts it, the intellect is driven to consent to a conclusion because of the efficacy of the demonstration.[4] The problem, then, is to determine what in fact constitutes an efficacious demonstration.

2. Science and Probability

Thomas's answer to this problem is that a demonstration is efficacious if it manifests the necessity of the conclusion, that is, that it cannot be other than it is. Put differently, the demonstrated conclusion is always true and cannot be sometimes true and sometimes false.[5] This, of course, provides a neat theoretical distinction between science and opinion; but it hardly helps one to know which is in fact which. The matter is, however, put somewhat more neatly by saying that a conclusion is demonstrated, and thus scientific, if its denial implies a

---

[1] *Q.D. de virt. card.* q. un., a. 2 c; *Q.D. de malo* 7. 7 c; *S.T.* I, 14, 1 obj. 2; 60, 2 c; I–II, 65, 1 c; 67, 3 c; II–II, 1, 1 c; 23, 7 ad 2; 51, 2 c.

[2] In the passages in question, namely those of the preceding note, these expressions seem almost interchangeable with yet another, *recta ratio*, which seems to indicate that Thomas is using none of the expressions in a very technical sense. This in itself, however, is interesting to us. For it lends weight to our contention that opinion and the terms expressive thereof serve as a kind of broad base for all of Thomas's epistemological doctrine.

[3] In Chapter 6 we shall find it necessary to found the certitude of first principles in God, who is thus for Thomas the ultimate guarantor of the value of human science.

[4] *Q.D. de ver.* 11, 3 ad 11.

[5] *In* VII *Met.* l. 15, nn. 1610–1612; *S.T.* I–II, 10, 2 ad 2.

denial of a principle.[1] In this way, the truth of a science as a whole reduces to the truth of its principles.

If, then, the principles are assumed to be true or even to be self-evident, then the truth of the science as a whole is guaranteed. All that one need do to increase the content of a given science (and this, of course, is a not insignificant task) is to show that the principles can be true only if the conclusion be also true.[2] In this way, the totality of the given science forms a kind of organic whole which stands or falls with the principles. If one grants the truth of the principles, then he must grant the truth of a demonstrated conclusion once he has in fact seen, through the demonstration, that there is a necessary connection between conclusion and principles, not, however, before he has seen this connection.[3]

However related a given proposition may be to the subject matter of the science, it does not enter into the structure of the science as such until it has been so demonstrated. Subjectively speaking, then, a given individual does not know that proposition scientifically unless or until he himself sees it to be necessarily connected with the principles of the science. All propositions not so seen are for him no more than opinions.[4]

(a) Demonstrative and Probable Argumentation

In other words, it is the reduction of a proposition to the principles of a science which makes that proposition properly scientific. The process of reasoning whereby this reduction is manifested is precisely what Thomas means by a demonstration. Thus is demonstration qualitatively set apart from all other arguments, which are called, for example, *ratio* or *probatio* or, as he says in one place, *processus* or *probatio rationalis*. These latter, which do not accomplish the ultimate reduction to principles, give one opinionative knowledge (*opinio* or *fides*) of the conclusion, but not science. Such arguments are, by comparison, probable rather than scientific. From this point of view, then, the probable is imperfect by comparison to the demonstrated, which is perfect knowledge. The former still calls for further discursive reasoning, the latter does not.[5] Both are in some way dependent upon

---

[1] *S.T.* I–II, 10, 2 ad 3; 13, 6 ad 1; *Q.D. de malo* 16, 7 ad 18.
[2] *Q.D. de ver.* 24, 1 ad 18.
[3] *S.T.* I, 82, 2 c; *Q.D. de malo* 3, 3 c.
[4] *In De Trin.* 6, 1 c; *In I Post. Analyt.* l. 44, n. 402; *Q.D. de ver.* 11, 1 c.
[5] *Q.D. de ver.* 15, 1 c; *S.T.* III, 9, 3 ad 2; *In I Post. Analyt.* l. 31, n. 258.

the first principles for their truth, but the probable, the opinionative, is not manifestly a necessary consequence thereof.[1]

Another difference between the demonstrated and the probable proposition is that the former may depend upon just one syllogism whereas the latter calls forth one's acceptance only on the basis of many syllogisms.[2] This difference is due to the fact that the demonstrative syllogism is efficacious or cogent, manifesting as it does a necessary connection with the principles, whereas the dialectical syllogism which supports a probable proposition does not accomplish this manifestation of necessity. Put differently, many middle terms are utilized in support of a probable proposition; but a demonstrated proposition, if truly demonstrated, might well be due to just one middle term which links that proposition to a principle. Stating the same thing from a more psychological point of view, many acts of reason are needed to establish opinionative knowledge (*habitum opinativum*) in the mind; but the possession of scientific knowledge can be brought about with just one act of reason, although subsequent acts may be necessary for the benefit of sense powers and memory.[3]

This reference to reason is of considerable importance, of course, since neither science nor opinion comes naturally, so to speak, as a result of knowing the principles.[4] Even with regard to what is known through demonstration, some conclusions follow at once (*statim*) from principles, others are not arrived at except through many middle terms.[5] And the more middle terms are needed to manifest a given proposition, the more likely it is that one or another of the links in the chain will be weak, thus rendering the whole proof inefficacious. For, if any one of the premises is false or even doubtful, the chain of reasoning is just as weak as this weakest link.[6] Moreover, the very fact that different conclusions are derived from the principles through different middle terms makes it possible for a person to know some conclusions of a science without knowing others.[7] The mere fact that a man is a grammarian, for example, does not mean that he can demonstrate all the conclusions of the science of grammar. Similarly, there might well be more con-

---

[1] *Q.D. de ver.* 11, 1 c; *Q.D. de virt. in comm.* q. un., a. 9 ad 11.

[2] *S.T.* I, 47, 1 ad 3; *Comp. theol.* c. 102, n. 196.

[3] *S.T.* I–II, 51, 3 c.

[4] *Q.D. de pot.* 2, 3 ad 7.

[5] *Q.D. de ver.* 8, 4 ad 12.

[6] *Q.D. de ver.* 14, 10 c. It should be noted that Thomas here makes this point in order to illustrate his contention that, because human instruments are fallible, one cannot have perfect certitude about the articles of faith.

[7] *S.T.* II–II, 5, 3 ad 2.

clusions demonstrable about a triangle than a given person knows.[1]

An obvious corollary of the foregoing is that a given proposition which is in itself demonstrable might be known only opinionatively.[2] This may be due to misapprehension of a principle or to inadequate or defective reasoning.[3] For example, a mathematical theorem which is in itself demonstrable might be known only on the basis of probable argumentation.[4] If, however, a given proposition is in fact demonstrable, then merely probable knowledge thereof is imperfect. For, the proposition is less well known than one can know it: the necessary, which can be known by way of necessity, is known only by way of probability.[5]

It is to be noted that the proposition known is in both cases the same; it is rather the mode of knowing which differs. One with only probable knowledge of a demonstrable proposition does in fact know the whole proposition, that is, he knows each of its parts, but he does not know that proposition totally, that is, as perfectly as it can be known. This perfect knowledge of a proposition by way of demonstration Thomas calls comprehension: one comprehends a proposition when he knows it as perfectly as it can be known. One who does not have this comprehensive knowledge which is attained by way of demonstration simply does not know it as perfectly as it can be known. He knows both subject and predicate and the connection between subject and predicate; but his knowledge is only imperfectly founded, upon probable argumentation. It is not at all irrelevant to our purposes to note, finally, that Thomas's standard reason for pointing out this difference between comprehensive and non-comprehensive knowledge of a proposition is in order to make a comparison between what we know of God in this life and what we shall know hereafter.[6]

One other question that here comes to mind in comparing demonstrative and probable knowledge of a proposition is whether or not one and the same person might have both types of knowledge of the same proposition. Early in his career, Thomas did not think so, on the grounds that one type of knowledge is opposed to the other as the doubtful to the non-doubtful.[7] But later on he came to hold that one could indeed know the same proposition by different means, that is, both through dialectical (or probable) and through demonstrative

[1] Q.D. de ver. 8, 4 c; S.T. I–II, 66, 1 c.
[2] In I Post. Analyt. l. 44, nn. 402–404; S.T. I, 2, 2 c.
[3] Q.D. de ver. 14, 6 c; 8, 4 c.
[4] Q.D. de ver. 8, 2 c.
[5] Comp. theol. c. 106, n. 213; S.T. II–II, 5, 3 c; C.G. I, 67; In De div. nom. c. 1, l. 1, n. 26.
[6] Q.D. de ver. 2, 1 ad 3; C.G. III, 55; S.T. I, 14, 3 c; 12, 7 c and ad 3.
[7] Q.D. de ver. 14, 9 ad 6. See also S.T. II–II, 1, 5 ad 4.

argument. Again it is interesting to note that this change of mind is stimulated by a theological need to explain how angels know the same things both by natural and by divinely infused knowledge (what Augustine had called morning and evening knowledge).[1]

(b) Opinion as Non-Demonstrated Knowledge

The probable knowledge of which we are speaking is, of course,, opinion, now seen in direct contrast to the demonstrated proposition that is science. As expressed in the *Posterior Analytics*, this is dialectical truth as compared to scientific truth. Similarities between the two are, however, numerous, to such an extent that in one place Thomas refers to opinion as a "lesser science." [2] According to Thomas's most rigorous definition of opinion, which he finds in Aristotle, it is the acceptance of or conviction as to an immediate non-necessary proposition: *acceptio, idest existimatio quaedam, immediatae propositionis et non necessariae.*[3] A brief consideration of the two characteristics of opinion, that is, (1) that it is non-necessary and (2) that it is immediate, will help to clarify its relationship to the scientific. But the latter, as we shall see, also raises a problem of no little importance.

That opinion is of the non-necessary means, as we recall, that it deals with that which can be (or is at least thought able to be) other than it is. Thus, certitude with regard to an opinion can vary considerably according to the extent to which the mind assents to the truth of the proposition in question.[4] By way of distinction between science and opinion, science is concerned only with what is *"semper verum,"* whether this is with regard to the necessary as such or some necessary aspect of the otherwise non-necessary, that is, the contingent. Thus, for Aristotle at any rate, knowledge of necessity in what is otherwise contingent is science and not opinion. This may be either art (*recta ratio factibilium*) or prudence (*recta ratio agibilium*). Opinion as such is directly concerned with contingents as contingent, and thus deals with what may be either true or false, that is, with propositions which may

---

[1] *Q.D. de pot.* 4, 2 ad 21, S.T. I, 58, 7 ad 3; 62, 7 ad 1; I–II, 67, 3 c. See also *In* I *Post. Analyt.* l. 13, n. 118; l. 42, n. 373; and, finally, S.T. III, 9, 3 ad 2, where Thomas uses basically the same illustration to clarify his contention that Christ had simultaneously infused knowledge and the knowledge of the beatific vision.

[2] *Q.D. de virt. in comm.* q. un., a. 9 ad 11. Because of the context, in which Thomas is already insisting upon the defective character of opinion, we translate the expression, *minor scientia*, not as "less than science" but as "a lesser science": ". . . opinio autem, licet sit minor scientia, non causatur in nobis per unum syllogismum dialecticum; sed requiruntur plures propter eorum debilitatem."

[3] *In* I *Post Analyt.* l. 44, n. 399.

[4] *In Post Analyt.* Proemium, n. 6.

be either true or false. Thus, whereas the demonstrator (one who demonstrates a proposition) always takes the true alternative of contradictory propositions, the dialectician takes both alternatives, since both are still open to consideration.[1] By way of a kind of summary of the difference of approach of the demonstrator and the dialectician, it can be noted that for the demonstrator the *dici de omni* must be true absolutely (*simpliciter*), that is, for all time; for the dialectician, on the other hand, the *dici de omni* is only taken in general (*communiter*), that is, as true for the time being ("*ut nunc*").[2]

This opinionative knowledge acquired by the dialectician is, however, taken to be genuinely true, at least for the most part (*ut frequenter*).[3] We shall have more to say about this further on. For now, the point is simply that one must not confuse such knowledge with science in the strict sense. A dialectical argument that is taken to be demonstrative is for that very reason sophistical. This is simply one step beyond the usual characterization of the sophistical argument as one which seems to be probable but in fact is not or which seems to be a syllogism but in fact is not.[4] On the other hand, merely because someone believes that a proposition to which he adheres is deserving only of opinion, this does not in itself make that proposition in itself opinionative, or merely probable. For, a proposition which is in fact susceptible of being demonstrated and thus of becoming the object of scientific certitude might at a given time or for a given individual be accepted only as an opinion.[5]

The second aspect of opinionative or probable knowledge mentioned above is that it is the adherence to an *immediate* proposition, that is, to a proposition which is not the conclusion of another syllogism but rather a kind of principle in that it is taken as basic. In other words, "immediate" here refers to the fact that there is "no other middle term" through which a given proposition might be reduced to a quasi-principle which is still more basic. This implies, in turn, that even on the level of probable or opinionative knowledge one reasons to some more or less basic principle which is taken as the justification for the proposition being asserted. As an example of an immediate proposition that is opinionative, Aristotle gives "the man is not moving," which

---

[1] *In* I *Post. Analyt.* l. 5, n. 47; l. 20, n. 172; l. 8, n. 71 bis.
[2] *In* I *Post. Analyt.* l. 9, n. 79.
[3] *In* I *Post. Analyt.* l. 42, n. 373.
[4] *In* I *Post. Analyt.* l. 13, nn. 114–115.
[5] Thus at *In* I *Post. Analyt.* l. 44, n. 402, Thomas says: "opinio est de his quae accipiuntur ut contingentia aliter se habere, sive sint talia sive non."

is held to be more basic and thus in some way a justification of or
argument for the mediate opinionative proposition, "the man is not
running." The immediate proposition gives a kind of reason for the
mediate proposition, thus establishing a kind of reasoned (*propter quid*)
opinion. A proposition of this kind is not science because it does not
state what is the proper (*per se*) cause of the observed event but only
a kind of quasi-cause (*causa per accidens*). A mediate proposition, that
is, one which can be reduced to another proposition which is still more
basic, is more a statement of the fact (*quia*) than a statement of the
reasoned fact (*propter quid*). Thus, the significance of Thomas's
characterization of opinion as a "lesser science"; for, in the domain of
opinion propositions imitate those of science by attempting to state a
fact or the reason for the fact. But whereas the scientific proposition
expresses the true, proper, intrinsic cause of an effect, the opinionative
or probable proposition, whether of a fact or of a reasoned fact, does not.[1]

Now, in view of all that has already been said about opinion, it should
be clear that by describing it as an *immediate* proposition in the sense
just explained, one severely limits its domain. For, as Thomas ordinarily
speaks of opinion (that is, *opinio, aestimatio, existimatio* or whatever),
he does not have in mind any such quasi-ultimate probable proposition.
Thus, in commenting upon the definition as given by Aristotle, he is
compelled to add at once that an opinion may nevertheless be the
acceptance of a *mediate* contingent proposition as well. "For," he argues
"opinion stands in relationship to the contingent as do *intellectus* [of
first principles] and *scientia* to the necessary." [2] In other words,
according to Thomas an opinion might be either a kind of conclusion
or a kind of principle with regard to what is or what is at least considered to be contingent.

Although Thomas does not make it clear at the point under discussion, it can nevertheless be seen from another passage in the same
work that opinion as here used is the culmination of dialectical disputation as is science the culmination of a demonstration. Opinion in this
sense, in other words, is the state of knowledge which one has of a given
proposition as a result of reducing it through disputation to a proposition which by virtue of its *probability* will be considered by the
audience to be self-evident and hence immediate. The text in which

---

[1] See *In* I *Post. Analyt.* l. 44, nn. 399, 402.
[2] *In* I *Post. Analyt.* l. 44, n. 399: "Sic enim se habet (opinio) circa contingentia, sicut
intellectus et scientia circa necessaria."

this view of opinion and probability is presented in contrast to the procedure of science is of sufficient importance to be quoted in full:

Since, then, the dialectical syllogism aims at producing *opinion*, the dialectician seeks only to proceed on the basis of the best opinions (*maxime opinabilia*), namely what is held by the many or especially by the wise. Let us suppose, then, that one encounter in dialectical reasoning some proposition which could in fact be proven through a middle term but which on account of its probability seems to be self-evident. The dialectician needs no more than this; hence he does not seek another middle term, even though the proposition is mediate, but, syllogizing on the basis of the proposition as given, constructs a dialectical syllogism adequate for his purposes.

But the demonstrative syllogism is meant to produce scientific knowledge of the truth. One seeking a demonstration is therefore constrained to proceed on the basis of what is really and truly immediate. If, then, the latter should be faced with a mediate proposition, he must prove it through a middle term proper [to the subject matter and continue so doing] until he arrives at an immediate proposition: nor is he satisfied with the probability of the proposition.[1]

Opinion, then, is indeed a "lesser science" or, if you will, an ersatz science. It is the best state of knowledge attainable or desirable under the circumstances. Such knowledge is, to be sure, probable, but it is not science.

(c) *Faith, Probability and Demonstration*

In the light of these comparisons between the probable and the scientific, it is now good to recall Thomas's conviction that no argument against the teachings of faith can be a demonstration but is only probable or even sophistical. Properly understood, this means in effect that the probable as well as the sophistical can be necessarily false.[2] For, since the teachings of faith are taken as necessarily true, any proposition contradictory to a teaching of faith, however probable, must be

---

[1] *In* I *Post. Analyt.* l. 31, n. 258: "Quia enim syllogismus dialecticus ad hoc tendit, ut *opinionem* faciat, hoc solum est de intentione dialectici, ut procedat ex his, quae sunt maxime opinabilia, et haec sunt ea, quae videntur vel pluribus, vel maxime sapientibus. Et ideo si dialectico in syllogizando occurat aliqua propositio, quae secundum rei veritatem habeat medium, per quod possit probari, sed tamen non videatur habere medium, sed propter sui probabilitatem videatur esse per se nota; hoc sufficit dialectico, nec inquirit aliud medium, licet propositio sit mediata, et, ex ea syllogizans, sufficienter perficit dialecticum syllogismum. Sed syllogismus demonstrativus ordinatur ad scientiam veritatis; et ideo ad demonstratorem pertinet, ut procedat ex his, quae sunt secundum rei veritatem immediata. Et si occurat ei mediata propositio necesse est quod probet eam per medium proprium, quousque deveniat ad immediata, nec est contentus probabilitate propositionis." It is interesting to compare this text, in which opinion based on probability is seen as an adequate culmination of dialectical disputation, with *In De Trinitate* 6, 1 c, where opinion is seen rather as a temporary state of knowledge on the way towards science. The difference is not one of doctrine but of point of view. In the *Posterior Analytics* the rhetorician's goal of persuasion is uppermost; in the *De Trinitate*, on the other hand, it is the goal of scientific demonstration that is under discussion.

[2] Nor is this contrary to Aristotelian teaching, at least as interpreted by Thomas. See *In* I *Post. Analyt.* l. 8, n. 71 bis; l. 27, n. 227.

false. Thus does theology reject as false any proposition which is repugnant to a proposition of faith, on the grounds that it is impossible to demonstrate the truth of a proposition which is contradictory to the word of God. Any argument presented for such a proposition is, therefore, in principle soluble.[1]

Arguments in favor of revealed truths are similarly only probable, since such truths transcend the capacity of human reason. But Thomas never says that the probable arguments in favor of truths of faith are soluble. To be consistent, of course, he would have to admit this, and in actual practice he does at times discredit arguments proposed in defense of one or another article of faith. But his guiding principle with regard to the teachings of faith is that, however weak our human arguments, all such teachings are in themselves capable of being demonstrated, even though in fact the necessary arguments remain hidden from us.[2]

In conclusion, then, the theory of argumentation and of demonstration is fairly clear in Thomas's mind, and the relationship between the two is rather neatly delineated. One is preparatory to the other, which, in its turn, is the fulfillment or culmination of the former. By virtue of a demonstration one transcends the opinionative, the merely probable, and attains a certitude founded upon the necessary, that is, upon what cannot be other than it is. If, of course, one does know that what he knows cannot be other than it is, he has extremely good reasons for being certain as to the truth of what he knows. And thus the distinction between the scientific and the opinionative is clearly justified in theory.

The troublesome problem that remains is just a bit more subtle: how know that what one is convinced cannot be other than it is, is in fact such that it cannot be other than it is? The answer to this problem is difficult enough just in the realm of formal logic; it is incomparably more difficult when considered with respect to the real world. For Thomas, however, the problem is somewhat less acute than it has been since the days of Kant; for to him the principles of thought are primarily and foundationally the principles of being: it is because things are the way they are that we think the way we do. This nonetheless, is still not an adequate solution, for one is at once invited to ask why things are in fact the way they are and not otherwise. What, in short, founds the order and regularity of things in such a way that

[1] *S.T.* I, 1, 6 ad 2; 1, 8; *C.G.* I, 9.
[2] *Q.D. de ver.* 14, 9 ad 1.

we are justified in convincing ourselves that any of our propositions are eternally true? As we shall see, Aristotle resolved this rather ultimate question by appealing to the stability, indeed, the eternity of the world and in particular of the heavenly spheres. Thomas's faith, however, will not permit him to accept such a solution, since for him the world is not eternal. Where, then, can he turn but to God?

We will consider this interesting aspect of Thomas's thought in a later chapter. But before taking up the question of ultimate foundations, we must first look into Thomas's ideas about how to deal with what is admittedly contingent, what is not eternal but quite frankly transient, temporary, even momentary. This is, after all, the proper domain of opinion, of the non-necessary, of that which can be known only with probability. As we shall see, however, he uses somewhat different terminology in dealing with the contingent as such. Speaking of what happens not always but only some of the time, he presents us, as had Aristotle, with what from a contemporary point of view might be described as a rudimentary "frequency theory" of probability.

CHAPTER V

THE QUASI-MATHEMATICS OF TRUTH:
SEMPER AND SOME OF THE TIME

Up to this point our consideration of the notion of probability in Thomas Aquinas has tended to show him as a kind of informal precursor of what is now called the logical theory of probability, namely that probability is a characteristic or qualificative of a proposition. For, generally speaking, it is either to a proposition or to the adherence to a proposition, in either case called "opinion," that Thomas applies the term "probable." As we have seen, this attribution of probability to an opinion has various connotations. In the first place, it refers to the authority of those who accept the given opinion; and from this point of view "probability" suggests *approbation* with regard to the proposition accepted and *probity* with regard to the authorities who accept it. In the second place, "probability" refers to the arguments which are presented in favor of the opinion in question; and from this point of view it suggests *provability*, that is, capacity for being proven (though not necessarily demonstrated). In the third place, "probability" takes on a somewhat pejorative connotation precisely insofar as the proposition in question is *merely* probable; for, from this point of view the proposition is only *probationary* and not strictly demonstrated as are propositions which are properly scientific. The second of these connotations, provability, is at least in theory the most basic and may be described as the *logical* aspect of probability. The first connotation, involving both approbation and probity, may be considered *sociological*. The third, which shows the probable to be merely probationary by comparison to the demonstrated, may be called *metalogical* or *critical*.

Having thus distinguished in the thought of Thomas three different connotations for the notion of probability, we could perhaps convince ourselves that we have now drawn out of our author all that he has to tell us for the history of the theory of probability. For, at least in terms of explicit statements, Thomas's usage of "probability" is fairly well encompassed within the three connotations to which we have just referred.

It would, however, be a gross historical blunder to deal with Thomas only within the narrow confines of explicit linguistic usage. For, here as elsewhere ideas are not the prisoners of any one terminological formulation. That Thomas does not use the term "probability" with explicit reference to frequency in nature is fairly clear. And yet, as we shall now see, everything he says about probability is in fact founded upon a recognition of some such frequency or regularity: to be specific, a frequency or regularity of what happens in less than all of the cases: some of the time, but not always.

As we have seen, a proposition for Thomas can be considered properly scientific only if it is known to apply universally, that is, always, with regard to what it is saying. The scientific, in short, is of the necessary: what cannot be other than it is and hence is such at all times. The non-scientific, on the other hand, is not known as necessary but only as contingent, as capable of being other than it is, capable of being false as well as true at moment $(t + 1)$ or, for that matter, even at moment t. This domain of the contingent, we recall, is properly that of *opinion* – indeed, of the opinionative "part" of the soul, which Thomas tends to identify with the practical intellect, the source of action and production. Thus to round out our consideration of opinion and probability in Thomas's thought, we must go beyond his language a bit to see what he has to tell us about what happens not always but only some of the time.

What we wish to do in this chapter, then, is to study Thomas's views about knowledge of the contingent. Our considerations in this regard will involve ethics and jurisprudence (C) as well as prophecy and scientific prediction (D). But to bring these topics into focus, we must first try to locate contingency and related notions within Thomas's general perspective as a theologian (A) and then show how he makes use of a quasi-statistical approach in order to relate cosmology to ethics (B). All of this, we shall see, is intimately related to his theory of probability. For, what is involved is in some ways a modification of "necessity" as a trait of the scientific proposition.

A. THE LOGICAL STRUCTURE OF THE CONTINGENT

Since we wish to consider knowledge of the contingent, it is appropriate that we begin by trying to show what Thomas means by the contingent. To this end, we shall contrast his notion of contingency with those of necessity and possibility. But before undertaking our discussion of these related notions we should like to set the tone for this whole chapter by pointing out the central problem that lies before us.

To begin with, it must be noted that Thomas recognizes the possibility of knowing the contingent scientifically – not precisely insofar as it is contingent but insofar as there are aspects of the contingent which are necessary. Thus he would say that with regard to knowledge itself science is only of the necessary, but that with regard to things known science may be either of the necessary or of the contingent.[1] Maintaining this staunch Aristotelianism even against the authority of Augustine, Thomas explains the latter's sceptical tendencies with regard to changing things by noting that to know them scientifically one needs in addition to the things themselves the light of the agent intellect, whereby the necessary aspects can be discerned.[2] There is in all of this a slightly Platonic tinge, of course, which is elsewhere expressed by saying that science is primarily or directly about the universal aspects of things and only secondarily or indirectly, by a kind of reflection, about the particular things of our experience.[3] Be that as it may, such knowledge could not be considered knowledge of the contingent *qua* contingent.

In the second place, however, Thomas does suggest in various ways that we do have some sort of intellectual knowledge of contingent things taken precisely insofar as they are contingent. It should be clear that this is quite another thing from knowing some necessary aspect of the contingent. For example, the case often used by Thomas himself: Socrates seated. The question is not to know Socrates *qua* man or *qua* acting; that is, it is not enough to tell about man or about action or about bodily position or whatever. The fact in question is this particular fleeting fact: this individual person, called Socrates, is at this moment seated. The fact is "there to be seen"; but it can change at any moment – and, for that matter, it might never have happened, at this moment or at any other. Is there, then, any real knowledge involved in "knowing" such a passing, unstable, transient event? If so, this is what we would mean by knowing the contingent as contingent.

Now, then, as we shall gradually come to see in the course of this chapter, it is not very easy to distinguish in Thomas's view between

<hr>

[1] *S.T.* I, 86, 3. See also *In* I *Post Analyt.* l. 16, nn. 136, 141; *In* VI *Ethic.*, l. 1, n. 1123; *S.T.* I, 84, 1 ad 3.

[2] *S.T.* I, 84, 6 ad 1. See Augustine, *Octoginta trium Quaest.* Q. 9; ML 40, 13.

[3] *In De Trin.* 5, 2 ad 4.

knowledge of the contingent *qua* contingent and knowledge of the contingent *qua* necessary. For, when speaking about our knowledge of the contingent, he invariably relies upon "the necessary" as a kind of model in terms of which "the contingent" is made as intelligible as possible. The model here in question is not explicitly mathematical; but as we shall maintain, it is mathematical at least implicitly. And thus we can discern in Thomas's thought what might be called an unformalized "calculus of probability."

This being said, we begin the defense of the assertion with a comparison between "contingency" and the related notions of "necessity" and "possibility."

1. Contingency and Necessity

In general, Thomas takes the contingent to mean that which is not necessary. The necessary being, according to Aristotle's synthetic definition, that which cannot be other than it is, the contingent is, from this point of view, that which *can* be other than it is.[1] To leave the comparison between necessary and contingent at that, however, is quite an over-simplification of Thomas's thought. For, he allows, as had Aristotle, for various meanings of "necessary," all of which are nonetheless related to what we have called Aristotle's synthetic definition. These other meanings are all what scholastics like to call analogous to the root meaning, expressing as they do some aspect of the root meaning.

For example, in his attempt to express the various nuances, the various shades and levels of meaning of "necessary," Thomas is led to speak of a different kind of necessity with regard to each of Aristotle's four causes (material, formal, final and efficient), which in turn reduce to intrinsic and extrinsic causes, thus suggesting intrinsic and extrinsic necessity.[2] Implied in these usages of "necessity," of course, is the conviction that there is a close relationship between processes of thought and processes in nature. For, by speaking of necessity in nature within the framework of Aristotle's fourfold causality, Thomas deliberately commits himself to saying that the structure of knowledge manifests at least in part the structure of things. But, on the other hand, the very fact that he resorts to a variety of meanings to cover the range of necessity in nature shows that he is

[1] See *In* IV *Met.* l. 7, n. 620; V, l. 6, nn. 827–841.
[2] *S.T.* I, 82, 1 c. See also *C.G.* II, 30.

aware, even painfully aware, of nature's adamant refusal to submit itself to neat and tidy laws of thought. Thus, Thomas sees no problem in attributing the synthetic definition of necessity to both principles and conclusions of demonstration in the strict sense.[1] But, according to his reading of Aristotle, he must content himself with saying that necessity in nature is *like* the necessity of scientific demonstration. With regard to Aristotle's teleological outlook, for example, the end or finality of a natural organism is in relation to that organism *somewhat like* a principle of demonstration in relation to a demonstrated conclusion.[2]

Thomas also tries to express the nuances of necessity by distinguishing between absolute and consequential necessity.[3] And in virtue of this and other related distinctions he tends to go beyond whatever physical determinism might be attributable to Aristotle's physical theory.[4] As for the distinction itself, absolute necessity amounts to a necessity that is expressed categorically; consequential necessity, in turn, amounts to a necessity that is best expressed by a conditional proposition, for example, the "necessity" of the contingent event. One has absolute (categorical) necessity if the predicate of the categorical implies the subject, or vice versa – which is, in effect, the characteristic of an Aristotelian demonstrated conclusion. Consequential necessity, on the other hand, is the necessity of that which, given certain conditions, cannot not happen. For example, if Socrates is in fact sitting. then it is necessary in this sense that Socrates be sitting.[5]

---

[1] *In* V *Met.* l. 6, n. 838.

[2] *In* II *Phys.* l. 15, nn. 273–274.

[3] *In* II *Phys.* l. 15; *C.G.* I, 67; *S.T.* I, 13, 6 ad 2; 19, 3 c and 8 ad 1.

[4] That Aristotle's physical theory is ultimately deterministic is, for example, the conclusion of Augustin Mansion's analysis of the *Physics*. See his *Introduction à la Physique Aristotélicienne*, 2e éd., revue et augmentée (Louvain-Paris, 1945), Chapitre IX, pp. 315–333.

[5] Making allowances for what is probably a misreading of the manuscript in the *Contra Gentiles*, the same example is used both at *S.T.* I, 19, 3 c and at *C.G.* I, 67, where the distinction in question is discussed. In the *Contra Gentiles* Thomas mentions that absolute necessity is called by some *necessitas consequentis*; the other type of necessity ("*sub conditione*") they call *necessitas consequentiae*. This latter Thomas describes as *ex suppositione* in the *Summa Theologica* (I, 19, 3 c; 23, 6 ad 2 and ad 3) and as *conditionalis* elsewhere in the *Contra Gentiles* (II, 29). It is tempting, of course, to translate this non-absolute necessity as "hypothetical," but modern usage of this term would only confuse what is involved in the scholastic distinction. For, what is really being distinguished is not two kinds of necessity but rather two kinds of propositions that express necessity, namely, a categorical and a conditional. As Thomas points out, it is most ambiguous to refer to the necessity of a contingent event by means of a categorical, (e.g. *Quod videtur sedere, necesse est sedere*). This ambiguity, however, is avoided by means of a conditional, e.g. *Si videtur sedere, (necesse est) quod sedet.* In particular, the categorical statement of contingent necessity is true if taken in the "*sensus compositus*" and "*de dicto*"; it is, however, false if taken in the "*sensus divisus*" and "*de re*", since it leads to the fallacy of composition and division. (See *C.G.*, I, 67; *S.T.*, I,

The example here given of consequential necessity, though perhaps trivial in itself, has implications of staggering proportions. For, it is to this kind of necessity that Thomas relates whatever happens as a result of God's will; and, even though Thomas would attribute the intelligible content of the universe (the order of essences) to God's intellect or, if you will, to the divine ideas, he would also attribute the very existence of the universe and of everything in it to God's creative choice.[1] One would think, therefore, that from this ultimate point of view Thomas could allow only consequential necessity in the universe. Indeed, if it be granted that the "absolute necessity" of the *Summa Theologica* is in fact logical, then we suspect that this theory might be pushed to that conclusion.

At the same time, however, we must grant Etienne Gilson that such a conclusion would be radically opposed to Thomas's own intentions. For, at one point in the *Contra Gentiles* Thomas goes to great lengths to show that there can be absolute necessity in the created universe.[2] What is most striking about Thomas's efforts here, however, is that his examples either involve faulty physical theory (e.g., the heavenly bodies and their effects or, in conjunction with theological data, the angels) or revert to the absolute or categorical necessity described above. Furthermore, Thomas's observations here about necessity in connection with the attainment of an end allow us to interpret the teleological necessity of the *Prima Secundae* as being also consequential.[3]

The problems here suggested, of course, would have to be treated at

14, 13 ad 3; I–II, 10, 4 ad 3.) Thus the advantage of the conditional to express the necessity appropriate to the contingent event. And, in view of these considerations, we think we come closest to what Thomas is really saying by referring to this non-absolute (i.e. non-categorical) necessity as *consequential* necessity, i.e. the formal necessity of a conditional proposition in which both antecedent and consequent are the same categorical: "If p, then p." In a broader sense, this consequential necessity is extended to a conditional of the type "If p, then q," given that q necessarily follows from p. For further details as to the distinction between a statement *de re* and a statement *de dicto* as well as that between the *sensus compositus* and the *sensus divisus*, see I. M. Bochenski, *A History of Formal Logic* (Notre Dame, Ind., 1961), pp. 182–187; William and Martha Kneale, *The Development of Logic* (Oxford, 1962), pp. 236–237.

[1] This inadequate summary of a complex and highly controversial subject might be supplemented by reference to Johann Stufler, *Why God Created the World; the Purpose of the Creator and Creatures, A Study in the Teaching of St. Thomas Aquinas* (tr. Edmund F. Sutcliffe) (Birmingham, England, 1937).

[2] The passage in question is *Contra Gentiles* II, 30, which Mr. Gilson finds to be a remarkable testimony to Thomas's harmonious blending of the world of theology and the world of physical science. See his *The Elements of Christian Philosophy* (New York, 1963), pp. 219–220.

[3] Though we are referring specifically to the end of *C.G.* II, 30, we might also quote *C.G.* II, 29: "Ea vero quae voluntate fiunt, necessitatem habere non possunt nisi ex sola finis suppositione." With regard, then, to Thomas's teleological *"necessitas"*, see especially *S.T.* I–II, 10.

much greater length if we were concerned *ex professo* with Thomas's doctrine of necessity and contingency. Since, however, we have broached these problems only as a means of developing Thomas's view of probability, we must leave their solution to others.[1] We might note in passing, though, that it is no longer possible to interpret what Thomas says about "absolute necessity" in nature without considerable reference to his ideas about the heavenly bodies.[2]

Allowing, then, for the inadequacy of our treatment of this subject, we must nevertheless take this occasion to put down a few impressions that are relevant to probability.

In the first place, it seems that Thomas's treatment of necessity and contingency is no more neatly organized than is that of Aristotle.[3] Indeed, his efforts to describe necessity in nature might almost be considered just a well nuanced description of the various ways in which men, including philosophers, speak of something as being "necessary." On the other hand, since Thomas makes much of "contingency" as a point of departure for an affirmation of the existence of God, it must be recognized that he hardly sees himself as the journalist of other people's ideas in this regard. It is, however, somewhat unfortunate that the clear distinctions between essence and existence in the *De Ente et Essentia* are seldom manifest in his treatment of necessity and contingency.

Secondly, we may apply to Thomas a critique first directed to Aristotle, namely, that his discussion of necessity and contingency suffers from a failure to distinguish clearly between the logical and the real.[4] The result, to say the least, is not such as to satisfy the rigorous standards of contemporary discussions in this area.

---

[1] See Innocenzo d'Arenzano, *Necessita e Contingenza nell' essere e sull' agire della natura secundo San Tommaso* (Piacenza, 1961). We also await with interest publication of doctoral research being done by J. Gevaert, at the Institut Supérieur de Philosophie of the University of Louvain, under the title, "Nécessité et Contingence d'après Saint Thomas."

[2] This, we think, is abundantly clear from Thomas Litt's *Les Corps Célestes dans l'Univers de Saint Thomas*, Paris-Louvain, 1963.

[3] See, however, Mansion, *Introduction à la Physique Aristotélicienne*, 2e éd. revue et augmentée (Louvain-Paris, 1945), Chapitre VIII, pp. 282–314, where the author resolves many problems concerning Aristotle's views on necessity and contingency by distinguishing between a broad and a strict sense for the notion of chance.

[4] See Mansion, *Introduction à la Physique Aristotélicienne*, p. 329. In ascribing Mansion's critique of Aristotle to Thomas we are not quite sure if we are saying the same thing or not. For, in the passage cited the author is not altogether clear. After distinguishing between real and logical necessity, he goes on (in accordance with his interpretation of determinism) to identify Aristotle's "contingency" with details not covered by the scientific system. Accordingly, for Mansion, Aristotle's "contingency" is equivalent to "uncertainty as to details", hence presumably causing a lack of "logical necessity". This suggests a confusion on Mansion's part between the logical and the psychological dimension of science. What we are saying, on the other hand, is that the systematic model of the universe is, precisely because

In our opinion, at any rate, when Thomas speaks of the contingent as that which is not necessary, as that which can be other than it is, either (1) he is in the realm of logic or (2) he is using a kind of convenient shorthand. As for the first, what we take to be his ultimate view of "absolute necessity" is basically essentialist or, as we would prefer to say, logical. As for the second, whether we cover the real world with "consequential necessity" or admit the notion of "absolute necessity," what is clear is that even for Thomas such necessity is not always the same, does not always have the same rigor. Thus his need to speak of different kinds of necessity, as, for example, the division based on fourfold causality.

Indeed, we are inclined to think that even consequential necessity, as described by Thomas, is more logical than anything else. From an empirical point of view, the consequentially necessary is just the contingent event which does in fact happen, in this particular instance or in a number of instances, or in the majority of cases – but not always. Thus the question of necessity in nature, in things, reduces empirically to the question of the contingent event, not *qua* contingent but *qua* event. That what happens is contingent is more or less obvious from the fact that it does not happen all the time (or is not known empirically to happen all the time). It is the fact that it happens at all that demands an explanation. But to say that because it happens, or is happening, it is therefore necessary – be that a consequential necessity or whatever – does not of itself explain anything. After all, what is this but a kind of theoretical "amen" to the given, glorified a bit with the impressive dignity of necessity? In effect, then, all that Thomas is really doing by thus extending the notion of necessity to nature is saying that what is, somehow must be. If, then, what is can be, he can go one step further and say that what can be must be if in fact it is.[1] Far from being terminological double talk, this is just a somewhat more roundabout way of stating a fundamental problem of being: why is there something rather than nothing – and what intelligible meaning does it have? [2]

of its *logical* rigor, an inadequate expression of the complex real. The logical necessity that obtains between a premiss and a conclusion is not the same as the necessity, however described, of natural events. Thus, if we must here speak of uncertainty, there is uncertainty not merely with regard to details but with regard to everything that is systematically described.

[1] As a matter of fact, Thomas comes very close to saying this if he does not in fact say it. See, for example, *C.G.* I, 67; III, 74; and especially *Q.D. de pot.* 1, 3 ad 9.

[2] Intended by these observations is our complete disagreement with Etienne Gilson's contention that there is no such thing as Leibniz's "theodicy" or the problem there implied in Thomas's thought. Still less are we of the opinion that this is just a "pseudo-problem." In any event, we shall shortly be pointing out how Thomas, to the detriment of probability theory, concerns himself with viewing the world if not as the best possible then at least as

2. *Possibility and Impossibility*

As just suggested, then, Thomas's attempt to put necessity in nature leads through the contingent event as such to the notion of possibility. For, in simplest terms, if something somehow *must* be, then in principle it is; and if it *is*, then it is *possible* that it be; the other way around, if something somehow *must not* be, then in principle it not only *is not* but *cannot possibly* be. We are very close to stating tautologies, perhaps; but what we moderns like to call modalities are just that closely interwoven. The necessary, however understood, implies the impossible as a correlative and the possible as a prerequisite. In other words, if something is necessary its contradictory is impossible in the same sense and it itself is manifestly possible.[1]

(a) *Physical versus Logical Possibility*

Thomas, of course, finds Aristotle struggling with this notion of possibility, as well as that of necessity, in the *Metaphysics*, where the Philosopher reduces a variety of different meanings – Thomas calls them "modes" – of possible and impossible to capacity or power and incapacity or impotence.[2] The analysis takes into consideration what is called active and passive power or ability, that is to say, the ability to act or to be acted upon, and in this way reduces possibility to causality: something is possible if intrinsic and extrinsic factors are such that it can be brought to be. But the attempt to describe the possible and the impossible as such resorts (inevitably, we think) to a logical comparison with the necessary.[3]

Thus, the impossible is described as that the contradictory of which is necessarily true, and the possible as that the contradictory of which is not necessarily false. The possible in this sense might be what is false but not necessarily so, or what is true but not necessarily so, or what is not true in this case although true in others like it.

But all of this, as noted above, is reduced to causality, to the

perfect *sub specie aeternitatis*. See Gilson, *The Elements of Christian Philosophy* (New York, 1963), pp. 185–186.

[1] *In* IX *Met.* l. 1, n. 1775; l. 3, nn. 1808–1814. For further details about this interesting aspect of scholastic thought, see I. M. Bochenski, "S. Thomae Aquinatis 'De modalibus' opusculum et doctrina," *Angelicum* 17 (April 1940), fasc. 2–3, pp. 180–218. The authenticity of the work in question is not universally admitted.

[2] *In* V *Met.* l. 14.

[3] For a more detailed consideration of these modal relationships in Aristotle's logical theory, see William and Martha Kneale, *The Development of Logic* (Oxford, 1962), pp. 84–86.

capability of existing factors to bring something about. For, a potentiality or possibility is defined with respect to an actuality or capability. As Aristotle maintains, a thing can be brought into being only if there is something in existence which is capable of bringing it into existence. Thus, for Aristotle at least, the potentialities or possibilities of natural things are limited by the actualities or capabilities of natural things, whatever the latter may be.[1] Since there is little awareness of any kind of evolutionary development either on the part of Aristotle or on the part of Thomas and the other medievals, this amounts to saying more or less that nature is capable of producing what it is known to produce or to have produced. If, then, something is to be brought into being beyond these more or less known capacities, this new effect would have to be due to a more competent – literally, a super-natural – cause.

The most, of course, that could be expected of such a cause is that it be capable of producing all that is not self-contradictory. But this, in short, is precisely Thomas's description of the causal capacity of God.[2]

(b) Logical or "Theological" Possibility

For Thomas, then, who sees all things in the light of God's creative power, the domain of the possible transcends the capacities of the material universe as such. To God, he insists, all is possible that is not strictly impossible, i.e. that is not ultimately self-contradictory. Thus it is precisely by recourse to divine omnipotence that Thomas can relate the full range of the logically possible to the world of nature. From this exalted point of view, he can distinguish between what is possible or impossible to this or that finite thing and what is possible or impossible to God. The latter, unlike the former, is in no way limited by the conditions of finite factors or circumstances but only by the principle of non-contradiction. For Thomas, in other words, God serves as an incontrovertible means of bridging the gap between the logically and the physically possible. In and through God, the totality of possibles is in principle capable of being actualized.[3]

This, says Thomas, must be the viewpoint of the theologian in considering the possible. Worldly philosophers, the wise of this world, decide what is possible or impossible only on the basis of "proximate"

---

[1] *In IX Met.* l. 4, nn. 1816–1817; l. 5; l. 7, n. 1846.
[2] *Q.D. de pot.* 1; 6, 1 ad 11, ad 15 and ad 16; *S.T.* I, 25, 3 c. This, however, should not be taken to imply that God himself can do whatever is logically possible. For the realization of a given possibility may be a mark of imperfection, which is excluded from God. Thus, for example, God as such cannot move or walk or sin. See *Q.D. de pot.* 1, 6.
[3] *Q.D. de pot.* 1, 3 c; 5, 3 c and ad 8; *C.G.* II, 39.

causes, that is to say, on the basis of natural capacities. But the theologian, mindful of God's omnipotence, recognizes as possible whatever is not in itself impossible, that is, whatever is not self-contradictory.[1]

Even the theologian, however, is compelled to recognize a considerable difference between what God *could* bring into being and what he *has in fact* brought into being. The universe does exist, and it exists in a rather definite way. And beyond what can be attributed to the "natural" course of events, there is also for the theologian an elaborate complex of "supernatural" possibilities which God has seen fit to bring into actuality. Without going into the fascinating problems which God's extraordinary intervention in the universe entails for Thomas, we may simply note here that he modifies his view of logical possibility enough to take account of possibilities that have been actualized.

The notion which allows Thomas to insert logical possibility into the world of actualities is, interestingly enough for Leibniz scholars, *compossibility*. On the basis of this notion, which Thomas uses in particular to resolve apparent conflicts between divine omnipotence and free will, he is able to point out that a given proposition, though *possible* taken by itself (*simpliciter*) may not be *compossible* with other propositions which God's inscrutable choice requires us to accept as true. For, generally speaking, even though each of two contradictories may be possible taken abstractly, the two may not be compossible in the concrete. On the supposition, then, that God has chosen one alternative, the theologian can consider the other alternative as possible only in principle and not in fact.

Thus, in addition to the possible which is also absolutely necessary, the theologian must also recognize the possible which is necessary in view of the facts or, to recall an expression, consequentially necessary: *necessarium ex suppositione*.[2]

In spite of these and other similar nuances, however, Thomas still insists that the totality of all that exists can be neatly divided into two non-overlapping subsets: the necessary on the one hand and the contingent on the other.[3] Both the necessary and the contingent, though, are to be understood in terms of their cause or causes, since

---

[1] *Q.D. de pot.* 1, 4 c, ad 1 and ad 4 in contrarium; 3, 14 c; *C.G.* II, 37.

[2] This doctrine, which is closely related to the distinction between absolute and consequential necessity, discussed above, will be found in one form or another in the following passages: *S.T.* I, 14, 13 ad 3; 19, 3 c; 23, 6 ad 2 and ad 3; I–II, 10, 4 ad 3; *Q.D. de malo* 6 a. un. ad 16; *Q.D. de ver.* 6, 3 ad 7 and ad 8; 23, 5 ad 3.

[3] *C.G.* III, 72.

whatever is, whether it be necessarily or only contingently, is because of what makes it to be. From this causal point of view, the necessary is *in*, that is, is within the capability of, its causes in such a way that it cannot but be; the contingent, though similarly in its causes, is so in such a way that it can either be or not be.[1]

The difference between the necessary and the contingent thus described is sufficiently significant, in Thomas's opinion, to justify attributing a different value or weight to the conclusions of a science which have to do with the necessary and those which have to do with the contingent.[2] And yet, when faced with the problem of justifying empirically that some things are necessary and others contingent, the best he can do, apart from appealing to the divine will, is to suggest what amounts to *a quasi-mathematical criterion*. The necessary, he says, is what happens all the time; the contingent, what happens only most of the time. Moreover, it is precisely the fact that the contingent can sometimes not occur that it is contingent and not necessary. It is, therefore, thanks to the occasional non-occurrence of the expected that one can speak of chance or fortune and not be compelled to admit that everything is necessary.[3]

It should go without saying, then, that our study of probability can hardly avoid this aspect of Thomas's thought.

B. THE QUASI-STATISTICS OF MORALITY

What we have referred to as a quasi-mathematical explanation of the contingent is not to be taken as a conscious attempt on the part of Thomas to utilize mathematical concepts as a means of describing natural events. Rather is it an unconscious or perhaps scientifically preconscious recourse to the mathematical. There is no conscious awareness of the fact that he is stating something about natural processes in a quantitative – one might almost say, statistical – way. But, consciously or not, it is just this that Thomas does, more or less following Aristotle in this regard.

It would, of course, be unfair to expect of him the precision of contemporary statistical procedures, especially since he has no explicit intention of proceeding statistically. Nevertheless, since the empirical basis of his distinction between the necessary and the contingent is at

---

[1] *C.G.* I, 67.
[2] *Q.D. de malo* 2, 6 ad 13; *In* VI *Met.* l. 1, n. 1149.
[3] *C.G.* III, 74.

least implicitly statistical, the judgments which he makes on the basis of this and related distinctions are open to the criticism of hasty generalization. But more about this later.

For the present, these remarks should suffice as an indication of what we mean by saying that Thomas's approach in this area is quasi-mathematical. It is not pseudo-mathematical, since he makes no pretense of proceeding mathematically; yet it is not non-mathematical, since the very basis of his approach is a measurement of discrete units. Thus we say "quasi-mathematical."

Also by way of clarification, although Thomas's approach is only unconsciously mathematical, this does not mean that he is unconscious of the possibility of a mathematical science of the real. Quite to the contrary, he has a fairly clear notion of such a science. The point is that he simply makes no connection between his theory of applied mathematics and his (quasi-mathematical) approach to the contingent. This, of course, is not surprising, since in his day there was no calculus of probability as we know it today. But, as we now hope to show, what Thomas does with the contingent (Section 2) can be viewed in retrospect as an illustration of his own theory of applied mathematics (Section 1).

1. Thomas's Theory of Applied Mathematics

It will be recalled that in speaking of the principles of a science we had occasion to refer to what Thomas calls a subalternate science, that is, a science whose principles, or axioms, are borrowed from and proven by a "higher" (more fundamental) science.[1] This notion of a subalternate science has reference primarily though not exclusively to what we would call applied mathematics. Since, at least in Thomas's eyes, it is to material things that pure mathematics is applied, applied mathematics as such stands somewhere between purely mathematical thought and thought about physical things which does not have recourse to mathematical concepts. Accordingly, he also calls such applied mathematical sciences *scientiae mediae:* intermediate sciences.[2] These *scientiae mediae* are considered to be materially physical but formally mathematical; that is, the objects with which they deal are the things of nature, but the formal reasoning about these objects

---

[1] See *In De Trin.* Proemium II, 2 ad 5 and ad 7; 5, 1 ad 5.
[2] *In De Trin.* 5, 3 ad 6.

proceeds on the basis of mathematical concepts.[1] As examples of *scientiae mediae*, Thomas usually refers to (theory of), music, which utilizes arithmetical notions, and astronomy, which utilizes notions taken from geometry.[2]

No less than Plato, Thomas recognizes that there is a considerable difference between abstract mathematics and mathematics as applied. But he does not seem to feel that this difference in any way distorts the epistemic value of the *scientia media* as such. He notes, for example, that in astronomy measurements are taken in such a way as to sacrifice perfect precision for the sake of simplicity. Thus in measuring the distance between the earth and the eighth sphere the astronomer takes as his points of reference the observer's position on the surface, rather than strive for a more accurate measurement from the center, of the earth.[3] Similarly, stars, which are in reality three-dimensional bodies, are for astronomical purposes taken to be points; the same is true of planets, and thus the paths which they trace in the heavens are considered abstractly to be circles, epicycles, and so on. This technique, Thomas maintains, does not distort what is given in sense experience; for, one can always make the necessary epistemic adjustments intellectually.[4]

Measurement, of course, suggests some quantitative relationship between the measure and the thing measured. But, in his interpretation of Aristotle, Thomas gives a meaning to measurement that, he feels, transcends the category of quantity. In this broader sense of measurement, what is involved is a comparison between entities one of which serves as the standard in terms of which the other is judged or evaluated.[5] Comparison between things from this point of view requires only that measure and measured be somehow related, that they be capable of coexisting in the same subject, and that they be somehow alike.[6]

Now, in this broader sense of measurement, Thomas speaks of the mind being measured by what it knows, insofar as facts are the criteria of truth. As often as he refers to this "measuring" of knowledge,

---

[1] *In De Trin.* 5, 3 ad 7; *S.T.* II–II, 9, 2 ad 3; *In II Phys.* l. 3, n. 164; l. 11, ln. 243.
[2] *In De Trin.* 5, 3 ad 6; *In I Met.* l. 13, n. 202. See also *In De Sensu* l. 1, nn. 14–17; *In I Post. Analyt.* l. 41, n. 358; l. 25, nn. 208–210. For a serious attempt to relate this notion of a *scientia media* to modern physical science, see Jacques Maritain, *The Degrees of Knowledge* (New York, 1938), pp. 76–82 165–247.
[3] *C.G.* III, 57.
[4] *In III Met.* l. 8, nn. 416 and 422.
[5] *In X Met.* l. 2, n. 1946. See also I, l. 14, n. 208.
[6] *In VII Phys.* l. 7, n. 936.

however, he never suggests that quantitative standards might be introduced to express, say, the degree of conformity to facts. With Aristotle, he puts the measure of truth not in the category of quantity but in the category of relation.[1] And in accordance with Aristotle's definition of truth as a conformity (*adaequatio*) of the mind to facts, Thomas insists that in this regard there can be no degrees, no more or less: the mind either judges things as they are or it does not. However, insofar as some *things* exist in a more perfect manner than others and thus have "more being," in knowing such things conceptually one knows "more truth" than in knowing other, inferior things.[2] In short, then, Thomas does allow for a certain gradation in knowledge, at least on the level of conceptualization. But he makes no explicit attempt to express this gradation mathematically.

More generally speaking, what Thomas has to say about applied mathematics and measurement has no counterpart in what he tells us about contingency in nature. Yet, if we may be permitted to view his ideas about contingency in retrospect, we will find that they can very well be interpreted as a kind of applied mathematics. For, *what Thomas does with the contingent is, in effect, to compare it with and thus in a way measure it in terms of the necessary*. And to the extent that he does this, we might even speak of his thought about contingent events as constituting a kind of rudimentary "frequency theory."

2. *Frequency as Determinant of Contingency*

As we have already seen, Thomas's manner of dealing with contingency is basically the same as that of Aristotle; but his perspective is quite different. For, Thomas is a theologian, and as such he is interested in this world mainly as a manifestation of and means towards the divine Wisdom which governs it all. This does not mean, however,

---

[1] *In* V *Met.* l. 17, nn. 1003 and 1027.

[2] *Q.D. de carit.* q. un., a. 9 ad 1. See also *In* I *Met.* l. 2, n. 43; IV, l. 8, n. 658; *S.T.* I, 79, 9 ad 3. It will be recalled that the passage here cited from the *Summa Theologica* has to do with Thomas's late view as to the manner in which the scientific aspect of the intellect is to be distinguished from the opinionative. As we saw in Chapter 2, Thomas here discards his earlier option for a distinction between powers in favor of a distinction between habits. What is most important in the present context, however, is that this passage of the *Summa* identifies the *necessary* as that which has perfect being and truth and the *contingent* as that which has only imperfect being and truth. It must therefore be added that we are now interpreting this distinction, on the basis of the *De Caritate*, in terms of judgment and conceptualization. It is by no means clear, however, that this is what Thomas wants to say. For, both "the necessary" and "the contingent" are, as we have seen, expressed propositionally, hence suggesting that each is known by way of judgment rather than merely by conceptualization. See Chapter 2, pp. 126–127.

that he disregards the tools of human science; it means rather that for him these tools have a transcendent dimension. And it is precisely in view of the transcendent that Thomas allows himself to "calculate" the contingent. For, whatever the ideal, the man in search of God must make his way through a universe which, at least in his eyes, is subject to the chance event.

(a) "Ut in Pluribus" *and* "Ut in Paucioribus"

In accordance with Aristotle's teaching, Thomas defines chance or fortune as being by accident, that is to say, things which happen in a minority of cases.[1] What happens naturally (rather than by chance) is that which happens either always or at least frequently. To state this in terms of Thomas's habitual formulae, the chance event is that which happens *ut in paucioribus;* the natural event occurs either *semper* or *ut in pluribus* (sometimes stated as *ut frequenter*).[2]

The same threefold division is also expressed with regard to the cause of an event. A cause which when posited produces a given effect, that is, a given kind of effect, either *always* or *most of the time* is a cause in the proper sense of the word (*per se*). A cause which when posited produces a given effect only *rarely* is an accidental cause, that is, a cause by accident, and the effect which it produces is said to happen by chance or, where human beings and their goals are in question, by fortune.[3]

Now, what is important here is that, abstracting from divine providence, Thomas takes this representation of causal frequency in nature to be sufficiently exhaustive from man's point of view; and thus he is able to classify types of human knowledge accordingly. Things which happen *always* are manifestly necessary and hence are susceptible to demonstration. Things which happen *most of the time* are also necessary if one postulate disturbing influences; hence these also are susceptible to at least hypothetical demonstration if one disregard exceptions. Things which happen only *occasionally*, however, are scientifically unknowable; for, from man's point of view they are chance or fortuitous events. But even these are at least indirectly intelligible insofar as they are referred to God's unlimited wisdom.[4]

That science is concerned only with what happens all the time or most of the time follows from the very fact that science, by definition,

---

[1] *In V Met.* l. 22, nn. 1139–1143; *Quodl.* 2, q. 3, a. 2 ad 1; *C.G.* III, 74.
[2] *In II Phys.* l. 13, n. 256; *Q.D. de ver.* 3, 1 c.
[3] *In II Phys.* l. 9, nn. 220–225. See l. 8, nn. 214-216; l. 10.
[4] *In II Phys.* l. 9, n. 238; *In VI Met.* l. 3, nn. 1215–1222.

demonstrates its conclusions. For, as we recall, demonstration requires a manifestation of necessity. But necessity is assured only with regard to what is always the case; and it can be presumed only with regard to what is usually the case. What happens only rarely, on the other hand, cannot be taken to be necessary. For, in Thomas's view, it cannot be systematically founded upon the universal principles of science; and thus, as we might say today, it is unpredictable.[1] In other words, what happens only rarely is judged to have occurred by chance or, in the case which involves human desires, fortuitously. Thus, for the sake of example, it is only fortuitously that an unskilled warrior (*qua* unskilled) should land good blows upon an enemy; and, this being the case, his good luck is not subject to scientific systematization. For, the consideration of the accidental can proceed to infinity, whereas a scientific demonstration must eventually reduce a proposition, by a finite number of steps, to some principle or axiom of the science in question.[2] Quite to the contrary, it is precisely with such accidental, or rare, occurrences that the sophist deals, making out of them arguments which are defective in that they involve the fallacy of accident.[3] In short, then, no science deals with the accidental as such; science is concerned only with what happens necessarily – that is, if not always then at least most of the time.[4]

Now, implied in this view of what may be taken as "necessary" for purposes of demonstration is a preference for the certitude of mathematics as opposed to that of physical science. For, it is mathematics which draws conclusions that are true always; physical science, on the other hand, often demonstrates only with regard to what happens frequently.[5] In the case of physical science, its premises often state what is the case most of the time, though not always; and thus the conclusion must be taken to apply not always but only most of the time. This, then, is not a demonstration in the strictest sense but only by way of extension (*secundum quid*).[6]

At the same time, however, it must be stressed that the notion of demonstration is thus extended so as to include the argumentations of

[1] *In* I *Post. Analyt.* 1. 42, nn. 373–374.
[2] *In* II *Phys.* l. 8, n. 214; *In* I *Post. Analyt.* l. 38, n. 335; *S.T.* I–II, 1, 4 ad 2.
[3] *In* VI *Met.* l. 2, nn. 1177–1179; XI, l. 8; I, l. 6, nn. 104 and 107.
[4] *In* VI *Met.* ll. 2–4; XI, l. 8. In the *Posterior Analytics* Aristotle speaks of a "particular demonstration"; but this is not to be understood as a demonstration of the particular as such. It is rather a demonstration which rests ultimately upon something evident to the senses, this being a kind of principle. See *In* I *Post. Analyt.* l. 16, n. 142; l. 38, n. 338.
[5] *In* VI *Met.* l. 1, n. 1149.
[6] *In* II *Post. Analyt.* l. 12, esp. nn. 524–525.

any science which can manifest at least what is the case *"ut frequenter,"* most of the time. For, implied in the recognition of a demonstration *ut frequenter* is a theoretical optimism which is both ontological and epistemological. Ontological, insofar as it assumes a certain stability in nature, founded upon the nature of things; epistemological, insofar as it assumes our ability to discover this stability, or regularity, by consideration of how often things happen in one way rather than in another. To this extent, at least, the contingent is considered to be knowable, and the knowledge thus obtained is, albeit in a wider sense of the term, scientific. But it must be emphasized that such knowledge can claim a grasp on "the necessary" only to the extent that things are naturally moved to act in a definite way (somewhat after the fashion of Popper's "propensity") and that therefore they do act in this way at least *"ut frequenter,"* at least more often than not.

(b) Monsters in a Divinely Ordered Universe

Let us grant, then, that the realm of science is considerably enlarged by the inclusion of the demonstration *ut frequenter.* But is this, we might now ask, enough of an enlargement? Is it really justifiable to exclude from science what happens only rarely, only *"ut in paucioribus?"* Does science, as it were, dare to be so haughty that it can neglect what is today often called the non-systematic divergence? More precisely, what is really called into question by the "exceptional" event, the event itself or the system?

The history of science since the time of Thomas Aquinas has taught us that, in spite of "dogmatic" claims of a given system, defenders of that system must either be ready to explain the "exceptions" to the system or else look for a more comprehensive system. The metascientific sophistication of our day, however, was still the "unthinkable thought" of the Middle Ages. For Thomas, in other words, the system, at least as far as it went, *was* the world, and there obviously was no other world which could serve in its place.

Thus for Thomas one of the main problems which led Aristotle to formulate the notion of what Thomas calls *"ut in paucioribus"* is the problem of the monster in nature. Were it not for the fact that in the process of generation, or reproduction, a monster is sometimes produced, the Philosopher would have had little reason to speak of anything but necessity in nature.[1] The existence of monsters, however, compelled

---

[1] It is to be noted that by stating the problem of chance in this way we considerably oversimplify Aristotle's theory. According to Augustin Mansion, Aristotle himself gradually

him to speak of natural processes as achieving their purpose only most of the time. The exceptions, which occur according to Thomas's expression *ut in paucioribus*, remained for Aristotle the scientifically unexplained. We may note in passing that, in spite of our vastly greater knowledge, such things still remain largely unexplained.

For Thomas, however, it was enough to refer all such aberrations from the norm to the infinite wisdom of God. From this exalted point of view, he can say that defects in men and in other creatures are for the good of the whole universe; that is, that though they may be contrary to the particular nature in question, they are not contrary to nature as a whole. Whether such a deviation from the norm is due to a defect in the acting power, or to some "indisposition" of matter, or to the interference of some more powerful agent, that deviation can always be ultimately understood and taken into account by reference to divine providence.[1]

Indeed, however modern scholars may wish to interpret Aristotle, Thomas at least is of the opinion that for the Philosopher not everything is determined, since he admits that celestial bodies produce their effects only *ut in pluribus* upon terrestrial things. Having thus interpreted Aristotle, Thomas explains Aristotle's position by the fact that he dealt only with proximate causes and did not, as does Thomas himself, reduce all causes to the first or divine cause which, as providence, arranges for both the necessary and the contingent, each happening in the way in which it does because God wants it to happen in that way.[2]

Thus, in the final analysis, Thomas accepts the reality of both contingent and necessary events as being part of God's vision of a perfect universe. For, quite simply, such a universe must have both necessary and contingent causes.[3] So also intellectual beings, that is, angels, are hierarchically related to one another because all things in

came to attribute the monster to chance only in a large sense of the term. The monster as such, he says, is of little significance for Aristotle's more rigorous notion of chance. However, as Mansion himself suggests, medieval commentators on Aristotle gave much more importance to the monster. And for Thomas, as we have seen, the monster becomes the type of deviations on all levels not only cosmological but intellectual (false opinion), religious (heresy) and moral (vice and sin). See Mansion, *Introduction à la Physique Aristotélicienne* (Louvain-Paris, 1945), pp. 301–302 and p. 308, fn. 50.

[1] *In* VI *Met.* l. 3, n. 1210; *C.G.* III, 99; *Q.D. de pot.* 6, 2 ad 8; *Q.D. de ver.* 5, 5 c. Mansion observes that by speaking of a failure in matter as a cause of the chance event, Thomas is interpreting rather than reading Aristotle. Admitting that this interpretation does not falsify Aristotle's thought, he nevertheless insists that it applies only to Aristotle's broader view of chance. See Mansion, pp. 298–299 and see preceding footnote.

[2] *In* VI *Met.* l. 3.

[3] *C.G.* I, 85.

the universe are arranged in an orderly way.[1] For the same reason, there is on the earth a hierarchy of plants, animals and men.[2] Again, contrary to Augustine's appeal to evolutionism, it is for Thomas sufficiently probable that the moon was created full, since this would be more perfect, more in keeping with due order.[3] Angels also, Thomas maintains, were created at the same time as other creatures; for, inasmuch as they too are a part of the universe, it is more fitting that they should have been created along with all other parts.[4] In like manner, although a miracle may be contrary to some particular nature, it is not contrary to the order of the whole universe.[5] This same principle of order, finally, is also responsible for the fact that Thomas rejects an earlier opinion of his and subscribes to the view that celestial bodies have an influence upon the terrestrial.[6]

This concern for the perfection of the universe is seen perhaps most clearly of all from Thomas's attitude towards the philosophers, particularly Aristotle, for having discovered and given proofs as to the existence of separate substances, or angels. He rejects their proofs for a variety of reasons (Aristotle's, for example, is based upon the assumption of perpetual motion, which for Thomas is untenable) and offers instead other ways of proving the same thing. Thomas's ways are based upon: (1) the perfection of the universe; (2) the order of things, which requires a medium between the complex and the simple; (3) the imperfection of our intellect as pointing to a more perfect created intellect.[7]

Thus does Thomas see the entire universe as a perfectly organized system, within which there are chance events only with respect to the particular cause; for, with respect to the universal cause, the supreme principle of all things, all are foreseen. Evil, chance, contingency, however mysterious from the human point of view, are perfectly subject to the order which derives from the universal cause, that is, subject to divine providence.[8]

In view, then, of this love for an orderly universe, it should not be too surprising that Thomas does not take as seriously as he might the

---

[1] *C.G.* III, 80. See also 81.
[2] *Q.D. de pot.* 5, 9 c.
[3] *S.T.* I, 70, 2 ad 5.
[4] *Q.D. de pot.* 3, 18 c and ad 8. See also 3, 16 c.
[5] *Q.D. de pot* 6, 1 obj. 21 and ad 21.
[6] *Quodl.* 6, q. 11, a. un. See also *C.G. III*, 82.
[7] *Q.D. de spir. creat.* q. un., a. 5 c.
[8] *Q.D. de pot.* 3, 6 c; *S.T.* I, 22, 2 c; 25, 3 ad 4; 103, 5 ad 1; 103, 7 c and ad objectiones; 115, 6; 116; *C.G.* III, 76–77; *Comp. theol.* c. 137, n. 278; cc. 139–140, nn. 280–281.

problematic character of the deviation, the abnormal, the non-systematic. For, "the system" is ultimately the Divine Mind; and the latter shall one day be manifest to the *beati* beyond this inscrutable world.

Thus it is primarily from the human point of view that Thomas allows himself to express in terms of Aristotle's rudimentary "frequency theory" the extent to which events approach or fall short of the ideal of absolute necessity. From this point of view, the necessary is equivalent to that which happens always, or every time. It is not enough to say, however, that because a thing is necessary, therefore it cannot be other than it is. The intention of Aristotle and of Thomas as well, we think, is quite the other way around. Aside from the comforting rigor of logical necessity, they wish to say that *from observation* it can be seen that there are things, or events, in this universe which happen always in the same way and that *therefore* these events are necessary. Other events fall short of perfect occurrence. But some of these still take place often enough so that one may assume necessity, thus making science of such things possible, by positing a defect in the cause or the intervention of a more powerful extraneous cause. In this case the expected event does not occur; in its stead there occurs a different event, which we might call the non-event or, to use a more contemporary expression, the complement of the event. Because of the very nature of things, the complement of an expected event occurs only by way of exception, this exception constituting the realm of chance or, where human goals are in question, fortune.

There is in this theory, then, an implicit reference to a kind of mathematical calculation, rough-shod though it may be. In fact, properly understood the theory is fundamentally mathematical, to such an extent that one might even symbolize it in accordance with the modern convention. The necessary event, which because it is necessary is the certain event, might then be said to have a probability of 1. The impossible event, which is impossible because its complement is necessary, might similarly be said to have a probability of 0. Between these two extremes one would then merely insert appropriate fractions to express, as precisely as experimentation would allow, the likelihood of the event which is said to occur *ut in pluribus* and the unlikelihood of the event which is said to occur *ut in paucioribus*.[1]

---

[1] It is important to note here a crucial difference between Thomas's feeble approach to events and the powerful instrument that we know now as the calculus of probability. In effect, Thomas allows for, or considers, only two values between 0 and 1. The calculus of probability, on the other hand, depends upon the assumption of a continuum of values, namely, all fractions between 0 and 1. This basic insight puts the calculus of probability far

This much at least would probably suffice for that part of the theory which Thomas takes over from Aristotle. To complete the formalization however, it would be necessary to express what might be called the meta-theory which Thomas introduces, on the basis of divine providence, in the hypothesis of a well-ordered universe. For, as we have seen, although Thomas recognizes the necessary and the contingent event, he nevertheless insists that to God each is a certain event. From this divine point of view, then, there are no intermediate events; whatever happens is, in God's eyes, a certain event.[1]

(c) Relative Frequency of Good and Evil

It will now be of interest to us to see how Thomas uses this quasi-mathematical breakdown of events which he has borrowed unhesitatingly from Aristotle. By way of introduction, however, it should be recalled that Thomas, unlike Aristotle, is not interested in physical science for its own sake. As a theologian, he is especially concerned with man's relationship to God; and, accordingly, the events with which he chooses to deal are mainly human actions, each of which by virtue of its moral content brings a man nearer to or farther away from God. Given, then, his particular point of view, it should not be surprising that the frequencies which are of interest to him are the frequencies of good and evil.

As we consider this troubling question with Thomas, however, we shall find it quite difficult to decide whether he is a moralistic snob overly influenced by Aristotle's act psychology or whether he is simply at odds with himself to find some intelligibility in the hideous reality of human iniquity. Fortunately for us, this not inconsiderable problem does not directly concern us. Regardless of Thomas's attitude towards the morality of the masses, we are interested only in the use which he makes of quasi-mathematical concepts in order to make that morality, or rather the lack of it, somehow meaningful. Be that as it may, even within the limits of our interest we shall be able to see that for Thomas, no less than for Job, the problem of evil remains truly a problem.

Now, with regard to this very problem, we recall, Thomas is not

beyond anything seen by Thomas. It is, then, for precisely this reason that when we speak of a *frequency theory* in Thomas's thought, we put the expression in quotation marks. For, Thomas obviously does not have in mind anything so sophisticated as a continuum of values to represent either *"ut in pluribus"* or *"ut in paucioribus."*

[1] See the commentary by William and Martha Kneale on *C.G.* I, 67: *The Development of Logic* (Oxford, 1962), pp. 237–238.

beyond appealing to the influence of the heavenly bodies in order to give a rational basis to what his theology tells him is due to original sin.[1] And, what is of great interest to us, it is precisely in this context that Thomas makes one of his rare uses of the term *probabile* to characterize a proposition based on frequencies. Making his usual observation that most of the time men follow their passions and that only the wise resist (the famous "*agere contra*"), Thomas calculates the effectiveness of planetary influence as follows: "It is more probable," he says, "that a given group will do that to which it is inclined by a heavenly body than that one single man would so act, since the latter might perhaps overcome the aforesaid inclination by reason." He then adds the factor of anger and says (still arguing from the "collective") that it is more likely that the group, perhaps the mob, would act out of this emotion than that any given individual would so act.[2]

It is also because of the fact that the many follow their passions that, according to Thomas, astrological predictions are verified more often than not: *ut in pluribus*.[3] That they are not always verified Thomas explains by comparing the causality of a heavenly body to that of a necessarily true major premiss in a syllogism. A necessary major, which is a kind of remote cause, cannot produce a necessary conclusion except through the mediation of an equally necessary minor; if the minor is contingent, the conclusion can only be contingent. Similarly, the causality of a heavenly body, though necessary, is only that of a remote cause. The proximate cause of terrestrial effects is the active and passive capabilities of the things on this earth, which produce their effects not necessarily (that is, always) but only contingently (that is, most of the time). Thus is physical determinism avoided and room left for the exceptional event which escapes the influence of celestial necessity.[4]

---

[1] See above, Chapter 2, pp. 59–60.

[2] *Q.D. de ver.* 5, 10 ad 7: "Multitudo ut in pluribus sequitur inclinationes naturales, inquantum homines multitudinis acquiescunt passionibus; sed sapientes ratione superant passiones et inclinationes praedictas. Et ideo magis est probabile de aliqua multitudine quod operetur id ad quod inclinat corpus caeleste, quam de uno homine singulari, qui forte per rationem superat inclinationem praedictam. Et simile esset, si una multitudo hominum cholericorum poneretur, non de facili contingeret quin ad iracundiam moveretur, quamvis de uno posset magis accidere." The argument which Thomas thus answers is to the effect that since the heavenly bodies can even induce large numbers of men to fight a war, *a fortiori* they can exert such an influence over an individual. Whence Thomas's appeal to a kind of moral law of large numbers. See *Q.D. de ver.* 5, 10 c.

[3] *S.T.* I–II, 9, 5 ad 3.

[4] *C.G.* III, 86. In this context Thomas restricts the necessary to that which happens always and considers as contingent what happens only most of the time. This usage, of course, is directly contrary to Aristotle's theory and, for that matter, to many of Thomas's own declarations, even in the same work. It is perhaps possible to attribute the rigorism of the passage

Now, the tone of the foregoing observations is already that of a Jeremias announcing the perdition of the masses. And the reason for this is not far to seek. Thomas, in effect, prejudices his moral statistics from the outset because of his basic contention that to be good a thing must be integrally good, in such a way that any defect makes the thing to that extent evil. It is obvious that the odds are against anything in this world, least of all a human action, being good in every possible respect, just as it is obvious that there is an unlimited number of ways in which something, especially a human action, can be somehow evil.[1]

From this somwehat computational point of view, one is left with the pessimistic conclusion that there is more evil than good in human actions. It might, of course, be objected that the reasoning here is specious in that it concentrates upon the accidental rather than the essential. But Thomas is not dissuaded. Even granting that the evil in question is as it were accidental, it can still occur most of the time or even always. To illustrate this point, Thomas reminds us that someone who goes into town with the express intention of shopping will inevitably meet a crowd of people: whatever his direct intention, the indirect or accidental consequence of his action has a frequency of most of the time or even always. Sad though it may be to contemplate, this illustration fairly well expresses man's chances of accomplishing the integral good in the midst of manifold possibilities of evil. To hit the golden mean of the virtuous is about as likely as would be the propelling of an arrow to the direct center of a target. In fact, for most men it is less likely, since they do not even know the true target, which is the good of reason, as well as they know the good of the senses.[2]

Because of the delicate precision of aim which is required, then, the frequency of evil in men is greater than that of good. This is in direct contrast to the subhuman things of nature, which attain their far simpler goals far more often than they are diverted to the production of a monster. Similarly, so long as one considers man only in terms of sense good, it can be said that he accomplishes the good more often than evil. It is only in introducing the level of reason (which, however, is the level proper to man) that the curve drops below the line. From this point on, it is only for the few who follow reason that the good is more frequent than evil.[3]

to Thomas's youth; but the distinction as given also seems related to that between absolute and consequential necessity. Be that as it may, it is at least clear that Thomas is not always consistent in what he has to say about "the necessary" and "the contingent."

[1] Q.D. de pot. 3, 6 ad 9.
[2] Q.D. de malo, 1, 3 ad 17.
[3] Q.D. de pot. 3, 6 ad 5.

For Thomas, then, the man who lives according to reason is rare and far between. And the direct result of this unhappy state of affairs is a rather limited population in the heavenly kingdom. Consider Thomas's argument. Most of the time, he says, men have the ordinary goods of nature and only occasionally fall short of this. The majority have enough knowledge to govern their lives; a smaller number (*pauciores*) are stupid or moronic; and still fewer (*paucissimi*) attain to a profound knowledge of things intellectual. Then, relating this quasi-statistical epistemology to the question of eternal happiness, which is perfect knowledge of God, Thomas concludes in accordance with his reading of Matthew 7:13–14 that few transcend the ordinary state of nature to achieve this great good.[1]

If Thomas is strict, however, it must nonetheless be said in his favor that he is not in this regard a misogynist. In a dialectical dispute as to whether there would have been as many females as there are males if Adam had not sinned, he feels that the argument for the affirmative makes the assertion probable. This, in turn, leads him to muse on both sides as to whether there is to be an equal number of males and females among the eternally blessed. Though open to correction, he favors equality.[2]

In general, then, this is not a very pleasant picture of the human condition. Nonetheless, Thomas is able to shift the balance in favor of the good by pointing out that if one take the universe as a whole, including as it does a vast majority of things for which natural defects constitute the only evil, then it can be said that good has the upper hand and that evil is but and small part of the whole universe.[3] It must be admitted, however, that though this may be consoling to the divine mind and to any other mind in tune therewith, it is hardly such to that unfortunate element of the universe which happens to be a human being and happens to be among the destitute majority who miss the dead center of reason's target.

Be that as it may, whatever man may say *about* the divine point of view, he is not under present circumstances fortunate enough to share that viewpoint himself. And Thomas, as we have already seen, knows this well enough. For Thomas, accordingly, the best that man can do is to state in his own way as well as he possibly can how things look as it were from above; as for the rest, he must fill in the gaps as circum-

[1] *S.T.* I, 23, 7 ad 3.
[2] *Quodl.* 3, q. 11, a. un.
[3] *S.T.* I, 49, 3 ad 5.

stances demand. In other words, there is a rather close parallel between Thomas's theory of practical knowledge and some of the contemporary philosophies of science. For, as Thomas sees it, all human knowledge is a kind of approximation to that ideal knowledge which is proper to God. What man knows and the way in which man states what he knows is always subject to improvement, and this is true even with regard to knowledge of divine revelation. This being the case, it is often necessary to make allowances for a certain margin of error, of inapplicability of the general to the particular, of the past to the present, of the present to the future. Into the gap left by this margin of error the individual must step with his own powers of reasoning in order to relate what is known in general to the particular problem of the moment. In so doing, he sometimes finds the general a sufficiently accurate expression of the particular. Yet at other times he is required to make adjustments in the light of the particular itself.

This process of tuning in, as it were, on the particular falls to what Thomas calls the virtue of prudence.[1]

C. MORAL DELIBERATION AND PROBABILITY

Our interest in probability, then, has led us through cosmological contingency to the realm of the ethical. And this is only appropriate. For, if Thomas's cosmology is in any way deterministic, this determinism is strictly theocentric. For Thomas himself, a mere man, the question of contingency remains of crucial importance, particularly with regard to matters of human decision.[2] For, man's intellectual limitations are such that he must act in a world which, for him at least, is filled with contingency; and thus he must often rely upon opinion or even conjecture. In other words, man's moral life consists largely of dealing with the contingent on the basis of probability. The ability to do this well is precisely what Thomas means by prudence.

Prudence taken integrally involves consideration of possible choices, decision, and the carrying out of that decision in action. There can be defects in any of the three stages, but of all defects failure to act is the very death of prudence.[3] This being said, however, we wish to con-

[1] See S.T. II–II, 47–56. See also Josef Pieper, *Prudence; The First Cardinal Virtue* (London, 1959).

[2] Thus for Thomas the importance of the virtue of *"gnome"*, which is, as it were, the intellectual pinnacle of prudence. For, if one is endowed with this virtue, he is thereby enabled to see beyond cosmological regularity into mysteries of the contingent which are ordinarily reserved to divine providence. See S.T. II–II, 51, esp. 4 c and ad 3.

[3] S.T. II–II, 47, 8.

centrate upon the first two steps of prudence, which are properly rational in a manner which Thomas likes to compare to reasoning in speculative sciences.[1] The principles of prudential reasoning are laws, here taken in a broad sense, and the process of reasoning has to do with finding appropriate particular propositions by means of which the general principles can be brought to bear upon the situation with which the individual is concerned.[2]

This rational deliberation through which the morality of the particular is brought to light can, in turn, take place on several different levels. On each of these levels, however, man seeks as it were to diminish the domain of the uncertain and the unforeseen with which he must deal in his concrete activity. And in this way, it will be noted, man somewhat haltingly approaches that breadth of intellectual vision which is proper to God and is shared by those closest to him.

The first and seemingly for Thomas the most important level of deliberation is that which results in human law. A second level is that of the individual moral agent conducting his own personal life. Constituting an intermediate level which is preparatory and ancillary to deliberation on each of the other levels is the dialectical inquiry which results in the various theoretical sciences, including, of course, ethics, which Thomas subsumes under theology.[3]

Since, however, actions are in the particular it is ultimately only on the level of concrete deliberate action that one can have adequate knowledge for moral choice. For, the realm of moral choice is precisely the realm of the contingent, of that which can be other than it is and which consequently cannot be predetermined outside of the concrete instance itself.[4] The task of law and of ethics is rather to expedite the attainment of such concrete truth by bringing to light in advance as

---

[1] See, for example, *Q.D. de ver.* 5, 1 ad 6. This question will be treated explicitly in Section 2, where we contend that a more valid comparison can be made between moral deliberation and dialectical disputation.

[2] *S.T.* I–II, 81, 3 c; 90, 1 ad 2.

[3] That moral theology or, if you will, ethics, is for Thomas only preparatory and ancillary to deliberation can be seen from *S.T.* I–II, 14, 6 c, where in fact this science is clearly supposed to be just one of many that contribute to the individual's reasoning about practical problems. Comparing the principles of moral deliberation to principles assumed by a subalternate science, Thomas here notes that the agent presupposes: (1) his ultimate goal, namely, happiness; (2) the data of sense experience; (3) the established truths of any science: "quaecumque sunt per aliquam scientiam speculativam vel practicam in universali cognita, sicut quod moechari est a Deo prohibitum, et quod homo non potest vivere nisi nutriatur nutrimento convenienti." One of the principles mentioned, it will be noted, would still be considered to be in the domain of theology, the other in that of biology. Whatever the source of such principles, however, they are not of themselves determinative of action: "Terminus autem inquisitionis est id quod statim est in potestate nostra ut faciamus."

[4] See *S.T.* II–II, 4, 2 obj. 3; 47, 5 c; *Q.D. de virt. in comm.* q. un., a. 12 c.

many stable factors of the human condition as possible. This task cannot, however, be perfectly fulfilled in the abstract; and hence both law and ethics as such remain incomplete and subject to interpretation in the light of concrete circumstances.

Indeed, if we may make explicit what for Thomas is only implicit, the very notion of circumstances is an abstraction and accordingly can itself be subjected to different levels of analysis. For purposes of law, man tries to grasp the general circumstances of a given time and place in human history. For purposes of ethics, man tries to grasp the somewhat more specific circumstances which are proper to various kinds of recurring moral problems. For purposes of immediate action, finally, the notion of circumstances must be taken in all the richness of concrete detail, whether the decision called for be in the public or in the private domain.[1]

It is, then, precisely because of the complexity of concrete circumstances that both legal and ethical propositions are able to state the truth only with regard to what is the case most of the time: *ut in pluribus*. The truth of the concrete situation can be determined only by means of the practical dialectic of what might today be called existential deliberation.[2]

In the light of these introductory observations, then, we can say all that need be said for our purposes by discussing the principles and the reasoning which go into a practical decision.

1. Laws as Practical Principles

For Thomas the principles of practical reasoning are, broadly speaking, laws. And, as we shall see, Thomas utilizes his notion of frequencies in his theory of law. Indeed, in some respects it is almost true to say that this theory of law *is* a theory of frequencies.

The basis of all law is what Thomas calls the eternal law, which for our purposes can be roughly described as God's plan for the universe. This eternal law as more or less naturally known by men constitutes

---

[1] Thomas's explicit teaching with regard to the notion of circumstances will be found in *S.T.* I–II, 7. The broader interpretation is based upon a variety of texts which will be discussed in detail. We might mention here, however, *S.T.* I–II, 97, 1 c, where Thomas speaks of the "*mutatio conditionum hominum*" and of the effect that this has upon morality, especially with regard to law.

[2] With regard to existential deliberation see *S.T.* I–II, 14, esp. 1 c; 57, 4 ad 2; II–II, 47, 4 ad 2; 49, 5 c and ad 2. With regard to the insufficiency of abstract ethical norms see the following: *In* IV *Sent.* d. 15, q. 3, a. 2; *S.T.* I–II, 84, 1 ad 3; 94, 4 c; 96, 1 ad 3 and 6 c; II–II, 70, 2 c; 88, 9 c; 120, 1 c; 147, 4 c; 152, 2 ad 3; 154, 2 c; *In* II *Ethic.* l. 2, nn. 258–259; l. 8, n. 334. The limitations of law will be discussed somewhat more directly in what follows.

what Thomas calls the natural law, that is to say, the basic principles of morality.[1] In addition to these basic principles naturally known, man also is aided in his moral reasoning by the supernatural principles revealed and contained in Sacred Scripture, these latter constituting what Thomas calls the divine law.[2]

Having thus stated the foundations of moral reasoning, we are at once compelled to add a qualification from the side of the subject. For, as Thomas indicates in various ways, knowledge of moral principles is not the same for all men. Some principles, he says, such as that one should love God and neighbor, are easily known to all; others, though somewhat more detailed, such as the Ten Commandments, are also easily known; still others require detailed study and consideration, and hence these are readily known only by the wise.[3]

One senses here a slight tone of intellectualism that would make of morality a matter of knowing the right propositions. But, however much Thomas involves himself in moral abstractionism, he is certainly aware of its limitations. For, in effect he is saying that the more remote a principle is from fundamental principles, the less certain it is and hence the less facile its application. Even more important, he recognizes that a given individual might acquire still other principles during the course of his life through education or simply through personal experience.[4] Since, however, not everyone profits equally from education or from personal experience, not everyone will have the same fount of principles or axioms on the basis of which to formulate practical judgments.

Implied here, of course, is the troubling fact that what really counts is not whether one has learned abstractly the right principles but whether he applies them in his actions. And Thomas suspects as much himself. As he puts it, it is only insofar as one is virtuous that he will think rightly (*recte opinari*) about principles of action.[5] Whence arises the Socratic problem which shall remain the theme of our discussion, the problem, namely, as to whether knowledge is virtue.

Be that as it may, Thomas has little confidence in either the knowledge or the virtue of the masses. Besides, he maintains, it is easier to make a good law than to make a good judgment about particular cases.

[1] *Q.D. de ver.* 5, 1 ad 6; 16, 1 c; *S.T.* I–II, 93. The ability in man to learn these principles Thomas calls, after Aristotle, *synderesis*. See *S.T.* I, 79, 12.

[2] *S.T.* I–II, 91, 4 c.

[3] *S.T.* I–II, 100, 1 c and 11 c.

[4] *S.T.* II–II, 47, 15 c and ad 2; 49, 1 c; 3 c and ad 2. See also II–II, 48, 1 c; *C.G.* III, 97; *Q.D. de ver.* 24, 11 ad 4. It is perhaps these personally acquired principles that Thomas has in mind when he says in *C.G.* III, 97, that principles of action are not always necessary.

[5] *Q.D. de ver.* 24, 11 ad 4.

Hence, he concludes, by means of law as little as possible should be left up to free choice.[1] But this obviously is just a convenient way to avoid the real problem. For, who under God has such good judgment as to make legislation itself an easy task?

As Thomas himself observes, laws cannot specify each and every possible situation which an individual might encounter. Man is simply incapable of thinking out every single case that might come up, and hence cannot put everything in the form of a law; nor would it be desirable to do so even if it were possible, in view of the confusion which would result. Accordingly, says Thomas, laws are to be made with a view to what happens most of the time – again, *ut in pluribus*.[2] Thus, for example, the Church's law of fasting is based upon the conviction that men in general benefit from fasting; and accordingly this law is binding in general upon all, but *only* in general and for the majority of cases: *communiter et ut in pluribus*.[3]

A law, in other words, is meant to state what is of benefit to the common welfare most of the time, that is, in view of what is usually the case. Since the very purpose of the law is the general welfare, the law is not to be observed if in a particular case its observance would be detrimental to that same general welfare. For example, notes Thomas, although it would be against the law to open the gates of a besieged city, the gates should nevertheless be opened to admit the leaders of the city, because they are, obviously enough, important to the welfare of all.[4] Thus does Thomas recognize the need to interpret a given law in the light of concrete circumstances.

But not only does a law need to be interpreted in the concrete; it might even need to be changed. For, laws like personal actions are not only to be decided upon, they are also to be critically evaluated. On the personal level, of course, it is clear enough that an individual not only decides upon a course of action but also deliberates subsequently as to whether what he has decided should have been done or should be done again.[5] A similar *post factum* critique is also of great importance with regard to existing laws. The public official, in other words, must deliberate as to whether these laws are adequate or should rather be changed or at least modified. That the deficiencies of earlier laws should be removed by subsequent modifications Thomas justifies on

[1] *S.T.* I–II, 95, 1 ad 2.
[2] *S.T.* I–II, 96, 6 ad 3.
[3] *S.T.* II–II, 147, 3 ad 1.
[4] *S.T.* I–II, 96, 6 c.
[5] See *Q.D. de ver.* 17, 1 c; *S.T.* I, 79, 13 c, ad 1 and ad 3; In II *Sent.* d. 24, q. 2, a. 4 c.

the grounds that human knowledge in general proceeds in the course of time from the less perfect to the more perfect. In addition to the advances in knowledge which make such changes desirable, he points to the fact that even good laws need to be changed when the conditions for which such laws were introduced have changed: *propter mutationem conditionum hominum.*[1]

For Thomas, in other words, a law is a standard (*mensura*) of action; but if the things with which it deals are changeable, the standard itself cannot be entirely unchanging. In this, he says, human laws differ from the demonstrative conclusions of the sciences; for, unlike the latter, they are not infallible.[2]

Now, what we have said so far pertains explicitly to laws made by man. But, as noted above, human laws are based upon what Thomas calls the natural law, that is to say, the eternal law of God as known by human reason. Can we, then, go one step further and say that even the natural law so understood is subject to modification? Though somewhat guardedly, Thomas nevertheless replies to this question in the affirmative.[3] Taken in general, he maintains, the principles of the natural law are indeed immutable. For, what is just and good, considered in abstraction (*formaliter*) is always and everywhere the same. But the more one takes into consideration the particular conditions of time and place, the more one sees the limitations of these general principles.[4] For, the principles taken by themselves do not specify in detail what is the good that is to be done or the evil that is to be avoided. This must always be determined in the light of prevailing circumstances, which is to say that reason must intervene to relate the principles to action here and now. Every act of virtue, insofar as it is virtuous, must be in accordance with the natural law, that is to say, in accordance with right reason; but this does not of itself mean that every such act is no more than a direct concretization of some abstract principle. Acts are in the particular, and as such are to be judged moral or immoral

---

[1] *S.T.* I–II, 97, esp. 1 c. On this point, then, Thomas distinguishes himself from what he takes to be Aristotle's position. See *In* II *Polit.* l. 12, nn. 293–295; III, l. 15, n. 512; IV, l. 4, n. 584; l. 12, n. 680.

[2] *S.T.* I–II, 91, 3 obj. 3 and ad 3; 97, 1 ad 2.

[3] See John W. Healey, *The Mutability of the Natural Law in Selected Texts of Saint Thomas* (unpublished Master's Thesis, Saint Louis University) (Saint Louis, Mo., 1954).

[4] *Q.D. de malo* 2, 4 ad 13 and *S.T.* I–II, 94, 4 c: "Etsi in communibus sit aliqua necessitas, quanto magis ad propria descenditur, tanto magis invenitur defectus . . . Et hoc tanto magis invenitur deficere, quanto magis ad particularia descenditur . . . Quanto enim plures conditiones particulares apponuntur, tanto pluribus modis poterit deficere . . ." See also *In* IV *Sent.* d. 33, q. 1, a. 2 c and ad 1; d. 26, q. 1, a. 1 ad 3; d. 33, q. 3, a. 2 ad 2; *S.T.* I–II, 100, 2 c; II–II, 57, 2 ad 1.

according as they are or are not proportionate to the particular conditions in which they are posited.[1]

In summary, then, the reasoning that results in moral decision is indeed based upon principles, and the principles are foundational in a way analogous to that of principles in the sciences. But, inasmuch as these moral principles are concerned with matters contingent and thus changeable, they lack the perfect stability of the principles of science.[2] Thus it might almost be said that for Thomas the general principles of morality are, as it were, empty schemata which must be given appropriate content by rational deliberation with regard to the way things are in time and place.

2. Moral Deliberation

Seeing, then, that moral principles alone do not suffice for an adequate moral decision, we must now consider the process of rational deliberation whereby an individual relates the universal to the particular, the abstract to the concrete.

(a) Deliberation as Dialectical

For this purpose, we may take as our point of departure the fact that Thomas compares existential deliberation to the reasoning processes which obtain in the speculative sciences. The basis of the comparison, according to Thomas, consists in the fact that in each case a syllogism is involved. In the practical order, says Thomas, one goes from a universal proposition to a conclusion, which is in effect the practical decision, by means of a singular proposition that relates the universal to the particular.[3] This, then, is the comparison which Thomas makes between scientific and moral reasoning. As we shall now attempt to show, however, his larger view of moral reasoning compares far more favorably with the reasoning appropriate to dialectical disputation.[4]

[1] S.T. I–II, 94, 3 c and ad 3; Contra Impugn. c. 5 (6), n. 243. See S.T. II–II, 31, 3 ad 3; Quodl. 6, q. 7, a. un. c. At this point, of course, one is reminded of Hegel's famous critique of Stoicism. See G. W. F. Hegel, La Phénoménologie de l'Esprit (Traduction de Jean Hyppolite: Paris, 1939), Tome I, pp. 169–171.

[2] It will be noted that we have not raised the question as to whether that law which Thomas calls divine is in any way changeable. To the best of our knowledge Thomas does not raise the question except to the extent that for him man's expression of divine revelation can be improved in the course of time. (See above, Chapter 3, pp. 118–119). Be that as it may, Thomas's views on this subject can well be considered outside the area of our research.

[3] In III De An. l. 16, nn. 840–846; Q.D. de ver. 10, 5 c; S.T. I, 80, 2 ad 3; I–II, 14.

[4] In approaching the subject in this way, we by no means deny the existence of passages where Thomas presents a seemingly more rigorous view. Indeed, at S.T. II–II, 51, 4 ad 2, Thomas states explicitly that moral reasoning includes both stages of argumentation, namely,

To begin with, Thomas tells us that in the process of moral deliberation (as in disputation) propositions of all kinds – speculative and practical, universal and particular, certain, probable and even conjectural – are brought to bear upon the problem at hand.[1] Thus in principle at least there is no limit as to how many things one might consider before arriving at a decision. Nonetheless, Thomas insists, the process is in practice limited both by the number of relevant principles, or axioms, which can be found and by the capacities of the moral agent.[2] At least under ordinary circumstances, then, one does complete the deliberation for better or worse and arrive at a decision. This decision, however, can hardly be any better than the profundity of the deliberation which has preceded it.

Next it must be noted that a proposition which is introduced into a moral deliberation is, precisely insofar as thus introduced, no more than probable.[3] For, however certain or necessary a given proposition might be taken by itself, it in no way follows from this fact alone that the proposition certainly applies to the practical problem at hand. For example, however certain one may be as to the proposition that murder is evil, he might well find himself faced with an urgent situation in which the content of that proposition would be terrifyingly inadequate. And however carefully he might deliberate in the time at his disposal, his decision and the act which follows from it would inevitably have about them that air of uncertainty which is proper to opinion.

The practical quandary just described is illustrative of the crucial point that moral deliberation has to do with the contingent. Since the contingent is by definition that which can be other than it is, the contingent as such can be known only opinionatively. Thus it is a characteristic of opinion that in adhering to it one recognizes that the truth of the matter might be other than one has taken it to be. Opinion, then, unlike science, is open to alternatives; and dialectical reasoning, unlike

---

disputation and demonstration. This, however, must be taken as an ideal. For, one looks in vain for a text in which Thomas clearly states that any particular moral deliberation arrives at a "demonstration". Be that as it may, the language of II–II, 51 as a whole is quite strong indeed.

[1] *S.T.* II–II, 48, 1 c. It is in this context that one must understand Thomas's definition of conscience as "the application of knowledge to some special act": *applicatio scientiae ad aliquam specialem actum* (*Q.D. de ver.* 17, 1 and 2). See also *S.T.* I, 79, 13 c; I–II, 19, 5; II–II, 19, 7 c; *In II Sent.* d. 24, q. 2, a. 4 c; *Quodl.* 3, q. 12, a. 26 c; *In III De An.* l. 14, nn. 813–814; 1. 15, n. 820; *Q.D. de ver.* 2. 8 c; 3, 3 c, ad 2 and ad 4. See below, p. 233 fn 1.

[2] *S.T.* I–II, 14, 6 c. See above, p. 214 fn. 3.

[3] It is in the light of this fact, we think, that one must understand Thomas's assertion of what might be called a negative corollary: "*quando conscientia non est probabilis, tunc debet eam deponere.*" For, as in the case of dialectical disputation so in the case of moral deliberation, an opinion must have probability in order to merit assent. See *Q.D. de ver.* 17, 4 ad 4.

scientific demonstration, must consider both alternatives. Since, therefore, moral deliberation has to do with the contingent and thus must be open to alternatives, it must be compared not so much with scientific demonstration as with dialectical disputation. And, as a matter of fact, Thomas tells us as much himself. Prior to acting, he notes, one is faced with opposite alternatives and therefore, aiming at the good as the dialectician aims at probability or as the rhetorician at persuasion, seeks to adopt the alternative which will most effectively lead in that direction.[1] It is not by accident, then, that the alternative proposition which is adopted as a result of deliberation is called by Thomas a *sententia*.[2]

As in the case of disputation, this *sententia*, or deliberated opinion, can be arrived at only by finding "arguments" in its favor.[3] In theory, of course, the arguments for either alternative might be so well balanced as to leave the mind as undecided as Buridan's ass. But Thomas is convinced that there is always the possibility of another point of view from which one can decide in favor of one alternative over the other.[4] This other point of view, as Thomas describes it, amounts to a higher (more fundamental) principle. So long as it is possible to reduce the proposition, or proposal, in question to a still more fundamental principle, moral deliberation (like dialectical disputation) remains "open." A decision to act, however, need not and in fact cannot arrive at demonstration in the strict sense. Deliberation as such can seldom acomplish more, from the subjective point of view, than resolution to what Thomas calls in his commentary on the *Posterior Analytics* an "immediate opinion."[5] This much accomplished, however, one is

---

[1] See *Q.D. de ver.* 22, 6 c and ad 4; *S.T.* I, 83, 1 c.
[2] See *S.T.* I–II, 13, 1 ad 2; 3 c; 6 ad 2; *In* II *Sent.* d. 24, q. 1, a. 3 ad 2 and ad 5; q. 2, a. 4 ad 2; *Q.D. de ver.* 17, 1 ad 4.
[3] *S.T.* I–II, 14, 4 c.
[4] *S.T.* I–II, 13, 6 ad 3. Thomas considers basically the same problem from a more cosmological point of view at *In* II *Phys.* l. 8, n. 109. Considering Aristotle's division of events into those which occur always or most of the time and those which occur only seldom, Thomas raises the question as to whether there might not be an event which is equally possible, that is, just as likely to happen as not. There are no such events in nature, he decides, since all natural things have a tendency to produce some effects rather than others and do in fact produce those effects unless occasionally hindered by extraneous causes. Human free choice, however, is such that alternative acts flowing from choice can be at least in theory equally likely. But, Thomas notes, so long as alternative choices are seen by the subject as being equally attractive, no act is posited. It is, he says, only when the will is able to prefer one over the other that a choice is made and an act posited. As posited, that act falls under Aristotle's breakdown of events into what happens always, most of the time, or occasionally. Whatever help this might be to Buridan's ass, it is of course little encouragement to the notion of a "random choice."
[5] See above, Chapter 4, pp. 183–184.

thereby entitled to commit himself to what we would perhaps call a final decision: *ultima* (or *finalis*) *sententia*.[1]

In short, reason deals with the practical in a manner analogous to that in which it deals dialectically with the speculative, and the end result is roughly the same: an opinion to which one adheres as the best expression of the truth obtainable under the circumstances.

Now, the reason why moral deliberation can produce only opinionative or probable conclusions is because the subject matter deliberated, namely, the concrete situation, is *contingent*, able to be other than it is. One might even say, then, that the concrete situation is non-systematic. This, of course, suggests quite a problem for the man who wants to make intelligent choices in his moral life; for, like it or not, he is almost driven by the way things are to "calculate" what is in all probability the right thing to do. Thomas, as we shall now see, resolves the problem at least in theory by determining what is probable on the basis of what happens *ut in pluribus*.

And by so doing, let us note well, Thomas performs a most interesting wedding between the quasi-statistical *ut in pluribus* and the logical *probabile*. Since we are as it were the official witnesses, we might be permitted to muse as to whether the marriage is one of love or one of convenience.

The rationale for it all goes something like this. To begin with, the very complexity of factors which are involved in a concrete situation is such that perfect certitude is humanly unattainable. Thus, the measure or criterion of judgment must be considerably more flexible than, say, is the case in mathematics (or, as we might interject, in *pure* mathematics). This being the case, it is enough for a morally licit action that one act in accordance with what can be probably estimated: *probabiliter aestimari potest*.[2] But this, in turn, is to be done by determining what occurs most of the time and fails to occur only rarely – or, according to an even more interesting formulation, what occurs probably and most of the time: *probabiliter et ut in pluribus*.[3]

Thus does Aristotle's cosmology of the contingent find its way into Thomas's moral theory. Its presence there, however, is not altogether felicitous. For, by relating judgments in the moral sphere to the physicist's laws about natural phenomena, Thomas in effect disregards his assertions as to the complexity of the concrete. The resulting fallacy

[1] *Q.D. de ver.* 15, 3 c; *S.T.* I–II, 14, 6 c; 74, 7 c.
[2] *S.T.* I–II, 96, 1 obj. 3 and ad 3; II–II, 62, 7 c.
[3] *S.T.* II–II, 32, 5 ad 3.

of hasty generalization is particularly unfortunate in that it tends to justify official contempt for the claims of the individual to personal rights and responsibilities. For, be it noted, it is not so much the individual as it is the State and the Church that Thomas wishes to instruct in the art of statistical probability.

(b) The Dialectic of Deliberation

As a general principle, then, Thomas assigns to the moral agent responsibility for all effects which follow either always or for the most part from a given type of action, but not for effects which follow only rarely or in a minority of cases, the latter amounting to what he calls a casual evil analogous to the casual defect in natural organisms. Thus, for example, a lumberjack who kills a man by felling a tree in a seldom traversed forest would ordinarily be inculpable; but someone who commits adultery cannot be exonerated from the injustice therein entailed.[1]

It is not, however, the role of the individual to apply this principle to his fellow man. Quite to the contrary, on the interpersonal level Thomas suggests that it is better to risk being deceived about others more often by having a good opinion of them than to risk misjudging someone even rarely by being generally suspicious of others. If, however, the iniquity of the other is clear, one's responsibility with regard to the other is more complicated. But, to begin with, one is not obligated to admonish another if it can be probably estimated that that person will not accept the correction but only become worse. Moreover, any such admonitions should be made in private so long as there is a probability of success. But once it becomes probable that further private admonitions would be fruitless, one may have recourse to public authority – except in the event that it can be probably estimated that such recourse would be equally unprofitable.[2]

Problems of religious life can also be illuminated by estimations of probability; and here the statistical element is somewhat more pronounced. The question at issue is how to deal with candidates for the religious life. Experience proves, says Thomas, that most of the time those who enter remain, and only occasionally does someone leave. Accordingly, he maintains, the question of encouraging vocations is to be determined in the light of what usually happens and not in the light of exceptions. For, what is true in an individual case should not

[1] *C.G.* III, 6; *Q.D. de malo* 1, 3 ad 15.
[2] *S.T.* II–II, 60, 4 ad 1; 33, 6 c; 8 ad 1.

be made a general rule. At the same time, he admits, what is generally true with regard to human actions should not be applied indiscriminately to the individual case.[1]

Granting, then, that there is some sort of calculation of probability, at least in a qualified sense, in personal affairs and even in religious life, it still seems that for Thomas this task falls chiefly to public authority. In support of this, we offer a few passages in which Thomas deals with jurisprudence.

As a general maxim, Thomas says that "testimony... does not have infallible certitude but (only) probable (certitude). And therefore anything which gives probability to the contrary renders the testimony inefficacious." [2] Accordingly, he feels called upon to provide a list of those whose authority lacks what we have called probity. This list, if we may say so, is an excellent illustration of what the French call *moyenageux*. Some, according to Thomas, lack probity because of their own guilt, others due to no guilt on their part. Included among the former are non-believers, those of bad reputation (*infames*), and public criminals. Included among the latter are three different groups: (1) those defective in reasoning power, namely, children, the mentally ill, and women; (2) relatives, domestics, and enemies of the accused; (3) individuals such as paupers and slaves who are subject to command and whom accordingly one could probably induce to give false testimony.

Of course, even with the set of acceptable witnesses thus restricted, the problem still remains as to how one shall evaluate the testimony of the acceptable. For this purpose, Thomas applies his quasi-statistical criteria in order to justify the juridical policy that the agreement of at

---

[1] *Quodl.* 3, q. 5, a. 1 c and ad 4; q. 4 a. un. c.

[2] *S.T.* II–II, 70, 3 c: "Testimonium ... non habet infallibilem certitudinem, sed probabilem. Et ideo quidquid est quod probabilitatem offerat in contrarium, reddit testimonium inefficax." A. Gardeil made much of this text to defend his thesis that for Thomas probability involves certitude and that hence there are no degrees of probability. As he sees it, for Thomas "il n'y a pas de moins probable. Il n'y a que du probable tout court." – "La Certitude Probable", *Revue des Sciences Philosophiques et Théologiques* 5 (1911): 264. As we have already seen from countless texts, Gardeil's rigorous interpretation is simply without foundation. But, like many other neo-scholastic theologians before and after him, Gardeil was interested much less in an objective study of Thomas's theory of probability than in defending a particular theory of moral casuistry. The effects of such an approach can, in fact, be seen from a careful consideration of the very text which Gardeil considered so beneficial to his cause. Thomas does not say here that arguments against someone's testimony destroy the probability of that testimony. All he says is that such arguments render that testimony inconclusive or inefficacious: *inefficax*. Thus, just as a demonstration of one alternative is possible only after all arguments for the other alternative have been answered, so also a legal judgment can be handed down on the basis of testimony only on the condition that there are no probable arguments against the truth of that testimony. Or, as American juries are advised, a verdict of guilty presupposes that there is "no reasonable doubt" as to whether the defendant might be innocent.

least two and preferably three witnesses is required for a legal judgment. In this regard apparently oblivious of the trial of Christ, Thomas says "it is more probable that the statement of many contains more truth than the statement of one." That demonstrative certitude is not thereby attainable he readily admits. But with regard to human affairs, he says, it suffices to have "probable certitude, which attains the truth most of the time (*ut in pluribus*) and misses the truth only occasionally (*ut in paucioribus*)." [1]

The same two points, somewhat more delicately nuanced, suffice to justify the same judicial practice among the ancient Hebrews. In the first place, Thomas points out, conjectural probability of the sort attainable by an orator suffices in human affairs. Secondly, although two or three witnesses might possibly conspire to lie, it is nevertheless neither easy nor probable that they would agree, especially when carefully examined as to details.[2]

It must be noted that Thomas has no illusions about the kind of certitude one can have on the basis of juridical testimony. Such certitude, he says, is not infallible but only "certitude which can be had probably." [3] This being Thomas's consistent position, it is all the more regrettable that he never warns against the wheels of justice

---

[1] *S.T.* II–II, 70, 2 c: "In actibus enim humanis, super quibus constituuntur judicia et exiguntur testimonia, non potest haberi certitudo demonstrativa; eo quod sufficit probabilis certitudo, quae ut in pluribus veritatem attingat, etsi in paucioribus a veritate deficiat. Est autem probabile quod magis veritatem contineat dictum multorum quam dictum unius." Of course, by attributing probability to the testimony of many witnesses rather than of one, Thomas seemingly contradicts his statements about the influence of celestial bodies upon human passions. For, with regard to the latter he says it is more probable that *one* will resist and follow reason than that many will do so. It must be noted, however, that there are additional factors involved in legal testimony and hence Thomas is not, as it were, dealing with the same set. For one thing, as we have just seen, Thomas eliminates from the court room large categories of "bad risks." Having thus restricted his set to the sub-set of more or less "virtuous", he further requires for probability that two or three be in agreement – and in detail. And perhaps most important of all in his eyes, he presumes that the witnesses are *speaking under oath*. For, the fear of God will presumably restrain the potential liar; and, for reasons that are not at all clear, by virtue of this "recourse to divine testimony" one is enabled to have "some certitude" about the future, the hidden thoughts of men, and "distant things". Anyway, this is what Thomas says. But he is careful to point out that this method of confirmation is in no way applicable in the sciences. "It would seem ridiculous," he says, "if someone in a disputation with regard to some science should wish to prove a proposition by means of an oath" "(*S.T.* II–II, 89, 1 c). See also II–II, 98, 4 ad 1. Also of great interest in this connection is the well documented article by Alessandro Giuliani entitled, "L'Element 'Juridique' dans la Logique Médiévale," in *Logique et Analyse* nouvelle série: 6e année, nn. 21–24: 540–570.

[2] *S.T.* I–II, 105, 2 ad 8. (See also II–II, 69, 3 ad 3.) One suspects that in making this observation about the difficulty of agreeing in detail Thomas has in mind the wise and compassionate Daniel, who saved the fair Susannah from undeserved death by skillful cross-examination of her accusers. See Daniel 13.

[3] *S.T.* II–II, 70, 2 ad 1.

grinding too small on the basis of *ut in pluribus*.[1] A conviction based on probability is for all that a conviction, and woe to the condemned man who falls into the category of *ut in paucioribus*.

The point is well illustrated by a particularly terrifying misuse of probability calculations. At issue is the now hotly controverted question of capital punishment, which for Thomas is simply a fact. Resisting the temptation to diverge on our own, we restrict ourselves to Thomas's theologico-probabilistic justification of the fact.[2] "Although the wicked," he says,

> so long as they are alive, are capable of changing for the better, this fact does not make it unjust to kill them. For, the peril (to others) that exists so long as they are alive is greater and more certain than the good which might be expected from their rehabilitation. Moerover, even at the very moment of death they have the opportunity to repent and be converted to God. If, therefore, they are so obstinate that even at the moment of death their hearts do not turn from malice, it can be estimated with sufficient probability that they would never turn away from malice.

Of course, the empirical test which Thomas here offers for his estimation of probability is somewhat inadequate by contemporary standards in that it can never be repeated. Moreover, more modern insights into the psychology of conversion would no doubt suggest that the intersubjective relationship of an execution is not the best means to the end desired. What is perhaps closer to the truth, we have here another example of Thomas's nostalgic desire to see everything, however unpleasant, from the viewpoint of God who understands all things.

As can be seen from these various examples, then, Thomas is able to elaborate some fairly acceptable applications of contingency theory to the realm of moral decision. Yet, as many contemporary students of ethics would note, there is something dangerously simplistic about Thomas's efforts in this direction. For, though he is by no means unaware of exceptions to the rule, Thomas leaves one with the impression

---

[1] Thomas admits the need for "*gnome*", a virtue whereby one goes beyond general rules to interpret the exceptional (*S.T.* II–II, 48, 1 c ad fin. and 51, 4). He even resolves Aristotle's dilemma about the relationship between legality and equality by saying that the virtue of "*epieikeia* est quasi superior regula humanorum actuum' (*S.T.* II–II, 120 and esp. 120, 2c). We are not aware, however, of any passage where Thomas suggests that a judge might not have these admirable virtues. Nor does he admonish the judge, as he does the witness, that he state as certain that about which he is certain and as dubious that about which he is dubious. (See *S.T.* II–II, 70, 4 ad 1.)

[2] *C.G.* III, 146: "Quod vero mali, quandiu vivant, emendari possunt, non prohibet qiun juste possunt occidi: quia periculum quod de eorum vita imminet, est majus et certius quam bonum quod de eorum emendetione expectatur. Habent etiam in ipso mortis articulo facultatem ut per poenitentiam convertantur ad Deum. Quod si adeo sunt obstinati quod etiam in mortis articulo cor eorum a malitia non recedit, satis probabiliter aestimari potest quod nunquam a malitia resipiscant."

that moral responsibility might be no more than the ability to calculate the odds. The harshness of this critique must be qualified by the acknowledgement that Thomas not only encourages intelligent modification of laws but also stresses the need for personal discretion. To the extent, however, that he involves himself in the quasi-statistics of contingency his ethics is woefully inadequate, and as such might serve as a warning to those who would make of probability theory or of the theory of games a tool for moral decision.[1]

3. Knowledge and Virtue

By applying the cosmology of the contingent to ethical decision Thomas, no doubt, hoped to close the gap somewhat between the systematic and what is in itself non-systematic by simply relating the former to the latter.[2] His attempt is not altogether satisfying. But this is not simply due to the fact that *his* system is inadequate; it is fundamentally due to the fact that *any* system is inadequate to the demands of concrete moral action. For, a system so-called is only abstract knowledge; and, in partial response to Socrates, such knowledge is *not* virtue. To close this section, then, we wish to consider briefly to what extent Thomas was aware of this disturbing fact.

Generally speaking, Thomas maintains that no concrete action can of itself negate the truth which one knows abstractly. In other words, even an erroneous (that is to say, an immoral) decision would not of itself alter a man's conviction as to the truth of the general principles which were the starting point of his deliberations. Accordingly, one may have a correct opinion in the abstract (*rectam existimationem in universali*) and still, for any of a number of different reasons, make a decision in the concrete which is not in accord with that opinion: *corrupta eius aestimatione in particulari*.[3]

In other words, as far as Thomas is concerned a man can certainly posit morally evil actions in the concrete even though he "knows better" in the abstract. How this is possible Thomas tries to explain by

---

[1] See, for example, R. B. Braithwaite, *Theory of Games as a Tool for the Moral Philosopher* (Cambridge, England, 1955); K. W. Deutsch, *Applications of Game Theory to International Politics; Some Opportunities and Limits* (Princeton, N.J. undated, mimeographed). For a complete picture of just how extensive this approach to moral decision has become, see the excellent bibliography in R. Duncan Luce and Howard Raiffa, *Games and Decisions: Introduction and Critical Survey* (New York-London, 1957). See also their summary of the contemporary state of the question, pp. 10–11.

[2] Indeed, he suggests as much himself in the important passage cited at the beginning of this section, S.T. II–II, 51, 4 c.

[3] S.T. II–II, 20, 2 c.

means of a distinction which is itself based upon the Aristotelian distinction between habits and acts. In view of the latter, Thomas points out that a man might possess a true opinion or even true science about some proposition and still, mainly due to the influence of passion, not act in accordance with that opinion. This can happen, says Thomas, because acts are directly contrary to acts and not to habits. Thus, a man cannot actively posit as true both a universal affirmative and a particular negative proposition; but he can be *habitually* convinced as to the truth of, say, the universal affirmative and still by way of concrete *action* posit as true the particular negative.[1]

This teaching Thomas likes to illustrate by comparing the failure of ethical knowledge in practice to the grammarian whose habitual knowledge of grammar is good but who nevertheless commits a grammatical fault in practice.[2] For, in this case as in the case of action not in accord with ethical convictions, it is not because of lack of knowledge but because of a choice in the concrete that one acts as he does. In other words, the failure to act in accordance with the truth as known is not to be attributed so much to an intellectual defect as to defective virtue.[3] If, then, one is to avoid such failures to apply what he knows in his actions, he must have virtue.

But just as an opinion cannot be solidified in the mind by one single dialectical syllogism but only by many (because each is weak taken by itself), so also virtue cannot be acquired by one single act (since each act is in itself weak) but only by many. The comparison here is more than merely illustrative; for, human action, not unlike opinion, is concerned with "the contingent and probable."[4] As far as the object is concerned, then, there is no difference between the virtuous and the non-virtuous; for, both must deal with the contingent. What makes the virtuous man stand out is that he deals with the contingent skilfully, even artfully, in such a way as to accomplish the good "promptly and infallibly most of the time": *prompte et infallibiliter ut in pluribus.*[5]

---

[1] *S.T.* I–II, 77, 2 ad 3; *Q.D. de malo* 3, 9 objs. 5–7 and ad 5. See also *Q.D. de ver.* 22, 5 ad 12.

[2] *Q.D. de virt. in comm.* q. un., a. 7 c and ad 5; a. 2 ad 11; *Q.D. de malo* 3, 1 c and 6 c.

[3] *In De div. nom.* c. 4, l. 23, n. 600: "Sicut enim opinari falsum est ex infirmitate intellectus ita desiderare malum est ex defectu virtutis desiderativae." See also *S.T.* I–II, 77, 2; 94, 6 c; I–II, 162, 4 ad 1; *In De div. nom.* c. 4, l. 22, n. 586; *Q.D. de ver.* 17, 2.

[4] *Q.D. de virt. in comm.* q. un., a. 9 ad 11: "Agibilia sunt contingentia et probabilia." See also a. 6 c.

[5] *Q.D. de virt. in comm.* q. un., a. 8 ad 6. See also *S.T.* I–II, 57, 4 ad 2 and II–II, 47, 4 ad 2, where prudence is compared to art on the basis of the fact that each deals with the contingent and hence requires deliberation.

With the reappearance of this familiar phrase, *ut in pluribus*, the circle is closed. Thomas may say, for example, that prudence is more than just knowledge.[1] But he cannot help explaining virtue in terms of knowledge. He admits that moral virtue is more regularly exercised than are the various intellectual virtues; but for him the latter have far greater dignity. Not only do they attain more certain knowledge but, even more significantly, they constitute as it were a beginning of that perfect knowledge which shall be the possession of the saints in heaven.[2]

As the phrase *ut in pluribus* suggests, Thomas's picture of moral excellence is a rather modest, human one. If only human, though, it is nonetheless patterned after the divine. For, the more one approaches God's knowledge of the singular, the better will he be able to lead a virtuous life. Since it is hardly possible for a man to achieve such knowledge all by himself, he does well, as does the dialectician in matters speculative, to take advantage of what others can teach him.[3] For somewhat the same reason, since an administrator cannot know all things at once as does God, he does well to leave details to his subordinates.[4] These modifications, however, do not change the ideal. The prudent man, almost by definition, is one who has come to know what happens or what is the case most of the time, and thus is able to reduce the infinity of singulars to something finite and therefore manageable.[5]

Implied, then, in this picture of the prudent man is the conviction that the most important function of prudence is to equip a man, on the basis of the past, to deal effectively with the future – or, to be specific, with future contingents.[6] From this point of view, reason is as it were the watchdog of the soul. It is the task of reason, in other words, to be cautious, to take into consideration the effects which it is possible to expect from a given action. Of course, what happens rarely or by chance as a result of a certain kind of action cannot be foreseen. But with care the number of mishaps can be greatly reduced.[7] In short, prudence makes the future less foreboding; for, in some way it brings a man closer to that knowledge which is proper to God.[8]

---

[1] *Q.D. de virt. in comm.* q. un., a. 6 ad 1. See also *S.T.* II–II, 47, 3 c and ad 1.

[2] *S.T.* I–II, 66, 3 ad 1. See also 63, 6; 57, 1 ad 2; 53, 1 ad 3.

[3] *S.T.* I–II, 14, 3 c; 102, 1 c; II–II, 3 c and ad 3; 4 c.

[4] *Comp. theol.* c. 131, n. 263.

[5] *S.T.* II–II, 47, 3 ad 2: "Tamen per experientiam singularia infinita reducuntur ad aliqua finita quae ut in pluribus accidunt, quorum cognitio sufficit ad prudentiam humanam." See also 49, 1 c.

[6] *S.T.* II–II, 49, 1 c and 6 c. See also 51, 4 c.

[7] *S.T.* II–II, 49, 8 ad 3.

[8] *S.T.* II–II, 51, 4 ad 3: "Omnia illa quae praeter communem cursum contingere possunt considerare pertinet ad solam providentiam divinam: sed inter homines ille qui est magis perspicax potest plura horum sua ratione dijudicare."

D. MAN'S KNOWLEDGE OF THE FUTURE CONTINGENT

It is, then, with a touch of epistemic fear and trembling that man, with his limited intellectual capabilities, approaches the contingent. For, insofar as the contingent can by its very definition be other than it is, even in the knowing of it one realizes that he has but caught a glimpse of a will-o'-the-wisp. The contingent is true, but its truth is fleeting, insecure, unstable.

Even at its best, in the discernible regularities of nature, the contingent (in this case presumed to be necessary) has a habit of occurring only most of the time: *ut in pluribus* or *ut frequenter*. This quasi-mathematical "most of the time" is also the best that can be expected with regard to the applicability of even the most carefully formulated human law. And so it is with regard to human affairs in general. By virtue of ethical reflection, one is able to narrow down the scope of the unforeseen both for purposes of law and for purposes of personal and social decision. But the closer one comes to the concrete, particular situation, the more one sees the limitations of the generalization. For, the contingent – and, consequently, the opinion whereby it is known – is open to alternatives.

Thus, not unlike the dialectician engaged in disputation, the moral agent must deliberate in the face of alternate possibilities so as to make the problem at hand as intelligible as possible in the light of accepted principles of action. In this way, he reduces one or the other alternative as closely as he can to a fundamental principle, and on the basis of this reduction he makes a final decision in terms of which he will act.

This, for the most part, is Thomas's view of the way in which man deals with the contingent. But it must at once be noted that our account is not yet complete. For, as suggested in our closing remarks about the value of prudence in dealing with the contingent, knowledge of the latter, if there be such, tends to imply some kind of knowledge of the future. This, at least, seems to follow from Thomas's position.

For, in the first place, the way in which he talks about knowledge of the contingent suggests a transcendence of the contingent. He denies the possibility of knowing the contingent as contingent by demonstration. But, as the whole preceding discussion shows, he does recognize some kind of knowledge of the contingent as contingent; for, this, after all, is what the practical order is all about. Yet everything Thomas tells us about the manner in which the contingent is known suggests that it is known not as contingent but only insofar as it conceals elements or hints of the necessary which the investigative mind uncovers. Knowledge of natural processes depends upon a postulated regularity, a corollary of which is that all exceptions to the rule are to be considered, at least in the light of divine providence, as non-systematic divergences. Moral deliberation, though focussed upon the concrete situation, is concerned not with any intelligibility of the situation as such but with the situation insofar as it can be seen to exemplify general principles. Thus the concrete situation is known, in accordance with Thomas's general epistemological stance, by a kind of indirect or reflex act of the mind turning towards the sense particular by way of the phantasm.

In short, we have here in all its essentials the thorny problem of induction. In Thomas's thought, however, this problem has a very special flavor. It will be recalled that for him future contingents are known with certitude only by God and by privileged creatures such as Christ and to some extent the prophets. For the ordinary man, the future can be known only insofar as one has demonstrated knowledge of the necessary. Thus, to take a banal example, man would know that in the future the acute angles of a triangle will equal one right angle (on the basis of the Euclidean postulates, of course). Such knowledge holds for the future, however, not because it is of the future but because it is of the necessary, which by definition holds always. The contingent, on the other hand, is not for always but only for some of the time, whether usually or occasionally. But even to say that a certain kind of event occurs "most of the time" implies a judgment which transcends the here and now, and the same is true of statements about "some of the time." These are essentially quantitative estimates which, though presumably based upon past observations, are obviously intended to hold in the present (for concrete moral decision) and in the future as well.

As Thomas himself tells us, such judgments involve probability rather than necessity. But, as we are here suggesting, in spite of Thomas's leanings towards a logical theory of probability, his quasi-statistical estimates tie "probability" to a kind of "frequency theory" about events in the world. And, like any frequency theory, Thomas's involves propositions the content of which goes beyond empirical data. This, however, presents no insurmountable difficulty for Thomas; for, as we shall see in the next chapter, he agrees with Augustine that truth is "eternal" insofar as it is in the intellect of God. This being the case, even if a true proposition has supra-temporal import that has not been and cannot be empirically established, it is nonetheless assured of a theo-centric foundation. Thus, that aspect of the problem of induction which many contemporary theorists would dispose of "horizontally" by defining frequency-probability as the limit of an infinite series Thomas escapes by means of a "vertical" reliance upon God.

In short, Thomas tends to view our knowledge of the contingent largely as a derivative of knowledge of the necessary; and the manner in which he speaks about our knowledge of the contingent suggests that there is a kind of necessity governing the contingent so as to make what is said of the past or present somehow valid for the future. Accordingly, to round out our discussion of the contingent we must consider a little more carefully how Thomas justifies whatever knowledge man does have of the contingent as future or, for short, of the future contingent.[1]

As we shall see, in spite of suggestions to the contrary in what Thomas says about the talents of the prudent man, his epistemology of the future contingent is quite consistent with his general view as to necessity and contingency in nature. Though he allows for supernatural knowledge in this area (prophecy and perhaps even divination), his view of natural knowledge of the future is basically Aristotelian. For, the latter is built upon distinctions between the necessary and the contingent, the actual and the potential, the universal and the particular. These distinctions he supplements with that between essence and existence.

In the light of these distinctions, Thomas maintains that men can have some natural knowledge about the universal aspects of future contingents. To the extent that a future contingent is a necessary effect of presently existing causes, it can be known (in the abstract) with certitude. If it is not in any way a necessary effect of presently existing causes it can only be known, in terms of its universal aspects,

---

[1] Commenting specifically on *C.G.* I, 67, William and Martha Kneale make the following observations of interest to us. "The problem of future contingents and divine foreknowledge, which Thomas discussed . . .," they say, "involves not only the theory of modality but also those questions about truth and the principle of excluded middle which exercised Aristotle when he wrote the famous chapter in his *De Interpretatione* about the naval battle. It is therefore not surprising that this problem was the subject of a great deal of discussion among medieval logicians. During the period of intense philosophical activity which lasted for about a century after the death of St. Thomas all the great schoolmen contributed opinions on the question at issue. But it can scarcely be said that the debate produced any new light on the puzzles that worried Aristotle, since it proceeded on the assumption that we can talk sensibly about a proposition as being true at a certain time." – *The Development of Logic* (Oxford, 1962), p. 238. For an analysis of Chapter 9 of *the De Interpretatione* see pp. 46–54. For references to studies on medieval views, see p. 238, fn. 1.

by way of "conjecture." [1] Considered precisely insofar as it is both singular and future, it cannot be known by natural knowledge but only with the help of supernatural intervention.

That scientific knowledge can to some extent penetrate the future Thomas explains on the basis of his distinction between essence and existence. In the *De Veritate*, after distinguishing between what a thing is (*quid est*) and whether it exists (*an est*), he goes on to note that things in the present and things that will be in the future do have similar properties. But the existence of the former, he points out, does not depend causally upon the existence of the latter. Consequently, to the extent that one possesses universal ideas about presently existing things he already knows something about what kinds of things will exist in the future; but he does not thereby know any individual thing that will exist in the future.[2] In other words, using the term essence somewhat loosely, by means of scientific knowledge one can know the essence of some future contingents but not their existence, since the former is determined whereas the latter is not.

This essential knowledge of the future, however, is not a Platonic given but is dependent upon what one has been able to glean empirically from the world of experience. As Thomas says, Aristotle's view of the way in which we come to know things is "truer" and "better" than Plato's. Accordingly, the Platonic attempt to justify knowledge of the future in terms of innate ideas just does not hold water. As Augustine had already pointed out, on this hypothesis the mere wish to know the future would suffice for knowing it, and this is contrary to fact: *Cur non semper potest, cum semper velit?* Following Aristotle, then, Thomas prefers to say that essential or notional knowledge of the future is limited to what one has learned from actual experience. But some men,

---

[1] As far as we have been able to determine. Thomas speaks of knowledge as being conjectural (*conjecturalis*) only with regard to what will take place in the future. As we shall see, all man's natural knowledge of the future is con-jectural inasmuch as it amounts to a projection of our knowledge of things in the present onto the future. But as Thomas uses this word, it refers specifically to a knowledge of causes which are not determined to produce a given effect. If the effect is determined, then in knowing the causes of that effect one has more than conjectural knowledge of the effect but, as will be pointed out, less than knowledge of what is occurring in the present. In short, knowledge of the future is "conjectural" to the extent that the future is contingent. It is therefore tempting to identify "conjectural" with "probable." But, as far as we know, Thomas does not do so himself; for, as our introductory remarks suggest, he was not clearly aware of the difficulties implicit in his quasi-statistical approach to the contingent. Had he been aware of these difficulties, he might have been driven to the conclusion that all knowledge of "the future," whether as "necessary" or as "contingent" is no more than probable. It is idle to speculate, however, about how a man might have answered a question if only the question had occurred to him.

[2] *Q.D. de ver.* 12, 3 ad 13.

he admits, will have greater predictive ability at this level because of their exceptional imaginative gifts and brilliance of intellect.[1]

Science, then, gives one insight into the future insofar as knowledge of universal aspects of the present world of experience can be considered a reliable guide to the *kinds* of things that will be in the world of the future. But precisely insofar as it is knowledge of universals, it does not give one knowledge of any singular thing that will exist or event that will occur in the future. On the basis of such knowledge, in other words, the future singular is not known as singular but only as a possible instance of a universal. For example, whether the knower be an angel or an astronomer, he does not know a future eclipse in the same way as he would know an eclipse actually occurring here and now. With regard to the future eclipse, all that one really knows are the causes (in this case the calculated paths of the celestial bodies in question) which will bring about an eclipse at a more or less accurately predictable time in the future. However accurate the prediction of such an eclipse might be, the eclipse as such, says Thomas, is not known in itself but only in general, or, as we might say, as an instance of universal laws.[2]

This restriction of science to the universal aspects of the future Thomas explains by pointing out that our intellect knows only universals and not singulars and that the distance is immense (*maxima*) between a thing as known intellectually and that same thing as existing materially and sensibly. Thus the rigorous conclusion which he draws from this sharp dichotomy between intellectual and sense knowledge: not even perfect intellectual knowledge of what we now call celestial mechanics would of itself suffice for true knowledge of a future singular as such. Even an accurate prediction as to time, place, and observable phenomena associated with an eclipse remains universal, in Thomas's eyes; "for," he says, "it is possible for such an eclipse to happen many times."[3]

For Thomas, then, if one have knowledge of universal aspects of the present he thereby has some knowledge of universal aspects of the future. This much being said, however, we must now ask if the certitude that is characteristic of science about the present is also transitive with regard to the future. In answer to this question we must again make a

---

[1] *S.T.* II–II, 172, 1 c.

[2] *S.T.* I, 57, 2 c.

[3] *Q.D. de an.* q. un. a. 20 c: "Nec ille qui cognoscit totum ordinem caeli, cognoscit hanc eclypsim ut est hic. Etsi enim cognoscat eclypsim futuram esse in tali situ solis et lunae, et in tali hora, et quaecumque hujusmodi in eclypsibus observantur; tamen talem eclypsim possibile est pluries evenire." Compare *S.T.* I, 89, 3 c.

few distinctions. That one's knowledge be truly scientific, that is, universal, is a necessary condition for certitude about the future; it is not, however, a sufficient condition. The sufficient condition for certitude about the future is that one's knowledge of the present include a necessary link between the present and the future. For, as is true of the present, some events in the future will follow only contingently from present causes and others will follow necessarily. It is this, in the final analysis, that puts the problem of the future *contingent* in a class by itself.

As Thomas consistently maintains, scientific certitude must be based upon a knowledge of causes. And thus men cannot have certitude about the future unless they know the causes of what will be in the future. If, however, the actual causes which are known are not strictly determined to produce a given effect, man's knowledge of that effect, of that *contingent* effect, cannot be certain. It can only be opinionative or probable knowledge more or less well founded upon experience of things as they are in the present.

This aspect of Thomas's epistemology of the future contingent is perfectly summarized in a brief expression found in his commentary on the *Physics:* "What actually exists," he says, "is more known than what exists potentially." [1] Thus he will say that the contingent can be known infallibly, with certain knowledge founded upon sense experience, provided only that the contingent be actually present to the knower.

It is only insofar as the contingent singular is not actually existing but only potentially, that is to say, insofar as it is only in the power of some cause or causes to bring it into existence, that it is not knowable with certitude. To use Thomas's favorite illustration, if Socrates is seen to be seated at this moment, one can here and now know with certitude that Socrates is in fact seated.[2] "For," as Thomas puts it, "the contingent is not repugnant to the certitude of knowledge except insofar as it is future, not insofar as it is present.... Therefore any knowledge which has to do with the contingent as present can be certain." [3] The difficulty, in short, is not with existing contingents, but with existing causes capable of producing a contingent in the future but not

---

[1] *In* VI *Phys.* l. 8, n. 829: "Quod est in actu est notius eo quod est in potentia".

[2] *S.T.* I, 14, 13 c; I–II, 14, 6 ad 3.

[3] *C.G.* I, 67: "Contingens enim certitudini cognitionis non repugnat nisi secundum quod futurum est, non autem secundum quod praesens est ... Omnis igitur cognitio quae supra contingens fertur prout praesens est, certa esse potest." See also *Comp. theol.*, c. 133, n. 272; *S.T.* I–II, 14, 6 ad 3.

determined to do so. To posit that the contingent in question will come to be in the future may turn out to be true, but then again it may not. And thus such knowledge is what Thomas calls conjectural.

In the light of the foregoing, it should now be clear what Thomas means by saying that man cannot know a future contingent with certitude, as well as what he does mean. He is in no way denying the universality of demonstrative propositions nor is he denying their necessity. Insofar as a proposition is scientific in the strict sense it applies to the future as well as to the present. But it applies only as a universal statement that such and such a cause necessarily produces a given kind of effect. To know an effect in its very individuality requires the sensible presence of that which is an effect – and this is not possible with regard to what is not occurring now but will rather occur in the future. As for other effects, those which will follow from their causes at most only contingently, these cannot be known with certitude even in the universal; they are known rather with conjectural knowledge, the degree of certitude of which depends upon how strongly those causes are inclined to produce the effects in question.

In short, however one chooses to look at it, our knowledge of the future as future cannot be more than opinionative. If it is in some way known scientifically, it is so known only insofar as it already exists potentially in presently, existing things which can or, better yet, will necessarily bring it about.[1]

Thus, unlike God, whose intuitive vision encompasses past, present and future, man on his own is restricted to knowing what it is possible to know in terms of the present. Accordingly, as Thomas notes, even when we speak of ourselves as foreknowing the future, it is more a knowledge of the present than of the future as such that is involved.[2] Nor is it irrelevant to observe in this regard that no self-consistent empiricist could disagree with this position, however much he might care to speak about scientific prediction; it is the present which is the key to the future, and the latter can be known only on the basis of the former. It would also be rather difficult to justify an assertion about future events without at least implying some form of causal relationship between the future and the present, that is to say, at the very least, some sort of necessity in things. And to the extent that such necessity, whether absolute or consequential, can be discovered in things,

---

[1] See *In IX Met.* ,l. 3, n. 1802; *C.G.* I, 63; *In De Mem.* l. 1, nn. 304–305, 309; *S.T.* I, 86, 4 c; *Comp. theol.* cc. 133–134, nn. 272–273; *Q.D. de ver.* 12, 10 ad 7.

[2] *Q.D. de ver.* 12, 10 c.

Thomas tends to regard any resulting predictions as not so much knowledge of the future as insight into the capacities – or, to use Popper's term, propensities – of what exists at the present.[1]

As a kind of corollary of this position, Thomas speaks (pejoratively) of divination only when it is a question of trying to know the future by means other than that of discovering genuine causal relationships. Divination – whether in the form of casting lots or of reading the stars or of invoking demons or whatever – is simply superstition and vain curiosity.[2] It must be admitted, however, that because of his theory about the influence of celestial bodies upon terrestrial events, Thomas is not ready to discredit such practices entirely. He is rather inclined to think that there is some validity to these methods, if not because of the methods themselves then because of contact with demons, who, like all angels, are better able to read the future in the present than are men.[2]

In fact, it is worth noting in this regard that most of Thomas's discussions about our knowledge of the future take as their point of departure some question about angelic (or, of course, divine) knowledge thereof. Only God knows the individual future contingent with the certitude with which we know Socrates to be seated here and now. But angels, fallen or otherwise, are shrewd analysts of the present, and hence, if reached by necromancy or whatever, can render assistance to man in his quest for more accurate knowledge of what lies ahead.[4]

Apart, then, from the scientific analysis of presently existing causes and whatever help can be obtained by contact with supra-human powers, there is no way in which man can come to a knowledge of the future unless God deigns to make such things known by some form of revelation. It is in this case that one has what Thomas calls prophecy in the strict sense of the word: a certain knowledge of the future which is possible to man only because of God. For example, only by a reve-

---

[1] Thus he says in *Q.D. de malo* 16, 7 c: "Cognoscere futuram in causa sua, nihil est aliud quam cognoscere praesentem inclinationem causae ad effectum."

[2] *Q.D. de ver.* 12, 3 c.; *S.T* II–II, 95, esp. 1 c, 2 c, ad 1 and ad 3.

[3] See *Q.D. de ver.* 12, 3 ad 5 and ad 7; *S.T.* I, 86, 4 ad obj.; II–II, 95, 3–7; *De Judiciis Astrorum*; *De Sortibus*, an interesting work which provides a detailed analysis of medieval methods of casting lots. The latter, by the way, Thomas considers perhaps foolish ("non videtur habere nisi forte vitium vanitatis") and at times even laudable, so long as it involves no superstitious dependence upon demoniacal powers (*S.T.* II–II, 95, 8 c). The qualifications thus suggested modify considerably F. N. David's monolithic view of the medieval Christian attitude towards casting lots. See his *Games, Gods and Gambling* (London, 1962), p. 30.

[4] *S.T.* I, 14, 13; 57, 3; 86, 4; II–II, 95, 1 c; *Q.D. de ver.* 8, 12; *Q.D. de pot.* 5, 6; *Q.D. de malo* 16, 7.

lation from God could one know the eternal destiny of individual men, or simply the future actions of men.[1]

In some cases, prophetic knowledge would be in the form of an imaginative vision, but for prophecy in the full sense of the word Thomas demands a truly intellectual insight into the future. For this is required what he calls a likeness of the divine fore-knowledge in the mind of the prophet, a kind of mirror of eternity.[2] To this end the prophet may be given to see old knowledge in a new way, in a new light, or he may even be given new knowledge, new concepts. Thus his knowledge might be somehow dependent upon abstraction from the senses, but more often it is not. For, the intellectual predispositions and even the morals of the prophet are of comparatively little importance: God can provide him not only with the knowledge but also with the dispositions of mind necessary to understand that knowledge, either at the very first instant of the prophet's existence or at the moment of prophetic revelation.[3] In any event, what really matters is not so much the intellectual abilities of the prophet himself but his contact with God. For, knowledge of the future is a divine prerogative, and the Spirit breatheth withersoever he wills.

Thus with Thomas's theory of prophecy we find ourselves having come full circle from our opening observations about the limitations of human knowledge. These limitations Thomas feels, to be sure, can be to some extent overcome by diligent application of the dialectical method of disputation. For, brought to its culmination, dialectic leads to scientific demonstration of necessary truths. But the domain of such demonstrations is small by comparison to the total range of propositions to which men give some degree of credence. On the hypothesis of regularity in nature and with the help of a quasi-statistical approach to the contingent, man can have some valid insights into what is not strictly necessary. When it comes to the vast and complex sector of human affairs, man can to some extent ape the divine vision by means of perfectible laws and ethical reflections; but the ultimate concrete action is and must be the product of prudential deliberation and decision. This process of moral deliberation does in fact give man some workable control over the future, at least with regard to ordinary expectation. But the future in itself, the concrete individual event which has yet to happen, remains for man ultimately and insurmounta-

---

[1] S.T. II–II, 174, 1 c.
[2] Q.D. de pot. 4, 2 ad 27; Q.D. de ver. 12, 11 c; S.T. II–II, 173, 1; 174, 2 c.
[3] S.T. II–II, 172, 3 and 4; 173, 2–4.

bly inscrutable. Only by virtue of a direct intervention on the part of God, gratuitously revealing his secrets to a prophet, can man have more than conjectural knowledge of what is not already determined to be produced by existing causes. And, when all is said and done, there is a limit to how much a man can be satisfied with the announcement that the sun will in fact rise again tomorrow.

In short, there is just no getting around it: Thomas suffers incurably from an epistemic nostalgia for the beatific vision, wherein man's cognitional limitations will be filled up with the plenitude of divine omniscience. Any knowledge short of this, however solid in itself, is by comparison but a feeble preparation for the perfection that lies beyond. For, it is then that the opinionative, the probable, the conjectural, even that which is believed on faith, will give way to certain and total vision. The world as we know it and all that is in it will pass away: only God and his saints will remain in the glorious heaven of clear and unshakeable certitude with regard to all that there is to know.

CHAPTER VI

THOMAS'S THEOCENTRIC PERSPECTIVE
ON PROBABILITY

We have come a long way in our study of Thomas's notion of probability. First from a psychological point of view, we were able to associate probability with opinion and thus with the possibility of error. Then from a socio-historical point of view, we noted the relationship between probability and traditional authority. We then abstracted from the sociological to elaborate the logical aspect of probability as a product of disputation and a preparation for demonstration. Then, in the preceding chapter, the logical theory was given a physical interpretation by means of a quasi-statistical approach to contingent events.

Throughout these various considerations, however, we have been compelled to make various qualifications in order to take into account the transcendent knowledge of God and of those specially instructed by God. Thus the psychological association of probability with fallible opinion had to be contrasted with the epistemic perfection of knowledge divine or divinely given. The socio-historical basis of the probable in human authority had to be qualified by the recognition that human authority is in part divinely guaranteed. The logical defense of the probable by argumentation had to be restricted so as not to compromise faith in divine revelation. And, finally the cosmological calculations of the probable had to be seen in contrast to the total vision of divine providence.

In effect, then, our study up to this point has suggested that Thomas's theory of probability can be perfectly founded neither in psychology nor in sociology nor in logic nor even in physical science. Whatever insights these various aspects of human knowledge provide as to Thomas's theory of probability, they remain for all that merely human aspects. The ultimate aspect of probability, as of all else, is for Thomas the *divine*.

Thus have we been developing in bits and pieces what might be called the theological dimension of Thomas's theory of probability. In different ways and from different points of view we have been leading towards the conclusion that Thomas's attitude towards cognitional imperfection is ultimately due to a literally theological orientation towards a culminating vision of all truth in God. It is, in other words, in view of this culminating or beatific vision that Thomas is able to regard present human knowledge as it were "within the proper perspective." The influence of this theotropic epistemology, if we may so speak, upon his theory of opinion and probability is already much in evidence. But to bring our investigations to their logical – or, shall we say, *theological* – conclusion, we must now show that neither science nor even faith is a sufficient remedy for the limitations of opinion and probability. For, "science" *is* capable of error, and thus is not essentially different from opinion; and faith is but a dimly lighted view of what still lies beyond. This amounts to saying, from our more limited perspective, that the summit of Thomas's theory of probability is the beatific vision; for, it is only in the perfect knowledge of God that human knowledge can ultimately transcend the probable.

This rather ultimate point of view might by some be considered critical in the modern sense of the term. We, however, are saying no more than that it is theocentric.[1] This theocentric aspect of Thomas's theory of probability involves what we might call, for lack of a better expression, the theological foundations of certainty. What follows,

---

[1] The point here is of sufficient importance to justify a few words of clarification. For, once again we are proposing to elucidate Thomas's views on probability by a consideration of what some would regard as properly "theological" questions, in particular, Thomas's notion of the beatific vision. If it makes any difference, we are willing to concede that this is what we are doing. But we insist that such "theological" questions are of the utmost relevance and that they have their counterpart in the "secularized" interpretations of probability which are more familiar in our own day. If we had chosen to end our discussion with Thomas's logical theory of probability and demonstration or even with his cosmological theory of contingency and divine providence, the resulting picture would have been an epistemic absolutism completely unrecognizable to scientists familiar with current approaches to the philosophy of science. For, we would have thus left undeveloped the very dimension of Thomas's thought which relativizes the seemingly absolutist formulations of more specific considerations. Accordingly, what has been frequently suggested above we now discuss *ex professo*, namely, the fact that for Thomas human knowledge is inadequate precisely to the extent that it is compared to the ideal, that is, to knowledge divine. From this point of view, we think, Thomas could well understand and perhaps even accept the assertion of a Reichenbach that all (human) knowledge is probable. Now, if anyone should like to conclude that this theological dimension makes Thomas's thought as a whole critical, he would be quite free to do so. Since, however, we do not identify a criticism of science with a critical approach to science, we refrain from any such generalization. All we are saying is that one has not exhausted the critical aspects of Thomas's thought without taking into consideration the theocentricism of his thought as a whole. For some interesting reflections on the critical aspects of medieval and especially Thomist thought, see Fernand van Steenberghen, *Epistémologie*, 3e éd. (Louvain-Paris, 1956), pp. 56–59.

then, is an attempt to show the importance of these theological foundations for a complete view of Thomas's theory of probability. For this purpose we shall proceed more or less according to what Thomas might call a *via negativa,* that is to say, by way of a process of elimination.[1] Reconsidering our material in inverse order, we shall thereby rejoin the observations of Chapter Two to the effect that human knowledge is ultimately stable and hence worthwhile to the extent that it leads one towards God.[2] And as we slowly spell out the implications of this theocentricism, we shall be led to the conclusion that for Thomas all human knowledge, *qua* human, is in a broad sense of the term probable. This sweeping generalization is by no means explicit in Thomas's thought; nor would his more limited usage of the term *probabilis* allow him to accept our generalization. Properly understood, however, the generalization is not alien to Thomas's perspective to the extent that this perspective is literally *sub specie aeternitatis.*

In particular, then, we shall maintain that for Thomas man's grasp on eternal truth cannot be adequately founded (A) cosmologically (Chapter 5); (B) logically (Chapter 4); (C) socio-historically (Chapter 3); or (D) psychologically (Chapter 2); but only (E) theologically, that is to say, in God. Our argument will consist of the following propositions:

(A) Since the duration of the world is finite, man's experience of the world as it is now does not of itself overcome opinion and probability independently of God;

(B) Since man's decisions as to what is or is not demonstrated are not justified by logic alone, the logical theory of demonstration does not of itself overcome opinion and probability independently of God;

(C) Since the authoritative claims of faith are by definition independent of all merely human authority and hence *sui generis,* human authority as such does not overcome probability independently of God;

(D) Since man's psychological conviction that his knowledge is certain differs from opinion in degree rather than in kind, man's claim to certainty does not overcome opinion and probability independently of God;

---

1 The *via negativa* as understood by Thomas himself is one of Pseudo-Dionysius' three methods of arriving at knowledge of God. In this case, the negative method involves denying of God whatever imperfections are found in creatures. In a very wide sense, our procedure in this chapter may be taken as a *via negativa* inasmuch as each consideration will lead us to God by way of default. In no sense of the word, however, are we suggesting that this constitutes a proof for the existence of God. For Thomas's notion of a *via negativa* see *In De div. nom.* c. 7, l. 4; *C.G.* I, 14, 24, 25, 29–34; *In I Sent.* d. 22, q. 1, a. 2 obj. 2; d. 35, q. 1, a. 1 c; *S.T.* I, 37, 2 c; 79, 9 ad 1; 88, 1 and 2 and esp. 2 ad 4.

2 See above, Chapter 2, pp. 77–78

(E) Since human knowledge *qua* human can only be, in a broad sense, opinionative or probable, such knowledge transcends the probable only insofar as it is founded in God, and definitively so in the beatific vision.

As a final word of introduction, we wish to make it clear that our development of these propositions will often be more a suggestion of what we feel is implicit in Thomas's thought than a simple exposition of his own overt convictions.

A. META-PHYSICAL ASPECTS OF TRUTH AS ETERNAL

Since the duration of the world is finite, man's experience of the world as it is now does not of itself overcome opinion and probability independently of God.

As we saw in Chapter Five, Thomas's theory of probability is at least indirectly founded in quasi-statistical aspects of natural phenomena. But the very recourse to quasi-statistical categories is, we recall, indicative of man's imperfect acquaintance with the order of the universe. That man is so limited in his knowledge of intra-mundane events is, however, due primarily to his confinement to a particular place and a particular time. It is, in particular, this spatio-temporal confinement which prevents man from knowing future contingents. Accordingly, for an intellect to transcend these epistemic limitations it is sufficient that it transcend space and time, as does the divine intellect. As we shall now see, however, this intellectual transcendence of space and time is also a necessary condition for durable knowledge. For, the world as man knows it is not here to stay.

What is at issue here is, to use scholastic terminology, materially Aristotle's arguments for the eternity of the world and formally Thomas's evaluation of these arguments. Very simply, Thomas takes it as an essential dogma of the Catholic faith that God and God alone is eternal and that therefore the world is not. This, in effect, predetermines Thomas's attitude towards Aristotle's position in this regard: where a teaching of faith is at stake, Aristotle must be shown to be wrong. The world is not eternal, and therefore the Philosopher could not have demonstrated that it is.[1]

---

[1] Interestingly enough, there is some basis for saying that Aristotle's insistence upon an eternal world was itself inspired by religious motives. See Friedrich Solmsen, *Aristotle's System of the Physical World: A Comparison with his Predecessors* (Ithaca, New York, 1960), p. 274.

That Thomas's position in this regard is in fact more in keeping with the findings of contemporary science than is that of Aristotle is, of course, interesting, but quite irrelevant. Thomas does not deal with the question simply on the level of cosmology; rather does he defend the truth of his faith against what is *a priori* a philosophical error. And in so doing, by the way, he provides us with an excellent illustration both of the indemonstrability of demonstration (Section B) and of the epistemic transcendence of faith (Section C).

There are involved in this question serious terminological difficulties, since what Thomas understands by eternity is based not on Aristotle but on Boethius, and Boethius' definition of this notion could be applied to the material universe as a whole only on the assumption of pantheism.[1] We need not involve ourselves in such linguistic pitfalls, however, since all that is here at stake is (explicitly) whether the world of our experience has always existed and (implicitly) whether it will continue to exist forever. Thus, eternity in this discussion may be taken to be equivalent to another term which Thomas also uses in this connection, namely that of *sempiternity:* duration infinite as to the past and as to the future. For Thomas, it is an article of faith that the world had a beginning in time; and he furthermore maintains as a doctrine of faith that the world as we know it will come to an end.[2]

---

[1] According to Boethius, "aeternitas est interminabilis vitae tota simul et perfecta possessio" – *De consolatione philosophiae* V, Prosa 6; ML 63; 858 A. See Thomas Aquinas, *In I Sent.* d. 8, q. 2, a. 1; *In De causis* l. 2; *S.T.* I, 10, 1. In a certain sense, Aristotle's view of the universe as eternal has overtones of a kind of pantheism insofar as he looks upon eternal and orderly motion as being somehow divine. Of much greater interest at this point, however, is the fact that Thomas's manner of posing the question about the duration of the universe follows Plato precisely where Aristotle does not. For, it was Plato who emphasized the contrast between time and eternity and sought to explain the former as an image of the latter. Aristotle, on the other hand, concentrated his attention upon time as it is known by man through measurement of motion; and from this point of departure he sought to show that the temporal *is* eternal and not merely a Platonic image of eternity. See Friedrich Solmsen, *Aristotle's System of the Physical World* (Ithaca, N.Y., 1960), pp. 144–159.

[2] *S.T.* I, 46, esp. a. 2; *In II Sent.* d. 1, q. 1, a. 5; *C.G.* II, 31–38; *Q.D. de pot.* 3, 11; *Quodl.* 12, q. 6, a. 1; *Opusc.* 24, *De aeternitate mundi.* These texts all have to do with the fact that the non-eternity of the world is not contrary to reason and is an article of faith. In this regard as well as with regard to the duration of the world, Etienne Gilson presents evidence for asserting that in Thomas's opinion material creatures will never be annihilated, although it is possible for God to bring this about: *The Elements of Christian Philosophy* (New York, 1963), pp. 214–221. His arguments (based primarily on *Q.D. de pot.* 5, 3; *S.T.* I, 104, 4; 65, 1 ad 1) we readily accept as showing that for Thomas created being as such has unlimited duration. But this, we maintain, commits Thomas to saying no more than that matter as such is incorruptible. As we shall see, Thomas also insist that the movements of the celestial bodies will come to an end; and, given his concept of celestial mechanics, this in itself amounts to saying that the world as we know it will come to an end. For, Thomas is convinced that the movements of material creatures are dependent upon those of the heavenly bodies. His eschatology, in turn, is based upon the biblical promise of a new heaven and a new earth. See Thomas Litt, *Les corps célestes dans l'univers de saint Thomas d'Aquin* (Paris-Louvain, 1963), pp. 110–254.

Accordingly, he cannot admit that the world is eternal even in the limited sense here indicated. His task with regard to Aristotle is, therefore, clear enough.

To begin with, Thomas does not accept the easy solution of some theologians that Aristotle does not in fact try to demonstrate the eternity of the world but merely presents probable arguments for both sides of the question. It is clear, says Thomas, both from Aristotle's method of procedure and from the use which he subsequently makes of his conclusion that he intends to prove the eternity of the world and thereafter supposes that he has done so.[1] Thus the problem for Thomas is to show that Aristotle's arguments, intended as a demonstration, are not in fact demonstrative. To put this another way, now familiar to us, he must show that the arguments are not necessary but only probable.[2]

Thomas admits that Aristotle proves by his arguments that things did not begin to be and to move as a result of any process found in nature. But this, says Thomas, in no way prevents one from saying, as faith teaches, that the whole of nature in which these processes are found was brought into being at some first instant by God.[3] This is not to say that the latter assertion can be demonstrated (Thomas does not think that it can), but simply that Aristotle's arguments in no way demonstrate the contrary. It is, then, from this point of view that Thomas sees the Philosopher's arguments as being merely probable. They are, in other words, *ad hominem* arguments. Though not strictly demonstrative of the eternity of the world, they are nonetheless efficacious against the position of those who maintained that the world has been somehow generated.[4] Indeed, argues Thomas, the very fact that Aristotle makes use of the testimony of his predecessors in these arguments indicates that the arguments are not demonstrative; for, appeal to authority is appropriate to dialectics, not to demonstration. Finally, the Philosopher himself, in the *Topics*, gives as an example of a dialectical problem (unresolved, of course) whether or not the world is eternal.[5]

In short, as far as Thomas is concerned neither the eternity nor the non-eternity of the world can be rationally demonstrated. To give just one minor example of what this means (an example interesting to us in

---

[1] *In* VIII *Phys.* l. 2, nn. 986–990.
[2] *C.G.* II, 34 and 35.
[3] *In* VIII *Phys.* l. 2, n. 987.
[4] *C.G.* II, 38; *Q.D. de pot.* 3, 17; *In* VIII *Phys.* l. 23, n. 1167; *In* XII *Met.* l. 5, nn. 2497–2499; *Comp. theol.* cc. 98–99, nn. 186–190; *S.T.* I, 46.
[5] *S.T.* I, 46, 1 c. See Aristotle, I *Topics* c. 11: 104, b, 12–16.

that it prefigures what is today so important: paleontological dating), Thomas points out at different times that the development of arts and sciences neither proves nor disproves a beginning in time. Human arts and sciences do seem to have begun a finite number of years ago. This, however, Aristotle explains by positing natural disasters which have necessitated repeated rediscovery. The position is unproven, of course, but it is enough to destroy any argument for a beginning in time that is based upon the finite development of human knowledge.[1] Such arguments, in other words, however well developed they may be remain ultimately inconclusive, no more than probable. Thus the teaching of faith that the world has a finite duration is, though not demonstrated, nonetheless safe from rational attack.

As for why the universe has a certain particular duration, no more and no less, this, says Thomas, cannot be demonstrated any more than one can demonstrate why the universe has the dimensions which it does have and no others. The ultimate reason for the duration as for the size of the universe is simply that God so wills it.[2] This means, in effect, that mathematics is of no help in resolving the question as to whether the universe has a finite or an infinite duration. Thus, says Thomas, the Philosopher does not try to prove the eternity of the world from the fact that planetary motions are circular: on the contrary, on the assumption that these motions are eternal, he shows that to be eternal they must necessarily be circular.[3]

Granting, then, that mathematics cannot resolve the problem, Thomas is not quite so willing to admit that theology has nothing to say on the subject.

Motion, says Thomas, is not natural to heavenly bodies as it is to the basic elements (which all tend toward their natural place). Thus, there must be some sufficient reason why the heavenly bodies move. This cannot be for the sake of motion as such or for the sake of something less noble than the heavenly bodies themselves; nor, thirdly, as we know on the authority of the saints, can this motion be infinite in duration. Stated positively, the heavenly bodies move for the sake of something other than themselves which is nobler than themselves, and this motion will come to an end. Some philosophers would say that the

---

[1] *In* II *Polit.* l. 12, n. 292; *In* XII *Met.*, l. 10, n. 2598; *Q.D. de pot.* 3, 17 ad fin. This example constitutes just one of many aspects of Aristotle's efforts to show that processes on earth imitate as far as possible the eternal regularity of the celestial bodies. For a thorough discussion of this cyclical regularity on earth, especially with regard to water, see Friedrich Solmsen, *Aristotle's System of the Physical World* (Ithaca, N.Y., 1960), pp. 420–439.

[2] *Q.D. de pot.* 3, 17 c.

[3] *Q.D. de pot.* 3, 17 ad 17. See *In* VIII *Phys.* l. 23, n. 1167.

purpose of celestial motions is simply to imitate divine causality. This, says Thomas, is reasonable; but his own opinion, which he says is more probable, is that the celestial motions have as their purpose to keep things going until and only until such time as the number of those destined for heaven has been fulfilled. In short, the celestial bodies will continue to move until heaven has been filled with the elect. This having been accomplished, motion will stop. For, all motion and variability must ultimately be reduced to the unmoving source of all motion, God.[1]

If, then, such is the ultimate fate of the universe, how can man claim that by knowing things in the universe he has truth which deserves to be called eternal? How can he boast of knowing "eternal truths"? That he might have knowledge which is true for today or even for the next several thousand years, this is readily admissible on Thomas's theory. But to say that a truth has longstanding validity is a far cry from saying that it is "eternal."

Indeed, Thomas admits that one could found the eternity of truth cosmologically, as does Avicenna, by positing that the world is eternal. For, he notes, this would safeguard at least abstract universals: species even though corrupted incidentally by the demise of one or another individual, could always be realized in some individual *ad infinitum*.[2] But, having rejected the eternity of the world on grounds of faith, Thomas cannot avail himself of Avicenna's solution. For Thomas, however durable the objects of knowledge may be, either individually or serially, they ultimately will or at least can pass out of existence; hence the mere knowing of such objects does not give one the right to claim knowledge of eternal truths.

For Thomas, then, the physical universe which it is man's privilege to know cannot be the basis of a claim to eternal truth. For him, in other words, eternal truth *qua* eternal cannot be justified in terms of the ordinary *objects* of human knowledge. This justification, if there is to be one, must be made in terms of a knowing *subject*. As we shall now see, however, this knowing subject cannot be the human intellect as such, because human knowledge is as susceptible to variation as are the things of nature and, moreover, the human soul is not eternal but only immortal. The only intellect, then, which can adequately found eternal truth is an eternal intellect, that is to say, the intellect which is God.

Thomas tells us, first of all, that human knowledge is variable in many different ways. One may learn something new or forget something

---

[1] Q.D. *de pot.* 5, 5. See also 5, 9 ad 8.
[2] Q.D. *de ver.* 1, 5 ad 14; 1, 6.

he formerly knew. One may give actual consideration to what he knows habitually, or in his reflections go from one thought to another.[1] Again, as we have seen at length, one may know something at first with probable knowledge (*per medium probabile*) and then with scientific knowledge (*per medium necessarium*). Also, one might retain an opinion which was once true even after a change in the object makes that opinion false.[2] One may also lose knowledge by giving adherence to an opinion contrary to the truth or by allowing himself to be deceived by sophistical reasoning. As Thomas says with regard to the latter, "a habit of true opinion or even of science can be corrupted because of false reasoning." [3] Finally, without actually losing knowledge, one may be rendered incapable of utilizing that knowledge as a result of physical damage, especially to the brain.[4]

For Thomas, then, human knowledge can be quite variable. This fact alone, of course, does not preclude the possibility of man's knowing eternal truth. But it does suggest that even if such truth is known by man, it is not eternal because of man's knowing it. And, as we shall now see, what is suggested by the variability of human knowledge is made explicit by virtue of a distinction between eternity and immortality.

To begin with, Thomas takes it to be scientifically demonstrated that the human soul is immortal. It is not to our purpose to go into Thomas's proofs for immortality, but we may note in passing that the principal proof is based upon the conviction that man is capable of immanent acts of intellection and volition which are independent of matter.[5] More directly of interest to us is Thomas's assertion that, since the knowledge of eternal truth is the soul's end or purpose, it can be shown that the soul must be immortal in order to fulfill its destiny.[6] For, in clarifying this theological approach to a proof of immortality, Thomas needs must insist that man's knowledge of eternal truth points to his goal rather than to his mode of being.

Faced with an argument that the soul is eternal because it knows necessary and eternal truths, Thomas qualifies the conclusion by saying that this shows the immortality but not the eternity of the soul.

---

[1] See *Q.D. de ver.* 1, 5 c.

[2] *Q.D. de ver.* 2, 13 c, ad 1, ad 8 and ad 10.

[3] *S.T.* I–II, 53, 1 c: "Per falsam rationem potest corrumpi habitus verae opinionis, aut etiam scientiae."

[4] *In* III *D e An.* l. 13, nn. 791–792; *In De Mem.* l. 4, nn. 354 and 358; *S.T.* I–II, 53, 1 ad 3.

[5] *S.T.* I, 75, 2 and 6; *In* II *Sent.* d. 19, a. 1; IV, d. 50, q. 1, a. 1; *C.G.* II, 79 ff.; *Quodl.* 10, q. 3, a. 2; *Q.D. de an.*, q. un., a. 14; *Comp. theol.* c. 84.

[6] *C.G.* II, 83 and 84.

This qualification he bases upon the following distinction. That the soul knows truths which are eternal, he says, does not imply that *that by which* such truths are known, namely, the human soul, is eternal, but rather that *that which* is known is ultimately founded in something eternal; and this foundation is the first truth, that is to say, God.[1]

In the light of this basic distinction, Thomas cannot entirely agree with Augustine's statements to the effect that in knowing certain truth we somehow know God; he will only admit – and at least in part by way of concession – that man's knowledge of certain truth constitutes a kind of image or reflection of divine truth.[2] That this admission involves a concession to the authority of Augustine can be seen from an important clarification which Thomas makes in this regard some thirteen years later.[3] Some propositions, he then says, are invariable because of "the necessary order of one term to another"; but this invariability does not make the propositions eternal except in the mind of God. Accordingly, Thomas goes on, when we know something eternal, such as grace, we are indeed beyond time from the viewpoint of the object; but, with all due respect to Augustine, from the viewpoint of the knowing subject we are still in time.

We see, then, that the basic principle behind Thomas's analysis of our rapport with eternal truth is that truth can be eternal only insofar as it is founded upon something eternal. On the basis of this principle he maintains – and Augustine would be in complete agreement – that this eternal foundation of eternal truth is neither in things nor in man's knowledge of things but in God. For, things may change and man's opinions about things may change; but God remains constant in himself and in his knowledge. In other words, truth is eternal only by virtue of the first truth, the cause of all truth, God.[4]

Also implied in this view, and for reasons that we have considered at some length, is that the eternal foundation of eternal truth is an intellect. Or, as Thomas himself expresses this idea, what is true or even necessary can be said to be eternal only insofar as it is in an eternal intellect, and this applies only to the intellect which is God. Stating the same thing negatively, "If no intellect were eternal, no truth would be eternal. Since, however, only the divine intellect is eternal, in it only does truth possess eternity."[5]

[1] *C.G.* II, 84.
[2] See *C.G.* III, 47.
[3] *Resp. de Art.* CVIII arts. 18 and 31, nn. 841 and 857. See *In I Sent.* d. 14, q. un., a. 1 ad 4.
[4] *S.T.* I, 14, 15 ad 3; *Q.D. de ver.* 1, 5 c.
[5] *S.T.* I, 10, 3 ad 3; 16, 7 c: "Unde si nullus intellectus esset aeternus, nulla veri tas esset

A subtle and significant consequence of this reduction of eternal truth to God is that eternal truth is ultimately unique. As Thomas puts it, there is only one eternal truth, and this is the first truth, the cause or exemplar of all that is true, God.[1] By way of corollary, then, any given proposition, whether demonstrated or not, can be said to be eternally true only insofar as it is somehow an expression, however partial, of one and the same truth: the truth that is in or, better, that *is* the divine intellect.

In summary, truth can be eternal only insofar as it is founded upon something eternal. But the world is not eternal; hence the eternal foundation of eternal truth must be an intellect. Since no created intellect is eternal, only the divine intellect can be the foundation of eternal truth. Accordingly, man's knowledge can be considered eternal only insofar as it is a participation in the knowledge proper to God.

B. METALOGICAL ASPECTS OF TRUTH AS DEMONSTRATED

Since man's decisions as to what is or is not demonstrated are not justified by logic alone, the logical theory of demonstration cannot of itself overcome opinion and probability independently of God.

As we saw in Chapter Four, the logical instrument of transcending opinion and probability is that perfect form of argumentation which Thomas calls a demonstration. Unlike dialectical disputation, which can only solidify the probability of one of two alternative opinions, demonstration reduces one alternative to principles of a special science which are themselves founded upon self-evident principles common to all sciences.

Such, at least, is the logical theory. But, as Thomas points out, one might accept as demonstrated what is not or consider as not demonstrated what in fact is. With regard to the latter case, no matter how logically rigorous a given argument might be, it cannot be a demonstration for a given individual, it cannot be "efficacious" for him, unless and until he recognizes that the argument shows the conclusion to be necessarily implied by incontrovertible premises. At times, we recall, Thomas explains non-acceptance of what has been demonstrated (somewhat like heresy) as being due to intellectual belligerence or inability to resolve merely sophistical arguments. Yet, as we said, he still

aeterna. Sed quia solus intellectus divinus est aeternus, in ipso solo veritas aeternitatem habet."
[1] *C.G.* III, 47; *S.T.* I, 16, 6 c; *Q.D. de pot.* 3, 17 ad 28.

admits the possibility of accepting as demonstrated what in fact is not; and, as we saw in the preceding section, this was precisely the error if not of Aristotle himself then of many Aristotelians with regard to arguments for the eternity of the world.

What Thomas here suggests, without alluding to it himself, is the troubling fact that *the demonstrativity of a demonstration is not itself demonstrable.* And thus one inevitably falls back upon other than purely logical criteria in accepting or rejecting a given argument as truly demonstrative. To show that Thomas himself is not entirely unaffected by this human predicament is the purpose of what follows.

As we have seen in various contexts, Thomas not infrequently speaks of a given proposition as having been proven; but, it must be recalled, proof does not necessarily mean demonstration. The difference is all the difference between probability and scientific certitude, and it is the latter that is here in question. Unfortunately, Thomas has no one single formula to indicate that a proposition has in his opinion been scientifically demonstrated. But his theory of demonstration is such that he could refer to the demonstrated proposition in a variety of ways. He might, of course, say that the proposition is "demonstrated," or that it is "necessary" or that it excludes all possibility of doubt, and so on. Thus on one occasion he speaks of the incorruptibility of the intellect as having been scientifically demonstrated.[1] Elsewhere he says that it can be concluded necessarily that the soul of a brute animal dies with the body.[2] And in the *De Potentia Dei* he uses the formula "without any doubt" to indicate how one should adhere to the propositions that God maintains all things in existence and that there are no accidents in God.[3]

On a much broader scale, Thomas refers in his commentary on the *De Trinitate* to the view of Avempace and Averroes that the speculative sciences are complete and perfect. Since this is used, however, merely as an argument from authority (*sed contra*), it tells us little about Thomas's own view of the matter.[4] Besides, there is ample evidence elsewhere to show that Thomas by no means considers the sciences to be so perfect.

In the first place, we have already seen in various contexts that Thomas recognizes an historical development with regard to the sciences. Thus, in commenting on Aristotle he has occasion to mention

---

[1] *Q.D. de ver.* 12, 2 c. See also *Quodl.* 10, 3, 2 c and 6, 4 c.
[2] *C.G.* II, 82. See also 81.
[3] *Q.D. de pot.* 5, 1 c; 7, 4 c.
[4] *In De Trin.* 6, 4 *sed contra.*

certain things which were not clearly understood at the time of the Philosopher but which he feels have since been explained. For example, Thomas calls attention to Aristotle's indecision as to whether choice (*electio*) is an intellectual or a volitional act.[1] Similarly, he notes that certain aspects of the knowing process were not clear at that time.[2] Again, he mentions certain doubts about the nature of mathematical entities, especially with regard to their connection with physical entities.[3]

This evolutionary aspect of science Thomas does not seem to have applied explicitly to any single author. At times, of course, he does either explicitly or implicitly change his own *opinion* on a given question.[4] But it does not occur to him that the *scientific* as such might be subject to similar evolutionary development. Nevertheless, he suggests as much in his commentaries on the thoughts of others. Time and time again he uses language which presupposes the conviction that some arguments are better, clearer, more obvious, more certain than others. This is especially but not exclusively the case in his commentaries on Aristotle. At numerous places in the *Physics* and the *Metaphysics*, for example, he notes that the subject there being treated by the Philosopher will subsequently be treated more thoroughly, more manifestly, with greater detail or with more efficacious arguments.[5]

Now, underlying these value judgments about arguments is, we think, Thomas's own distinction between the probable and the demonstrated. For, since the latter is in principle definitively established, only the former requires more and better arguments. And, indeed, Thomas does apply this distinction in his critique of "science." The only problem is that his opinion as to which qualification should be applied to which proposition is not always in agreement with the opinion of others.

To begin with, there is hardly any need any more to point out that Thomas qualifies many propositions as merely probable, and for a variety of reasons. We might mention, however, that he even seems to suggest in one place that the hallowed theory of four elements is only hypothetical in the modern sense: *qualia sentimus*.[6] More generally, we have seen that on occasion Thomas speaks of astronomical systems as

---

[1] *S.T.* I, 83, 3 c, *Q.D. de ver.* 24, 6 c.
[2] *In* III *De An.* l. 5, n. 639.
[3] *In* VI *Met.* l. 1, nn. 1160–1163; *Q.D. de spir. creat.* q. un., a. 3 ad 14.
[4] See, for example, *S.T.* III, 62, 6 ad 3; *In* IV *Sent.* d. 1, q. 2, a. 4; q. 1, a. 3; *Q.D. de ver* 2, 10 c, ad 2 and ad 2 *in contrarium*.
[5] See, for example, *In* IV *Phys.* l. 8, n. 493; VI, l. 12, n. 875; VIII, l. 9, nn. 1040–1041; *In* I *Met.* l. 7, n. 123; XII, l. 10, n. 2586; *In* II *De An* l. 8, n. 376.
[6] *C.G.* IV, 30.

being hypothetical. It is now of interest to show that his critique of astronomy and, by application, of theology as well is considerably more refined than that.[1]

With regard to astronomy, Thomas seems to admit as demonstrated that the celestial bodies move with uniform velocity; but he grants only probability to explanatory systems, such as that of Ptolemy, which provide what we would call a mathematical model of the paths which these bodies follow. That the explanatory system is epistemically inferior to what has been strictly demonstrated Thomas attributes to the different roles played by what he calls a *radix*: literally, a root, or radical proposition. If we may translate this as *thesis*, then the scientific would be distinguished from the probable according as the thesis in question is itself demonstrated or, without being demonstrated, merely serves as the axiomatic basis of an explanatory system. Applying this distinction to theses about God, Thomas considers the proposition that there is one God to be demonstrated; but the proposition that there are three persons in God is, from the viewpoint of systematic theology, an undemonstrated axiom from which other implied propositions are deduced.

This same basic distinction between the necessary and the probable, the scientific and the opinionative, is similarly presupposed in Thomas's criticism of what others have or have not demonstrated or, more basically, in his assertions as to what can or cannot be demonstrated. As examples of the former, Thomas denies scientific status to arguments for the Platonic theory of separate substances, or Ideas, as well as to arguments which support the contention that angels and human souls are of the same species.[2] As the most typical examples of the latter, Thomas refuses demonstrative status to any argument against the existence of God that is based upon sense objects; yet, at the same time, he insists that only arguments from effect to cause can demonstrate anything about God.[3]

It is quite clear, then, that Thomas is genuinely critical in his evaluation of what is or is not strictly "scientific." But, as noted above, his critique is not always in accord with that of others. In particular, Thomas often finds himself in disagreement with others as to the type of argument which Aristotle presents or as to its efficacity.

---

[1] *S.T.* I, 32, 1 ad 2. See *In* II *De Caelo et Mundo*, l. 17; *C.G.* III, 23; *Q.D. de pot.* 6, 6 ad 9; *In* XII *Met.* l. 9, n. 2565. See also above, Chapter 3, pp. 133–138; Chapter 5, pp. 200–201.

[2] *Q.D. de an.* q. un., a. 7 ad 14; *In* I *Met.* l. 14, n. 210; *In De div. nom.* c. 11, l. 4, n. 933. See also *Q.D. de ver.* 6, 1 ad 6.

[3] See, for example, *In De div. nom.* c. 4, l. 2, n. 690; *Q.D. de pot.* 7, 3 c ad fin.

On the one hand, he sometimes defends as demonstrative in the strict sense an Aristotelian argument which others consider no more than probable. Against the views of others, for example, Thomas insists that Aristotle has in fact demonstrated that substance as such is not subject to change and that whatever is moved is moved by another.[1]

On the other hand, an argument which others consider to be efficacious in the strict sense Thomas might consider efficacious only with respect to the opposite opinion being attacked. This, as we saw in the preceding section, is the case with regard to Aristotle's arguments for the eternity of the world. Here we might add as instances of the same thing Aristotle's arguments in the *Physics* for the non-separability of a vacuum and against the infinite potentiality of a finite magnitude.[2]

Finally, Thomas might accept one part of Aristotle's position as established and yet insist that another part has only probability. For example, Thomas accepts as established Aristotle's position as to the number of separate substances which move celestial bodies; but, for theological reasons of his own, he rejects as no more than probable Aristotle's further attempt to restrict the total number of separate substances to those engaged in celestial mechanics.[3] Not unrelated to this approach is Thomas's appeal to the First Cause (divine providence) in order to go beyond Aristotle's views about chance, which he feels are quite valid if considered only on the level of secondary or physical causality.[4]

We see, then, that whatever Thomas may say in theory about the perfection of science, his writings indicate, both implicitly and to some extent explicitly, a certain dissatisfaction with what merely human science can accomplish. In spite of his Aristotelian exclusion of the opinionative or probable from the realm of science as such, the exclusion is by no means as absolute as theoretical posture might suggest. To be precise, Thomas's theoretical image of demonstration loses something of its absolutivity when one realizes that Thomas himself finds it quite a problem to distinguish in practice between what is and what is not demonstrated. Accordingly, the theoretical insistence that science is characterized by certainty might well need some phenomenological qualifications. But this may be more appropriately left to our subsequent consideration of psychological foundations.

For the moment, the point we want to make is simply that Thomas's

---

[1] *In* V *Phys.* l. 3, n. 664; VII, l. 1, nn. 887–890.
[2] *In* IV *Phys.* l. 12, n. 536; VIII, l. 21, n. 619. See also *Q.D. de pot.* 3, 17 ad 15.
[3] *C.G.* II, 92; *In* XII *Met.* l. 9, n. 2557. See also *Q.D. de spir. creat.* q. un., a. 8 ad 10.
[4] See above, Chapter 5, pp. 196–199, 202–209.

judgments about what is demonstrated and what is not demonstrated are not motivated by purely logical considerations. What he defends as having been demonstrated he often needs for theological reasons, as, for example, to prove the existence of God or to guard the immortality of the soul. What he reduces to probability, on the other hand, is often felt to be somehow incompatible with the teachings of faith. This, in turn, reminds us once again that the teachings of faith are for Thomas epistemically superior to the merely human knowledge of "the philosophers." And for precisely this reason Thomas is often compelled to use logic in order to go beyond the merely logical.

For, as Thomas sees it, God is intimately involved in all man's efforts to attain truth, however "rational" these efforts might be. Truth, to be sure, is the good of the human intellect; but all good comes from God, and hence all truth comes from God.[1] Whether it be a question of conclusions or of principles, of opinion or of science, to the extent that one has truth one is ultimately dependent upon God for that truth. On the level of proximate causes, admittedly, the certainty of conclusions depends entirely upon the certainty of principles; but the very light of reason whereby man has certainty about principles comes to him directly from God.[2] Indeed, Thomas even goes so far as to say that the necessity of the principle of non-contradiction, from which other principles derive their necessity, depends ultimately upon the providence and "disposition" of God.[3]

Given, then, Thomas's metalogical concern for the divine, it is to be expected that his regard for reason will never be so great as to allow him to turn his back on revelation. For, in the background of Thomas's critique of science is his conviction that man has a transcendent destiny about which he can know and towards which he can direct his life only with the help of truths divinely given. That there is what is called the

---

[1] *Q.D. de ver.* 1, 8.

[2] *Q.D. de ver.* 11, 1 ad 13 and ad 17; 11, 3 c; *Comp. theol.*, c. 129, n. 258.

[3] *Q.D. de ver.* 5, 2 ad 7: "Necessitas principiorum dictorum (quae neque etiam Deus potest mutare, sicut hoc principium quod non est de eodem affirmare et negare) consequitur providentiam divinam et dispositionem: ex hoc enim quod res productae sunt in tali natura, in qua habent esse terminatum, sunt distinctae a suis negationibus: ex qua distinctione sequitur quod affirmatio et negatio non sunt simul vera, et ex hoc principio est necessitas in omnibus aliis principiis, ut dicitur in IV Metaphysicorum." Understood in the best light, what Thomas is here saying is that the principle of non-contradiction is known by man because it has first been put into the world by God. But however understood, Thomas's desire to preserve the universal scope of divine providence involves him in a needless confusion between the logical and the real. For a more thorough presentation of Thomas's views about God as the source of "distinction" in things see Edmund F. Byrne, *The Thomistic Metaphysics of Unity and Multiplicity and its Role as a Foundation for the Doctrine of Distinction*, unpublished Master's Thesis, Loyola University, Chicago, Ill., 1956.

economy of salvation or that God has in fact revealed this to men Thomas does not attempt to demonstrate. But as a believing Christian he presupposes both; and on the basis of this twofold presupposition he seeks to show that it is in fact reasonable or credible.

In particular, he gives a variety of reasons for the fact that God did well to reveal truths to men, which reasons he borrows from Moses Maimonides. Asking in the *Contra Gentiles*, for example, why revelation is needed, Thomas gives as one of three reasons the fact that men left to themselves have great difficulty attaining certainty, especially with regard to knowledge about God. Because of the weakness of our intellect, he says, we often fall into error. The masses remain in doubt even about what has truly been demonstrated, and all the more so because they see that not even the wise can agree with one another. Moreover, it sometimes happens that something false is mixed in with a demonstrated truth, or that an argument which is only probable or even sophistical is taken to be a demonstration. For these and other reasons, Thomas concludes, men need to believe in divine revelation if they are to have untarnished truth and certainty about God.[1]

Such revelation, Thomas adds, is an excellent remedy for human presumption. For, it shows the would-be rationalist that there are truths which totally surpass the capacity of man's intellect.[2] At least with regard to these transcendent truths, then, the real key to certainty is not science but faith in divine revelation. And, in view of the difficulties of demonstration, one might even go so far as to suggest that were it not for these truths divinely given, Thomas would be hard pressed to say what he knows and knows to be incontrovertibly certain outside of a few basic principles.

C. METAHISTORICAL ASPECTS OF TRUTH AS AUTHORITATIVE

Since the authoritative claims of faith are by definition independent of all merely human authority and hence *sui generis*, human authority as such cannot overcome opinion and probability independently of God.

As we saw in Chapter Three, Thomas like all of us is heavily dependent upon the opinions of his forebears for what he accepts as true or rejects as false. But he does not receive all opinions handed down to him with equal hospitality. To the extent that tradition as such helps

---

[1] *C.G.* I, 4. See also *S.T.* II–II, 2, 4 c. With regard to Thomas's dependence upon Maimonides in this matter see Etienne Gilson, *The Elements of Christian Philosophy* (New York, 1963), p. 312.
[2] *C.G.* I, 5. See also *In Symb. Apost.* Prologus, nn. 864–866.

Thomas to make up his mind about what is or is not probable in the sense of approvable, Thomas attributes greater probity to Aristotle than to other "philosophers" and still greater probity to "the saints." We have insisted at some length that this cultural categorization of opinions is an inadequate basis even for the determination of probability. But, whether adequate or not, Thomas himself is quite clear as to the fact that even the opinions of the saints *qua* saints yield *no more than probability* so long as the proposition which they accept does not pertain to faith. If, on the other hand, the proposition in question does pertain to faith, it is *ipso facto* free of the fallibility of human testimony. A proposition that states a dogma of faith is absolutely certain and incontestable.

Accordingly, if tradition as such is capable of providing man with a way to transcend opinion and probability this can only be in connection with those very special propositions which, though true, are neither opinionative nor demonstrated, namely, those which state the dogmas of faith. To show, then, that tradition cannot of itself enable man to overcome opinion and probability we need only show that for Thomas the teachings of faith cannot be explained simply as opinions which, like any other opinions, have been argumentatively defended or demonstrated down through the ages. In other words, we must show that for Thomas faith is an absolutely unique ingredient of man's cultural tradition; or, in short, that it is metahistorical and thus *sui generis*. In so doing, we shall find ourselves once again before the throne of God.

Having thus set the goal we may take as our point of departure what was suggested by the preceding consideration, namely, that faith in divine revelation affords man greater certainty than he can attain by his unaided powers of reasoning. At one point, in fact, Thomas even goes so far as to say that faith is not subject to doubt or questioning; and this he proves from the solidity of faith as compared to human opinion, from the believer's awareness of this solidity, and from the example of the Apostles.[1]

Now, anyone who has ever been inclined to doubt or even to reject religious teachings (in our case, those of Christianity) might well be astonished at Thomas's assertions as to the certainty of faith. It is well to bear in mind, therefore, that such eulogies of faith derive more from Thomas's conviction as to the divine basis of the Christian tradition than from a serious analysis of faith as an existential reality. Besides,

---

[1] *In De div. nom.* c. 7, l. 5, nn. 737–740.

the phenomenon of agnosticism, which in our day is perhaps the rule rather than the exception, was relatively unknown within the social structure of thirteenth century Europe. Deviations from the norm, however dramatic, amounted to divergent interpretations of the religious given rather than outright rejection of the given as such. For Thomas, at any rate, the Moslem, the Jew, or even the Orthodox Christian existed more in theory than in flesh and blood. Thomas's concrete milieu was one in which however well or badly one lived his life it would hardly have occurred to him to reject commonly accepted dogmas as such. Not surprisingly, then, Thomas gives no evidence of ever having encountered a "non-believer" who by his very life might call into question the absolutivity of accepted Christian formulations. In short, having as it were located faith in the speculative intellect, Thomas was never pressed by facts to the contrary to defend the certainty of faith. This certainty was, for all practical purposes, a sociological given.

It must be noted at once, however, that Thomas is by no means a fool; and in the course of his life he does give some evidence of recognizing that faith entails a certain psychological problem precisely insofar as it is said to be certain. He readily admits, for example, that faith does not involve clarity of knowledge: and, what is more important, on occasion he even tries to take account of the fact that men do have doubts about the teachings of faith.[1] But for the most part his explanation of these facts is so theoretically remote from the facts themselves that he succeeds only in avoiding rather than in clarifying the problem of a believer's doubts.

Now, the remoteness of what Thomas says about a believer's doubt is, we think, due to two principal reasons. In the first place, Thomas is more concerned with defending the divine origin of faith than with exploring the implications of experiential data. Thus, in the second place, for Thomas the psychological or epistemic problem of faith is largely one of distinguishing faith from any form of knowledge recognized by mere philosophers, in particular by the Philosopher himself.

In view of the divine origin of faith, Thomas feels he must insist that faith is more certain than merely human knowledge.[2] That one can doubt about the teachings of faith Thomas explains by saying that faith is more certain from the viewpoint of God, even though merely

---

[1] See, for example, *Q.D. de ver.* 10, 12 ad 6, where he says that faith is certain with respect to firmness of adherence though not with respect to satisfaction or fulfillment of the intellect.

[2] *In De div. nom.* c. 1, l. 1, nn. 7–9; *Q.D. de ver.* 14, 1 ad 7.

human knowledge, such as science, is more certain from man's point of view.[1] As we shall see in the next section, this theocentric notion of certainty is of fundamental importance in Thomas's thought. But, be that as it may, it really sheds little light on the concrete problem of a believer's doubts. For, in effect, by means of this distinction Thomas makes certainty a characteristic not of the believer's knowledge but of God's, in such a way that the believer's doubts have no foundation except in the weakness of his intellect. That about which the believer doubts is certain – perhaps not to him, but to God, who understands what he does not.[2]

Now, what is for us a most important consequence of Thomas's theocentric foundation of faith is that for him faith cannot possibly be identified with any merely human form of knowledge. In effect, this means distinguishing faith from the types of knowledge recognized by Aristotle. Since for Thomas faith is a habit in the speculative intellect, he must therefore set it apart from other such habits and, in particular, both from "perfect" and from "imperfect" intellectual knowledge: both from science and from opinion.[3]

The manner in which Thomas carries out this task of distinction varies from one place to another, especially, it would seem, because of the fact that he comes to grant more importance to the will in formally intellectual acts. This development, in turn, is perhaps due to increasing familiarity with Aristotle's thought at first hand.[4] But in any event the attempt to guard the uniqueness of faith is already present in Thomas's early works.

In the *De Veritate*, for example, Thomas seems to be concerned above all to show the unique character of supernatural faith in comparison to other modes of knowledge discussed by philosophers. To this end he first gives us a kind of logico-psychological analysis of natural faith as defined by Augustine, then follows this up with a similar analysis of supernatural faith as described in the Epistle to the Hebrews.[5]

As Thomas understands Augustine's definition (*"credere est cum assensione cogitare"*), belief combines assent with continued inquiry.[6] So Thomas describes doubt as a fluctuation between alternatives,

---

[1] *S.T.* II–II, 4, 8 c.
[2] *S.T.* II–II, 4, 8 ad 1 and ad 2.
[3] For Thomas's view that faith is a habit in the speculative intellect, see his treatment of the question at *In* III *Sent.* d. 23, q. 2, a. 3, q. 1a 1; *Q.D. de ver.* 14, 4; *S.T.* II–II, 4, 2.
[4] In *S.T.* II–II, 1, 5 ad 4, for example, Thomas considers the relationship between faith, opinion, and science with explicit reference to Aristotle's *Posterior Analytics*.
[5] *Q.D. de ver.* 14, 1 and 2.
[6] Augustine's definition will be found in his *De praedestinatione sanctorum* II (PL 44: 963).

opinion as the acceptance of one alternative without real assent, and conviction (*sententia*) as an assent to one alternative. The assent, he says, may involve no reasoning, as in the case of understanding first principles, or it may involve reasoning. If the reasoning *culminates* in assent, then one has science; if reasoning is still possible even after assenting, then one has belief. So much, then, for natural faith.

Turning next to supernatural faith as described in the Latin Vulgate of *Hebrews*, Thomas builds his analysis around *argumentum*, which he here takes to mean a determination of the intellect and "the substance of things to be hoped for." [1] Because with faith the intellect is determined, faith is thus distinct from doubt and opinion. Because supernatural faith has reference to things hoped for this – it is not altogether clear why – distinguishes such faith from faith in the wide sense of a strong opinion (*vehementer opinamur*).

In the following article, Thomas then points out that if an intellectual virtue be taken to involve the will, then neither opinion nor science but only faith is an intellectual virtue. (That opinion is independent of the will he will later deny.) If, however, an intellectual virtue be taken as a perfection of knowledge, then, says Thomas, neither opinion nor faith are virtues but only science.[2] In short, already in this early work Thomas shows us his desire to isolate supernatural faith by contrasting it with natural types of knowledge.

By the time he comes to write the *Secunda Pars* of his *Summa Theologica*, that is, some twelve or thirteen years later, he has managed to work out the contrasts much more neatly. As we have seen in other contexts, Thomas likes to describe faith as a medium between opposite heresies in much the same way as truth is the medium between opposite errors and (true) opinion the medium between contrary (false) opinions.[3] But the relationship which Thomas seems to consider the most appealing is that which he finds expressed by Hugh of Saint Victor: "Faith is a kind of certainty of the mind which is about what is otherwise unknown (*de absentibus*) and which is superior to opinion and inferior to science." [4]

Thomas describes quite rigorously how he visualizes this intermediate

---

[1] The Vulgate definition of faith upon which Thomas bases his analysis reads as follows: "Est autem fides sperandarum substantia rerum, argumentum non apparentium." (*Hebrews* 11:1).

[2] *Q.D. de ver.* 14, 3 ad 5.

[3] *S.T.* I–II, 64, 3 ad 3; 4 ad 3; *C.G.* III, 108.

[4] Hugh of St. Victor, *De sacramentis* l. I, part. 10, c. 2: "Fides est certitudo quaedam animi de absentibus supra opinionem et infra scientiam." See Thomas Aquinas, *S.T.* II–II, 1, 2 sed contra; 2, 1 c; 4, 1 c.

position of faith in answer to the question as to whether one will have faith after this life on earth.[1] To make his case, he points out that knowledge may be imperfect either because the thing known is imperfect (contingent) or because the medium of knowledge is imperfect (probable as opposed to demonstrative knowledge) or, finally, *because of imperfections in the knower*. Taking the latter as the reason for faith's imperfection as knowledge, Thomas can then admit that whereas scientific knowledge has both vision and firmness and opinion has vision but not firmness, faith has firmness but not vision.

Further on in the same work, when dealing explicitly with faith, he breaks down the epistemic relationships on the basis of the manner of assent.[2] One may assent to a proposition, he says, either because of the object or because of volitional choice. Objective assent may be either immediate (*per seipsum cognitum*), as in the acceptance of first principles, or mediate (*per aliud*), as in the case of scientific conclusions. If the assent depends upon an act of volition, this assent may include doubt and respect for the opposite alternative, which is the case with opinion, or the assent may involve certitude and no concern about the opposite, and this is the case of faith in the strict sense.

Soon afterwards, Thomas makes another attempt at categorization by saying that faith involves firm assent, and is thus like science and the understanding of principles, and also involves lack of vision, in which it is like opinion, doubt, and suspicion.[3]

Now, it is to be noted from our brief consideration that in attempting to relate faith to the Aristotelian classification of knowledge, Thomas presupposes (1) that faith is essentially a perfection of the intellect and (2) that faith must be somehow clearly distinct from any form of knowledge known to a mere philosopher, even one of the stature of Aristotle. And thus we find Thomas placing faith in a position somehow or other intermediate between opinion and science. This, in turn, suggests three interesting observations.

In the first place, it will be recalled, Thomas had great difficulty with Aristotle's distinction between the scientific and opinionative functions of the soul, and in time tended to identify the two, respectively, with the intellect as speculative and the intellect as practical. Thus we are presented with the remarkable fact that implicit in

---

[1] S.T. I–II, 67, 3.

[2] S.T. II–II, 1, 4 c.

[3] S.T. II, II, 2, 1 c. There are numerous other passages in the works of Thomas in which he attempts to guard the unique character of faith while leaving it with its intellectual neighbors. See, for example, S.T. I–II, 112, 5 c and ad 2; II–II, 1, 5 ad 4; 2, 9 ad 2; 4, 8.

Thomas's thought, apparently without his alluding to it himself, is a tendency to identify faith as a function of the intellect intermediate between that of reflection and that of action. In the light of contemporary religious thought this tendency is of considerable interest. But it is interesting enough even within the confines of Thomas's own thought: there is here suggested a similarity between faith and prudence, since the role of the latter is precisely to bring the speculative or necessary into the realm of the practical or contingent.[1]

In the second place, then, Thomas's attempt to define faith by contrasting it with the various elements of Aristotle's schema of the intellect results in an extremely important modification of the Philosopher's theory of knowledge. For, in particular, the very fact that from the viewpoint of the knower faith is considered intermediate between science and opinion quite simply destroys the science-opinion dichotomy so dear to Aristotle as well as to others before and after him. That neither Thomas himself nor his followers is quite aware of what he has done in no way alters the fact that he has done it. Thomas may continue to posit between opinion and science a theoretically absolute dichotomy; but, almost as though by subconscious wish, he himself bridges the gap by virtue of his psychology of faith.

Our third and principal observation flows from the preceding two and brings our discussion to a close. In briefest terms, faith is neither fish nor fowl, that is, neither opinion nor science, nor, for that matter, any other merely human form of knowledge. Hence it cannot possibly

---

[1] We are not suggesting here that Thomas wished to consider faith as complete or perfect without any reference to action. Quite to the contrary, Thomas considers faith *"informata"* so long as it is not activated by love or charity. The point is, rather, that for Thomas faith as such is essentially a speculative virtue, whereas prudence is simultaneously speculative and practical. In other words, one can on this theory have faith without acting upon it; but one cannot have prudence without acting upon it. The difference could, perhaps, be explained away as a matter of terms, and this is in part the case. But it is only a part, as can be seen especially from Thomas's theory of heresy. For the relationship between faith and charity, see *In* III *Sent.* d. 23, q. 2, a. 4, q. 1a 1; q. 3, a. 1, q. 1a 1 and 2; a. 4, q. 1a 1, 3; *Q.D. de ver.* 14, aa. 3, 5–6, and 7; *Q.D. de virt. in comm.* 1, 7; 2, 3; *S.T.* I–II, 65, 4; II–II, 4, 3–5; 23, 8. For an interesting attempt to preserve the intellectuality of Thomas's theory of faith without the harsh consequences of heresy-hunting, see Olivier A. Rabut, *La Vérification Religieuse: Recherche d'une spiritualité pour le Temps de l'Incertitude* (Paris, 1964). A far more critical view of an intellectualized faith, which depends among other things upon a distinction between *"foi"* and *"croyance,"* is that of Francis Jeanson, *La Foi d'un Incroyant* (Paris, 1963). This not unusual expression of distaste for overly formalized religion is, in turn, nowhere better answered than in the remarkable work of Wilfred Cantwell Smith, *The Meaning and End of Religion: A New Approach to the Religious Traditions of Mankind* (New York, 1962). If exception be made for the ecumenical outlook of the latter work, Smith's concept of faith as transcending its cultural expression can, we think, be shown to be not unrelated to Thomas's theory. For, in spite of his completely different cultural milieu and vastly inferior acquaintance with non-Christian religions, Thomas by his separation of faith from all human forms of knowledge is pointing precisely at the transcendence of faith.

be subjected to the human dialectic of argumentative pro and con – except, as we recall, insofar as men might use such human means to find human arguments in support of divine revelation. This being the case, faith as Thomas understands it cannot be explained in terms of the cultural data of merely human tradition.[1] Since faith, however, was the only candidate in our quest, it must be concluded that human tradition as such provides no escape from opinion and probability.

This, of course, is not to be taken as a reason for despair. For, what cannot come to us on the horizontal level of human history can come to us vertically in our rapport with God. Through God's gift of the intellectual *habitus* of faith, man is supernaturally endowed with a means of transcending the dichotomy between science and opinion, between the necessary and the contingent, thus imitating in his own way the intuitive vision of divine providence. Or, to read the suggestions somewhat differently, through faith the human intellect attaches itself somehow to the ultimately Necessary while remaining in the midst of the contingent. And this, after all, is in accordance with Thomas's epistemological dream. Prominent figures in that dream are, we recall, not only Adam, the prophets and Jesus but even angels; and to this group we can now add also the perfectly prudent man. Each of these is an epistemological hero, if we may so speak, precisely because of and to the extent that he (or it) is in rapport with the divine mind.

The mere philosopher, of course, can through diligent study approach the divine insofar as he comes to contemplate separate substances; but the rest of his knowledge, however demonstrative it may be, is of passing value if he does not see it as a reflection of the First Truth. For, the material universe which is the very object and source of his knowledge will not endure. Accordingly, it is only by direct participation in knowledge divine, partially in this life through faith and perfectly hereafter in the beatific vision, that man can definitively transcend the contingent.

---

[1] We know of just one instance where Thomas addresses himself to the question here posed, and in his reply he insists that it is not tradition as here understood but God that causes faith in the believer. Against an appeal to Augustine that *"scientia"* generates and fosters faith, Thomas replies: "Per scientiam gignitur fides et nutritur per modum exterioris persuasionis, quae fit ab aliqua scientia. Sed principalis et propria causa fidei est id quod interius movet ad assentiendum (gratiam Dei)." – *S.T.* II–II 6, 1 ad 1. See also 1 c.

D. METAPSYCHOLOGICAL ASPECTS OF TRUTH AS CERTAIN

Since man's psychological conviction that his knowledge is certain differs from opinion in degree rather than in kind, man's claim to certainty does not overcome probability independently of God.

As we saw in Chapter Two and recalled just above, though Thomas accepts Aristotle's distinction between the opinionative and the scientific parts of the soul, he has some difficulty figuring out just what to make of these distinctions. Thus he eventually gives up the idea that there are two different faculties, or powers, in question and contents himself with saying that the intellect simply forms different habits according as the things which it knows are necessary or contingent. That Thomas thereby tends to associate scientific-opinionative with speculative-practical is relevant at this point but may be overlooked; our thoughts lead us in a somewhat different direction. For, still unanswered is the fascinating question as to how a man can be *certain* that what he takes to be necessary is necessary and that what he takes to be contingent is contingent.

The psychological distinction as given would suggest, of course, that this question simply does not arise. For, implied in Aristotle's tidy arrangement of intellectual furniture is the understandable desire that there be a one-to-one correspondence between psychological states and physical events. Hence in accepting this arrangement Thomas also asserts as an ideal that what the mind takes to be necessary is in fact necessary and that what the mind takes to be contingent is in fact contingent.

As we have seen from many different points of view, however, for Thomas this ideal is in fact realized only in the divine mind. Only God, in the final analysis, is certain both about what is necessary and about what is contingent, since it is he who has established some things as necessary and others as contingent. Man, on the other hand, can and does err by taking the necessary for contingent or the contingent for necessary. This is, after all, the common failing of the ordinary man with regard to all kinds of things. To go one step farther, even if a man wishes to learn science, he must still accept on (natural) faith what his teacher presumably knows by way of demonstration. Even then, however, he cannot be sure that his psychic state will be corrected, for the simple reason that some men are more gifted than others at grasping a process of reasoning productive of scientific certainty.[1] In the case of someone like Thomas, of course, we are dealing neither with a neophyte nor with a mediocre mind but rather with perhaps the greatest intellect of his day. And yet, as we have seen, Thomas must struggle mightily to convince himself and others that one or another proposition is in fact demonstrated and hence incontrovertibly certain. How, then, is it possible for Thomas to speak so facilely about an intellectual habit of the necessary and an intellectual habit of the contingent? Even more, what possible relationship can there be between man's certitude and certitude divine?

To approach this delicate problem, let us start with the assumption that it is possible to defend the distinction between opinion and science on the level of human psychology. For this purpose, then, one might explain the distinction simply as an expression of the fact that man has certitude, or certain knowledge, about some things and only opinion, or probable knowledge, about others.

We see at once, though, that this explanation is too simple as it stands, for at least two reasons: (1) Thomas is not adverse to talking about "probable certitude"; (2) in speaking of heretics he makes allowances for what he calls "certitude of adherence." [2] Whatever else these expressions may involve, they at least suggest that when Thomas is concerned about certitude as a psychological state which may be or is objectively unfounded, he tends to state as much by qualifying his term for certitude, *certitudo*, with some appropriate modifier. And thus he tells us in effect that this is not what he would consider real or objective or justifiable certitude. *In what follows, therefore, we shall avoid the suggestion of unfounded personal conviction by speaking not of "certitude" but only of "certainty." This "certainty," in turn, must be presumed to be justified.*

Having thus modified our tentative assumption of psychological foundations, we now propose a parallelism between mental probability (opinion) and "certainty" on the one hand and real probability (contingency) and necessity on the other. And to defend this parallelism we take it as sufficient to establish that opinion has as it were a parameter of values as does the contingent whereas certainty is a constant as is necessity.[3] Since we may consider the first part as already established we proceed directly to the second part.

---

[1] *C.G.* II, 73; III, 152; *S.T.* I–II, 52, 2 c; II–II, 2, 3 c; *Q.D. de ver.* 8, 10 c; 20, 5 c; *Q.D. de spir. creat.* q. un., a. 9 ad 6; *In* II *De An.* l. 11, n. 372.

[2] See above, Chapter 3, pp. 122–123; Chapter 5, pp. 224–225.

[3] In reality, the condition(s) which we here set forth is by no means sufficient to establish

As a matter of fact, there is some reason to think that Thomas supports our parallelism, because on occasion he contrasts probability with certainty. Thus, for example, he tells us that one cannot have certainty but only probability as to his possession of grace and/or charity or as to the merit of his works.[1] With observations of this kind we might also associate Thomas's contention that one can be certain, as was St. Paul, that he is a minister of Christ without being certain that he is just or, in other words, that he is in a state of grace.[2] Also relevant in this regard is Thomas's assertion that one who has science can have certainty as to his possession of science.[3]

In all the foregoing observations, however, including those which explicitly contrast certainty with probability, Thomas uses certainty in a restricted sense. For, what he has in mind in these instances is certainty as to the existence of a thing (an est) rather than certainty as to its explanation (quid est). Applying this distinction to man's knowledge of his soul, Thomas dimly foreshadows Descartes by maintaining that certainty as to its existence is basic to man, whereas certainty as to its explanation is acquired only with great difficulty.[4] To the first kind of certainty, which is imperfect in comparison to the second, we can relate the certainty of sense experience and hence also certainty about sensibly present contingent events, such as our old friend Socrates seated. It is only the second kind of certainty, however,

---

the proposed parallelism; but it is a necessary condition. A little explanation should make this clear. Suppose that one wants to establish a relationship of correspondence between the mental states of opinion and certainty on the one hand and the contingent and the necessary event on the other. Since in principle both opinion and the contingent event are variable whereas both certainty and the necessary event are constant, one would postulate that opinion should be matched with contingency and certainty with necessity. Now, to verify this hypothesis, one would have to show: (1) that both opinion and the contingent event are in fact variable; (2) that both certainty and the necessary event are in fact constant; (3) that the variability of opinion is a function of the variability of the contingent event; (4) that the constancy of certainty is a function of the constancy of the necessary event; (5) that the psychic commitment of opinion varies in direct proportion to the relative frequency of the contingent event; and, most important of all, (6) that the variability in question can be effectively measured. Conditions 1 and 2 are necessary; conditions 3–6, if properly developed, would seem to be sufficient. Here then, we assume on the basis of Thomas's theory of probability that condition 1 is established, and thus go on from there to consider condition 2. For the sake of simplicity we disregard the quite relevant question as to whether the "necessary" event is in fact constant and ask only if certainty is constant.

[1] Q.D. de ver. 6, 5 ad 3; 10, 10 c, ad 1–5 and ad 9; Quodl. 3, q. 4, a. 1 c. This view places Thomas in the somewhat awkward position of maintaining that even though one cannot be certain that he has charity, nevertheless he is obliged to love out of charity. See Q.D. de carit. q. un., a. 8, ad 16.

[2] S.T. III, 82, 5 c.

[3] Quodl. 3, q. 4, a. 1 c; S.T. I–II, 112, 5 c and ad 2.

[4] Q.D. de ver. 10, 8 c and ad 8 and 12 ad 7: "Nullus potest cogitare se non esse cum assensu: in hoc enim quod cogitat aliquid, percipit se esse." See also Q.D. de ver. 10, 9; C.G. III, 46; S.T. I, 87, 1 c and 2 c; In XII Met. l. 11, n. 2617.

that is scientific in the strict sense. Accordingly, if we are to maintain our parallelism we must show that mental certainty, or science, about *quid est* is to necessity as is mental probability, or opinion, to contingency.

Now, as a matter of fact, Thomas is somewhat encouraging in this regard; for, in at least one place he describes human certainty in such a way as to restrict it to the certainty which derives from knowledge of the necessary. To begin with, he gives a definition of *certainty of knowledge* which makes such certainty practically indistinguishable from truth. As he puts it, one has certainty of knowledge when one's thoughts about a thing square with the way the thing is in itself.[1] Of the utmost importance, however, he goes on to say that one has such knowledge (*certa existimatio*) especially as a result of knowing a thing in the light of its causes. Whence, he maintains, the notion of certainty refers in the first instance to the ordered relationship of cause to effect. Certainty in this sense, which he calls *certainty of order*, obtains when a cause infallibly produces a given effect. As we have already seen, however, this is the case only with regard to what is necessary, that is to say, what does in fact or at least should in theory happen *always*.

Thus is Thomas's ultimate meaning of certainty tied to necessity and sempiternity. In this primordial meaning of certainty, it is the necessary, what happens always, that is certain in itself; if the causal order which guarantees such necessity does not obtain, neither the object in question nor man's knowledge of it can be certain in this strict sense. It is, therefore, in the light of this certainty in the real world that mental certainty, or "certitude," must be judged, since the latter is justified only to the extent that its object approaches the certainty of the necessary.

This focussing of the notion of certainty upon real causal relationships is, to be sure, motivated by ontological considerations. But it must be noted that Thomas is also moved in this direction by reasons that are properly theological; and it is at precisely this point that our attempt to justify a psychological basis for certainty begins to break down.

In the passage considered at length in the preceding paragraph, Thomas is concerned to show that in addition to God's foreknowledge of the future destiny of all men, which is certain *qua* knowledge, divine predestination, that is, God's plan for the salvation of the elect, is certain both as to knowledge and as to the ordering of causes to effects.

---

[1] *Q.D. de ver.* 6, 3 c: "Cognitionis quidem certitudo est, quando cognitio non declinat in aliquo ab eo quod in re invenitur, sed hoc modo existimat de re sicut est."

In other words, since some men are obviously wicked and God is obviously good, Thomas likes to say that God's knowledge of future free acts of men is universally certain *qua* knowledge but not *qua* ordering of causes to effects.[1] The problem of free will here suggested need not detain us, since all that we want to point out is what such a problem does to the notion of certainty. In view of the intellectual capacities of God, Thomas will admit that the notion of certainty refers primarily to a cognitive power (in the case of providence, to the divine intellect); but he insists that it refers "by way of participation" to what is governed by intellect. It is from this point of view that the processes of nature can be said to function "certainly" (*certitudinaliter*); and, in view of God's gift of faith to the human intellect, the appetitive virtue of hope, which is based upon faith, can be said to be certain.[2]

We see, then, that for a proper view of Thomas's attitude towards human certainty it is necessary to distinguish between the certainty of determinate events and the certainty of man's knowledge of those events. One might for short speak of objective and subjective certainty; but on the whole this manner of speaking is inadvisable. With the tranquillity of a pre-Kantian realist, Thomas presupposes that at least under ordinary conditions scientific knowledge is certain because one knows the necessary relationship of effect to cause and knows furthermore that the relationship as he knows it is such in reality.[3] In other

---

[1] *Q.D. de ver.* 6, aa. 3–4. As Pius Servien has correctly noted, the problem of divine foreknowledge and predestination, which sorely tested theologians of the seventeenth century, is an important element in the intellectual milieu which brought forth the first attempts at a mathematical calculus of probability. These very problems, however, have roots deep in the history of Christian speculation, a fact that is particularly well illustrated by these articles from the *De Veritate*. As Thomas tells us in Article 3, he must bolster God's knowledge as he does because of "the authority of the Scriptures and the sayings of the saints." Article 4, in turn, is a veritable classic in terms of medieval theory of probability. The problem before Thomas in this article is in general whether the *number* of predestined is certain and in particular Augustine's observation that the number of the elect is certain only if the default of one man makes room for the election of another. Albert the Great, it must be noted, had interpreted Augustine's statement as meaning that the number taken formally is certain but taken materially it is not. In other words, it might be certain that 100 have been predestined, but not certain as to which members of the set of all men would constitute that subset of 100 predestined. Thomas's argument, in turn, consists in showing that with regard to God himself this solution is inadequate, for the reason that God knows the number not only formally but also materially, and that moreover he is causally responsible for the subset of the predestined. Here, then, we see some basis for F. N. David's contention that the medieval doctrine of divine providence prevented development of a calculus of probability. What David overlooks, however, is the fact that it was precisely men who discussed this doctrine and thus were compelled to deal with problems which the calculus tries to solve. There is, in other words, a wealth of meaning in the assertion that early mathematical probabilists were attempting to play God. For Augustine's observation see his *De correptione et gratia* XIII (PL 44: 940). For Albert's interpretation see his *In I Sent.* d. 40, *a.* 11 (BO 26; 319).

[2] *S.T.* II–II, 18, 4 c.

[3] We recall once more that Thomas does in fact speak of "probable certitude" with regard

words, the certainty which man acquires through science derives not from the knower but from the reality known. This being the case, Thomas attributes human certainty to the real rather than to knowledge of the real, that is, to the objective basis of scientific certainty rather than to its psychic reverberations.

There is implicit in this approach the recognition of a great gap between man's certainty and certainty divine. What we have here is a case of what Thomists would call analogy. Both God and man have certainty about the world; but whereas God's certainty is an automatic consequence of his being the First Cause of all causes, man's certainty is dependent upon his ability to discover for himself at least some of the causes which God has activated in the world.

From this point of view, then, the only absolutely stable certainty is that which coincides perfectly with the way things are, whether they be necessary or contingent, in the real world. But perfect coincidence between cognitional certainty and real events (contingent or necessary) is the prerogative of God alone. Accordingly, the parallelism which we have tentatively proposed *can* be said to apply perfectly – – *not*, however, to man's knowledge of the world but to God's. Hence, lest anyone make too hasty an application of Thomas's views to the contemporary debate over interpretation of quantum physics, we must proceed at once to a description of man's certainty as a mere approximation to the ideal.

That man's certainty only approximates the divine ideal is seen especially from the fact that this certainty is as subject to gradation or, if you will, to a parameter of values, as is probability. And this in turn sugests that certainty as a characteristic of human science differs from opinion or probable knowledge not in kind but only in degree. If, however, this is in fact the case, then everything which Thomas says about man's dialectical flight from the less true to the more true can be applied, though perhaps on a higher level, to the "less certain" and the "more certain."

To begin as it were at the bottom, we must note that Thomas recognizes a gradation of certainty even on the level of sensation. On the assumption that the more "spiritual" organ of sensation is capable of greater certainty, Thomas agrees with Aristotle that among the various senses some, and in particular sight, are more certain than

to knowledge of the contingent and "certitude of adhesion" with regard to the heretic. But the very rarety of such qualifications indicates that when Thomas speaks of "*certitudo*" without qualification he presupposes that the state of mind said to be certain is objectively founded.

others. But reason, he insists, yields greater certainty than do the senses.[1]

That man can attain to certainty on the level of reason is due primarily if not exclusively to reason's ability to arrive at scientific demonstrations. But demonstrations as such depend upon principles. And in this regard Thomas would agree with Aristotle that science proceeds from what is "more certain to us" to what is "more certain in itself." [2] As for what he would consider "more certain to us," this depends upon the subject matter in question. Some principles are more certain to us because they are more apparent to the senses (the principles of physical science), others because they are in themselves more simple and primordial (the principles of mathematics), others because they are more readily known by men (the principles of ethics).[3] Moreover, just as the certainty of principles so also the certainty of conclusions is dependent upon the subject matter in question. Accordingly, in some sciences one can attain greater certainty, in other sciences less.[4]

For the most part, the gradation of sciences according to the degree of certainty which they attain is based on the criterion of simplicity in conjunction with that which is essentially another form of the same thing, the criterion of spirituality, or detachment from matter. Thus arithmetic, which depends only upon the principle of unity, is thought to be more certain than geometry, which adds to the notion of unity that of the point or, as we might say, locus. Following the same criterion, metaphysics, which studies simply being, is thought to be more certain than mathematics, which studies being insofar as it is quantified, and still more certain than natural science, which studies being insofar as it is subject to motion.[5] By simplicity, in other words, is meant a conceptual simplicity, in such a way that one might almost say: the greater the comprehension the less the certainty, and the greater the extension the greater the certainty.

Thus we find that the criterion of simplicity, or of spirituality, is in effect a criterion of universality: the more universal the principle, or the object of the science, as the case may be, the greater the certainty attainable. By way of corollary, then, the closer man approaches the particularity and multiplicity of concrete things, the less he can attain

---

[1] *In* VII *Polit.* l. 5, n. 1127; *In* I *Met.* l. 1, n. 6; *In* II *De An.* l. 19, nn. 479–482; *In De Sensu* l. 9, n. 120.

[2] *In* l *Phys.* l. 1.

[3] *In* VI *Met.* l. 1, n. 1146.

[4] *In* I *Ethic.* l. 3, n. 36; *In* XI *Met.* l. 7, n. 2249.

[5] *In* I *Met.* l. 1, nn. 24–28; l. 2, n. 47; *In De Trin.* 6, 1 c.

certainty about what he is studying. Art is only an apparent exception to this rule, since in fact the principles of art are not in matter as such but are in the mind of the artist; his practical function, very simply, is to impose these immaterial principles, or ideas, upon the matter at his disposal.[1] As we have seen, however, human actions are concerned precisely with the concrete particular; and thus Thomas says that "the certainty of prudence is never so great as to remove all solicitude." [2]

We see, then, that the degree of certainty which a science can attain is directly proportional to the simplicity or universality of its object (more technically, its formal object). But, be it noted, this criterion applies only for the most part. There is an exception, and this exception sheds a great deal of light upon Thomas's view of certainty with respect to human knowledge. In his commentary on the *De Trinitate*, Thomas says that mathematics is more certain than physics or the practical sciences, but it is also more certain than science about divine things.[3] Now, that mathematics should be considered more certain than physics or the practical sciences is a clear application of the criterion of simplicity as explained above. For, the greater certainty attained in mathematics is said to be due to the fact that the objects considered by mathematics, unlike those considered in physics, are detached from matter and motion. But that mathematics should be considered more certain than *scientia divina* or theological science (as here used, referring to metaphysics in the sense of natural theology) would seem to be a clear departure from the criterion of simplicity. For, in Thomas's mind, the object or objects of metaphysical theology are ontologically, that is to say, in themselves, simpler than the objects of mathematics. Be that as it may, Thomas explains at considerable length that for man mathematics is more certain; and he justifies this position on the grounds that the concepts of mathematics, unlike those of the science of divine things, have a content which is imaginable. In other words, for man the study of the divine is less certain than that of mathematics precisely because of the fact that the former unlike the latter transcends the imagination. This amounts to saying – and this is the whole tenor of the discussion – that mathematics is more certain

---

[1] *S.T.* II–II, 49, 5 ad 2.
[2] *S.T.* II–II, 47, 9 ad 2: "Quia vero materiae prudentiae sunt singularia contingentia, circa quae sunt operationes humanae, non potest certitudo prudentiae tanta esse quod omnino sollicitudo tollatur."
[3] *In De Trin.* Proemium; Lect. II, Proemium; 6, 1 ad 1 and ad 2.

to man because it proceeds in a manner more appropriate to human cognition than does the science of divine things.[1]

That certainty about God is so difficult to obtain by comparison to certainty about mathematicals is not, however, a reason to disregard the divine. Apart from the help man receives through revelation, he can make some progress towards knowledge of God by the use of his reason. And where certainty is lacking, probability can fill in. For, as we recall, the maxim which Aristotle applies to knowledge of the soul, of the heavenly bodies, and of things metaphysical, Thomas applies directly to knowledge about God: it is better to have probable knowledge about nobler objects than certainty about the less noble.[2]

In short, when Thomas speaks of certainty from the human point of view, he suggests in many ways that some propositions that are "certain" are "more certain" than others. But to say that proposition A is "more certain" than proposition B is to say that B is "less certain" than A. And this, in turn, leads one to wonder what might be the "least certain" of less certain propositions. Might it not be precisely that proposition which Thomas tells us is deserving of only "probable certainty?" But if this latter be considered as a kind of point of overlap between certainty and probability, what is to prevent us from saying that the probable is "less certain" and that the certain is "more probable?" Put somewhat differently, if for man there are degrees of certainty, as is so often indicated in Thomas's writings, what is it precisely that distinguishes the mentally or psychologically certain from the probable, the mentally or psychologically scientific from the opinionative? The theoretical answer, of course, is demonstration; but, as we have seen, some propositions seem to be more clearly demonstrated than others – and thus we are again faced with a gradation in knowledge.

In the light of these considerations, we must conclude that our parallelism is a failure from the viewpoint of human psychology. Certainty in human knowledge is not a constant but takes on a parameter of values as does probability; and, even more, there is reason to suspect that the values of one are continuous with the values of the other. And thus we could say that in a broad sense all human knowledge is "probable" insofar as it never achieves perfect assurance as to its grasp of the object, whether that object be considered "neces-

---

1 See also *In* II *Met.*, l. 5, n. 336 for a fairly equivalent description of mathematics as most certain from the human point of view (*quoad nos*).
2 *In* I *De An.* l. 1, nn. 4–6; *In* VI *Met.* l. 1, nn. 1166–1168; *S.T.* I–II, 101, 2 ad 2.

sary" or "contingent." However many arguments a man may propose as "disputative" or even "demonstrative" defense of a proposition, the proposition continues to call for still better defense. That he chooses to consider one proposition (or argument) probable and another certain depends upon many different factors, among which real "contingency" or "necessity" may not be the most important. That man's scientific certainty should map onto necessity and his probable opinion onto contingency is, of course, an interesting ideal. But it is not borne out in the writings of Thomas Aquinas.

Divine knowledge, on the other hand, is never lacking in perfect assurance and thus is never in need of better arguments. Whatever God knows, and he knows all, is rigorously and rightly certain both with regard to the necessary and with regard to the contingent. For God, in short, mental certainty, or science, is all-embracing and mental probability, or opinion, simply does not obtain. To the extent that anything exists or occurs in any way at all, whether "contingently" or "necessarily," it is known to God within the full panorama of its causes.

Admittedly, there is in man what Aristotle called the light of the agent intellect, and this is an accurate instrument of knowing truth; but it is accurate precisely because of the fact it is immediately impressed in us by God and is thus a kind of derivative of the divine mind.[1] Thus the fact that man is capable of attaining certainty is in the last analysis due to our intellect's somehow participating in the infallibility of the divine intellect. But if this is in fact the case, then a man would have more certain knowledge about any given thing by knowing it directly in and through God than by knowing it as it were indirectly through scientific demonstration.[2] Whence the extreme good fortune of the prophets, to some extent of the faithful, and *par excellence* of the blessed in heaven.

E. GOD AS THE CULMINATION OF RATIONAL DIALECTIC

Since human knowledge *qua* human is in a wide sense only opinionative or probable, such knowledge transcends the probable precisely insofar as it is founded in God, and definitively so in the beatific vision.

---

[1] *C.G.* III, 154; *S.T.* I, 87, 1 c; II–II, 171, 5 c and 6 ad 2; *Q.D. de spir. creat.* q. un., a. 10 c. That Thomas is in this respect more influenced by Augustine than by Aristotle he realizes full well; but he does not feel that by referring the light of reason to the divine light he has in any way distorted the thought of the Philosopher. See *Q.D. de spir. creat.* q. un., a. 10 ad 8.

[2] *Q.D. de ver.* 2, 4 ad 5.

As we have seen from our consideration of the theological or theocentric dimension of Thomas's theory of probability, he gives us ample reason to conclude that man cannot overcome opinion and probability independently of God. On the level of secondary causes, to be sure, man makes successful and even prodigious efforts in this direction. But working within him and drawing him on is the First Cause of all causes, the First Truth, the unique Eternal Truth in whom alone the yet unknown does not obtain. Here, then, must man go if he would find definitive respite from the blight of ignorance and error.

The full implications of this epistemic dependence upon the divine Thomas works out in greatest detail in his *Contra Gentiles*. Taking Augustine's theme of the restless heart that cannot rest until it rests in God, Thomas modulates that theme to read rather, "the restless intellect." The question which he raises for consideration is that of man's ultimate happiness. This, he insists, must consist primarily in intellectual fulfillment, since it is the intellect which makes man properly man. But the intellect is fulfilled neither by knowledge of principles nor by science, but only by contemplative wisdom. The question, therefore, becomes: in what kind of contemplation will man be intellectually fulfilled? Obviously, for Thomas, it must be a contemplation of God.[1]

But contemplative happiness is hardly to be found in the ordinary man's knowledge about God.[2] Perhaps, then, it is to be found in scientific demonstrations about God. Decidedly not, answers Thomas; and, of great interest to us, he gives five reasons why demonstrations about God do not suffice for happiness.[3] In the first place, he says, few attain to such knowledge. Secondly, what knowledge is thus attained is always imperfect and subject to improvement. Thirdly, there is almost always some error mixed in with what has been demonstrated; for, even those who have acquired demonstrative truth about God tend to follow their own opinions where demonstration is lacking. Fourthly, the very divergences of opinion about God indicate how uncertain is such knowledge. And, finally, whatever one does know scientifically about God, he still desires to know the yet unknown.

Thomas then shows that knowledge of God by faith is inadequate for fulfillment of the intellect.[4] For, by the very nature of faith, the believer attributes more perfect knowledge to the one believed, in this

---

[1] *C.G.* III, 37.
[2] *C.G.* III, 38.
[3] *C.G.* III, 39.
[4] *C.G.* III, 40.

case, of course, God. Thus, whether the believer is justified or (*per impossibile*) deceived in his estimation of what God knows, in either case faith can hardly be perfect knowledge about God.

Then, after a lengthy analysis of various opinions about whether separate substances can be known in this life, Thomas concludes on the authority of Aristotle that such knowledge is extremely imperfect and, in any event, is attained by very few.[1]

Thus by a process of elimination Thomas arrives at the conclusion that intellectual fulfillment is not possible in this life. For, he says, in addition to failures of virtue to which we are all to some extent subject, there is no one in this life who has not in some way been deceived or, if he is not ignorant of, then at least is capable of no more than opinion about what he would like to know with certainty.[2] Human knowledge, in short, is marked by a tendency towards ever greater perfection.[3] But the intellectual perfection towards which man tends can be attained only in the unending union with God which is the beatific vision.[4]

God, in other words, is the fulfillment of man's desire to know. Being, according to one of Thomas's richest summaries, "the fount and source of all being and truth," God "would so fulfill the natural desire of knowing that nothing else would be sought and one would be blessed."[5] It is, then, in the beatific vision of God that one attains the philosopher's dream of knowing the whole universe and its causes. All other knowledge, however exalted, is by comparison imperfect and needs must be imperfect, since the human intellect of itself is incapable of learning all things. This it can do only by being united somehow to God, the source of all truth.[6]

Indeed, not only must the intellect be united to the source of all truth, but it must know with certainty that it shall remain thus united for all eternity. For, if man is to be truly happy, he must no longer be

---

[1] *C.G.* III, 41–45.

[2] *C.G.* III, 48: "Nullus enim invenitur qui non aliquando inordinatis passionibus inquietetur; qui non aliquando praetereat medium, in quo virtus consistet, vel in plus vel in minus; qui non etiam in aliquibus decipiatur; vel saltem ignoret quae scire desiderat; aut etiam debili opinione concipiat ea de quibus certitudinem habere vellet. Non est igitur aliquis in hac vita felix."

[3] *C.G.* III, 48.

[4] *C.G.* III, 50.

[5] *S.T.* I, 12, 8 ad 4: "Si tamen solus Deus videretur, qui est fons et principium totius esse et veritatis, ita repleret naturale desiderium sciendi, quod nihil aliud quaereretur, et beatus esset."

[6] *Q.D. de ver.* 2, 2 c; 8, 1; *In De Trin.* 6, 4 ad 3 and ad 5; *Q.D. de an.* q. un., a. 5 ad 9; *Comp. theol.* cc. 104–107, nn. 207–215. See also *In* IV *Polit.* l. 10, nn. 625–626; VII, l. 1, n. 1058.

subject to false opinion, which is the evil of the intellect. He must have the opinion that he is happy in the perfect and unending possession of truth, and his opinion must be true and certain.[1] In beatitude, that is to say, there is no room for error, for doubt, or for the chance event to which man is subject in the present life.[2] Beatitude must be a total victory of the intellect, or it will be no victory at all.

Man's knowledge is imperfect. It is a mixture of darkness and light, of prejudice and good judgment, of error and truth. Dependent upon the evidence of his senses, man can of himself learn no more than what is somehow implied in this sense experience. Yet, different from all other animals, he is endowed with reason; and by virtue of his reason he is able to move, however haltingly, towards a broader and deeper understanding of the universe around him and within him. Capable of little as an isolated individual, he nonetheless profits greatly from the cooperative assistance of others. In particular, he has ever at his disposal what has been handed down by his predecessors – either the fruits of their own reflections or the record of divine revelation. The latter remaining the standard of truth for the former, man can then consider the opinions on any subject and evaluate their probability on the basis of arguments which can be presented in their favor. This process of dialectical disputation, which has as its end to make a problem as clearly understood as possible, is a preparation for scientific demonstration. Through demonstration, in turn, what dialectic had shown to be probable is shown to be necessary and thus certain in the light of certain principles. This, of course, is not always possible – indeed, never possible where it is a case of the contingent as such. Nevertheless, there is a certain regularity even in the contingent, and this can be estimated for purposes of theory as well as of practice – at least up to a point. Beyond that point, where lies the chance event, one must trust in the wisdom of divine providence.

As for the conclusions of scientific demonstration, these are more or less certain according to the certainty of the principles involved and the rigor of the reasoning. The latter varies according to human ingenuity and the former, however certain, are ultimately dependent upon the one first truth, which is God. Besides, the universe as it is now, which is the object of human sciences, is of limited duration at best, and thus nothing known about it is eternally true from our point

[1] *S.T.* I–II, 5, 4 c.
[2] *C.G.* I, 102.

of view. Eternal truth must therefore be founded in God. This being the case, the best knowledge for man to have is knowledge about God. To some extent, science can attain to this knowledge, and the conclusions of science might well be quite certain from our point of view. But far outstripping science in its reach towards God is faith, which, after all, depends directly upon the source of all truth and is therefore in itself more certain than science. Even faith, however, like all forms of knowledge possible to man in this life, is limited; though surpassing the firmness of opinion, it lacks the vision of science. The epistemic value of faith, then, is not so much what it is in this life, that is, in comparison to other temporal knowledge, but what it is in respect to the life to come. For, through faith one transcends the limits of the rationally knowable and draws nearer to the source of all truth.

At last, what faith only approaches the beatific vision makes a reality: perfect and unending fulfillment of the intellect. Whatever else heaven may be, it is at least unqualified certainty unlike anything of which man is capable on this earth. To be beyond the vicissitudes of this world, forever one with Truth Eternal! In this way and in this way only will man surmount the vagaries of opinion and the mark of opinion's imperfection, mere probability.

Such, then, is Thomas's total vision of what we have called opinion and probability in human knowledge. It is not, should it be necessary to say it, precisely the vision of all who have taken it upon themselves to interpret the thought of the Angelic Doctor for later generations. But, then, there are few men in this world who would be willing to say of their own intellectual endeavours that all they have written is as straw. This, we contend, Thomas did say – if not in fact, then at length in his writings themselves. He said it, however, not so much because he considered truth unattainable, but because he felt it is ultimately attainable only in Him who is Truth.

The vision of Thomas Aquinas, like that of all of us, was limited. But in and even because of the very limits of that vision there is still much to be learned, by believer and nonbeliever alike. For, there is something of straw about every man's pretensions to learning. Fortunately for all of us, however, straw has been known to burn with incomparable brilliance and splendor. For all his sufferings, the accomplishment of Prometheus has not been in vain.

ON THE HISTORICAL DIMENSION
OF "PROBABILITY"

It is quite generally believed that no meaningful or, better, significant rapprochement is possible between medieval thought and modern thought. For, the usual argument goes, the modern world is to a great extent a world made by man rather than by God – and made by him not only since the close of the Middle Ages but in large measure since the close of the nineteenth century. On this view, in other words, there is between us and the medieval an unbridgeable gap that has been forged among other things by the development of the mathematical and now more recently the logical sciences.

As a result of this historical transformation, it is contended, thought patterns have also been transformed, and to such an extent that they would no longer be understandable to the medieval man. For, in general, our thought is sophisticated whereas that of the medieval was naive. The latter thought in terms of absolutes; we think in terms of approximations. He was fond of uniformity; we pride ourselves on being able to adapt ourselves to pluralism on all levels of life. He looked for simplicity in things; we remain ever conscious of complexity.

In short, we are thus presented with two radically different universes of thought. And, as Badi Kasm has observed, a particular universe of thought is systematically closed in upon itself and hence can only be judged on its own terms.[1] But if this be the case, then it would seem to follow that any supposed rapprochement between medieval and modern thought is at best artificial and at worst misguided.

To put all this somewhat differently, the ghost of Jacob Burckhardt has not yet been laid to rest. Too willing to take some writers of the Renaissance at their word, this nineteenth century historian concluded that all that was good and noble about the "new birth" of intellect was

---

[1] Badi Kasm, *L'Idée de Preuve en Métaphysique*, Paris, 1959.

due to a return to the Greeks.[1] This view, to be sure, has been considerably modified by subsequent research. But to a great extent it remains the accepted conviction of most contemporary philosophers: the Muse of today's philosopher speaks not Latin but Greek – and perhaps even something more ancient than that.

It is interesting to note, therefore, that what some historians of philosophy have tried in vain to show the philosopher, historians of science are making ever more palatable to the interested scientist. The prodigious growth of the history of science in the past fifty years and, in particular, in the past ten years has clarified and qualified but never destroyed Pierre Duhem's thesis of continuity between medieval and Renaissance (or Newtonian) science. The results of research along these lines are well illustrated in the convincing work of John Henry Randall, Jr., entitled, curiously enough, *The Career of Philosophy*.[2]

Now whatever one may think of this gradually developing view of historical continuity between medieval and Renaissance science, he cannot fail to see that even if there be continuity during that period, it has only limited significance. For, it is anything but obvious that there is much important continuity between Newtonian science and the science of today. The revolutionary effect of Einstein's reformulation of celestial mechanics is a case in point. But no less important is the reformulation of terrestrial mechanics on the basis of the calculus of probability.

In briefest terms, it is generally felt that the introduction of "relativity" and "probability" into scientific thought has brought down the Newtonian absolutes and thus in effect cut the last tie between our world and the world of the medieval. In the place of absolutes, whether considered as conceptual or as propositional, man now deals with an "optique" or, if you will, a horizon of thought which is interpreted as a manifestation of his particular spatio-temporal condition. In the shadow of Einstein, all thought is described as being somehow or other "relative." And in the shadow of the quantum physicists, propositions are often viewed not as "true" but only as more or less effective approximations to truth. The absolute, however described, remains at best what Kant would call a transcendental ideal. In short, the new sophistication is upon us, and from it flow such bountiful blessings as freedom of conscience and a growing spirit of ecumenical rapproche-

---

[1] Jacob Burckhardt, *The Civilization of the Renaissance in Italy*, New York, 1921.
[2] The full title of this work, already cited in the first chapter, is *The Career of Philosophy from the Middle Ages to the Enlightenment* (New York and London, 1962).

ment. But at the same time, it is felt, with the denouement of the absolute our last tie with medieval thought has been definitively cut.

The principal purpose of our study has been to question this supposed dichotomy between medieval and modern patterns of thought. This we have done by taking as our focal point the notion of probability, as expressed today and as expressed in the Middle Ages. To limit our task to the humanly possible, we have chosen to compare representative views of the twentieth century with the view of the best known of all medieval thinkers, Thomas Aquinas.

Our method has consisted primarily of studying what is said precisely in the hopes of describing the ideological universe which has made it acceptable to say such things. It is, if you will, two ideological universes which we have tried to describe, our own and that of the medieval. We recognize full well the differences between these two universes, and even more between the kinds of statements possible in each. But at the same time *we claim to have found important similarities between these ideological universes which suggest, in turn, the possibility of an historical continuity with regard to the notion of probability*.

To spell out in detail what has here been suggested, we propose to defend consecutively five major conclusions. Each of these conclusions, we think, can be drawn independently from the study which we have made; but some are more clear cut and obvious than others. Accordingly, we have staggered our conclusions from the most to the least obvious and thus from the most trivial and readily acceptable to the most important and controversial. In this way we hope to use the stronger in order to build support for the weaker. Our conclusions, then, are the following:

I. There is a similarity between the structure of Thomas's thought patterns and modern thought patterns.

II. There is a similarity between Thomas's notion of opinion, or probable knowledge, and modern notions of non-demonstrative knowledge.

III. There is a similarity between Thomas's disputation and the modern calculus of probability.

IV. There is a similarity (A) between Thomas's theory of probability and the contemporary logical theory of probability and (B) between Thomas's theory of contingency and the contemporary frequency theory of probability.

V. There is a relationship between (A) Thomas's distinction between *scientia* and opinion-probability and (B) the modern problem of probability in science.

These, then, being our conclusions, we proceed at once to their elaboration.

I. *There is a similarity between the structure of Thomas's thought patterns and contemporary thought patterns.*

On the surface, at least, our approach to Thomas Aquinas has not differed remarkably from that of many other commentaries on the thought of the medieval master. And, as for these commentaries, we quite readily admit that more often than not they will contain a far more thorough treatment of most of the topics which have entered into our discussion. From a logical point of view, at any rate, the presentation of these topics in scholastic manuals will manifest the results of centuries of reflection upon and development of principles and procedures set forth in the writings of Thomas himself. Precisely because of ideological trends since the time of Aquinas, his thought has undergone a great deal of refinement especially with regard to ontology and epistemology in general and the theory of science and of demonstration in particular. On the whole, no doubt, these developments of Thomas's thought were, at least for their time, all for the good; and, properly understood, they still have a contribution to make to contemporary thought.

It is our opinion, however, that studies of Thomas's thought have in general been overly absolutist in their interpretation of the Angelic Doctor. And, as a result, Thomas has perhaps been systematized far better than he has been understood. It has been our impression, at least, that the rationalistic formulations of many so-called Thomistic manuals make the thought of Thomas himself, when seen at first hand, seem by comparison the cautious estimates of a neophyte before the unknown.

In contrast to the view of Thomas which these manuals usually present, we maintain that (A) the basic distinction of Thomas's theory of knowledge is, broadly, that between creator and creature or, more narrowly, between God and man; and that (B) from this distinction flows the basic distinction of his theory of human knowledge; broadly, that between the certain and the probable or, more strictly, between the scientific and the opinionative, the demonstrated and the probable.

A. *The basic distinction* of Thomas's theory of knowledge, in terms of which all else is to be judged, might *most properly* be described as *that between the absolutely necessary, the creator, and what is by comparison contingent, the creature.* But because of the specific bent of our investigations we prefer to speak of this distinction *somewhat more narrowly* as that *between the divine and the human.*

It is this distinction between the divine and the human which is at the heart of Thomas's division of all man's knowledge into natural (or, more loosely, reasoned) and revealed; and the latter, in turn, forms the basis for his evaluation of the two traditions, that of the saints and that of the philosophers. Still more broadly than this, we have seen that Thomas looks upon all human knowledge as imperfect by comparison to the divine, and for this reason paints a glowing picture of what is known by those who are closer than most to God: angels in general and such men as Adam, the prophets, and above all Christ. For Thomas, accordingly, the whole purpose of human specualtion is to approach as closely as possible in this life to that divine knowledge which is shared to perfection by the blessed in heaven. This orientation towards the divine (not surprising, of course, for a theologian) tends to distract Thomas from a closer investigation of the contingent in favor of a panoramic view of the way things must look to God. And thus Thomas's "frequency" approach to the contingent – not only in cosmology but also in his theory of disputation and of practical deliberation – is best seen within the context of God's providential knowledge of all particulars, past, present, and future. This is in no way intended to negate the value of what Thomas does say about these various human problems. Rather does it underline the element of relativity which permeates all that he says about such problems precisely because he is speaking as a mere man who does not have that clear vision which is the prerogative of God.

We realize full well that by introducing Thomas's theological views about God into a discussion of his theory of probability we satisfy neither the Thomist who likes his philosophy and theology neatly distinguished nor the probabilist who likes his science neatly isolated from "religious" considerations. But the place of probability in Thomas's thought is such that it cannot be adequately presented except within the full context of the divine and the human. For, in Thomas's view, the probable is proper to human, that is to say, to *merely* human knowledge; the range of the probable is reduced by scientific demonstration, and is ultimately transcended in the beatific vision.

At the risk of being criticized for hopelessly confusing areas of thought which are radically different one from another, we maintain that, *mutatis mutandis*, this theological vision of human knowledge is not unlike the vision of many modern scientists who have expressed themselves on the subject. For, whether one talk about God or about a beatific vision or about an ultimate comprehension of the universe, the epistemic goal remains the same, and opinionative knowledge of the probable is man's most familiar means of approaching it. The scientist as such, of course, does not speak about God, nor does the theologian as such speak about degrees of confirmation or relative frequency. But each is in some way aware of a postulated culmination of human reasoning which, however he may care to describe it, gives finality to his intellectual endeavors. Indeed, it is only in the light of this postulated perfection of knowledge that he can speak at all meaningfully about the imperfections of what he already knows. In short, however others may choose to speak about cognitional limitations, Thomas does so within a theocentric context. Accordingly, if one wishes to grasp the full significance of what he is saying, one must be willing to accept him on his own terms (transposing, to be sure, if he is so inclined) – and these terms are theocentric.

B. In view, then, of the absolute superiority of divine knowledge over all merely human knowledge, Thomas maintains that whatever man knows, and in whatever way he knows it, his knowledge is but an imperfect approximation to God's comprehensive vision of all things.

However, within the horizon of the imperfect as such, some of man's knowledge is less imperfect than the rest. For, though man has only probable knowledge about many things, he does have certain knowledge about some things. Thus, without losing sight of God's epistemic superiority, Thomas still maintains a clear distinction *between that part of man's knowledge which is certain and that part of his knowledge which is only probable.*

To be sure, man's certainty may be unfounded, as in the case of heretics. But to the extent that man's certainty is founded in fact, it is due to his having to some extent approached the wisdom of God by determining the cause or causes of something through scientific demonstration. For, God's wisdom is, after all, a knowledge of the causes of things. Thus, again in view of the perfection of divine knowledge, the distinction in human knowledge between the certain and the probable *reduces to that between the scientific and the opinionative, the demonstrated and the probable.* This distinction, in turn, is hypothetically taken to be at least a rough approximation to that between the necessary and the contingent.

Applying metahistorical categories to history, unfortunately, Thomas uses these distinctions to sort out in the world those who have the truth and those who do not. The "extraneous" or "heretical" opinion is recognized from the fact that it is contrary to what is known to be true. Such over-zealous absolutism is, of course, easy to criticize; but the would-be critic could spend his time more profitably by trying to determine what are *his own* metahistorical absolutes. We are reminded, for example, of the case of the American who would dare to call himself a Communist or of the white South African who would dare to call himself an integrationist.

Be that as it may, as a corollary of this interpretation, we further maintain that for Thomas other distinctions between various branches of learning are of quite secondary importance. Even more, inasmuch as his notions of science and of opinion cut across the dividing lines of all human disciplines, he would find it difficult to understand a distinction between "philosophy" and "science" and impossible to understand a distinction between *philosophia* and *scientia*.

II. *There is a similarity between Thomas's notion of opinion, or probable knowledge, and modern notions of non-demonstrative knowledge.*

Having already noted a broad similarity between Thomist and modern thought patterns in general, we now wish to limit our attention to that part of these thought patterns which corresponds to Thomas's notion of opinion, or probable knowledge. This, in turn, restricts our attention to what might be called, in modern terms, the logic of science. Our purpose being once again to point out an important similarity, we take as our point of departure Thomas's notion of *probabilis*.

In Thomas's usage, *probabilis* applies in general to the class of all propositions which are (1) neither demonstratively false (2) nor demonstratively true. The adherence to such a proposition is an opinion, which accordingly is characterized precisely by the fact that it may be either true or false. Thus *the medieval notion of probability is essentially metascientific in that (1) it presupposes criteria of demonstration and (2) it implies with regard to a given proposition that these criteria are not fulfilled.*

In the second place, we find in modern thought, though not under the aegis of "probability," a recognition of the non-demonstrative which, *mutatis mutandis*, is not unlike that implied by Thomas's *probabilis*. To cite just a few examples of what we have in mind, we are reminded of Popper's characterization of science as *"doxa,"* Polanyi's search for "the personal" in science, and Perelman's analyses of argumentation in terms of "the preferable."

In the third place, we note Rudolf Carnap's insistence that one of what he considers the two basic meanings of *probability* which scientists have sought to explicate is that of "degree of confirmation." This sense of *probability*, he maintains, is the proper concern of what he calls "inductive logic." But inductive logic as understood by Carnap is precisely the logic of non-demonstrative reasoning. And thus the modern notion of probability is at least in part linked to the notion of the non-demonstrative.

From the foregoing, then, we see that it is historically unsatisfactory to consider "probability" simply and solely as an interpretation of one particular mathematical system. For, this would leave us with the conclusion that Thomas's view was much broader in that it took into account the whole range of the opinionative or non-demonstrative. And this, in turn, would make inexplicable the many and varied contemporary studies of the non-demonstrative which more often than not make no explicit reference to "probability."

In the light of these considerations, then, we shall attempt to establish a similarity between Thomist and modern logic of science in terms of what we shall call *opinion-probability*. To do this, we shall proceed in three steps. First (A), we shall propose a general definition of the notion of opinion-probability which includes both Thomas's *probabilis* and the *explicandum* of Carnap's *probability*$_1$. Secondly (B), we shall distinguish between the notion of probability and both explanations of it and instruments developed to deal with it. Thirdly (C), we shall use the first two steps as a basis for developing a criterion whereby the notion of opinion-probability can be recognized.

A. *The Notion of Opinion-Probability.* First of all, by "notion of opinion-probability" we shall mean *notion of the non-systematic*. *Notion* is here taken in a general sense broader than that of concept and is meant to imply, without further precision, awareness of or consciousness of. *Non-systematic* is also taken in a broad sense and is meant to imply non-necessary, or non-certain, or non-demonstrated, or even non-scientific in the Thomist sense which is not unrelated to the modern "indeterminate." Being negative, *non-systematic* is meant to imply also *"with respect to a given system."* In general, then, by "notion of opinion-probability" we mean *conscious or reflective awareness of the opinionative.*

B. *Explanations of and Instruments for Opinion-Probability.* Secondly, we wish to distinguish the notion of opinion-probability thus described both from explanations of the fact of opinion-probability and from instruments (conceptual or physical) developed to deal with it. For, it is one thing to recognize the non-systematic, it is another thing to attempt to explain or give the reason for the non-systematic thus recognized, and it is yet another thing to propose or develop an instrument to deal with the non-systematic.

To clarify what we mean here, we begin by recalling that we take "notion of the non-systematic" to imply *with respect to a given system,* S. In other words, the recognition of the non-systematic is essentially a recognition of the limits of S beyond which lies what is non-systematic, or non-demonstrated, with respect to S. And thus the recognition of the non-systematic suggests the need (1) to explain why there is a "non-systematic" with respect to S and (2) to develop some means – call it an instrument – of dealing with what is non-systematic with respect to S.

We deliberately avoid being too precise as to what constitutes a "system"; and, in particular, we avoid specifying whether "system" implies formalized or not, or whether it implies content or not. What is important, and all that is important in this context, is that *only what is "systematic" is considered demonstrated and that, accordingly, the "non-systematic" implies non-demonstrated.* Thus, what one will consider "non-systematic" is a function of what he considers "systematic." For example, if one takes Aristotelian physics as S, then any physical events not explained by that physics will be considered non-systematic *with respect to S.* Similarly, if one takes Newton's mechanics as S, then whatever relevant phenomena are not explained by Newton's system are non-systematic *with respect to S.* Recalling, finally, that systematic here implies demonstrated, we note that one might consider only formal theories in the strict logical sense to be "systematic" (in our sense) and hence anything extra-logical to be non-systematic in the sense of non-demonstrated.

Trusting, then, that we have sufficiently indicated the wide sense in which we take "systematic" and "non-systematic," we now wish to clarify somewhat what we mean by (1) an explanation of the non-systematic and by (2) an instrument for opinion-probability.

B. 1. *Explanation of Opinion-Probability.* An explanation of the non-systematic with respect to S is, in general, a meta-scientific reason for the fact of the non-systematic with respect to S. The reason given might refer to limits of S or to limits of its user or to planetary influences or to the divine will or whatever. What is important is that the reason is not itself a part of S but is a meta-judgment about S.

B. 2. *Instrument for Opinion-Probability.* Now, having recognized the non-systematic, non-S, with respect to a given system S, one might with or without explanation, propose or develop an instrument to deal with non-S. This instrument, physical or conceptual, might in principle be simply S itself but it is more likely to be some analogue or model of S, associated with S by more or less rigorous rules of correspondence, or even some modification of S. What is important here is that *since only S is considered demonstrative, the instrument non-S is not.* Thus, if we must refer to this instrument as being also a system, it is nonetheless, *qua* instrument for the non-systematic, *a non-demonstrative system* as opposed to the demonstrative S.

The distinctions thus made between the notion of, the explanation of, and the instrument for opinion-probability can be illustrated first from the example of Thomas Aquinas and then from the example of some modern writers.

Thomas Aquinas in recognizing the non-systematic sees it precisely as that about which one does not have demonstrative knowledge. That demonstration is not possible in all cases he explains physically in terms of contingency in terrestrial events and theologically in terms of man's lack of divine vision. Seeing that the contingent, unlike the necessary, is that which can be other than it is, he characterizes non-demonstrative knowledge as that which, unlike science, can be other than it is. Having thus pointed to the fact that the non-demonstrative is open to alternatives, he accepts as man's best instrument for dealing with the non-demonstrative a modification of demonstrative argumentation. This modified form of argumentation is dialectical disputation, in which, precisely, the two alternatives of any question are argumentatively opposed and evaluated. Since, finally, the practical order is concerned with the contingent as defined above, Thomas feels free to consider moral deliberation as a kind of disputation with regard to alternative courses of action. Aware, however, that both disputation and deliberation have to do with the non-demonstrative, Thomas notes that these methods arrive at the truth, somewhat like the occurrence of the physically necessary, only most of the time: *ut in pluribus.*

Among the moderns, Karl Popper's notion of *doxa* involves a recognition that the extra-logical is non-systematic; he explains this situation by appealing to the downfall of Newtonian absolutism; and, not unlike Thomas, he proposes the conjecture and refutation of logical theories as an instrument to deal with the non-systematic. Polya points to the non-systematic with respect to mathematics in terms of "plausibility" and, without explanation, elaborates a variety of logical techniques of "plausible reasoning." Perelman recognizes "the preferable," explains the need for recognizing it along the lines of Gonseth's "open philosophy," and proposes to deal with it by developing a theory of argumentation. Polanyi calls attention to the non-systematic with respect to physical science, explains it as being due to factors overlooked by those who exaggerate the ideal of "objectivity," and thus proposes the need to develop a social psychology of "the personal" in science. Others, more imbued with that very ideal of "objectivity," see the non-systematic simply as that which is still beyond the reach of logic and/or mathematics. Thus Borel, for example, urges prudent application of the calculus of probability to personal affairs and Carnap insists upon developing a logic of the non-demonstrative. Servien, finally, in recognizing the non-systematic as the extra-mathematical, proposes to deal with the latter by an elaboration of his distinction between the language of mathematics and the language of literature.

C. *How to Recognize the Notion of Opinion-Probability.* Turning now to our third step, we propose to elaborate a criterion on the basis of which the notion of opinion-probability can be recognized.

In preparation for this task, we note that though an instrument be addressed to "the non-systematic," it is nonetheless constructed according to the best available systematization of the non-systematic. The problem is simply that the non-systematic cannot in principle be *demonstratively* systematized. Whence it happens that an instrument addressed to the non-systematic will in principle encounter what are often referred to as non-systematic divergences. In view, then, of these non-systematic divergences, it is incumbent upon the constructor of the instrument to safeguard the efficacity of the instrument before the non-systematic by providing the instrument as much as possible with systematic means to adapt itself to non-systematic divergences. To do this, he adds to the instrument certain self-correcting devices by means of which non-systematic variations can be more or less effectively neutralized. These self-correcting devices amount to qualifications of the instrument and constitute the manifestation in that instrument of the notion of the non-systematic.

From these observations we now draw three conclusions which are subordinate one to the other. First of all, precisely insofar as the non-systematic is non-systematized, it will involve variables not systematically represented by the instrument addressed to it. Secondly, these unsystematized variables can and in many cases will diminish the effectiveness of the instrument as applied to the non-systematic. Thirdly, the effectiveness of the instrument before the non-systematic is therefore directly proportional to its ability to neutralize the effect of non-systematic variables.

In general, then, awareness of the non-systematic is manifested precisely by the fact of taking precautions against and thus attempting to neutralize the effect of non-systematic variables. This, in turn, reveals the non-demonstrative character of the system serving as an instrument and thus allows us to suggest the following as *a criterion on the basis of which the notion of opinion-probability can be recognized: The notion of opinion-probability is manifested whenever the results (or conclusions) obtained by utilization of an instrument are in some way qualified, thus qualifying indirectly the system on which the instrument is based.*

That this criterion applies to Thomas's notion of opinion-probability has already been suggested, but it will be useful to spell out the suggestion in some detail. Thomas's basic presumption with regard to instruments addressed to the non-systematic is that the non-systematic can be represented disjunctively. Thus he divides contingent events into those which occur *ut in pluribus* and those which occur *ut in paucioribus,* he sets up a disputation according to opposite sides of a question, he portrays deliberation as a consideration of alternative choices. Yet in practice he often satisfies himself that the true opinion, theoretical or practical, is a golden mean between extremes. Because of the complexity of the problems involved, however, he is forced to admit (still, be it noted, within the confines of a dichotomous representation) that these instruments attain the truth only *ut in pluribus.*

That this criterion applies to all modern notions of opinion-probability is, of course, more difficult to establish, since there are so many different formulations. Here, then, we presume no more than to point out that it applies both independently of the calculus of probability and in connection with the calculus of probability.

First of all, on the basis of Carnap's association of the non-demonstrative with "degree of confirmation," we identify as manifestations of opinion-probability Polya's reference to "plausibility" in connection with mathematics, Popper's reference to "doxa" and Polanyi's reference to "the personal" with regard to science, Perelman's reference to "the preferable" with regard to argumentative method, and so on.

Secondly, we find manifestations of opinion-probability in discussions about the calculus of probability. We find it, for example, in Gendre's observations about the practical need to qualify Bernoulli's theorem with Stirling's formula, in Russell's breakdown of non-mathematical meanings of probability and in particular in his reference to *probable* probability with regard to applications of the calculus, in Borel's cautions about the applicability of the calculus to practical life, in Polanyi's insistence that as applied in these areas the calculus is a maxim like other maxims, in Boll's rather irresponsible statements about probability as the law of the universe, in Reichenbach's insistence that all knowledge is probable, and, in general, in the innumerable discussions about the probability of induction.

III. There is a similarity between Thomas's disputation and the modern calculus of probability.

Having already proposed a similarity between Thomist and modern *thought-patterns* in general and between Thomist and modern *notions of opinion-probability* in particular, we now begin to specify similarities involving directly the calculus of probability. And first of all we propose that *the calculus of probability, like medieval disputation, was originally viewed as an instrument to deal with the non-demonstrative.* The elaboration of this proposal will amount to what we shall call *the historical meaning* of "the calculus of probability."

In brief, at first, we take "calculus" to refer to an *instrument* and "probability" to refer explicitly to *the notion of the non-systematic* and implicitly to *a new way of expressing the non-systematic.* To explain what this involves, we shall: (A) extend the notion of the non-systematic so as to make room not only for the qualification of an instrument but also for the replacement of one instrument by another; (B) consider abstractly the ideological universe in which the notion of a "calculus of probability" originated: (C) consider concretely the evidence of this ideological background in Laplace's *Philosophical Essay on Probabilities.*

A. *Replacement of one instrument by another.* We have suggested in the preceding discussion that the notion of the non-systematic tends to generate an explanation as to why there is this non-systematic and this in turn tends to generate an instrument to deal with the non-systematic. We have further noted that the effectiveness of such an instrument is directly proportional to its ability to neutralize the effects of non-systematic divergences. Now we wish to add as a corollary that if the neutralizing capacity of the instrument, however qualified, is minimal with regard to a given problem, the need arises to replace that instrument with another one.

As examples of how this might apply to the contemporary history of ideas, we refer to just three which are rather well known. First of all, we call attention to the fact that repeated failures to establish the Euclidean axioms led eventually to modifications of the axioms which made possible non-Euclidean systems of geometry. Secondly, we note that the inability of classical mechanics to deal effectively with certain problems led to reformulations which we now know as quantum physics. Thirdly, we recall that efforts to provide a perfect formalization of arithmetic uncovered problems which eventually led to recognition both of internal limitations of a formal system and of the need for richer languages. Each of these examples in some way (more or less strictly according to the case) involves what might be called a recognition of incompleteness. And thus on this level of replacement of one instrument by another we are suggesting a connection between the notion of incompleteness and that of the non-demonstrated or non systematic.

In what follows, then, we shall propose that the calculus of probability came to replace medieval dichotomous instruments as a more effective means of dealing with the non-systematic. We shall also observe, however, that this new-born instrument was in its childhood considered precisely as an instrument of the non-systematic rather than as a demonstrative system in its own right.

B. *Ideological Origins of "Calculus of Probability."* Having just recognized the possibility of replacing one instrument by another, we now prepare the way for a kind of meta-history of the calculus of probability by viewing it as a new instrument of the non-systematic parallel with a new system gradually replacing the old on which had been based medieval instruments of the non-systematic.

To begin with, we note that the notion of opinion-probability was much more universally covered by *probabilis* than is the same notion today by *probable*. Today, a variety of other terms (including "personal," "preferable," etc.) substitute in one way or another for the medieval *probabilis*. That this is largely due to expropriation of *probability* by mathematicians is relevant but not directly to the point. The point is rather that said expropriation had not yet taken place at the time when "the calculus of probability" took, as it were, its first baby steps. The world of Cardano, even the world of Pascal and Fermat, and even the world of the Bernoullis and of Laplace was still in some ways more "medieval" than many of us would care to admit. For, Thomas's picture of man's approximation to divine knowledge as well as his distinction between the demonstrative and the probable were still at least implicitly acknowledged. What gradually and sometimes dramatically changed was man's view as to what was in fact "probable" and what was in fact "demonstrative."

This, after all, was the very heart of the controversy over Copernican astronomy. Scholars like Bellarmine opposed Galileo not for favoring the Copernican system but for insisting that it was scientific (that is, demonstrative) rather than merely probable. Without approving of methods adopted to persuade Galileo, we nevertheless are today closer to Bellarmine's view than to that of Galileo – and thus closer to Thomas's evaluation of empirical science than to the post-Newtonian. But absolutism reigned in between. Galileo's word in time became law with the triumph of Newton's *Principia Mathematica Philosophiae Naturalis*. The general blueprint of natural motion had been definitively demonstrated not merely with regard to what happens *ut in pluribus* but with regard to what happens *semper*. The system, in short, was perfect: it was, as had been Aristotle's cosmology before it, the new *scientia* of the macrocosm.

Though perfect, however, the system was not exhaustive. A realm of *ut in pluribus* and *ut in paucioribus* was still being subjected in the schools to the dichotomous instrument of disputation, which was becoming with each passing year more and more a stranger in a new world built by mathematics. Here, then, alongside of *scientia*, was the realm of the non-systematic, the non-demonstrative, the *probabilia*.

There was, then, a clear notion of *probabilis* in the schools. This notion, in turn, presupposed both a notion and a theory of demonstration. On the basis of the notion and theory of demonstration, the notion of the non-demonstrated was closely linked with that of the contingent, that is, that which can be other than it is. Operating on a principle of disjunction, the scholastic successors of Thomas Aquinas divided the contingent into what occurs *ut in pluribus* and what occurs *ut in paucioribus*, attacked the contingent with the dichotomous instrument of disputation, and proposed that one deliberate his practical decisions by consideration of alternative choices. Results obtained by these instruments, in contrast to those of the demonstrative syllogism, had to be qualified. And thus was kept alive the notion of *probabilis*, of the non-systematic.

In the course of time, Cardano and then Pascal and Fermat came to recognize that gambler's rules already in existence might provide a more effective instrument with which to deal with the contingent. These gambler's rules they and then others developed and systematized.

That this more or less systematic instrument of the non-systematic came to be known as a *calculus* is due not only to its character as a mathematical instrument but to imitation and adulation of the great new instrument of the systematic, the calculus of Leibniz and Newton. (For Pascal, still under the influence of Descartes, it was rather a "geometry of chance.")

That this *calculus* of the non-systematic came to be called a calculus of *probability* is due to ingredients of the intellectual milieu which go back deep into the Middle Ages. To uncover in detail how these ingredients were kept before the minds of the first mathematical "probabilists," one might study in detail developments after Thomas with regard to (1) the Aristotelian theory of demonstration; (2) divine providence and foreknowledge in the face of man's free will; and (3) moral systems of resolving practical doubt.

As for the calculus itself, the new instrument thus inaugurated was eventually systematized by Laplace according to standards of his day and by Kolmogorov and others according to standards of our day. But it is important to bear in mind that what is now a demonstrative system in its own right began as *an instrument to deal with the non-systematic on the basis of a new theory about how to express the non-systematic:* not disjunctively but in terms of a continuum of values between what happens always and what never happens.

C. *Historical Meaning of "Calculus of Probability."* We have just proposed that the notion of a "calculus of probability" is in part traceable to medieval ideology, and that the part which is medieval is precisely the "probability." It would require another book to prove that Thomas's usage of *probabilis* remained current throughout the developmental period of the calculus of probability. In lieu of this, we shall here indicate only that the greatest nineteenth century "probabilist," *Pierre Simon, Marquis de Laplace* (1749–1827) not only addressed himself to the notion of opinion-probability but in effect saw his instrument as a replacement for the medieval method of disputation. Our remarks are based on his *Essai philosophique sur les probabilités* (1819), which served as an introduction to the third edition of his great *Théorie analytique des probabilités* (1820).[1] Our purpose is to show that for Laplace (1) probability is a mark of imperfect knowledge; (2) proba-

---

[1] More specifically, we follow the translation into English of the sixth French edition by Frederick Wilson Truscott and Frederick Lincoln Emory entitled, *A Philosophical Essay on Probabilities* (New York, 1951). We have taken the liberty to correct their translation where we find it deficient. This work will be cited as *Philosophical Essay*.

bility is non-demonstrative knowledge; (3) the calculus of probability is an instrument of the non-systematic.

C. 1. *Probability as Mark of Imperfect Knowledge.* Laplace begins his *Philosophical Essay on Probabilities* by noting that "nearly all our knowledge is problematical" and that even "the small number of things which we are able to know with certainty... are based on probabilities."[1] After this humble beginning, which differs little from the (theocentric) attitude of a Thomas Aquinas, he goes on, in spite of his ignorance of medieval thought, to present a view of the cosmos not unlike that of Thomas. The old ideas of "final causes" or "chance," he says, have gradually been replaced by the idea of an orderly universe based upon Leibnitz's principle of sufficient reason.[2]

C. 2. *Probability as Non-Demonstrative Knowledge.* Of many examples in Laplace's work which compare favorably with Thomas's notion of probability, we cite just two.

First of all, speaking with regard to the tides, he notes that Kepler was aware of a tendency of waters towards the moon but "he was able to give on this subject only a probable idea. Newton," Laplace goes on, "converted into certainty the probability of this idea by attaching it to his great principle of universal gravity." [3] Laplace then goes on to say that his own calculations give

a probability that the flow and the ebb of the sea is due to the attraction of the sun and moon, so approaching certainty that it ought to leave room for no reasonable doubt. It changes into certainty when we consider that this attraction is derived from the law of universal gravity manifested by all the celestial phenomena.[4]

Secondly, after observing that it is difficult to evaluate the probability of the results of induction, Laplace goes on to present a basically Thomist (Aristotelian) view of the preparatory character of induction. "Induction," he says,

in leading to the discovery of the general principles of the sciences, does not suffice to establish them absolutely. It is always necessary to confirm them by demonstrations or by decisive experiments.[5]

[1] Laplace, *Philosophical Essay*, p. 1.
[2] Laplace, *Philosophical Essay*, pp. 3–4. This form of determinism, which for the objectivist Popper would amount to a "conspiracy theory" of ignorance, is briefly traced through history and defended by John Maynard Keynes in his *Treatise on Probability*, Part IV; chapters xxiv and xxv: pp. 281–323 (ed. New York, 1962).
[3] Laplace, *Philosophical Essay*, pp. 89–90.
[4] Laplace, *Philosophical Essay*, pp. 92–93.
[5] Laplace, *Philosophical Essay*, pp. 176–177.

C. 3. *An Instrument of the Non-Systematic.* Given then, human fallibility and the resulting need for demonstration, Laplace tends to identify demonstration about the cosmos with Newton's mechanics. What
the latter has not encompassed must be approached by instruments
directed to what is non-systematic with respect to Newtonian mechanics. His own instrument, he finds, is particularly suited for this
purpose. For, he points out,

In the midst of numerous and incalculable modifications which the action of
the causes receives... from strange circumstances these causes conserve always
with the effects observed the proper ratios to make them recognizable and to
verify their existence. Determining these ratios and comparing them with a
great number of observations, if one finds that they constantly satisfy it, the
probability of the causes may increase to the point of equalling that of facts in
regard to which there is no doubt.[1]

Thus, says Laplace,

The analytic formulae of probabilities... may be viewed as the necessary
complement of the sciences... (and) ...are likewise indispensable in solving a
great number of problems in the natural and moral sciences. The regular causes
of phenomena are most frequently either unknown, or too complicated to be
submitted to calculus; again, their action is often disturbed by accidental and
irregular causes; but its impression always remains in the events produced by
all these causes, and it leads to modifications which only a long series of
observations can determine. The analysis of probabilities develops these
modifications; it assigns the probability of their causes and it indicates the
means of continually increasing this probability.[2]

In particular, Laplace notes that the analysis of probabilities has a
very useful application in that it serves to determine "the mean values
which must be chosen among the results of observations."[3] But,
perhaps in keeping with the spirit of the French Revolution, he is most
delighted with the possibilities of his instrument for the moral sciences.
Thus, for example, not unlike Thomas Aquinas's moral statistics,
Laplace rejoices in the utility of his instrument for determining "the
probabilities of testimonies"[4] and "the probability of the judgments
of tribunals."[5]

That Laplace is thereby putting in his own mouth the Thomist
theory of contingency together with its corollary of a postulated
necessity for what happens *ut in pluribus* is, we think, undeniable. Also

---

[1] Laplace, *Philosophical Essay*, p. 89.
[2] Laplace, *Philosophical Essay*, p. 195.
[3] Laplace, *Philosophical Essay*, p. 191.
[4] Laplace, *Philosophical Essay*, pp. 109–125.
[5] Laplace, *Philosophical Essay*, pp. 132–139.

undeniable is the fact that he wishes to apply his instrument to the same kinds of problems to which Thomas's theory of contingency was directed. That he places much more emphasis upon empirical observation than does Aquinas is also clear, and that the instrument which he addresses to these problems is superior to Thomas's bivalent system is not in question.

We need only add that there are clear indications in Laplace that he sees his mathematics as a replacement for medieval disputation. In one place, he cries forth an encomium of Francis Bacon for "insisting, with all the force of reason and eloquence, upon the necessity of abandoning the insignificant subtleties of the school, in order to apply oneself to observations and to experiments" and for "indicating the true method of ascending to the general causes of phenomena." [1] Yet at the same time Laplace admonishes:

Let us enlighten those whom we judge insufficiently instructed; but first let us examine critically our own opinions and weigh with impartiality their respective probabilities.[2]

For Laplace, however, the best method of doing this is by use of "the theory of probabilities." For:

It leaves no arbitrariness in the choice of opinions and sides to be taken; and by its use can always be determined the most advantageous choice. Thereby it supplements most happily the ignorance and the weakness of the human mind.[3]

To conclude this brief look at the ideology behind the "calculus of probability," we recommend most serious reflection upon the motives behind Laplace's name for his mathematics. In a chapter entitled "Concerning the Analytic Methods of the Calculus of Probability," he reviews the contributions of his predecessors, refers to all kinds of mathematical developments since Descartes, especially that of integral and differential calculus, and winds up with the most important historical observation of all:

I have named the ensemble of the preceding methods the *Calculus of Discriminant Functions:* this calculus serves as a basis for the work which I have published under the title of the *Analytical Theory of Probabilities.*[4]

IV. *There is a similarity (A) between Thomas's theory of probability and the modern logical theory of probability and (B) between Thomas's theory of contingency and the modern frequency theory of probability.*

After having explained a similarity between Thomas's notion of

---

[1] Laplace, *Philosophical Essay*, pp. 179–180.
[2] Laplace, *Philosophical Essay*, p. 9.
[3] Laplace, *Philosophical Essay*, p. 196.
[4] Laplace, *Philosophical Essay*, p. 48.

probability and modern notions of non-demonstrative knowledge, we then showed that this notion of opinion-probability is very much in evidence in Laplace's views on probability. We also noted in Laplace, however, a similarity between his ideas about the cosmological basis of probability and Thomas's notion of contingency. For, in the view of Laplace as well as in Thomas's view a proposition about a contingent event is probable to the extent that it occurs with some determinable regularity. Thomas, of course, was content to say of such an event that it occurs (for example) *ut in pluribus*. But, with his mathematical sophistication as a guide, Laplace insisted on establishing with much more precision just what this *ut in pluribus* might be. Like his medieval predecessor, however, he was willing to grant that if an event occurs with sufficient regularity one might attribute exceptions to disturbing factors and thus postulate the existence of a necessary cause of such an event. But his conviction as to the absolutely demonstrative character of Newton's mechanics is such that he does not seem to admit what Thomas would call a demonstration *ut frequenter*.

Now it is of the utmost importance to note that in speaking about the frequencies with which more or less irregular events occur, Laplace refers quite often to their "probabilities." Though he does not seem to be consciously aware of what he is doing, he is in fact giving another sense to "probability" than the sense of opinion-probability which he explicitly discusses along lines not unlike that of Thomas Aquinas. This second sense of "probabilities" as relative frequencies gradually became, as Rudolf Carnap tells us in detail, a second *explicandum* for the interpretation of the calculus of probability.

Thus, while John Maynard Keynes and others continued to view "probability" as a characteristic of a proposition, as had Aquinas, others, including notably Richard von Mises, Hans Reichenbach, and the school of statisticians now represented by Ronald Fisher, have concentrated upon "probability" in the sense of relative frequency. Summing up the development, Carnap identifies "relative frequency in the long run" as *probability$_2$* and identifies "degree of confirmation" as *probability$_1$*. The former constitutes the *explicandum* for the "mathematical" theory of probability, and the latter constitutes the *explicandum* for the "logical" theory of probability.

The differences between these two theories are not inconsiderable. To use the simple summary of Polanyi, the logical theory concentrates upon a *"probable" proposition* about events whereas the mathematical theory concentrates upon a proposition about *"probable" events*. The latter is a manifestation of the great modern ideal of "objectivity" in that it shuns any suggestion of "subjective" or "psychological" adherence. But the logical theory is no less "objective," since it is concerned with logical properties of a proposition and not with what a subject "thinks" or "feels" about that proposition.

In short, much has happened since the time of Laplace. And the most important thing that has happened is the formalization of the calculus of probability. For, as a result of this formalization it is now possible to introduce into a consideration of the calculus of probability several extremely important distinctions which were not clearly recognized at the time of Laplace. What these distinctions are can be summarized as follows. A careful analysis of formal systems has led to rather general agreement that (1) a formal system may be considered without regard to any interpretation, and that (2) a formal system of any importance is open to more than one interpretation. In more precise terms, these two points mean, respectively, that (1) there is an important distinction to make between a formal system and an interpretation of that system, and that (2) there is an equally important distinction to make between interpretation as such and a set of statements which interpret or are taken to interpret a given formal system.

We shall return to these points directly, but it will be useful beforehand to make three contrasting observations about Laplace. In the first place, Laplace seems to have viewed the calculus of probability somewhat naively (though not necessarily erroneously) as a direct representation of certain kinds of events now often referred to as aleatory. Secondly, he was aware of the fact but not of the significance of the fact that the mathematical instrument which he directed to such events was based upon the concepts and methods developed by Newton and others to represent the "systematic." Thirdly, he was implicitly involved in but not explicitly aware of two different interpretations of his instrument: the "logical" (probable propositions) and the "mathematical" (probable events).

Now, then, to show that the contemporary view of formal systems brings considerable clarity into the muddled thinking of a Laplace, we shall use the distinctions made above in order to analyze a particularly relevant statement by Bertrand Russell. The latter, after noting general agreement about the calculus of probability as such and general disagreement about its interpretation, suggests the following as an escape from discord. "In such circumstances," he says, the simplest course is to enumerate the axioms from which the theory can be deduced, and to decide that *any concept which satisfies these axioms has an equal right, from the mathematician's point of view, to be called "probability."* If there are many such concepts, and if we are determined to choose between them, the motives of our choice must lie outside mathematics.[1]

What is to be noted in the first place about Russell's statement is a clear distinction between an uninterpreted (or, as it is sometimes called, abstract) formal system and an interpretation of that system. Considered precisely as uninterpreted, the formal system has no extra-logical meaning. But, according to Russell, it can be given a meaning as it were indirectly by establishing a correspondence between statements in the formal system and statements which are "meaning-ful" or which have *content*. These latter, then, might be called *contensive* statements as opposed to the abstract statements of the formal system.

In the second place, we note that Russell allows for the possibility of more than one "interpretation" of the formal system. Thus, it is advisable to make a clear distinction between interpretation of a formal system and a particular set of contensive statements which "interpret" those in the formal system. For, a particular contensive statement which interprets a formal statement does not exhaust the possible interpretations that might be found for that same formal statement. For the sake of clarity, then, some logicians prefer to speak of an interpreting statement as an *interpretant*. Speaking somewhat loosely, we shall here refer to a set of interpreting statements as an interpretation.

In the third place, we note that Russell speaks about satisfying the axioms of the formal system, and thus in effect demands that the interpretation be *valid*. An interpretation is valid only if each contensive statement corresponding to a theorem of the formal system is true. And this, apparently, is what Russell demands when he says that a given "concept" must satisfy the axioms of the formal system.[2]

---

[1] Bertrand Russell, *Human Knowledge: Its Scope and Limits* (New York, 1962), p. 339 (italics added). The following analysis of Russell's statement is based upon the consistent position of Haskell B. Curry as stated in: *A Theory of Formal Deducibility* (Notre Dame, Ind., 1950), pp. 9–10; *Leçons de Logique Algébrique* (Louvain-Paris, 1952), pp. 26–27; "The Interpretation of Formalized Implication," *Theoria* 25 (1959): 13–16; *Foundations of Mathematical Logic* (New York-Toronto-London, 1963), pp. 48–49, 59–60. Similar though less developed views will be found in Alfred Tarski, *Introduction à la Logique* (Louvain-Paris, 1960), n. 37, pp. 106–115; Morris R. Cohen and Ernest Nagel, *An Introduction to Logic* (New York-Burlingame, 1962), pp. 137–142. The author is particularly indebted at this point to Jean Ladriere and to Madeleine Sergant for assisting him materially in the delicate task of expressing technical definitions with non-technical precision. He alone, however, assumes responsibility for the accuracy of his presentation.

[2] Earlier in the same work, Russell considers the notion of interpretation *ex professo*, and there makes it clear that what he demands of an interpretation is that it be *valid*. "Our formulas," he says, "are not regarded as 'true' or 'false.' but as hypotheses containing varia-

These demands, to be sure, are rigorous enough; but it is well to point out that they might be made even more rigorous. For one thing, the notion of a valid interpretation does not eliminate the possibility of having true contensive statements which, though relatable to a formal statement, do not correspond to a theorem of the formal system. In such a case, the interpretation would still be valid but it would not be *adequate*. This, in turn, suggests the possibility of a stronger formal system which could allow for an adequate interpretation. An interpretation is adequate, then, if each formal statement shown to correspond to a true contensive statement is a theorem of the formal system.

One might further inquire as to whether all possible valid interpretations of a given system are isomorphic. Stating the matter briefly, when a system is based on the first-order predicate calculus, it is possible to build a certain kind of interpretation which is called, in the strict sense of the word, a model. Between models it is possible to define a relation of isomorphism, that is to say, similarity of structure. A system admitting models is then said to be categorical if all its models are isomorphic or, in other words, if it determines its models up to an isomorphism.

That the calculus of probability is not a categorical system can be seen from the many and sometimes heated discussions between proponents of the "logical" and proponents of the "relative frequency" interpretation. Even more, relative frequency has been expressed in terms of both finite and infinite series. And thus is indicated in a general way that the reality in question is still too complex for the formal system (the calculus of probability) which is used in various ways to represent it.

We see, then, that the notion of interpretation is, among other things, a matter of degree. Interpretation as here used always involves a correspondence between statements. But the correspondence in question might be more or less exhaustive and thus, if you will, more or less perfect. To some extent, then, factors extrinsic to logic itself will determine how rigorous a correspondence shall be required. The degree of correspondence which one requires will then determine whether or not a given interpretation is *acceptable*.

bles. A set of values of the variables which makes the hypotheses true is an 'interpretation'"
... The axioms consist partly of terms having a known definition, partly of terms which, in any interpretation, will remain variables, and partly of terms which, though as yet undefined, are intended to acquire definitions when the axioms are 'interpreted.' The process of interpretation consists in finding a constant signification for this class of terms." *Human Knowledge*, p. 343.

We may, however, leave the delicate problem of the standards for an acceptable interpretation of the calculus of probability to people such as the quantum physicists, for whom it is of more immediate importance. For, our concern for the moment is elsewhere.

What we want to draw out of the preceding considerations is the fact that an interpretation of a formal system does not of itself establish a "meaning" for the formal system. All it really establishes is a more or less perfect *logical correspondence* between contensive statements and the abstract statements of the formal system. And thus, we think, Russell is saying perhaps even more than he intends to say when he notes that "the motives of our choice must lie outside mathematics." The point at issue, then, is simply this: if a formal system has no extralogical meaning, then an interpretant of an abstract statement in that formal system, *considered precisely as an interpretant*, has no meaning either. For, interpretation determines correspondence and not meaning. And thus, if a statement that is (or that is taken to be) an interpretant of an abstract statement has contensive meaning, this meaning is quite independent of the logical correspondence that is called interpretation.

Therefore, since the extra-logical meaning of the formal system entitled "the calculus of probability" comes neither from the formal system itself nor from its interpretation, the extra-logical meaning must come from some third source. What, then, is this source of the extra-logical meaning of the formal system entitled "the calculus of probability?"

The third source, we propose, is what we have called the historical meaning which is packed into the (extra-logical) name of the formal system called "the calculus of probability": namely, *the cultural tradition which has been associated with this instrument of the non-systematic from its origins.*

As a sign of this cultural source of meaning, we point to an inconsistency in Russell's otherwise excellent analysis of "probability" as an interpretation of the formal system. According to Russell, we recall, whatever satisfies the axioms of the formal system can be called "probability." *But why, we should like to know, is it called "probability" if the system interpreted has in principle no meaning?* For all his logical clarity, Russell is caught in a vicious circle, from which, we think, the only escape is along the lines of Pius Servien's insistence that the formal system as such might just as well be called a Calculus of Sensations or, for that matter, "gindlegob." For, the name given to the formal system is *not* a part of the system but is rather a summary of the historical meaning given to that system in its developmental stages.

More specifically, while it is in principle true that any number of interpretations can be found for the calculus of probability, in actual fact only two important interpretations have been found:

(1) *the "logical" interpretation:* probability (degree of confirmation) of a proposition;

(2) *the "mathematical" interpretation:* probability (relative frequency) of a class of events.

It is possible to maintain, no doubt, that it is purely by chance that these two interpretations rather than others have been found for the calculus of probability. But the fact that the respective notions basic to these two interpretations are already present (one explicitly, the other implicitly) in Laplace's thoughts on the subject makes chance an unlikely explanation. Chance becomes even more unlikely when we realize that Laplace's two usages of *probability* correspond to Thomas Aquinas's usages of:

(1) *probabilis:* argumentatively supported (proposition);

(2) *contingens:* what happens (an event) either *ut in pluribus* or *ut in paucioribus.*

This being said, we consider our point as having been made. For, though it is perfectly obvious that neither of these notions served as the *explicandum* for an interpretation of a formal system during the Middle Ages, nevertheless the notions themselves, however refined they may have become, are essentially the *explicanda* of interpretations subsequently "found" for the calculus of probability.

V. *There is a relationship between Thomas's distinction between* scientia *and opinion-probability and the modern problem of probability in science.*

We have pointed out first in the abstract and then by a concrete consideration of Laplace that it was to a notion like Thomas's of opinion-probability that early probabilists directed their new instrument for the non-systematic. This new instrument, in turn, was felt to be concerned precisely with what was non-systematic with respect to the Newtonian system of celestial mechanics. The latter, in other words, was viewed as replacing medieval *scientia* and the former was viewed as replacing medieval disputation as a means of determining and increasing the probability of the opinionative. Moreover, since this new instrument was concerned primarily with physical events which fell short of the regularity requisite for *scientia*, its use in this regard gradually gave to "probability" a second meaning which embraced the *ut in pluribus* and *ut in paucioribus* whereby Aquinas characterized the *contingens*.

These points having been made, we are now in a position to bring out the full significance of our insistence that the calculus of probability was originated and developed *as an instrument to deal with the non-systematic*. In other words, we now want to make relevant to contemporary thought the fact that the calculus of probability was viewed during its formative years as a replacement for medieval disputation, that is to say, as the new preparation for or auxiliary to *scientia*.

In briefest terms, what is of the utmost importance about the present role of the calculus of probability is precisely the fact that it is no longer viewed as a preparation for or auxiliary to *scientia*. On the one hand, the *scientia* that was the Newtonian celestial mechanics has given way to Einstein's theory of relativity, and in the process man has lost his confidence in the absolutivity of *scientia*. On the other hand, and almost simultaneously, that which had been viewed as the propadeutic to *scientia* has suddenly found itself as the systematic representation of a large and important sector of *scientia* itself. And thus the new quantum physics has come to represent, from an historical point of view, a kind of wedding between *opinio* and *scientia*.

The resulting ideological crisis as to the meaning of this strangest of all weddings is still unresolved and will no doubt remain so for a long time to come. But it can already be observed that the crisis itself is due at least in part to an inadequate historical perspective and also in part to an exaggerated dichotomy between subject and object.

According to the traditional view – the view of Laplace as well as of Keynes – the imperfect, the merely "probable" was, qua imperfect, attributable to limitations on the part of the *subject*. The perfect, the "scientific," by contrast, achieved full *objectivity* or, so to speak, met the world on its own terms.

In the wake of quantum physics, this traditional view – essentially the same as that of Thomas Aquinas – was supposedly overturned. For, what had been for centuries two neatly distinct types of knowledge now seemed to be inextricably intermingled. The heretofore subjective "probable" was now projected upon the objective "scientific." Probability, science and objectivity were now thought to be all of one piece. And thus one could no longer say with Keynes and his forebears that the universe was determinate and that probability referred to gaps in our knowledge of that universe. One now had to say, rather, that the universe itself is indeterminate and that probability is simply an expression of that indeterminacy, without any reference to the (non-scientific) subject.

However, in spite of great dedication to the cause of objectivity, "the probable" has still not been successfully abstracted from "the subjective." Reichenbach, for example, still likes to insist that all knowledge is probable, and Popper tells us that it is *doxa* or verisimilitude. Thus, neither object nor subject qualifies any longer as the locus of certitude. This, for many, has withdrawn into a realm which presumably transcends the dichotomy of subject and object: the realm, namely, of logic as such. Certitude, if such there be, is to be found today only in the formal system.

This reaction to the calculus of probability, though unprecedented in its complexity, is nonetheless a familiar by-product of the introduction of a new mathematical instrument into man's efforts to harness the universe. The Pythagoreans and the Greeks in general, fascinated by the new geometry, saw geometrical design everywhere, and for this were eventually taken to task by Sextus Empiricus. The medieval followers of Ptolemy saw spheres and even epicycles in the heavens, and by way of reaction Kepler saw more heavenly harmony than was there. The founding fathers of the calculus tended to see "integrals" and "differentials" in the universe until Bishop Berkeley took time off from tar water to point out to them their inconsistencies.

Whatever the value of "the calculus of probability" as an instrument for nuclear research, this much at least seems clear. The universe is no more "determinate" or "indeterminate" today than it was a hundred years ago. Whether or not one considers the present formulation of quantum physics to favor one view over the other perhaps has something to do with the mathematics in question, but it has far more to do with one's views about the extent to which mathematics does more than merely measure. These views, in turn, are not derived from the formal system that persists in being called "the calculus of probability" but from a host of other factors which, *pace* positivists, can well be described as meta-physical.

In short, discussions about the calculus of probability and its applications have in one way or another been operating under the assumption that there has been in effect a wedding between *scientia* and *opinio*. And this assumption, which only now is beginning to be attacked at its roots, presupposes an ideology which goes back through Thomas Aquinas to the beginnings of Western thought.

This being said, we may consider as accomplished our task of pointing out the relevancy of medieval thought to post-medieval theories of probability. We have, to be sure, spoken as an interested layman about a subject that is not ours by profession. Since, therefore, we have surely failed in detail, we trust that we have not failed in perspective. For, we have been encouraged in our study by these century-old words of John Venn:

No science can safely be abandoned entirely to its own devotees. Its details of course can only be studied by those who make it their special occupation, but its general principles are sure to be cramped if it is not exposed occasionally to the free criticism of those whose main culture has been of a more general character.[1]

---

[1] John Venn, *The Logic of Chance*, 1st ed. (London, 1866), Preface. Quoted by J. P. Day, *Inductive Probability* (New York, 1961), p. x.

SELECTED BIBLIOGRAPHY

I. PRINCIPAL WORKS OF THOMAS AQUINAS

I. 1. *Marietti Editions* (whose arrangement and numerical divisions of the texts we have utilized for all the following works with the single exception of "Questions 5 and 6" of *In de Trinitate*, which is based on Wyser's critical edition, I. 2):

In Aristotelis Libros Peri Hermeneias et Posteriorum Analyticorum Expositio. Rome and Turin, 1955. Cited respectively as *In Peri Herm.* and *In Post. Analyt.*

In VIII Libros Physicorum Aristotelis Expositio. Rome and Turin, 1954. Cited as *In Phys.*

In Aristotelis Libros De Caelo et Mundo, De Generatione et Corruptione, Meteologicorum Expositio. Rome and Turin, 1952. Cited respectively as *In De Caelo, In De Generat.*, and *In Meteor.*

In Aristotelis Librum De Anima Commentarium, editio quarta. Rome and Turin, 1959. Cited as *In De An.*

In Aristotelis Libros De Sensu et Sensatu, De Memoria et Reminiscentia Commentarium, editio tertia ex integro retracta. Rome and Turin, 1949. Cited respectively as *In De Sensu* and *In De Mem.*

In XII Libros Metaphysicorum Aristotelis Expositio, tertia editio stereotypa attente recognita. Turin, 1935.

In X Libros Ethicorum Aristotelis ad Nichomachum Expositio, editio tertia. Rome and Turin, 1964. Cited as *In Ethic.*

In Libros Politicorum Aristotelis Expositio. Rome and Turin, 1951. Cited as *In Polit.*

In Librum de Causis Expositio. Rome and Turin, 1955. Cited as *In De causis.*

In Librum Beati Dionysii De Divinis Nominibus Expositio. Rome and Turin, 1950. Cited as *In De div. nom.*

Opusculum De Ente et Essentia, editio tertia diligentissime recognitum. Rome, 1957. Cited as *De ente.*

Opuscula Theologica, 2 vols. (Rome and Turin, 1954), including *inter alia:*
Compendium Theologiae ad Fratrem Reginaldum. Cited as *Comp. theol.*
Contra Errores Graecorum ad Urbanum IV Pontificem Maximum. Cited as *Contra Errores Graecorum.*
Contra Impugnantes Dei Cultum et Religionem. Cited as *Contra Impugn.*
Contra Pestiferam Doctrinam retrahentium homines a religionis ingressu. Cited as *Contra Retrah.*

De Articulis Fidei et Ecclesiae Sacramentis ad Archiepiscoporum Panormitanum Cited as *De art. fidei.*

De Judiciis Astrorum ad Fratrem Reginaldum socium suum carissimum. Cited as *De Judiciis Astrorum.*

De Rationibus Fidei contra Saracenos, Graecos et Armenos ad Cantorem Antiochenum. Cited as *De rat. fidei.*

De Sortibus ad Dominum Jacobum de Burgo. Cited as *De Sortibus.*

In Librum Boetii de Hebdomadibus Expositio. Cited as *In De hebdom.*

In Librum Boetii de Trinitate Expositio. Cited as *In De Trin.*

In Symbolum Apostolorum scilicet "Credo in Deum" Expositio. Cited as *In Symb.*

Responsio ad Fr. Joannem Vercellensem Generalem Magistrum Ordinis Praedicatorum de Articulis XLII. Cited as *Resp. de Art. XLII.*

Responsio ad Joannem Vercellensem Generalem Magistrum Ordinis Praedicatorum de Articulis CVIII sumptis ex opere Petri de Tarantasia. Cited as *Resp. de Art. CVIII.*

Responsio ad Lectorem Bisuntinum de Articulis VI. Cited as *Resp. de Art. VI.*

Responsio ad Lectorem Venetum de Articulis XXX; Epistola prior ad lectorem venetum seu textus A. Cited as *Resp. de Art. XXX.*

Responsio ad Lectorem Venetum de Articulis XXXVI; Epistola altera ad lectorum venetum seu textus B. Cited as *Resp. de Art. XXXVI.*

Quaestiones Disputatae, editio nona revisa, 2 vols. (Rome and Turin, 1953), including *inter alia:*

Quaestio Disputata de Anima. Cited as *Q. D. de an.*

Quaestio Disputata de Caritate. Cited as *Q. D. de carit.*

Quaestio Disputata de Spiritualibus Creaturibus. Cited as *Q. D. de spir. creat.*

Questio Disputata de Virtutibus Cardinalibus. Cited as *Q. D. de virt. card.*

Quaestio Disputata de Virtutibus in Communi. Cited as *Q. D. de virt. in comm.*

Quaestiones Disputatae de Malo. Cited as *Q. D. de malo.*

Questiones Disputatae de Potentia (Dei). Cited as *Q. D. de pot.*

Quaestiones Disputatae de Veritate (Fidei). Cited as *Q. D. de ver.*

Quaestiones Quodlibetales, editio nona. Rome and Turin, 1956. Cited as *Quodl.*

Summa Contra Gentiles. Rome and Turin. 1934. Cited as *C. G.*

Summa Theologiae, 3 vols. Rome and Turin, 1948–1950. Cited as *S. T.* followed, according to the case, by I (Prima Pars), I–II (Prima Secundae), II–II (Secunda Secundae), III (Tertia Pars).

I.2. *Other Editions*

In Librum Boethii de Trinitate Questiones Quinta et Sexta, edited by P. Wyser. Louvain and Fribourg: Nauwelaerts and Société Philosophique, 1948. Cited as *In de Trin.* 5 or 6.

Scriptum Super Libros Sententiarum Magistri Petri Lombardi, 4 vols., edited by R. P. Mandonnet and M. F. Moos. Paris: Lethielleux, 1939–1947. Cited as *In Sent.*

"S. Thomae Aquinatis 'De modalibus' opusculum et doctrina," by I. M. Bochenski, in *Angelicum* 17 (1940), fasc. 2–3, pp. 180–218. (The authenticity of this work is not universally admitted.)

I.3. *English Translations*

Aristotle, On Interpretation; Commentary by St. Thomas Aquinas and Cajetan; a translation of the *In Aristotelis Liber Peri Hermeneias* with introduction by J. T. Oesterle. Milwaukee, Wis.: Marquette University Press, 1962.

Commentary on Aristotle's Physics; a translation of the *In VIII Libros Phy-*

sicorum Aristotelis Expositio by R. J. Blackwell and others with introduction by V. J. Bourke. London: Routledge & Kegan Paul, 1963.

Commentary on the Metaphysics of Aristotle, 2 vols.; a translation of the *In XII Libros Metaphysicorum Aristotelis Expositio* by J. P. Rowan. Chicago: Regnery, 1961.

On Being and Essence; a translation of the *Opusculum De Ente et Essentia* by A. Maurer. Toronto: Pontifical Institute of Mediaeval Studies, 1949.

On the Power of God; a translation of the *Quaestiones Disputatae de Potentia* (Dei) by English Dominican Fathers. Westminster, Md.: Newman Press, 1952.

On the Truth of the Catholic Faith, 5 vols.; a translation of the *Summa Contra Gentiles* by A. C. Pegis (L. I), J. Anderson (L. II), V. J. Bourke (L. III) and C. S. O'Neill (L. IV). Garden City, N.Y.: Hanover House, 1954–1956.

Summa Theologiae; Latin text and English translation, introduction, notes, appendices and glossaries (general editors: T. Gilby and P. K. Meagher). Vol. I (T. Gilby), Vol. 2 (T. McDermott), Vol. 3 (H. McCabe), Vol. 4 (T. Gornall), Vol. 13 (E. Hill), Vol. 22 (A. Kemy). London: Eyre & Spottiswoode, 1964 –.

The Compendium of Theology; a translation of *Compendium Theologiae* by C. Vollert. St. Louis, Mo.: B. Herder, 1947.

The Division and Methods of the Sciences, 3rd revised edition; a translation of Questions V and VI of the *In Librum Boetii de Trinitate Expositio* by A. Maurer. Toronto: Pontifical Institute of Mediaeval Studies, 1963

Treatise on Separate Substances; a Latin-English edition of a newly-established text based on 12 medieval MSS of the *Quaestio Disputata de Spiritualibus Creaturibus*, with introduction and notes, by F. J. Lescoe, West Hartford, Conn.: St. Joseph College, 1960.

Truth, 3 vols.; a translation of the *Quaestiones Disputatae de Veritate* (Fidei) by R. W. Mulligan (Vol. 1), R. W. Schmidt (Vol. 2), and J. V. McGlynn (Vol. 3). Chicago: Regnery, 1952–1954.

I.4. *Structure, Lexicology and Chronology of the Works*

Deferrari, R. J., and others. *A Lexicon of St. Thomas Aquinas*. Washington, D.C.: Catholic University of America Press, 1948.

Editio Leonina S. Thomae Aquinatis Operum, Tome XVI.

Eschmann, I. T. "A Catalogue of St. Thomas's Works: Bibliographical Notes," in E. Gilson's *The Christian Philosophy of St. Thomas Aquinas* (New York: Random House, 1961), pp. 381–437.

Indices in Summa Theologiae et in Summa Contra Gentiles S. Thomae Aquinatis, extractum ex Tomo XVI editionis Leoninae. Rome: Marietti, undated.

Paris, G. M. *Divisio schematica Summa Theologiae S. Thomae Aquinatis ac ad Tertiam Partem Supplementi ad usum professorum atque studentium*. Turin: Marietti, 1931.

Schütz, L. *Thomas-Lexikon: Sammlung, Übersetzung und Erklärung der in sämtlichen Werken des h. Thomas von Aquin vorkommenden Kunstausdrücke und wissenschaftlichen Aussprüche*. New York: Ungar, 1957.

Walz, A. *Saint Thomas d'Aquin*, translated into French and corrected by P. Novarina. Philosophes medievaux, t. V. Louvain and Paris: Nauwelaerts and Beatrice-Nauwelaerts, 1962.

II. SOME WORKS RELEVANT TO THOMAS'S THEORY OF PROBABILITY

Abelson, P. *The Seven Liberal Arts: A Study in Medieval Culture.* New York, Columbia University Press, 1906.

Adler, M. J. *Saint Thomas and the Gentiles.* Milwaukee: Marquette University Press, 1938.

Anderson, J. P. "Was St. Thomas a Philosopher?" *The New Scholasticism* 38 (1964): 435–444.

Arenzano, I. d'. *Necessità e contingenza nell' essere e nell' agire della natura secondo San Tommaso.* Piacenza: Fac. Philos. P.U.G., 1961.

Aristotle. *The Works of Aristotle Translated into English,* 11 vols. Edited by W. D. Ross and others. Oxford: Clarendon Press, 1908–52.

Aristote et Saint Thomas d'Aquin: Journées d'études internationales. Paris and Louvain: E. Nauwelaerts, 1957.

Becker-Freysing, A. *Die Vorgeschichte des Philosophischen Terminus "contingens"; Die Bedeutungen von "contingere" bei Boethius und ihr Verhältnis zu den Aristotelischen Möglichkeitsbegriffen.* Heidelberg: Bilabel, 1938

Bennett, O. *The Nature of Demonstrative Proof according to the Principles of Aristotle and St. Thomas Aquinas.* Washington: Catholic University of America Press, 1943.

Bittremieux, J. "Ideae Divinae de possibilibus." *Ephemerides Theologicae Lovanienses* 3 (1926): 57–62.

Blanche, F. A. "Le vocabulaire de l'argumentation et la structure de l'article dans les ouvrages de S. Thomas." *Revue des Sciences Philosophiques et Théologiques* 14 (1925): 167–187.

Blic, J. de. "Probabilisme," in *Dictionnaire Apologétique de la Foi Catholique,* Tome 4, cols. 302–340.

Bochenski, I. M. *A History of Formal Logic.* Notre Dame: University of Notre Dame Press, 1961.

Boehner, P. *Medieval Logic; An Outline of its Development from 1250 to c. 1400.* Chicago and Manchester: University of Chicago Press and Manchester University Press, 1952.

Bonnefoy, J.-F. *La Theologie comme Science et l'Explication de la Foi selon saint Thomas d'Aquin.* Paris and Bruges: J. Vrin and Ch. Beyaert, 1939.

Brown, P. "St. Thomas's Doctrine of Necessary Being." *The Philosophical Review* 73 (1964): 76–90.

Bruckman, W. D. "The Natural and Supernatural End of the Intellect." *The New Scholasticism* 5 (1931): 219–233.

Brunet, A.-M. "Science et Certitude selon Aristote." *Philosophie* (Ottawa) 1 (1936): 67–77.

Byrne, E. F. *The Thomistic Metaphysics of Unity and Multiplicity and Its Role as a Foundation for the Doctrine of Distinction.* Unpublished Master's Thesis, Loyola University. Chicago, 1956.

Callahan, J. *Four Views of Time in Ancient Philosophy* Cambridge, Mass.: Harvard University Press, 1948.

Campanini, G. "Legge e ragione pratica nel pensiero tomistico." *Rivista internazionale di Filosofia del Diritto* 39 (1962): 447–461.

Carro, V. "La distinción del orden natural y sobranatural según Santo Tomás y su transcendencia en la teología y en el derecho." *La Ciencia Tomista* 26 (1942): 274–306.

Cathala, M.-R. "Du Probable et de l'Opinion." *Revue Thomiste* n.s. 6 (1923): 102–112.

Chenu, M.-D. "Les 'philosophes' dans la philosophie chrétienne médiévale." *Revue des Sciences Philosophiques et Théologiques* 26 (1937): 27–40.

— "Le plan de la Somme." *Revue Thomiste* 43 (1939): 93–107.

— *Introduction à l'Etude de saint Thomas d'Aquin*, 2nd ed. Paris: Librairie Philosophique, J. Vrin, 1954.

— *La Théologie comme Science au XIIIe Siècle*, 3rd ed. Paris: Librairie Philosophique, J. Vrin, 1957.

Choisnard, P. *Les Précurseurs de l'Astrologie scientifique et la Tradition: Ptolémée, S. Thomas d'Aquin et Kepler*. Paris, 1929.

Chroust, A.-H. "Some Reflections on the Origin of the Term 'Philosopher.'" *The New Scholasticism* 38 (1964): 423–434.

Cioffari, V. *Fortune and Fate from Democritus to St. Thomas Aquinas*. New York: Columbia University Press, 1935.

— *The Conception of Fortune and Fate in the Works of Dante*. London: Oxford University Press, 1941.

— *Fortune in Dante's Fourteenth Century Commentators*. Cambridge, Mass: Harvard University Press, 1944.

Clagett, M. *The Science of Mechanics in the Middle Ages*. Madison: University of Wisconsin Press, 1960.

Clark, G. H. "Spontaneity and Monstrosity in Aristotle." *The New Scholasticism* 8 (1934): 31–45.

Collins, J. D. *The Thomistic Philosophy of the Angels*. Washington: Catholic University of America Press, 1946.

Congar, Y. "Théologie," in *Dictionnaire de Théologie Catholique* Tome 15, cols. 342–502.

— *La Foi et la Théologie*. Tournai: Desclée, 1962.

Conley, K. *A Theology of Wisdom; A Study in St. Thomas*. Dubuque: Priory Press, 1963.

Conway, P., and G. Q. Friel. "Farewell, Philosophy." *The New Scholasticism* 24 (1950): 363–397.

Copleston, F. *A History of Philosophy*, vol. II: *Medieval Philosophy: Augustine to Scotus*. Westminster, Md.: Newman Press, 1952.

Crombie, A. C. *Robert Grosseteste and the Origins of Experimental Science, 1100–1700*. Oxford: Clarendon Press, 1953.

— *Augustine to Galileo: The History of Science A.D. 400–1650*, 2nd ed. Cambridge Mass.: Harvard University Press, 1959.

Crowe, M. B. "St. Thomas against the Gentiles." *Irish Theological Quarterly* 29 (1962): 93–120.

Cunningham, F. A. "*Certitudo* in Saint Thomas Aquinas." *The Modern Schoolman* 30 (1953): 297–324.

David, F. N. *Games, Gods and Gambling: The Origins and History of Probability and Statistical Ideas from the Earliest Times to the Newtonian Era*. New York and London: Hafner and Griffin, 1962.

De Ghellinck, J. *Le Mouvement théologique au XIIe Siècle*, 2nd ed. Paris, 1948.

Deman, T. "Sur l'organisation du savoir moral." *Revue des Sciences Philosophiques et Théologiques* 23 (1934): 258–280.

— "Probabilisme," in *Dictionnaire de Théologie Catholique*, Tome 13, part i, cols. 417–619.

De Voght, K. "De natuurlijke levenswet en het scheppen van zedelijke normen in de moraal van St. Thomas." *Bijdragen* 23 (1962): 302–311.

Dockx, S. "Du désir naturel de voir l'essence divine selon saint Thomas d'Aquin." *Archives de Philosophie* 27 (1964): 49–96.

Dougherty, K. *The Subject, Object and Method of the Philosophy of Nature according to Thomas Aquinas.* Unpublished doctoral dissertation, Catholic University of America. Washington, 1951.

Dozois, C. "Sources patristiques chez saint Thomas d'Aquin." *Revue de l'Université d'Ottawa* 33 (1963): 28*–40*.

Dreyer, J. L. E. "Medieval Cosmology." *Theories of the Universe* (ed. M. K. Munitz; New York: Free Press of Glencoe, 1957), pp. 115–138.

Duhem, P. *Le Système du Monde; Histoire des doctrines cosmologiques de Platon à Copernic,* 10 vols. Paris: A. Hermann et Fils, 1954–1959.

Duroux, B. *La Psychologie de la Foi chez saint Thomas d'Aquin.* Tournai: Desclée, 1963.

Eslick, L. J. "The Thomistic Doctrine of the Unity of Creation." *The New Scholasticism* 13 (1939): 49–70.

Espositio, M. "Sur quelques écrits concernant les hérésies et les hérétiques aux XIIe et XIIIe siècles." *Revue d'Histoire Ecclésiastique* 36 (1940): 143–162.

Fabro, C. "La nozione tomista di contingenza." *Rivista di Filosofia Neo-scolastica* 30 (1938): 132–149.

Ferland, J. "La méthode de S. Thomas d'Aquin." *Le Canada français* 18 (1931): 361–379, 478–489.

Freundlieb, M. "Zur Entstehung des Terminus 'contingens'." *Philosophisches Jahrbuch* 47 (1934): 432–440.

Gardeil, A. "La certitude probable." *Revue des Sciences Philosophiques et Théologiques* 5 (1911): 237–266, 441–485.

Garrigou-Lagrange, R. "La prudence: sa place dans l'organisme des vertus." *Revue Thomiste* n.s. 9 (1926): 411–426.

— "Hasard ou finalité? Sens commun et philosophie." *Revue Thomiste* n.d. 14 (1931): 662–680.

Gevaert, J. *Contingent en Noodzakelijk Bestaan in de Wijsbegeerte van de H. Thomas van Aquino.* Unpublished memoir for the licentiate, Institut Supérieur de Philosophie. Louvain, 1956.

Gilbert, N. W. *Renaissance Concepts of Method.* New York: Columbia University Press, 1960.

Gilleman, G. *The Primacy of Charity in Moral Theology.* Westminster, Md.: Newman Press, 1961.

Gilson, E. *Reason and Revelation in the Middle Ages.* New York: C. Scribner's Sons, 1938.

— *History of Christian Philosophy in the Middle Ages.* New York: Random House, 1955.

— *The Christian Philosophy of St. Thomas Aquinas.* New York; Random House, 1956.

— *The Elements of Christian Philosophy.* New York: New American Library (Mentor-Omega), 1963.

— "Sur la problématique thomiste de la vision béatifique." *Archives d'Histoire Doctrinale et Littéraire du Moyen Age* 31 (1964): 67–88.

Giuliani, A. "L'Elément 'Juridique' dans la logique médiévale." *Logique et Analyse* n.s. 21–24 (1963): 540–570.

Glorieux, P. *Répertoire des Maîtres en Théologie de Paris au XIIIe Siècle,* 2 vols. Paris: J. Vrin. (Etudes de phil. méd.), 1933–34.

Glutz, M. A. *The Manner of Demonstrating in Natural Philosophy.* River Forest, Ill.: Dominican House of Studies, 1956.

Godin, G. *L'Admiration, Principe de Recherche philosophique d'après saint Thomas d'Aquin.* Paris, 1960.

Gorce, M.-M. "Le jugement pratique." *Revue des Sciences Philosophiques et Théologiques* 17 (1928): 5–37.

— "La méthode historique du Maître de la Théologie." *Revue Thomiste* 18 (1935): 557–567.

Grabmann, M. "Le fondement divin de la vérité d'après S. Augustin et S. Thomas." *Revue de Philosophie* 35 (1928): 517–529; 36 (1929): 7–30, 125–155.

— "Der Wissenschaftsbegriff des hl. Thomas von Aquin und das Verhältnis von Glaube und Theologie zur Philosophie und weltlichen Wissenschaft," *Publikation der Görres-Gesellsch. zur Pflege der Wissenschaft* (Bonn, 1934), pp. 7–44.

— "De theologia ut scientia argumentativa secundum S. Albertum Magnum et S. Thomam Aquinatem." *Angelicum* 14 (1937): 39–60.

— "Scientific Cognition of Truth: Its Characteristic Genius in the Doctrine of St. Thomas Aquinas." *The New Scholasticism* 13 (1939): 1–30.

Grabowski, S. J. *The All-Present God; A Study in St. Augustine.* St. Louis, Mo.: B. Herder, 1954.

Granger, G.-G. *La Raison.* Paris: Presses Universitaires de France, 1958.

Groblicki, J. *De Scientia Dei futurorum contingentium secundum S. Thomam ejusque sequaces.* Cracow: Universitas, 1938.

Guitton, J. *Le Temps et l'Eternité chez Plotin et saint Augustin.* Paris: Boivon, 1933.

Hart, C. A. *The Thomistic Concept of Mental Faculty.* Washington: Catholic University of America Press, 1930.

Healey, J. W. *The Mutability of the Natural Law in Selected Texts of Saint Thomas.* Unpublished Master's Thesis, Saint Louis University. St. Louis, Mo., 1954.

Heath, T. R. "St. Thomas and the Aristotelian Metaphysics." *The New Scholasticism* 34 (1960): 438–460.

Henle, R. J. *Saint Thomas and Platonism: A Study of the Plato and Platonici Texts in the Writings of Saint Thomas.* The Hague: Martinus Nijhoff, 1956.

Henry, J. "L'Imputabilité de l'erreur d'après S. Thomas d'Aquin." *Revue Néo-scolastique* 26 (1925): 225–243.

Hirschenauer, F. R. *Die Stellung des hl. Thomas von Aquin im Mendikantenstreit an der Universität Paris.* St. Ottilien, Overbayern: Missionsverlag, 1934.

Hoenen, P. "De philosophia scholastica cognitionis geometriae." *Gregorianum* 19 (1938): 498–514.

Hopper, V. F. *Medieval Number Symbolism: Its Sources, Meaning and Influences on Thought and Expression.* New York: Columbia University Press, 1938.

Horst, V. "Das Wesen der 'auctoritas' nach Thomas von Aquin." *Münchener Theologische Zeitschrift* 13 (1962): 155–172.

Isaye, G. *La Théorie de la Mesure et l'Existence d'un Maximum selon saint Thomas.* Paris: Beauchesne, 1940; reprinted, 1944.

Ivanka, E. von. "Das Stoische Fatum und der Scholastische 'ordo universi.'" *Theologie und Glaube* 25 (1933): 15–24.

Janssens, E. "Le probabilisme moral et la philosophie." *Revue Néoscolastique* 25 (1923): 209–219.

— "A propos de la logique de l'opinion." *Revue Néoscolastique* 26 (1924): 68–81.

Janssens, L. *Liberté de Conscience et Liberté religieuse.* Paris: Desclée De Brouwer, 1964.

Jean de Dieu. "Le probabilisme moral." *Etudes Franciscaines* 35 (1923): 382–399.

Jeanson, F. *La Foi d'un Incroyant.* Paris: Editions du Seuil, 1963.

Junkersfield, M. J. *The Aristotelian-Thomistic Concept of Chance.* Lithoprinted. Ann Arbor, Mich.: Edwards Bros., 1945.

Katz, J. *Exclusiveness and Tolerance: Studies in Jewish-Gentile Relations in Medieval and Modern Times.* Scripta Judaica. London: Oxford University Press, 1961.

Keeler, L. W. *The Problem of Error from Plato to Kant; A Historical and Critical Study.* Analecta Gregoriana, 6. Rome: Universita Gregoriana, 1934.

Kendzierski, L. H. "Wisdom, Synderesis and Practical Principles." *Proceedings Am. Cath. Phil. Assoc.* 26 (1951): 168–179.

Klibansky, R. "The Rock of Parmenides: Medieval Views on the Origin of Dialectic." *Medieval and Renaissance Studies* 1 (1941–1943): 178–186.

Klubertanz, G. P. "St. Thomas and the Knowledge of the Singular." *The New Scholasticism* 26 (1952): 135–166.

Kneale, W. and M. *The Development of Logic.* Oxford: Clarendon Press, 1962.

Kolski, H. *Ueber die Prudentia in der Ethik des hl. Thomas von Aquin.* Würzburg: University Press, 1934.

Kossel, C. G. *Relation in the Philosophy of Saint Thomas Aquinas* (especially with regard to Thomas's distinction between *esse* and *ratio,* pp. 65–127). Unpublished doctoral dissertation, University of Toronto. Toronto, 1944.

Koyré, A. *From the Closed World to the Infinite Universe.* New York: Harper, 1958.

Krempel, A. *La Doctrine de la Relation chez saint Thomas.* Paris: J. Vrin, 1952.

Kuebler, C. G. *The Argument from Probability in Early Attic Oratory.* Reproduced from typewritten copy. Chicago: University of Chicago Press, 1944.

Labourdette, M.-M. "Connaissance pratique et savoir moral." *Revue Thomiste* 48 (1948): 143–179.

Lafont, G. *Structure et Méthode dans la Somme Théologique de Saint Thomas d'Aquin.* Paris: Desclée De Brouwer, 1961.

Le Blond, J.-M. *Eulogos et l'Argument de convenance chez Aristote.* Paris: Les Belles Lettres, 1938.

— *Logique et Méthode chez Aristote.* Paris: J. Vrin, 1939.

Leclercq, Jacques. *La Philosophie morale de S. Thomas devant la Pensée contemporaine.* Paris: J. Vrin, 1955.

— *La Liberté d'Opinion et les Catholiques.* Paris: Editions du Cerf, 1963.

Leclercq, Jean. *The Love of Learning and the Desire for God.* New York: 1962.

Lee, H. D. P. "Geometrical Method and Aristotle's Account of First Principles." *Classical Quarterly* 29 (1935): 113–124.

Le Goff, J. *Les Intellectuels au Moyen Age.* Paris: Editions du Seuil, 1960.

Legrand, J. *L'Univers et l'Homme dans la Philosophie de saint Thomas d'Aquin,* 2 vols. Paris and Brussels, 1946.

Lenz, J. W. "Necessity and Possibility in Aristotle's Philosophy" (abstract). *The Journal of Philosophy* 59 (1962): 674.

Lewinsohn, R. *Science, Prophecy and Prediction,* translated by A. J. Pomerans. New York: Harper, 1961.

Litt, T. *Les Corps célestes dans l'Univers de saint Thomas d'Aquin.* Paris and Louvain: Nauwelaerts, 1963.

Lopez, U. *Thesis Probabilismi ex Sancto Thoma Demonstrata.* Rome: Gregorian University, 1937.

Lorenzo, R. "La certitude en matière morale." *Laval Théologique et Philosophique* 19 (1963): 120–170.

Lottin, O. "L'Ordre moral et l'ordre logique d'après S. Thomas d'Aquin." *Annales de l'Institut Supérieur de Philosophie* (Louvain) 5 (1924): 303–399.

— "Raison pratique et foi pratique." *Ephemerides Theologicae Lovanienses* 34 (1958): 21–34.

Madden, E. H. "Aristotle's Treatment of Probability and Signs." *Philosophy of Science* 24 (1957): 167–172.

Maier, H. *Die Syllogistik des Aristoteles*. Tübingen: H. Laupp'sche Buchhandlung 1900.

Mansion, A. *Introduction à la Physique Aristotélicienne*, 2nd ed. revised and augmented. Paris and Louvain: Nauwelaerts, 1945.

Marlé, R. *Le Problème théologique de l'Herméneutique: Les grands axes de la recherche contemporaine*. Paris: Editions de l'Orante, 1963.

Mason, Sr. M. E. *Active Life and Contemplative Life; A Study of the Concepts from Plato to the Present*. Milwaukee: Marquette University Press, 1961.

McKian, J. D. "What Man May Know of the Angels: Some Suggestions of the Angelic Doctor." *The New Scholasticism* 29 (1955): 259–277.

McWilliams, J. A. *Physics and Philosophy: A Study of Saint Thomas's Commentary on the Eight Books of Aristotle's Physics*. Washington: Catholic University of America Press, 1945.

Mondolfo, R. *L'Infinito nel Pensiero dei Greci*. Florence: F. Le Monnier, 1934.

Mullahy, B. I. "Practical Knowledge and Relativity." *Proceedings Am. Cath. Phil. Assoc.* 22 (1947): 151–166.

Mulligan, R. W. *"Ratio superior* and *ratio inferior:* The Historical Background." *The New Scholasticism* 29 (1955): 1–32.

Munitz, M. K. (ed.) *Theories of the Universe from Babylonian Myth to Modern Science*. New York, Free Press of Glencoe, 1957.

Muniz, F. P. *The Work of Theology*, translated by J. P. Reid. Washington: Catholic University of America Press, 1953.

Naus, J. E. *The Nature of the Practical Intellect according to St. Thomas Aquinas*. Rome: Libreria Editrice dell' Università Gregoriana, 1959.

Nivard, M. "Autour du probabilisme." *Archives de Philosophie* 2 (1924): 142–160.

O'Mahony, J. E. *The Desire of God in the Philosophy of St. Thomas Aquinas*. Cork, Ireland: Purcell, 1929.

Owens, J. *The Doctrine of Being in the Aristotelian Metaphysics*. Toronto: Pontifical Institute of Mediaeval Studies, 1951.

Peghaire, J. *Intellectus et Ratio selon saint Thomas d'Aquin*. Paris: J. Vrin, 1936.

Pegis, A. C. *St. Thomas and Philosophy*. Milwaukee: Marquette University Press, 1964.

Persson, P. E. *Le Plan de la Somme théologique et le Rapport Ratio-Revelatio*. Paris, 1958.

Petitot, H. "La mort de S. Thomas d'Aquin." *Vie Spirituelle* 10 (1924): 312–336.

Petrin, J. *Connaissance spéculative et Connaissance pratique*. Ottawa: *Editions de de l'Université d'Ottawa*, 1948.

Pichette, H. "Considerations sur quelques principes fondamentaux de la doctrine du speculatif et du pratique." *Laval Théologique et Philosophique* 1 (1945): 52–70.

Pieper, J. *The Silence of Saint Thomas*. New York: Pantheon Books, 1957.

— *Prudence: The First Cardinal Virtue*. New York: Pantheon Books, 1959.

— *Scholasticism: Personalities and Problems of Medieval Philosophy*, translated by R. and C. Winston. New York: Pantheon Books, 1960.

Price, E. F., Jr. *The Renaissance Idea of Wisdom*. Cambridge, Mass.: Harvard University Press, 1958.

Rabut, O. A. *La Vérification religieuse: Recherche d'une Spiritualité pour le Temps de l'Incertitude*. Paris: Editions du Cerf, 1964.

Rahner, K. *Geist in Welt; Zur Metaphysik der endlichen Erkenntnis bei Thomas von Aquin.* Innsbruch: Rauch, 1939.

Rashdall, H. *The Universities of Europe in the Middle Ages,* rev. ed., 3 vols. Oxford: Clarendon Press, 1936.

Regatillo, E. F., and M. Zalba. *Theologiae Moralis Summa,* 3 vols. Madrid: Biblioteca de Autores cristianos, 1952–1954.

Regis, L.-M. *L'Opinion selon Aristote.* Paris and Ottawa: J. Vrin and Institut d'Etudes médiévales d'Ottawa, 1935.

Richard, T. *Le Probabilisme moral et la Philosophie.* Paris: Nouvelle Libr. Nationale, 1922.

— "Théorie de la certitude morale." *Revue Thomiste* n. s. 6 (1923): 155–178.

— "Philosophie du probable." *Revue Thomiste* n.s. 7 (1924): 174–191.

— "A propos d'un article récent sur le probabilisme." *Revue Thomiste* n.s. 7 (1924): 404–415.

— "Probabilité unique ou douteuse; précisions et réponses." *Revue Thomiste* n.s. 8 (1925): 452–473.

— "Autour de la probabilite unique." *Revue Thomiste* n.s. 10 (1927): 165–195.

— "L'Imperfection et la doctrine de S. Thomas." *Revue Thomiste* n.s. 14 (1931): 131–156.

Rimaud, J. *Thomisme et Méthode.* Paris: Beauchesne, 1925.

Riquet, M. "Thomas et les 'Auctoritates' en philosophie." *Archives de Philosophie* vol. III cah. 2 (Paris- Beauchesne, 1925), pp. 117–155.

Rolland-Gosselin, M.-D. "Béatitude et désir naturel d'après S. Thomas d'Aquin." *Revue des Sciences Philosophiques et Théologiques* 18 (1929): 193–222.

Rousselot, P. *The Intellectualism of Saint Thomas.* New York: Sheed and Ward, 1935.

— *Quaestiones de Conscientia.* Paris and Brussels: Desclée De Brouwer, 1937.

Royal, E. P. "On Determinacy in Human Knowledge." *The New Scholasticism* 37 (1963): 1–27.

Salman, D. "La conception scolastique de la physique." *Revue Néoscolastique de Philosophie* 39 (1936): 27–50.

Sarton, G. P. *The Appreciation of Ancient and Medieval Science during the Renaissance.* Philadelphia: University of Pennsylvania Press, 1953.

Schwientek, A. "La ciencia moral en la doctrina de Santo Tomás de Aquino.' *La Ciencia Tomista* 62 (1942): 146–168.

Sentroul, C. "Le vraisemblable du probable." *Revue Néoscolastique de Philosophie* 25 (1923): 311–328.

— "Encore la logique de l'opinion. Réplique à M. E. Janssens." *Revue Néoscolastique de Philosophie* 26 (1924): 81–84.

Sergescu, P. *Les Mathématiques à Paris au Moyen Age.* Paris: Gauthier-Villars, 1938.

Sesmat, A. "Controverses médiévales sur la valeur des hypothèses astronomiques." *Revue de Philosophie* 38 (1938): 381–409.

Simon, Y. "Reflexions sur la connaissance pratique." *Revue de Philosophie* n.s. 3 (1932): 449–473, 531–555.

— *Prévoir et Savoir; Etudes sur l'Idée de la Nécessité dans la Pensée scientifique et en Philosophie.* Montreal: Editions de l'Arbre, 1944.

— "Introduction to the Study of Practical Wisdom." *The New Scholasticism* 35 (1961): 1–40.

— and K. Menger. "Aristotelian Demonstration and Postulational Method." *The Modern Schoolman* 25 (1948): 183–192.

Simonson, S. 'The Aristotelian Form of Disputation." *The New Scholasticism* 18 (1944): 385–390.

Sleva, V. *The Separated Soul in the Philosophy of St. Thomas Aquinas.* Washington: Catholic University of America Press, 1940.

Smith, G. *Natural Theology.* New York: Macmillan, 1951.

Smith, I. "The Place of Authority in Philosophy according to St. Thomas Aquinas." *Proceedings Am. Cath. Phil. Assoc.* 3 (1927): 89–102.

Smith, W. C. *The Meaning and End of Religion: A New Approach to the Religious Traditions of Mankind.* New York: Macmillan, 1963.

Solmsen, F. "Aristotle and Cicero on the Orator's Playing upon the Feelings." *Classical Philology* 33 (1938): 390–404.

— "The Aristotelian Tradition of Ancient Rhetoric." *The American Journal of Philology* 62 (1941): 35–50.

— *Aristotle's System of the Physical World; A Comparison with his Predecessors.* Ithaca, N.Y.: Cornell University Press, 1960.

Southern, R. W. *Western Views of Islam in the Middle Ages.* Cambridge, Mass.: Harvard University Press, 1962.

Stahl, W. H. *Roman Science: Origins, Development and Influence to the Later Middle Ages.* Madison, Wis.: University of Wisconsin Press, 1961.

Suerdmont, P. *Tabulae schematicae cum Introductione de principiis et compositione comparatis Summae Theologicae et Summa contra Gentiles Sancti Thomae.* Turin: Marietti, 1943.

Suess, W. *Ethos; Studien zur Altgriechischen Rhetorik.* Leipzig, 1910.

Symposium Aristotelicum. *Aristote et les Problèmes de Méthode.* Paris and Louvain: Nauwelaerts, 1961.

Taylor, F. S. *The Attitude of St. Thomas to Natural Science.* Oxford: Blackfriars, 1945.

Thiry, L. *Speculativum-Practicum secundum S. Thomam: Quomodo Se Habeant in Actu Humano.* Rome: Scuola Salesiana del Libro, 1939.

Thorndike, L. *A History of Magic and Experimental Science,* 6 vols. New York: Macmillan, 1923–1943.

Tshibangu, T. *Théologie positive et Théologie speculative; Position traditionelle et nouvelle Problématique.* Paris and Louvain: Nauwelaerts, 1965.

Turner, W. H. "St. Thomas's Exposition of Aristotle: A Rejoinder." *The New Scholasticism* 35 (1961), 210–224.

Van Ackeren, G. F. *Sacra Doctrina: The Subject of the First Question of the Summa Theologica of St. Thomas Aquinas.* Rome: Catholic Book Agency, 1952.

Vanni Rovighi, S. "Concezione aristotelico-tomistica e concezione moderna dell' induzione." *Rivista di Filosofia Neoscolastica* 26 (1934): 578–593.

Van Riet, O. *L'Epistémologie Thomiste: Recherches sur le Problème de la Connaissance dans l'Ecole Thomiste contemporaine.* Louvain: Editions de l'Institut Supérieur de Philosophie, 1946.

— *Problèmes d'Epistémologie.* Paris and Louvain: Nauwelaerts, 1960.

— "Y a-t-il chez saint Thomas une philosophie de la religion?" *Revue Philosophique de Louvain* 61 (1963): 44–81.

— "Le probleme de Dieu chez Hegel: athéisme ou christianisme?" *Revue Philosophique de Louvain* 63 (1965): 353–418.

Van Steenberghen, F. *Aristotle in the West: The Origins of Latin Aristotelianism.* Paris and Louvain: Nauwelaerts, 1955.

— *The Philosophical Movement in the Thirteenth Century.* Edinburgh; Nelson, 1955.

— *Ontologie,* 3rd ed. Paris and Louvain: Nauwelaerts, 1961.

— *Histoire de la Philosophie: Période chrétienne.* Paris and Louvain: Nauwelaerts, 1964.

— *Epistémologie,* 4th ed. Paris and Louvain: Nauwelaerts, 1965.

Vignaux, P. *La Pensée au Moyen Age.* Paris: A. Colin, 1938.
Wallace, W. A. *The Scientific Methodology of Theodoric of Freiberg.* Fribourg, Switzerland: University of Fribourg Press, 1959.
— *The Role of Demonstration in Moral Theology; A Study of Methodology in Saint Thomas Aquinas.* Washington: Catholic University of America Press, 1962.
Walz, A. "De S. Thomae Aquinatis e vita discessu." *Xenia Thomistica* (Rome, 1925), Tome III, pp. 41–45.
Wartman, C. *The Scholastic Doctrine of the Elision of Probability.* Rome: Scuola typogr. missionaris Domenicana S. Sisto Vecchio, 1936.
Webering, D. *Theory of Demonstration according to William Ockham.* St. Bonaventure, N.Y., Louvain and Paderborn: Franciscan Institute, 1953.
Weisheipl, J. A. *The Development of Physical Theory in the Middle Ages.* New York: Sheed and Ward, 1959.
Weiss, H. *Kausalität und Zufall in der Philosophie des Aristoteles.* Basel: Verlag Haus zum Falken, 1942.
Well, J. von. *Ueber das Verhältnis des intellectus speculativus und des intellectus practicus zueinander bei Thomas von Aquin.* Bonn: University Press, 1933.
White, V. *Holy Teaching: The Idea of Theology according to Thomas Aquinas.* Oxford: Blackfriars, 1958.
Windass, G. S. "The Consecration of Violence; Reflections on the Crusades." *Cross Currents* 15 (1965): 9–18.
Wright, B. "Necessary and Contingent Being in St. Thomas." *The New Scholasticism* 25 (1951): 439–466.

III. SOME WORKS INVOLVING POST-MEDIEVAL THEORY OF PROBABILITY

Adler, I. *Probability and Statistics for Everyman: How to Understand and Use the Laws of Chance.* New York: John Day, 1963.
Bachelard, G. *Le nouvel Esprit scientifique.* Paris: Librairie Felix Alcan, 1934.
— *La Formation de l'Esprit scientifique.* Paris: J. Vrin, 1938.
Bachelier, L. J.-B. *Les Lois des grands Nombres du Calcul des Probabilités.* Paris: Gauthier-Villars, 1937.
Barker, S. F. *Induction and Hypothesis; A Study of the Logic of Confirmation.* Ithaca, N.Y., and London: Cornell University Press and Oxford University Press, 1957.
Barnes, L. "Probability and the Logic of Induction." *Scripta Mathematica* 11 (1945): 192–196.
Barnett, S. "Philosophy and Probability." *The Philosophical Review* 30 (1921): 585–601.
Bass, W. A. *Some Difficulties in the Theory of Probability.* Ann Arbor, Mich.: University Microfilms (Microfilm AC–1 no. 7953; A 55–3233), 1954.
Becknell, E. A. "Probability: A Function of Ideology." *American Journal of Psychology* 53 (1940): 604–609.
Bergmann, P. G. *Basic Theories of Physics; Heat and Quanta.* New York: Prentice Hall, 1951.
Bertrand, J. *Calcul des probabilités.* Paris: Gauthier-Villars, 1907.
Birkhoff, G. D. "Intention, Reason and Faith in Science." *Science* n.s. 88 (1938): 601–609.
Bohr, N. *Atomic Theory and the Description of Nature.* New York: Macmillan, 1934.

— *Atomic Physics and Human Knowledge*, New York: Interscience, 1958.
Boole, G. *Studies in Logic and Probability*, reprinted. London: Watts, 1952.
— *An Investigation of the Laws of Thought*, reprinted. New York: Dover, 1951 and 1962.
Borel, E. "A propos d'un traité des probabilités." Review of J. M. Keynes' *A Treatise on Probability*. *Revue Philosophique France Etranger* 98 (1924): 321–336.
— (ed.) *Traité du Calcul des probabilités et ses applications*, 4 vols. Paris: Gauthier-Villars, 1925.
— "Les lois physiques et les probabilités." *Revue Scientifique* 65 (1927): 225–228.
— *Le Jeu, la Chance et les Théories scientifiques modernes*. Paris: Gallimard, 1941.
— *Les Probabilités et la Vie*. Paris: Presses Universitaires de France, 1943; English translation, New York and London: Dover and Constable, 1962.
— *Probabilité et Certitude*. Paris: Presses Universitaires de France, 1950; English translation, New York and London: Walker, 1963.
Born, M. *Natural Philosophy of Cause and Chance*. Oxford: Clarendon Press, 1949.
— *Experiment and Theory in Physics*. Cambridge, England: University Press, 1954.
Boyer, C. B. *History of Analytic Geometry*. New York: Scripta Mathematica, 1956.
— *The History of the Calculus and its Conceptual Development*, 2nd ed. New York: Dover, 1959.
Braithwaite, R. B. *Scientific Explanation*. Cambridge, England: University Press, 1953.
— *Theory of Games as a Tool for the Moral Philosopher*. Cambridge, England: University Press, 1955.
Bridgman, P. W. *The Logic of Modern Physics*. New York: Macmillan, 1928.
Broad, C. D. "Theorems connecting Probability with Induction." *Mind* 53 (1944): 193–214.
Broglie, L. de. *Physics and Microphysics*. New York: Pantheon Books, 1955.
— *New Perspectives in Physics*. New York: Basic Books, 1962.
Brown, G. S. *Probability and Scientific Inference*. New York: Longmans, Green, 1957.
Bunge, M. "What is Chance?" *Science and Society* 15 (1951): 209–231.
— *The Place of the Causal Principle in Modern Science*. Cambridge, Mass.: Harvard University, 1959.
— *Intuition and Science*. Englewood Cliffs, N.J.: Prentice-Hall Spectrum, 1962.
Burke, K. *A Grammar of Motives and a Rhetoric of Motives*. Cleveland: World, 1962.
Burtt, E. A. *The Metaphysical Foundations of Modern Physical Science*, rev. ed. London: Routledge & Kegan Paul, 1932.
Caldin, E. F. *The Power and Limits of Science*. London: Chapman and Hall, 1949.
Čapek, M. *The Philosophical Impact of Contemporary Physics*. New York, London Toronto et al.: Van Nostrand, 1961.
Cardano, G. *The Book on Games of Chance: "Liber de Ludo Aleae,"* translated by S. H. Gould and others. New York: Holt, Rinehart and Winston, 1961.
Carnap, R. "On Inductive Logic." *Philosophy of Science* 12 (1945): 72–97.
— "Probability as a Guide in Life." *The Journal of Philosophy* 44 (1947): 141–148.
— "What is Probability?" *Scientific American* 189 (1953): 128–130.
— *Logical Foundations of Probability*, 2nd ed. Chicago: University of Chicago Press, 1962.

Castelnuovo, G. "Determinismo e probabilità." *Scientia* 53 (1933): 1–12.
— *La Probabilité dans les différentes Branches de la Science.* Paris: Hermann, 1937
Cesari, P. *Les Déterminismes et la Contingence.* Paris: Presses Universitaires de France, 1950.
Chambers, L. P. "Search for Certainty." *Monist* 38 (1928): 481–493.
Child, A. "Problem of Truth in the Sociology of Knowledge." *Ethics* 58 (1947): 18–34.
Churchman, C. W. "Probability Theory." *Philosophy of Science* 12 (1945): 147–173.
Chwistek, L. *The Limits of Science: Outline of the Logic and Methodology of the Exact Sciences.* London: Harcourt, Brace, 1948.
Cohen, I. B. *The Birth of a New Physics.* Garden City, N.Y.: Anchor, 1960.
— "'Quantum in se Est': Newton, Kepler, Galileo, Descartes and Lucretius." *Proceedings Am. Cath. Phil. Assoc.* 38 (1964): 36–46.
Cohen, J. "Subjective Probability." *Scientific American* 197 (1957): 128–130.
— *Chance, Skill and Luck; The Psychology of Guessing and Gambling.* Baltimore: Penguin Books, 1960.
— and M. Hansel. *Risk and Gambling; The Study of Subjective Probability.* New York: Philosophical Library, 1956.
Comp, B. H. "Definitions of Probability." *American Mathematical Monthly* 39 (1932): 285–288.
Compton, A. H. "Do We Live in a World of Chance?" *Yale Review* n.s. 21 (1931): 86–99.
Copeland, A. H. "Fundamental Concepts of the Theory of Probability." *American Mathematical Monthly* 48 (1941): 522–530.
Cournot, A.-A. *Exposition de la Théorie des Chances et des Probabilités.* Paris, 1843.
— *Considérations sur la Marche des Idées et des Evénements dans les Temps modernes,* reprinted, 2 vols. Paris: Boivon, 1934.
— *An Essay on the Foundations of our Knowledge.* First French edition, Paris, 1851; English edition, New York: Liberal Arts Press, 1956.
Cousin, D. R. "Carnap's Theories of Truth." *Mind* 59 (1950): 1–22.
Cox, R. T. *The Algebra of Probable Inference.* Baltimore: Johns Hopkins University Press, 1961.
Crissman, P. "Causation, Chance, Determinism and Freedom in Nature." *Scientific Monthly* 61 (1945): 455–464.
Curry, H. B. *A Theory of Formal Deducibility.* Notre Dame Mathematical Lectures, No. 6. Notre Dame, Ind.: Notre Dame University Press, 1950.
— *Leçons de Logique Algébrique.* Paris and Louvain: Gauthiers-Villars, 1952.
— "The Interpretation of Formalized Implication." *Theoria* 25 (1959): 1–26.
— *Foundations of Mathematical Logic.* New York, London, Toronto et al.: McGraw-Hill, 1963.
Czuber, E. *Die philosophischen Grundlagen der Wahrscheinlichkeitsrechnung.* Leipzig and Berlin: Teubner, 1923.
Dampier, W. *A History of Science and its Relations with Philosophy and Religion,* 4th. ed. Cambridge: University Press, 1949.
Darwin, C. G. "Logic and Probability in Physics." *Discovery* n.s. 1 (1938): 332–344. Same abbreviated, *Nature* 142 (1938): 381–384.
Day, J. P. *Inductive Probability.* New York: Humanities Press, 1961.
Delhomme, J. *La Pensée Interrogative.* Paris: Presses Universitaires de France, 1954.
De Morgan, A. *An Essay on Probabilities.* London, 1838.

Deutsch, K. W. *Applications of Game Theory to International Politics; Some Opportunities and Limits.* Mimeographed. Princeton, N.J.: Princeton University, Center of International Studies, undated.

Dijsterhuis, E. J. *The Mechanization of the World Picture.* Oxford: Clarendon Press, 1961.

Dingle, H. "The Meaning of Probability." *Nature* 136 (1935): 423–436. Replies by W. Barrett and T. Smith, with rejoinder: *Nature* 136 (1935): 604–605.

Dorolle, M. *Le Raisonnement par Analogie.* Paris: Presses Universitaires de France, 1949.

Dotterer, R. H. "Ignorance and Equal Probability." *Philosophy of Science* 8 (1941): 297–303.

Dubs, H. H. "The Principle of Insufficient Reason: Reply to R. H. Dotterer." *Philosophy of Science* 9 (1942): 123–131.

Ducasse, C. J. "Some Observations concerning the Nature of Probability." *The Journal of Philosophy* 38 (1941): 393–403.

Dugas, R. *A History of Mechanics.* New York: Central Book, 1955.

Eddington, A. S. *The Nature of the Physical World.* New York: Macmillan, 1928.

— *The Philosophy of Physical Science.* New York: Macmillan, 1939.

Einstein, A., and L. Infeld. *The Evolution of Physics; The Growth of Ideas from the Early Concepts to Relativity and Quanta.* New York: Simon and Schuster, 1938.

Eisenhart, C., and M. Zelen. "Elements of Probability," in *Handbook of Physics* (eds. E. U. Condon and H. Odishaw; New York: McGraw-Hill, 1958), Part I, ch. xii, pp. 134–164.

Ellis, L. *The Mathematical and Other Writings of Leslie Ellis.* Cambridge, England, 1863.

Erismann, T. *Wahrscheinlichkeit im Sein und Denken; eine Theorie der Wahrscheinlichkeit und ihrer Geltung im Naturgeschehen.* Vienna: A. Sexl, 1954.

Evans, H. P., and S. C. Kleene. "Postulational Basis for Probability." *American Mathematical Monthly* 46 (1939): 141–148.

Feller, W. *An Introduction to Probability Theory and its Applications,* 2nd ed., 2 vols. New York and London: Wiley, 1957.

Fellner, W. "Distortion to Subjective Probabilities as a Reaction to Uncertainty." *Quarterly Journal of Economics* 75 (1961): 670–689. Reply by K. R. W. Brewer, *ibid.* 77 (1963): 59–61.

Fischer, R. A. "Uncertain Inference." *American Academy of Arts and Sciences Proceedings* 71 (1936): 245–258; *Scientific Monthly* 43 (1936): 402–410.

— *Statistical Methods and Scientific Inference,* 2nd ed. rev. London and Edinburgh: Oliver, 1959.

Frank, P. *Between Physics and Philosophy.* Cambridge, Mass.: Harvard University Press, 1941.

— *Modern Science and its Philosophy.* Cambridge, Mass.: Harvard University Press, 1949.

— *Philosophy of Science.* Englewood Cliffs, N.J.: Prentice-Hall, 1957.

Frechet, M. R. *Le Calcul des Probabilités à la Portée de Tous.* Paris: Dunod, 1924.

Fry, T. C. "Fundamental Concepts in the Theory of Probability." *American Mathematical Monthly* 41 (1934): 206–217.

Frye, A. M., and A. W. Levi. *Rational Belief.* New York: Harcourt, Brace, 1941.

Gardner, M. *Logic Machines and Diagrams.* New York: McGraw-Hill, 1958.

Gell-Mann, M., and E. P. Rosenbaum. "Elementary Particles." *Scientific American* July, 1957.

—, G. F. Chew and A. H. Rosenfeld. "Strongly Interacting Particles." *Scientific American* February, 1964.

Gendre, J.-L. *Introduction à l'Etude du Jugement probable*. Paris: Presses Universitaires de France, 1947.

Gillespie, C. C. "Intellectual Factors in the Background of Analysis by Probabilities," in *Scientific Change* (ed. A. C. Crombie; London: W. Heffer, 1963), pp. 431–453.

Ginzburg, B. "Probability and the Philosophic Foundations of Scientific Knowledge." *The Philosophical Review* 43 (1934): 258–278. Reply by H. D. Roelofs, *ibid*. 44 (1935): 484–487.

Gnedenko, B. V. *The Theory of Probability*. New York: Chelsea, 1962.

— and A. Khinchin. *An Elementary Introduction to the Theory of Probability*, translated by L. F. Boron. New York: Dover, 1962.

Gonseth, F. (ed.) *Philosophie Néo-Scolastique et Philosophie ouverte*. Paris: Presses Universitaires de France, 1954.

Good, I. J. *Probability and the Weighing of Evidence*. London: C. Griffin, 1950.

— "Kinds of Probability." *Science* 129 (1959): 443–447.

Goodfellow, L. D. "The Human Element in Probability." *Journal of General Psychology* 23 (1940): 201–205.

Goodstein, R. L. "On Von Mise's Theory of Probability." *Mind* 49 (1940): 58–62.

Graves, H. F. *Argument: Deliberation and Persuasion in Modern Practice*. New York: Cordon, 1938.

Grunbaum, A., and M. Scriven. "Symposium: Determinism in the Light of Recent Physics." *The Journal of Philosophy* 54 (1957): 713–741.

Gurvitch, G. *Dialectique et Sociologie*. Paris: Flammarion, 1962.

Halmos, P. R. "Foundations of Probability." *American Mathematical Monthly* 51 (1944): 493–510.

Harding, T. S. "Science versus Absolutism: Science Approaches Truth by a Series of Approximations." *Sewanee Review* 44 (1936): 472–481.

Hawkins, D. "Existential and Epistemic Probability." *Philosophy of Science* 10 (1943): 255–261.

Hay, W. H. "Professor Carnap and Probability." *Philosophy of Science* 19 (1952): 170–177.

Hegel, G. W. F. *La Phénoménologie de l'Esprit*, translated by J. Hippolyte, 2 vols. Paris: Aubier, Editions Montaigne, 1939–1941.

Heisenberg, W. *Philosophic Problems of Nuclear Physics*. London: Faber and Faber, 1952.

— *Physics and Philosophy*. New York: Harper, 1958.

— *The Physicist's Conception of Nature*. New York: Harcourt, Brace, 1958.

Hogben, L. T. *Statistical Theory: The Relationship of Probability, Credibility and Error. An Examination of the Contemporary Crisis in Statistical Theory from a Behaviorist Viewpoint*. London: Allen and Unwin, 1957.

Hosiasson, J. L. "Induction et analogie: comparaison de leur fondement." *Mind* 50 (1941): 351–365.

Jeans, J. H. *Physics and Philosophy*. New York and Cambridge, England: Macmillan and The University Press, 1943.

Jeffreys, H. "On Some Criticisms of the Theory of Probability." *Philosophy of Mathematics* 22 (1936): 337–359.

— "Science, Logic and Philosophy." *Nature* 141 (1938): 672–674, 716–719, 977.

— *Theory of Probability*. Oxford, 1939; 3rd ed.: Clarendon Press, 1961.

— "Probability and Quantum Theory." *Philosophy of Mathematics* n.s. 7 (1942): 815–831.

— "Bertrand Russell on Probability." *Mind* 59 (1950): 313–319.

Kac, M. *Probability and Related Topics in Physical Sciences*. New York: Interscience, 1959.

— "Probability." *Scientific American* September 1964: 92–108.
Kasm, B. *L'Idée de Preuve en Métaphysique*. Paris: Presses Universitaires de France, 1959.
Katsoff, L. O. "Modality and Probability." *The Philosophical Review* 46 (1937): 78–85.
Katz, J. J. *The Problem of Induction and its Solution*. Chicago: University of Chicago Press, 1962.
Kerr, H. P. *Opinion and Evidence: Cases for Argument and Discussion*. New York: Harcourt, Brace & World, 1963.
Keynes, J. M. *A Treatise on Probability*. Oxford, 1921; New York: Macmillan, 1948.
King, A. C., and C. B. Read. *Pathways to Probability; History of the Mathematics of Certainty and Chance*. New York: Holt, Rinehart and Winston, 1963.
Kline, M. *Mathematics and the Physical World*. New York: Crowell, 1959.
Kneale, W. C. *Probability and Induction*. Oxford: Clarendon Press, 1949.
Knight, F. H. "Virtue and Knowledge: The View of Professor Polanyi." *Ethics* 59 (1949): 271–284.
Kolmogorov, A. N. *Foundations of the Theory of Probability*, 2nd English ed. New York: Chelsea, 1956.
Koyré, A. *Etudes Galiléennes*, 3 vols. Paris: Hermann et Cie., 1939.
— *La Révolution astronomique*. Paris: Hermann et Cie., 1960.
— *Concept and Experience in Newton's Scientific Thought*. Cambridge, Mass.: Harvard University Press, 1965.
Kuhn, T. S. *The Structure of Scientific Revolutions*. Chicago: University of Chicago Press, 1962.
— "The Function of Dogma in Scientific Research," in *Scientific Change* (ed. A. C. Crombie; London: Heinemann, 1963), pp. 347–369.
Kyburg, H. E. *Probability and the Logic of Rational Belief*. Middletown, Conn.: Wesleyan University Press, 1961.
— and H. E. Smokler (eds.) *Studies in Subjective Probability*. New York: Wiley, 1964.
Lachelier, J. *Du Fondement de l'Induction*. Paris: Alcan, 1924.
Ladriere, J. *Les Limitations internes des Formalismes: Etude sur la signification du théorème de Gödel et des théorèmes apparentes dans la théorie des fondements des mathématiques*. Paris and Louvain: Nauwelaerts, 1957.
Laguna, T. de. "On Keynes' Theory of Probability." *The Philosophical Review* 39 (1930): 227–242.
Lalande, A. *Les Théories de l'Induction et de l'Expérimentation*. Paris: Boivon, 1929.
— (ed.) *Vocabulaire Technique et Critique de la Philosophie*, 7th ed. revised and augmented. Paris: Presses Universitaires de France, 1956.
Laplace, P. S. Marquis de. *A Philosophical Essay on Probabilities*, translated from the 6th French ed. by F. W. Truscott and F. L. Emory. London: Constable, 1951.
Lavelle, L. *La Dialectique du Monde Sensible*, 2nd ed. Paris; Presses Universitaires de France, 1954.
— *Manuel de Méthodologie dialectique*. Paris: Presses Universitaires de France, 1962.
Leblanc, H. "Two Probability Concepts." *The Journal of Philosophy* 55 (1956): 679–688.
Leclercq, R. *Histoire et Avenir de la Méthode Expérimentale*. Paris: Masson, 1960.
Levinas, E. *Totalité et Infini: Essai sur l'Extériorité*. The Hague: Martinus Nijhoff, 1961.

Levinson, H. C. *Chance, Luck and Statistics; The Science of Chance.* New York: Dover, 1963.

Levy, P. *Calcul des Probabilités.* Paris: Gauthiers-Villars, 1925.

— "Les Fondements du Calcul des probabilités." *Revue de Métaphysique et de Morale* 68 (1963): 25–56.

Lewis, G. N. "The Scientific Meaning of Chance." *Yale Review* n.s. 15 (1926): 672–686.

Linfoot, E. H. "On the Law of Large Numbers." *Royal Society of London Philosophical Transactions* 227 ser. A (1928): 417–451.

Logic of Personal Knowledge. New York: Free Press of Glencoe, 1961.

Lonergan, B. J. F. *Insight: A Study of Human Understanding,* rev. student ed. New York and London: Longmans, Green, 1958.

Luce, R. D., and H. Raiffa. *Games and Decisions: Introduction and Critical Survey.* New York and London: Wiley, 1957.

Mac Kinnon, E. M. "Understanding according to Bernard J. F. Lonergan, S.J." *The Thomist* 28 (1964): 97–132, 338–372.

Maher, P. T. "Proof that Pure Induction Approaches Certainty as its Limit." *Mind* 42 (1933): 208–212.

Malcolm, N. "Certainty and Empirical Statements." *Mind* 51 (1942): 18–46. Reply by M. Black, *ibid.*, 361–367.

Margenau, H. " Probability and Causality in Quantum Physics." *Monist* 42 (1932): 161–188.

— *The Nature of Physical Reality.* New York: McGraw-Hill, 1950.

Maritain, J. *The Degrees of Knowledge.* New York, 1938.

— *Philosophy of Nature.* New York: Philosophical Library, 1951.

Marling, J. M. "The Dialectical Character of Scientific Knowledge," in *Philosophical Studies in Honor of the Very Reverend Ignatius Smith, O.P.* (ed. J. K. Ryan; Westminster, Md.: Newman Press, 1952), pp. 3–13.

Martin, N. M. "The Explicandum of the Classical Concept of Probability." *Philosophy of Science* 18 (1951): 70–84.

Matisse, G. "Le mécanisme du déterminisme." *Revue Philosophique* 123 (1937): 176–194.

Maxwell, G. "The Ontological Status of Theoretical Entities," in *Minnesota Studies in the Philosophy of Science,* vol. 3 (eds. H. Feigl and G. Maxwell; Minneapolis, 1962), pp. 3–27.

Mayo, B. "The Existence of Theoretical Entities." *Science News* 32 (1954): 7–18.

— "More about Theoretical Entities." *Science News* 39 (1956): 42–55.

McCormick, T. C. "Note on the Validity of Mathematical Probability in Sociological Research." *American Sociological Review* 10 (1945): 626–631.

McDougall, W. "Mechanism, Purpose and the New Freedom," *Philosophy* 9 (1934): 5–18.

Meyerson, E. "Les mathématiques et le divers." *Revue Philosophique France Etranger* 177 (1934): 321–334.

Montessus de Ballore, R. de. "Les phénomènes physiques et la loi de probabilité simple." *Revue Générale des Sciences Pures et Appliquées* 39 (1928): 293–299, 333–340.

— "Quelques points obscurs du calcul des probabilités." *Revue Générale des Sciences Pures et Appliquées* 40 (1929): 199–202.

Morgenbesser, S. "On the Justification of Beliefs and Attitudes." *The Journal of Philosophy* 51 (1954): 565–576.

Nagel, E. "The Frequency Theory of Probability." *The Journal of Philosophy* 30 (1933): 533–554.

— Verifiability, Truth and Verification." *The Journal of Philosophy* 31 (1934): 141–148.

— "The Meaning of Probability; with discussion." *American Statistical Association Journal* 31 (1936): 10–30.

— Review of H. Reichenbach's *Wahrscheinlichkeitslehre*. *Mind* 45 (1936): 501–514.

— *Principles of the Theory of Probability*. International Encyclopedia of Unified Sciences vol. 1 n. 6. Chicago: University of Chicago Press, 1939.

— Review of H. Jeffreys' *Theory of Probability*. *The Journal of Philosophy* 37 (1940): 524–528.

— *The Structure of Science: Problems in the Logic of Scientific Explanation*. New York and Burlingame: Harcourt, Brace and World, 1961.

— and J. R. Newman. *Gödel's Proof*. New York: New York University Press, 1958.

— and M. R. Cohen. *An Introduction to Logic*. New York and Burlingame: Harcourt, Brace and World, 1962.

Nidditch, P. H. *The Development of Mathematical Logic*. New York: Free Press of Glencoe, 1962.

— *Propositional Calculus*. New York: Free Press of Glencoe, 1962.

Nisbet, R. H. "Foundations of Probability." *Mind* 35 (1926): 1–27.

Oliver, R. T. *Psychology of Persuasive Speech*, 3rd ed. New York: Longmans, Green, 1957.

Ovink, B. J. H. *Philosophie und Sophistik*. The Hague: Van Stockhum, 1940.

Parratt, L. G. *Probability and Experimental Errors in Science: An Elementary Survey*. London: Wiley, 1961.

Parzen, E. *Modern Probability Theory and its Applications*. New York and London: Wiley, 1960.

Perelman, C. *La Nouvelle Rhétorique; Traité de l'Argumentation*, 2 vols. Paris: Presses Universitaires de France (Logos), 1958.

— and L. Olbrechts-Tyteca. *Rhétorique et Philosophie: Pour une Théorie de l'Argumentation en Philosophie*. Paris: Presses Universitaires de France, 1952.

Piaget, J., and B. Inhelder. *La Genèse de l'Idée de Hasard chez l'Enfant*. Paris: Presses Universitaires de France, 1951.

Planck, M. *The Universe in the Light of Modern Physics*. New York: Norton, 1931; Philosophical Library, 1949.

— *The Philosophy of Physics*. New York: Norton, 1936.

— *Scientific Autobiography*. New York: Philosophical Library, 1949.

Plummer, H. C. K. *Probability and Frequency*. New York: Macmillan, 1940.

Poincaré, H. *Calcul des Probabilités*, 2nd ed. Paris: G. Carré, 1912.

— *La Science et l'Hypothèse*. Paris: Flammarion, 1929.

Poirier, R. *Remarques sur la Probabilité des Inductions*. Paris: J. Vrin, 1931.

Polanyi, M. *Personal Knowledge: Towards a Post-Critical Philosophy*. Chicago: University of Chicago Press, 1958..

Pollard, W. G. *Chance and Providence: God's Action in a World Governed by Scientific Law*. London: Faber and Faber, 1958.

Polya, G. "Heuristic Reasoning and the Theory of Probability." *American Mathematical Monthly* 48 (1941): 450–465.

— *Mathematics and Plausible Reasoning*, 2 vols. Princeton: Princeton University Press, 1954.

Pommaret, M. C. "Valeur scientifique de la méthode statistique." *Revue Générale des Sciences Pures et Appliquées* 47 (1936): 241–246.

Popper, K. R. *The Logic of Scientific Discovery*. New York: Basic Books, 1959.

— *The Poverty of Historicism*. London: Routledge and Kegan Paul, 1957, 1961.

— *Conjectures and Refutations; The Growth of Scientific Knowledge.* New York: Basic Books, 1962; London: Routledge and Kegan Paul, 1963.

Randall, J. H., Jr. *The Career of Philosophy from the Middle Ages to the Enlightenment.* New York: Columbia University Press, 1962.

Reichenbach, H. *The Theory of Probability.* German ed., Leiden, 1935; English translation with new additions, Berkeley, Cal.: University of California Press, 1949.

— "Are Phenomenal Reports Absolutely Certain?" *The Philosophical Review* 61 (1952): 147–159.

Reiser, O. L. "Physics, Probability and Multi-Valued Logic." *The Philosophical Review* 49 (1940): 662–672.

Ritchie, A. D. "Induction and Probability." *Mind* 35 (1926): 301–318.

Ritter, W. E. "Logic in our Common Knowledge or Logic in the Light of Common Sense, Common Knowledge and Common Understanding." *Philosophy of Science* 11 (1944): 59–81.

Ruddick, C. T. "Cournot's Doctrine of Philosophical Probability." *The Philosophical Review* 49 (1940): 415–423.

Russell, B. "Probability," in *Human Knowledge: Its Scope and Limits* (New York: Simon and Schuster, 1962), part V, pp. 333–418.

Sauvy, A. *L'Opinion Publique.* Paris: Presses Universitaires de France (Que Sais-Je?), 1961.

Schrödinger, E. *Science, Theory and Man.* New York: Dover, 1957.

— *Mind and Matter.* Cambridge, England: University Press, 1958.

Segond, J. *Hasard et Contingence.* Paris: Hermann, 1938.

Servien, P. *Le Choix au Hasard: Mesure d'Egalités physiques et Calcul des Probabilités.* Paris: Hermann, 1941.

— *Base physique et Base mathématique de la Théorie des Probabilités vers une nouvelle forme de la théorie.* Paris: Hermann, 1942.

— *Probabilités et Physique.* Paris: Hermann, 1945.

— *Probabilités et Quanta.* Paris: Hermann, 1948.

— *Hasard et Probabilités.* Paris: Presses Universitaires de France, 1949.

— *Science et Hasard.* Paris: Payot, 1952.

Sheldon, W. H. "Science, Philosophy and Certainty." *The Philosophical Review* 39 (1930): 243–257.

Singer, C. *A Short History of Science to the Nineteenth Century.* Oxford: Clarendon Press, 1941.

Smart, J. J. C. "The Reality of Theoretical Entities." *Australasian Journal of Philosophy* 34 (1946): 1–12.

Smith, G. H. "Belief in Statements Labeled Fact and Rumor." *Journal of Abnormal Psychology* 42 (1947): 80–90.

Smith, M. B., and others. *Opinions and Personality.* New York: Wiley, 1963.

Stebbing, L. S. *Philosophy and the Physicists.* London: Methuen, 1937.

Sterne, T. E. "Mathematical and Physical Meaning of Probability." *Science and Progress* 31 (1936): 250–257.

Strong, E. W. *Procedures and Metaphysics; A Study in the Philosophy of Mathematical-Physical Science in the Sixteenth and Seventeenth Centuries.* Berkeley, Cal.: University of California Press, 1936; Cambridge, England: University Press, 1937.

Sullivan, J. W. N. *The Limitations of Science.* New York: Viking Press, 1933.

Swenson, D. F. "Objective Uncertainty and Human Faith." *The Philosophical Review* 37 (1958): 433–459.

Tarski, A. *Introduction à la Logique.* Paris and Louvain: Gauthiers-Villars, 1960.

Taton, R. *Reason and Chance in Scientific Discovery*. London: Hutchinson, 1957.

Todhunter, I. *History of the Mathematical Theory of Probability from the Time of Pascal to that of Laplace*, reprinted. New York: Chelsea, 1949.

Toulmin, S. *The Uses of Argument*. Cambridge, England: University Press, 1958.

— *Philosophy of Science*. New York: Harper, 1960.

— *Foresight and Understanding; An Enquiry into the Aims of Science*. Bloomington, Ind.: Indiana University Press, 1961.

Tovani, F. "Maynard Keynes on Probability." *English Review* 34 (1922): 485–490.

Venn, J. *The Logic of Chance*, 4th ed. (unaltered reprint of 3rd ed. of 1888). New York: Chelsea, 1962.

Von Mises, R. *Probability, Statistics and Truth*. German ed., Vienna, 1928; 1st English ed., New York, 1939; 2nd rev. English ed., New York and London: Macmillan and G. Allen and Unwin, 1957.

Walker, E. R. "Verification and Probability." *The Journal of Philosophy* 44 (1947): 97–104.

Wallace, W. A. "The Reality of Elementary Particles." *Proceedings Am. Cath. Phil. Assoc.* 38 (1964): 154–166.

Weaver, R. M. *The Ethics of Rhetoric*. Chicago: Regnery, 1953.

Weaver, W. "The Reign of Probability." *Scientific Monthly* 31 (1930): 457–466.

— *Lady Luck: The Theory of Probability*. Garden City, N.Y.: Doubleday Anchor, 1963.

Weizsacker, C. F. von, and J. Juilfs. *The Rise of Modern Physics*. New York: Braziller, 1957.

White, M. G. "Probability and Confirmation." *The Journal of Philosophy* 36 (1939): 323–328.

Wiener, P., and A. Nolan (eds.) *The Roots of Scientific Thought*. New York: Basic Books, 1957.

Williams, D. C. "On the Direct Probability of Inductions." *Mind* 62 (1953): 465–483.

Wittgenstein, L. *Tractatus Logico-Philosophicus*. New York: Harcourt, Brace, 1922.

Wolf, A. *A History of Science, Technology and Philosophy in the Eighteenth Century*. London: Allen and Unwin, 1938.

Wright, G. H. von. Review of Carnap's *Logical Foundations of Probability*. *The Philosophical Review* 60 (1951): 362–374.

— *The Logical Problem of Induction*, 2nd rev. ed. New York and London: Macmillan and Blackwell, 1957.

— *Treatise on Induction and Probability*. New York: Littlefield, 1960.

INDEX